Oct. 2015

P9-DCD-572

WITHDRAWN

Genealogy Online

FOR DUMMIES®

A Wiley Brand

7th Edition

by Matthew L. Helm
and
April Leigh Helm

Algonquin Area Public Library
2600 Harnish Dr.
Algonquin, IL 60102
www.aapld.org

Genealogy Online For Dummies®, 7th Edition

Published by: **John Wiley & Sons, Inc.,** 111 River Street, Hoboken, NJ 07030-5774, www.wiley.com

Copyright © 2014 by John Wiley & Sons, Inc., Hoboken, New Jersey

Published simultaneously in Canada

No part of this publication may be reproduced, stored in a retrieval system or transmitted in any form or by any means, electronic, mechanical, photocopying, recording, scanning or otherwise, except as permitted under Sections 107 or 108 of the 1976 United States Copyright Act, without the prior written permission of the Publisher. Requests to the Publisher for permission should be addressed to the Permissions Department, John Wiley & Sons, Inc., 111 River Street, Hoboken, NJ 07030, (201) 748-6011, fax (201) 748-6008, or online at http://www.wiley.com/go/permissions.

Trademarks: Wiley, For Dummies, the Dummies Man logo, Dummies.com, Making Everything Easier, and related trade dress are trademarks or registered trademarks of John Wiley & Sons, Inc. and may not be used without written permission. All other trademarks are the property of their respective owners. John Wiley & Sons, Inc. is not associated with any product or vendor mentioned in this book.

LIMIT OF LIABILITY/DISCLAIMER OF WARRANTY: THE PUBLISHER AND THE AUTHOR MAKE NO REPRESENTATIONS OR WARRANTIES WITH RESPECT TO THE ACCURACY OR COMPLETENESS OF THE CONTENTS OF THIS WORK AND SPECIFICALLY DISCLAIM ALL WARRANTIES, INCLUDING WITHOUT LIMITATION WARRANTIES OF FITNESS FOR A PARTICULAR PURPOSE. NO WARRANTY MAY BE CREATED OR EXTENDED BY SALES OR PROMOTIONAL MATERIALS. THE ADVICE AND STRATEGIES CONTAINED HEREIN MAY NOT BE SUITABLE FOR EVERY SITUATION. THIS WORK IS SOLD WITH THE UNDERSTANDING THAT THE PUBLISHER IS NOT ENGAGED IN RENDERING LEGAL, ACCOUNTING, OR OTHER PROFESSIONAL SERVICES. IF PROFESSIONAL ASSISTANCE IS REQUIRED, THE SERVICES OF A COMPETENT PROFESSIONAL PERSON SHOULD BE SOUGHT. NEITHER THE PUBLISHER NOR THE AUTHOR SHALL BE LIABLE FOR DAMAGES ARISING HEREFROM. THE FACT THAT AN ORGANIZATION OR WEBSITE IS REFERRED TO IN THIS WORK AS A CITATION AND/OR A POTENTIAL SOURCE OF FURTHER INFORMATION DOES NOT MEAN THAT THE AUTHOR OR THE PUBLISHER ENDORSES THE INFORMATION THE ORGANIZATION OR WEBSITE MAY PROVIDE OR RECOMMENDATIONS IT MAY MAKE. FURTHER, READERS SHOULD BE AWARE THAT INTERNET WEBSITES LISTED IN THIS WORK MAY HAVE CHANGED OR DISAPPEARED BETWEEN WHEN THIS WORK WAS WRITTEN AND WHEN IT IS READ.

For general information on our other products and services, please contact our Customer Care Department within the U.S. at 877-762-2974, outside the U.S. at 317-572-3993, or fax 317-572-4002. For technical support, please visit www.wiley.com/techsupport.

Wiley publishes in a variety of print and electronic formats and by print-on-demand. Some material included with standard print versions of this book may not be included in e-books or in print-on-demand. If this book refers to media such as a CD or DVD that is not included in the version you purchased, you may download this material at http://booksupport.wiley.com. For more information about Wiley products, visit www.wiley.com.

Library of Congress Control Number: 2013954204

ISBN 978-1-118-80810-8 (pbk); ISBN 978-1-118-80816-0 (ebk); ISBN 978-1-118-80818-4 (ebk)

Manufactured in the United States of America

10 9 8 7 6 5 4 3 2

Contents at a Glance

Table of Contents

Part II: Bringing Your Ancestor to Life 131

Introduction

· ·

*T*here could be any number of reasons that you picked up this book. Maybe you've become curious about genealogy after watching a television show. Perhaps you've always been interested but you didn't have the time to pursue it until now. Possibly, you're a student with a project to complete on your family history. No matter what the reason, you probably need some help getting started, and we're here to help!

The number of family history resources that are available online has skyrocketed in the 15 years since we wrote the first edition of this book. This is an exciting time because scanned images of key records are coming online at an unprecedented rate. Also, new technologies such as DNA testing have been refined and are now invaluable tools to confirm evidence from paper records.

Although the technology and amount of material available online has changed over the years, you still need a solid foundation for your research. We've written *Genealogy Online For Dummies* to give you the necessary resources and advice to balance online sources with traditional research to ensure you are successful every step of the way.

If you're a repeat reader of *Genealogy Online For Dummies,* we think you'll be pleased to find all sorts of new and updated information. And if you're brand new to genealogy, we think you'll be equally pleased with easy-to-understand directions and information about the resources that await you.

At this point, we feel obligated to give you a couple of warnings or reminders. First, genealogy is an addictive pursuit and a long journey. You might find yourself staying up all hours of the night chasing down that elusive ancestor. Please don't blame us if you start falling asleep at work due to your genealogical research routine. Also, on a more serious note, keep in mind that online research is merely one tool among others for finding information about your family. To thoroughly research your genealogy, you must use a number of tools — many of which we talk about throughout this book.

Now that the disclaimers are out of the way, put the kids to bed, let your pets out, and boot up that computer. Your ancestors are just waiting to be found!

About This Book

If you type in the word *genealogy* into a popular search engine like Google, you'll see millions upon millions of pages that mention the subject. In fact, at the time we wrote this, such a search returned 182,000,000 results. With so many choices, it's impossible to know where to start without a map. That's what this book is all about. Although we won't cover every available resource, we will point you toward the sites and technologies that'll give you the best chance for researching many different family lines.

You're probably asking yourself how this book differs from the many other genealogy books on the shelf. Some books tell you only the traditional methods of genealogical research that have you traveling hundreds of miles to visit courthouses and archives in other states. Unfortunately, these books neglect the many opportunities that online research and new technologies provide. Other books that do cover online genealogy tend to group resources by how users access them (all link-based sites are listed together, all subscription sites are listed together, and so on), rather than telling you how you can integrate the many online resources to achieve your genealogical goal. As genealogists, we understand that researchers don't conduct searches by trying all the link sites, then all the subscription sites. We search by looking for surnames or places anywhere we can find them — through websites, blogs, e-mail, or any other source.

Web addresses (or URLs) throughout the book are in a `different font` to set them apart from regular text. This way, you can easily see the sites we recommend that you visit to try something or read more online. Additionally, to make it easier for you to follow a set of specific instructions, when you should type something, **bold type** indicates what to type.

Foolish Assumptions

In writing and revising this book, we made a few assumptions. If you fit one of these assumptions, this book is for you:

- You're psyched up and ready to jump into researching your family history with both feet.

- You have at least a little computer experience, are now interested in pursuing your family tree, and want to know where and how to start.

- You have a little experience in genealogy and some experience with computers, but you want to find out how to put them together.

- You're an experienced genealogist or family historian and you're looking for ways to make your research more efficient.

You can have a lot of computer experience and be a novice to genealogy or online genealogy and still benefit from this book. In this case, you may want to dive right into the chapters about strategies for finding online resources.

Icons Used in This Book

To help you get the most out of this book, we created some icons that tell you at a glance whether a section or paragraph has important information of a particular kind.

The Remember icon marks important genealogical stuff, so don't forget it.

When you see the Tip icon, you know we're offering advice or shortcuts to make researching easier.

Look out! The Warning icon indicates something tricky or unusual to watch for.

Beyond the Book

We've provided additional information about genealogy online to help you on your way:

✔ **Cheat Sheet:** Check out www.dummies.com/cheatsheet/genealogyonline.

✔ **Online articles:** On several of the pages that open each of this book's parts, you'll find links to what the folks at *For Dummies* call Web Extras, which expand on some concept we've discussed in that particular section. You'll find them at www.dummies.com/extras/genealogyonline.

Where to Go from Here

Depending on where you're reading this introduction, your next step is one of the following:

- ✔ You need to go to the front of the bookstore and pay for this book so that you can take it home and use it.

- ✔ If you've already bought the book and you're at home (or wherever), you can go ahead and start reading in depth, following the steps for the online activities in the book as they come along.

We don't expect you to read this book from cover to cover, in the order we wrote it. It definitely doesn't hurt our feelings knowing you may skip through the sections looking for only the information that you're interested in at a particular moment! Each section in each chapter can stand alone. If we think something relevant in another section can supplement your knowledge on a particular topic, we provide a note or reference telling you the other place(s) we think you should look. However, we tried hard to do this referencing in a manner that isn't obnoxious to those of you who choose to read the book from cover to cover. We hope we've succeeded in addressing both types of readers!

Now that we've explained a bit about the book, are you ready to get started and to become an official genealogist? You might be asking yourself, "What are the requirements for becoming an official genealogist?" You simply need an interest in your ancestry and a willingness to devote time to pursuing information and documents. So dive in and start collecting the puzzle pieces of your family history and remember to have fun!

Part I
Getting Started with Genealogy Online

In this part...

- ✔ Learn how to use information that you know on yourself to begin your online research.

- ✔ Discover how primary sources can jump-start your genealogical journey.

- ✔ Locate large collections of records that you can use to find details on the lives of your ancestors.

- ✔ Learn how census records can be used to track the movements of your ancestors every ten years.

- ✔ Discover how you can use primary sources to find the details of your ancestors' lives.

Chapter 1

Beginning Your Ancestral Journey

In This Chapter

▶ Starting research with yourself

▶ Getting familiar with a genealogical database

▶ Creating an online family tree

▶ Entering data with an app

*W*e know you're ready to go! You have a mouse in hand and are set to learn all there is to know about your ancestors. However, we need to go over a few useful things before that mouse runs wild.

If you're new to genealogy, we strongly suggest that you begin your journey with this chapter. (That's why we made it Chapter 1.) We'll walk you through the basics of recording genealogical data by starting with a very familiar person — you! Then we'll explore how to get valuable information from relatives, locate key documents around the house, how to use photographs to further your research, and explore easy ways to get organized.

Sketching Yourself

Late one night, you decide to start looking for information on your great-great-grandfather Absalom Looney. After booting up your computer and connecting to the Internet, you put good old Absalom's name into your favorite search engine. Within a couple of seconds, a page appears telling you there are more than 51,000 results for Absalom Looney. How can you possibly sift through all the Absaloms onscreen and find the one you're looking for? Well, before you go any further, we should let you in on a little secret: Instead of starting your journey with Absalom, it's better to begin with the information you have about someone you know better — yourself.

Regardless of what your spouse thinks, we're convinced that you're really the expert on you. You know your birth date, place of birth, parents' names, and where you've lived. (We recognize that not everyone knows all this information; adoptions or other circumstances may require you to do the best you can with what you know until you can discover additional information about yourself.) Knowing some things about yourself, it's time to start sketching out your life — and, at the same time, learning some good research skills that will help you delve into the lives of others.

When working on your life's sketch, we recommend beginning with current events and working back through your life. This is the method you'll likely use when researching an ancestor. First, note the basics: your current marital or family status, occupation, residence, and activities. Then move back to your last residence, occupation, and so on until you arrive at your birth date. Make sure that you include milestones such as children's birth dates, marriage dates, military service dates, educational experience, religious affiliations, participation in organizations and sports, and other significant events in your life. If you prefer, you can cover your life by beginning with your birth and working forward to the present. Either way is fine, as long as you list all the important events.

You have several ways to store your sketch. Some people prefer to start with index cards, placing a particular event on each card — or, if you want to use a digital tool, you can store notes in a product such as Evernote (www.evernote.com) or Microsoft's OneNote (office.microsoft.com/en-us/onenote). Others use a database or word processor to write up things that they recall over a certain period of time. If you don't have time to type something out, why not use a digital voice recorder to record all those nuggets of information? Using any of these methods, you can begin to arrange historical events to form the basis of your biographical sketch.

The biographical sketch that you create now may become an important research tool for one of your descendants who decides to conduct research about you in the future. So, when you have the time, turn that sketch into a full-blown autobiography. This way, your descendants not only know the facts about your life, but also gain some insight as to why you chose the paths you did throughout your life.

Using an online resource

Because this book deals with online resources, we wouldn't be doing our job if we didn't mention an online resource for writing your biographical sketch. One site that assists you with creating your autobiography is Story of My Life (www.storyofmylife.com). Story of My Life contains a simple way to assemble chapters together to form your biographical sketch.

To begin your biographical sketch on Story of My Life, follow these steps:

1. **Point your browser to `www.storyofmylife.com`.**

2. **In the top-right corner, click the Register Now image to register for free.**

   Fill out the Personal Info form. You can check the availability of your Story of My Life ID by clicking the Check Availability button. Also, make sure you read the Terms of Service and Privacy Policy, and select the appropriate box for the level of notifications that you would look to receive. Keep in mind that you can opt out of receiving notifications by deselecting the Notifications check boxes.

3. **Click the Continue button.**

   The confirmation page appears. You should also receive an e-mail confirmation. To progress to the next step of the registration process, confirm your e-mail address.

4. **Go to your e-mail program and open the confirmation e-mail from Story of My Life.**

   The title of the e-mail is Registration | Email Validation. Open the e-mail and locate the link to validate your e-mail.

5. **Click the link in the e-mail to validate your e-mail address or copy and paste the validation link into your web browser.**

   The web page shows that your e-mail address has been verified. The page also allows you to choose a Forever Space package, which requires payment. Don't panic! You don't have to purchase a plan to use the site. If you're not interested in purchasing a package, just make sure to choose the I Will Buy Later. Continue with My FREE Story Account option.

6. **Click the green Continue button near the bottom of the screen.**

   The next page in the registration process is the Checkout page. If you don't want to order anything, make sure the package is set to Free and the total at the bottom of the page is $0.00.

7. **Click Continue.**

   The My Story page appears, shown in Figure 1-1.

8. **Click the Click Here link (in the middle of the page, under the Stories tab) to begin writing your story.**

   You can add chapters or categories by using the prompts under the My Story menu on the left.

Figure 1-1:
The My
Story page
on Story of
My Life.

Using genealogical software

You can use a biographical website to document your life (as described in the previous section), but another option is to use a tool of the genealogy trade from the beginning — genealogical software. Over time, you'll collect a lot of information on your ancestors. You need something to help you keep everything straight and make sense of it all. Not only can genealogical software keep track of the names, dates, and places of your ancestors, but it can also show you the gaps in your research and point you where to go next.

Several software programs on the market can store and manipulate your genealogical information. They all have some standard features in common. For instance, most serve as databases for family facts and stories, have reporting functions to generate predesigned charts and forms, and have export capabilities so that you can share your data with others.

Each software program also has a few unique features (for example, the capability to take information out of the software and generate online reports at the click of a button or integrate with data stored on subscription genealogical websites) that make it stand out from the others. Here's a list of some simple features to look for when evaluating software packages:

- **How easy to use is the software?** Is it reasonably intuitive from a graphics standpoint so that you can see how and where to enter particular facts about an ancestor?

- **Does the software generate the reports you need?** For instance, if you're partial to Family Group Sheets, does this software support them?

- **Does the software allow you to export and import a GEDCOM file? What other formats does it export to?** *GEDCOM* is a file format that's widely used for genealogical research. For more info about GEDCOM, see the nearby sidebar "GEDCOM: The genealogist's standard."

- **How many names can this software hold?** Make sure the software can hold an adequate number of names (and accompanying data) to accommodate all the ancestors about whom you have information.

  Keep in mind that your genealogy continues to grow over time.

- **Can your current computer system support this software?** If the requirements of the software cause your computer to crash every time you use it, you won't get very far in your genealogical research.

- **Does this software provide fields for citing your sources and keeping notes?** Including information about the sources you use to gather your data — with the actual facts, if possible — is an important and a sound genealogical practice. Take a look at later parts of this chapter, as well as in Chapter 11, for more information about the importance of citing sources and understanding how to do so.

- **Does this software have utilities that warn you of incorrect or incomplete data?** For example, some software can check the place-name that you enter against a database of locations and suggest a standard way of spelling the location.

- **Does this program integrate with genealogical websites?** Integrating content between websites and genealogical software is an easy way to build your genealogical database, as well as to share your findings with others.

GEDCOM: The genealogist's standard

As you probably have already discovered, genealogy is full of acronyms. One such acronym that you'll hear and see repeatedly is *GEDCOM (GEnealogical Data COMmunication)*. GEDCOM is the standard for individuals and software manufacturers for exporting information to and importing information from genealogical databases. Simply put, GEDCOM is a file format intended to make data transferable among different software programs so that people can share their family information easily.

The Church of Jesus Christ of Latter-day Saints developed and introduced GEDCOM in 1987. The first two versions of GEDCOM were released for public discussion only and were not meant to serve as the standard. With the introduction of version 5.*x* and later, however, GEDCOM was accepted as the standard.

Having a standard for formatting files is beneficial because you can share the information that you collect with others who are interested in some (or all) of your ancestors. It also enables you to import GEDCOM files from other researchers who have information about family lines and ancestors in whom you're interested. And you don't even have to use the same software as the other researchers! You can use Reunion for Macintosh, and someone with whom you want to share information can use Family Tree Maker; having GEDCOM as the standard in both software programs enables each of you to create and exchange GEDCOM files. Similarly, GEDCOM enables you to transfer data from your smartphone genealogical application to your home computer.

To convert the data in your genealogical database to a GEDCOM file, follow the instructions provided in your software's manual or Help menu. You can create the GEDCOM file relatively easily; most software programs guide you through the process with a series of dialog boxes.

In addition to creating GEDCOM files to exchange with other researchers, you can generate GEDCOM files to submit to larger cooperatives that make the data from many GEDCOM files available to thousands of researchers worldwide. You can also convert your GEDCOM file to HTML so you can place the data directly on the web for others to access.

Although GEDCOM has been a reliable standard for a while, the implementation of it in some genealogical software products has been less than ideal. As a result, some genealogical software developers have created products that can import files made from one software package into software that uses a different file format — without the need to save the file to GEDCOM. One such product is GenBridge, which is part of the Family Tree SuperTools product from Wholly Genes Software (www. whollygenes.com/Merchant2/ merchant.mvc?screen=FTST). Before purchasing a converter product, check the documentation that came with your genealogical software to ensure that your software doesn't already have the conversion capability built into it.

Although GEDCOM has been around for a while, efforts are underway to engineer the future of the standard. GEDCOM X (www.gedcomx. org) is a project to develop a new model to improve the capability of genealogical software and websites to share data.

Entering Information into RootsMagic Essentials

To help you get a better idea of how software can help you organize your records and research, and to help you figure out what features to look for in particular software packages, this section examines how to use RootsMagic, a popular genealogy program.

You can download a free trial version of RootsMagic Essentials software and install it on your computer:

1. **Open your web browser and go to the RootsMagic site at** `www.rootsmagic.com/Products`.

2. **Scroll down to the RootsMagic Essentials section and click the Free Download button.**

3. **Complete the information fields, including typing your name and your e-mail address. Enter your e-mail address again in the Verify E-mail field shown in Figure 1-2.**

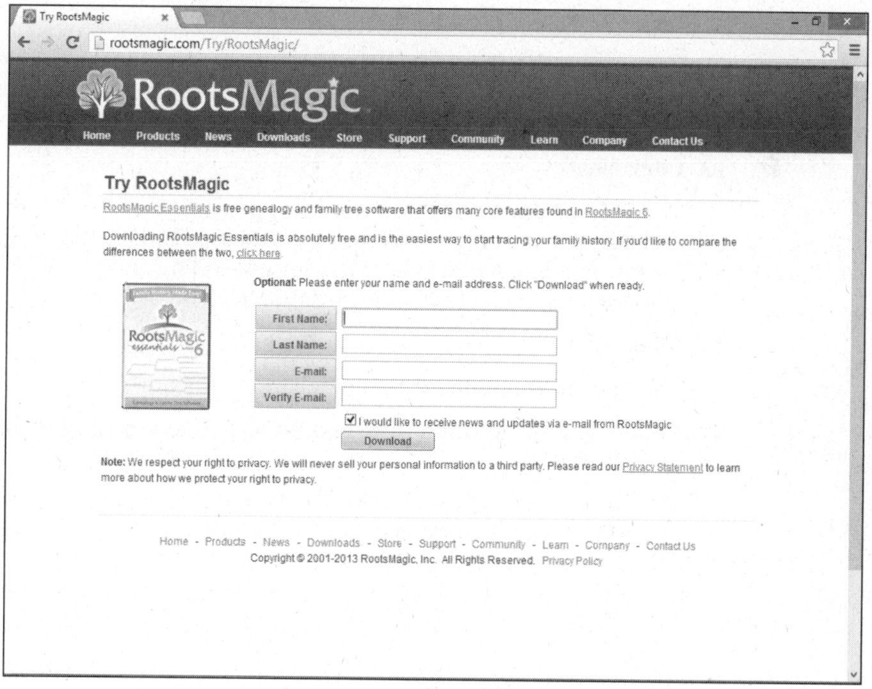

Figure 1-2:
Information fields for the RootsMagic install.

4. **Select the check box if you want to receive e-mails from RootsMagic.**

5. **Click Download.**

   The instructions for downloading the product appear.

6. **Click the RootsMagic Essentials Installer link.**

   The software downloads to a directory on your computer.

7. **To begin the installation, double-click the downloaded file.**

   When we installed it, the filename was RM6Setup.exe. The Welcome to RootsMagic Setup wizard pops up.

8. **Click Next.**

   The license agreement appears.

9. **Read through the licensing agreement. If you agree to its terms, click the I Accept the Agreement option and then click Next.**

   In the window that appears, choose where to have the RootsMagic Essentials software stored on your computer.

10. **Identify where to store the software and then click Next.**

    The Select Start Menu Folder field appears. This enables you to identify where to put shortcuts for the program. The default location is a folder called `RootsMagic`.

11. **If you want the shortcuts listed in `RootsMagic`, leave the default location in the field. If you prefer to have shortcuts in another folder, browse and select the folder or enter the location.**

12. **Click Next.**

    The Select Additional Tasks window opens. If you want to set up any additional tasks (such as creating a desktop icon for the program or downloading a place database for geocoding and gazetteer components), select the appropriate check box.

13. **Click Next.**

    The final information for the installation appears.

14. **Review the installation information and, if everything looks correct, click Install.**

    The software installs on your computer. When it's finished installing, the Completing the RootsMagic Setup Wizard box appears.

15. **If you want to open RootsMagic now, select the Launch RootsMagic check box and click the Finish button.**

   A window opens welcoming you to the software and asking you to identify which version of the product you're opening.

16. **Click the RootsMagic Essentials — Free Version link.**

Now that you have the RootsMagic Essentials software installed on your computer, let's get down to the nitty-gritty and start entering data. When you open the application for the very first time, you get a RootsMagic News window containing links to various announcements and stories of interest to RootsMagic users. If you want to read any of these, you can click the links; otherwise, just click Close.

When the RootsMagic News box closes, you see a Welcome to RootsMagic screen. To begin your family tree, follow these steps:

1. **Click Create a New File.**

   A box appears, enabling you to do several things:

   - Identify the new filename.

   - Determine the location for the file.

   - Set options, including the date format for the file, whether to display a number after a name, whether to display surnames in all capital letters, and whether to set up and support some additional fields for the Latter-day Saints and FamilySearch family tree support.

   - Choose whether to start a file from scratch or import data from another program.

2. **Enter the new filename in the New File Name box, set any of the optional formatting items, and identify whether you're starting a new file or importing an existing one; then click OK.**

   In our case, we're starting a family tree for the Abell family, so we entered **Abell** as the filename. We set the date format and selected the option for starting a new file.

3. **Click OK.**

   The database is created and the Pedigree view opens, as shown in Figure 1-3.

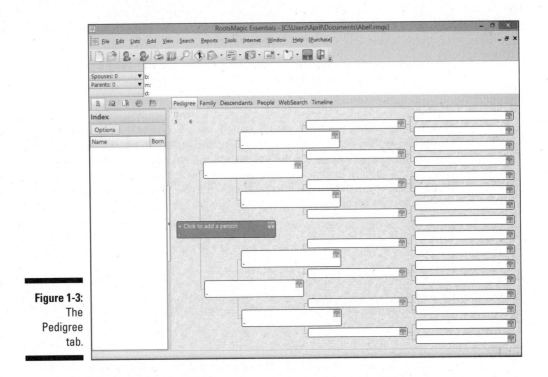

Figure 1-3:
The
Pedigree
tab.

You can start entering information about yourself in the Pedigree chart (presuming that you choose to start with yourself). Then you can add information for four additional generations.

Completing the Pedigree page

Usually, it's easiest to enter information about yourself, your spouse, and your children, and then work backward through your parents, grandparents, great-grandparents, and so on. After you complete your direct lines back as far as you can, enter information about each of your siblings, nieces and nephews, cousins, and other relatives. Always enter as much information as you can in each of the fields in the Add Person dialog boxes. Follow these steps to fill in the Pedigree page:

1. **Select the Click to Add a Person box in the Pedigree chart.**

   The Add New Person dialog box appears, and then you can fill in details about yourself or an ancestor.

2. **Complete the Add New Person box and click OK.**

   Type the first and middle names in the Given Name(s) field and the last name in the Surname field. Then complete the remaining fields to the extent that you know the biographical facts about that person. Remember to use your maiden name if you're female — regardless of your marital status. Of course, we want to set a good example in this book when it comes to privacy for living relatives, so rather than typing information about one of us, we type in Matthew's great-great-grandfather, Samuel Clayton Abell Jr.

   After you click OK, the Edit Person dialog box appears.

3. **Complete the Edit Person dialog box and click Save.**

   You can add more facts about yourself or an ancestor by clicking these buttons in the edit window — Notes, Sources, Media, Address, and To Do. You can also add or delete facts by clicking the appropriate button and then following the prompts in the Fact Types box that appears. After you finish adding the details, click Save.

   Make sure that you use the four-digit year when you enter dates in RootsMagic. If you inadvertently use only two numerals for the year, the software accepts the year as is, leaving it ambiguous for anyone who references your database in the future.

4. **Click Close.**

After you've entered your first person, you can click the next person box you want to complete or click the Add People to the Database icon on the toolbar and enter information for people related to the individual, such as spouse, children, and parents. You can keep track of family units by clicking the Family tab.

Sourcing your information

As you enter information about people, it's critical that you cite your data sources. Most genealogical software programs, including RootsMagic, allow you to enter source information. For specific instructions on how to enter info in your particular software, see the Help file or user's manual that comes with the software. In RootsMagic, you add sources through the Edit Person box.

To add a source for your information, follow these steps:

1. **From the Pedigree chart, double-click the person that the source references.**

   We have the source documents for the marriage of Samuel and Martha. So for this example, we double-click Samuel Clayton Abell Jr. The Edit Person box appears.

2. **Select the fact or event that you want to source.**

   We select the marriage fact in the left side of the box.

3. **Click the Sources button in the lower-right side of the box.**

   The Citation Manager opens for the marriage fact.

4. **Select Add New Source.**

   The Select Source Type box appears, as shown in Figure 1-4.

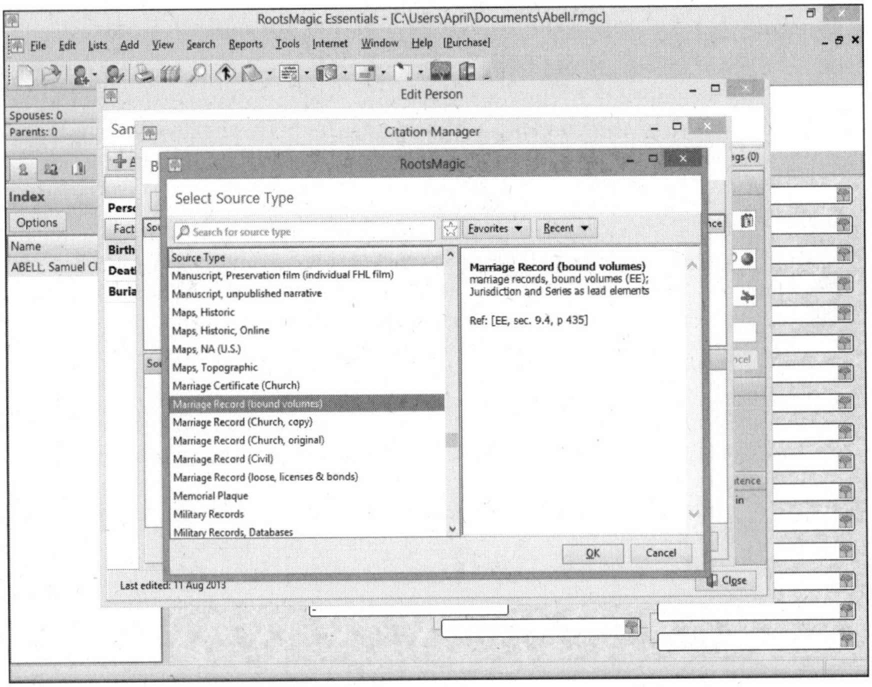

Figure 1-4:
The Select
Source Type
box.

5. **Select from the list of source types.**

   In our case, we search for the source type Marriage and then select one of the results — Marriage Record (Bound Volumes). If you can't find an existing source type to fit your need, select Free Form and enter your own source type.

6. **Click OK.**

   Enter details about the source of your information. You should complete as many of the fields as you can for every source.

7. **Complete the Edit Source fields and click OK.**

   You should now see a check mark under the Source icon in the Edit Person box.

You may have already noticed another way to get to the Source Manager. Choose Lists⇨Source List, click the Add a New Source button, and follow the preceding steps. This enables you to add a source that's not necessarily tied to one specific event in that person's life. If your ancestor kept a diary or memoirs of sorts, you might prefer to use this method of citing sources. Similarly, you have functionality to add sources that pertain to more than one person (called Family Sources in the drop-down list accessible from the Sources icon).

After you've used RootsMagic Essentials for a while, you may find that you need more features. You can compare the features between RootsMagic and RootsMagic Essentials at `www.rootsmagic.com/RootsMagic/Features.aspx` to determine whether you need an upgrade.

Creating the Virtual You

If you're going to be researching using a variety of computers, perhaps a better option is to use an online genealogical database rather than a genealogical database stored on one computer. One full-featured online genealogical database is Ancestry.com. Not only can you enter genealogical information, but you can also upload media files and integrate your data with the content found on the Ancestry.com subscription site through the Hints function.

To get started, try the following:

1. **Point your web browser to** `www.ancestry.com`.

   The Ancestry.com home page appears.

2. **In the upper-left corner of the home page, click the Family Trees button on the menu bar to open the Family Trees page.**

   A new page appears labeled Start your tree. Organize facts. Find answers.

3. **Near the top of the page, enter your first name and last name, select your gender, and click Start Your Tree.**

   The resulting page shows a three-generation Pedigree chart with you as the first person on the left side; see Figure 1-5. Note the helpful tips along the right side of the chart.

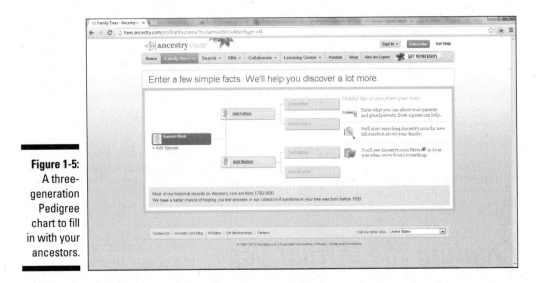

Figure 1-5:
A three-generation Pedigree chart to fill in with your ancestors.

4. **Add the name of a family member to the tree by clicking the Add Spouse link, the Add Father link, or the Add Mother link.**

   In the pop-over box that appears, enter the first and middle names, maiden (or last) name, gender, birth date, birthplace, and, if applicable, death date and death place. A *pop-over box* is similar to a dialog box except that you must complete its fields and click a button to make it disappear. When you begin to enter a location in the Birthplace field, a list of potential matching locations appears beneath the field. You can select from the list to enter the information more quickly. You can also use this list to standardize the location that makes searches easier in the Ancestry.com database.

5. **Click Save.**

   The Save and Build Your Family Tree pop-over box appears. To save the family tree, complete all of the fields on the form, including the tree name and your first name, last name, and e-mail address. You can also choose to allow others to view the tree by selecting the check box. If you don't want others to view it, deselect the check box. You may also want to review the privacy policy by clicking the link on the right side of the box.

6. **Click the Save My Tree button.**

   If your e-mail address matches a registered user of Ancestry.com, the Provide a Password page appears. Type your existing password to continue. If your e-mail address is new to the site, Ancestry.com automatically registers you and gives you a default user name and password. To change the default user name and password (randomly assigned values that you aren't likely to remember), click the link. The family tree you just created is displayed. A pop-up box may also appear describing the Ancestry Hints feature. After reading it, click the X in the upper-right corner. If you want to see the hints, click View Hints. In our case, we clicked the X to continue to the Pedigree chart.

7. **Add information about other family members by clicking the Add Father, Add Mother, or Add Relative links.**

   Clicking any of these links opens a pop-over box. Enter the individual's first name, middle name, last name, gender, birth date, birthplace, death date, and death place. Click the Save button when you're finished.

8. **The Pedigree page is shown again with the names of the new family members.**

   If you see the green shaky leaf symbol, as shown in Figure 1-6, Ancestry.com has found a hint, meaning that Ancestry.com has searched its databases and thinks it has found further information on that particular individual. Sometimes the hint applies to the person and sometimes it doesn't.

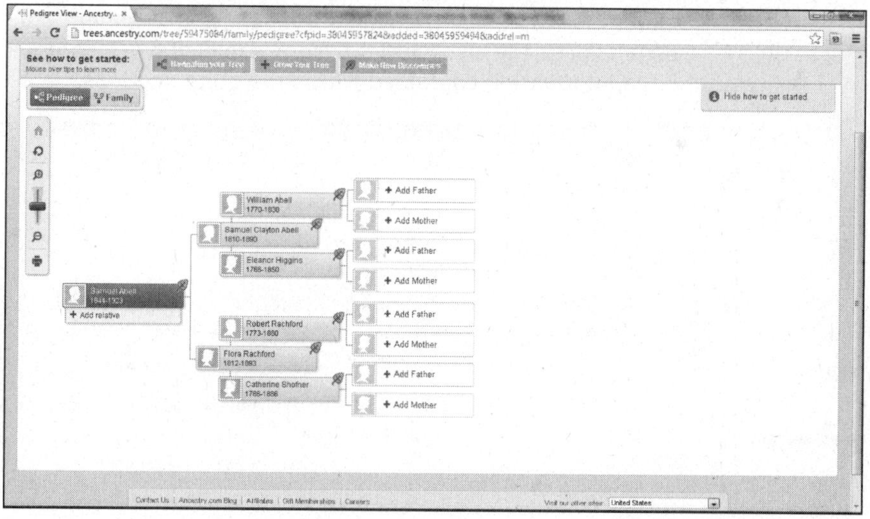

Figure 1-6:
Shaky leaves indicate a hint about your ancestor.

9. **Click the leaf symbol to see the hint. When you finish reading the hint, click the gray Return to Tree box.**

   Not every individual triggers a hint, so don't be concerned if you don't see one. If you follow a hint that leads to part of the paid subscription database, the site prompts you to subscribe to the Ancestry.com site.

10. **As time allows, add more generations to your family tree.**

Beefing up your profile

Just like your ancestors' lives, your life is a lot more than just names and dates. To get a better picture of you, or your ancestor's life, you need to include details about important events such as marriages, buying a house, starting a new job, moving to a new town, and so on. To add some facts, try the following:

1. **If your family tree isn't onscreen, place the mouse cursor over the Family Trees button at the top of the Ancestry.com home page. A secondary menu drops down showing the family tree you created. Click the family tree name to display your family tree.**

    Your family tree is displayed with the Pedigree view.

2. **Place the mouse cursor over the name of a person on your family tree.**

    A pop-over box appears with more information about the person on your family tree.

3. **Select View Profile.**

    Several tabs are available on the Profile screen: Overview, Facts and Sources, Media Gallery, Comments, Hints, and Member Connect. As you might expect, the Overview tab, shown in Figure 1-7, shows a summary of the information contained within the other sections.

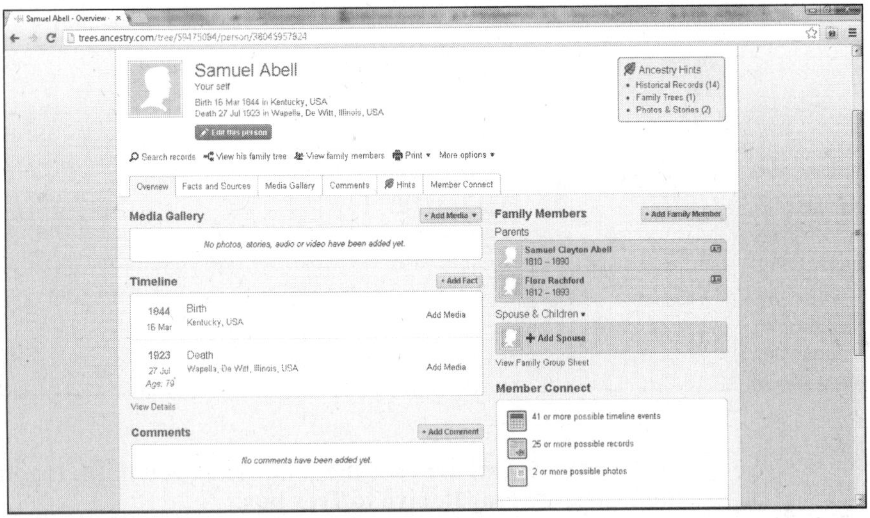

Figure 1-7:
The Family
Tree
Overview
tab.

4. **Click the Facts and Sources tab.**

    The new page contains some basic facts that you already entered, such as gender, birth, and death.

5. **Click the Add a Fact button on the right side of the green menu bar.**

   The Add a New Fact or Event page appears.

6. **Click the Add a New Fact or Event drop-down box and select an event, as shown in Figure 1-8.**

   One or more fields appear on the page depending on the event that you selected.

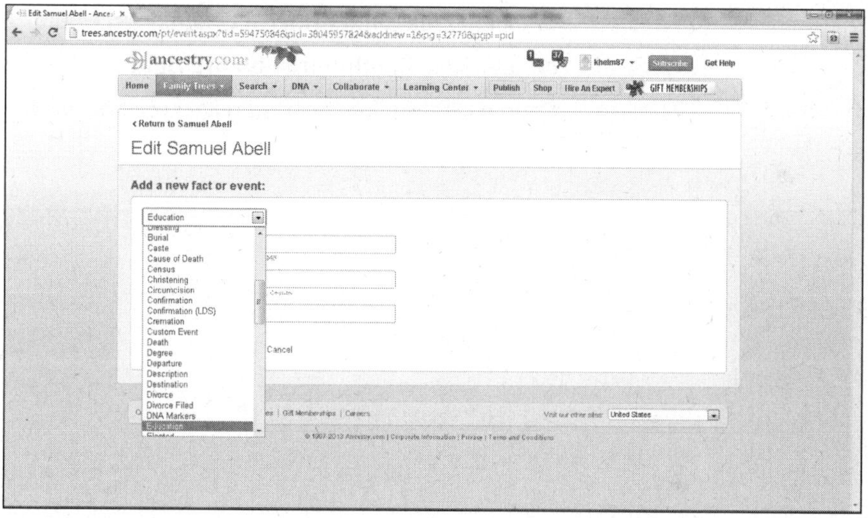

Figure 1-8:
The Add a
New Fact or
Event drop-
down box.

7. **Fill out the fields and click Submit.**

   The information that you entered now appears on the Facts and Sources tab.

Citing your sources

A *source* is any material (book, document, record, or periodical, for example) that provides information for your research. We strongly encourage you to cite the sources of all facts and information that you enter into profiles on your family tree.

Keeping track of sources helps you remember where you discovered the information and helps other researchers retrace your steps. If you find conflicting information later, returning to the source can help you sort out the reliability of your information.

Follow these steps to cite a source for a fact you've added to your tree:

1. **Display the profile page for the person you want to cite a source for.**

   Follow Steps 1 through 3 in the earlier section "Beefing up your profile."

2. **Click the Facts and Sources tab.**

   The Facts and Sources page appears.

3. **Click the Source Citations button.**

   The button is located just under the Facts and Sources tab.

4. **Click the Add a Source Citation link on the right.**

   The Create Source Citation Information page appears, as shown in Figure 1-9.

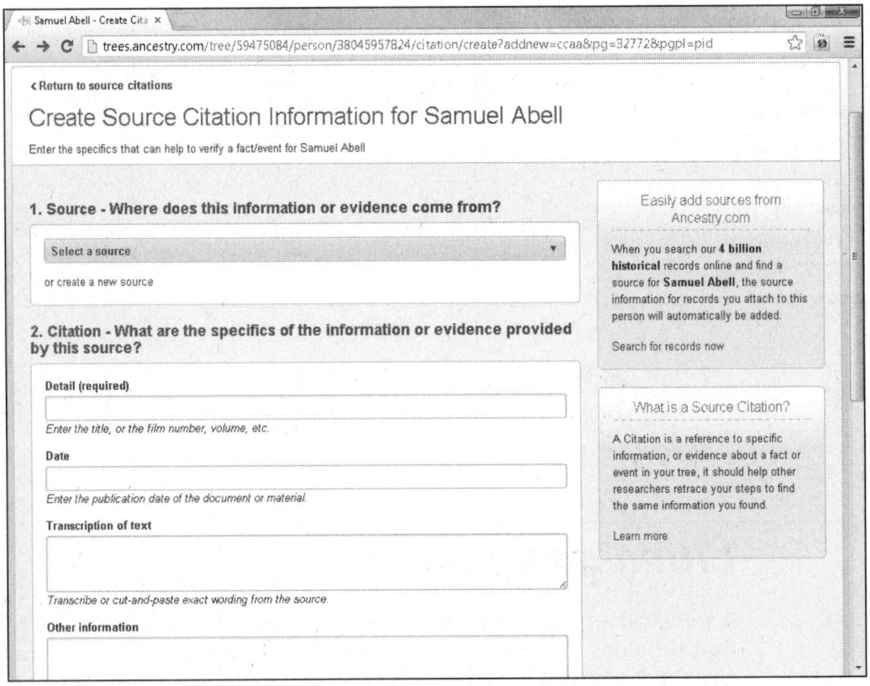

Figure 1-9: Create Source Citation Information page.

5. **Click the Create a New Source link under Step 1 onscreen.**

   The link appears just below the Select a Source drop-down box. The Create a New Source page appears.

6. **Fill out fields for the source of the information.**

   You don't have to fill out all fields. The only required field is Title.

7. **Near the bottom of the page, click the Create a New Repository link.**

A *repository* is a place that holds the source that you're citing, such as a library or a person's house, in the case of the location of family photos. The Create a New Repository page appears.

8. **Fill out the fields to describe the repository. When you're finished, click the Save Repository button to save the repository and return to the Create a New Source page.**

   Note that after you've created a repository once, it's then available for you to use in future citations.

9. **Click the Save Source button.**

   The source title is now reflected in the drop-down box under Step 1 on the Create Source Citation Information page; see Figure 1-10.

10. **Complete the fields under the Citation portion of the source (Step 2 on the Create Source Citation Information page).**

    The Detail field is the only required field in this section.

11. **If you have a scanned document, an audio recording, or a video recording that you want to include as part of the source, click the Yes radio button under Step 3 on the Create Source Citation Information page.**

12. **Under Step 4 on the Create Source Citation Information page, select the box next to the fact or event that you want the source to document.**

13. **Click the Save Source Citation button.**

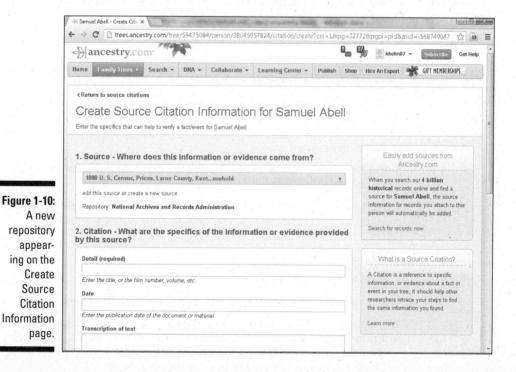

Figure 1-10: A new repository appearing on the Create Source Citation Information page.

Getting the full media experience

To provide a rich experience for your sources, consider adding media. For example, you can scan a birth record of an ancestor and add the image of the actual record as part of your source citation. Follow these requirements to upload media to Ancestry.com:

✔ **Photo:** A photo must be in .bmp, .gif, .jpeg, .jpg, .png, or .tiff format. No individual photo can be larger than 15 megabytes (MB).

✔ **Story:** Type your anecdotal story on the site, or upload it in .doc, .docx, .pdf, .rtf, or .txt format. No individual story can exceed 15 megabytes (MB).

✔ **Audio:** Add audio recordings directly via the Ancestry.com site.

✔ **Video:** A video must be recorded using a webcam and the Ancestry.com site. Videos must be less than 12 minutes long.

Follow these steps to add media to your Ancestry.com family tree:

1. **Display your family tree and open the personal profile to which you want to add media.**

2. **Click the Media Gallery tab.**

3. **Click the Add Media button on the right side of the screen.**

   On the drop-down menu shown in Figure 1-11, you can choose to upload media from your computer (either a photo or a word processing file), type a story, record audio, or record video.

4. **Select Upload Media from Computer.**

   The Upload Media page appears.

5. **Click the Content Submission Agreement link.**

   Read the submission agreement so that you know the terms and limitations of posting content to the Ancestry.com site. Click the Close button (the X in the upper-right corner of the pop-up screen) to close the content submission agreement.

6. **Select the check box labeled I Accept the Content Submission Agreement.**

   Agree only if you have read it and you're comfortable with its terms and conditions. If you choose not to accept it, you cannot submit media to Ancestry.com.

7. **Click the Select Files button.**

   The Open dialog box appears.

8. **Select the files you want to upload and then click the Open button.**

   While the files are uploading, you'll see the progress bar on your screen. After the upload is complete, the Add Details to Your Media page opens.

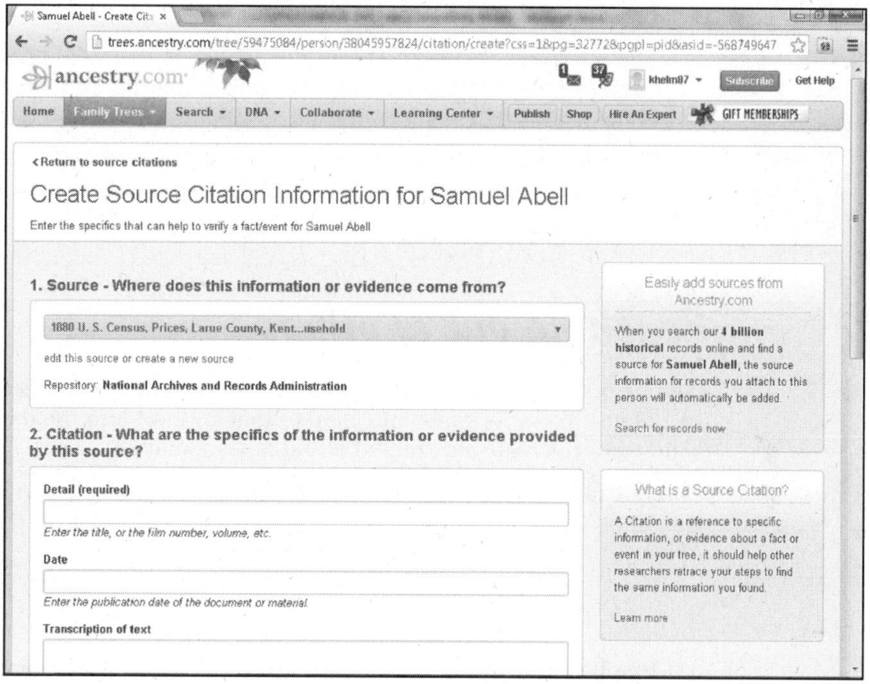

Figure 1-11:
The Add Media drop-down menu.

To select multiple files to upload at the same time, hold down the Ctrl key in Windows or the Command key on a Mac.

9. **Replace the title of the image in the Title field.**

   The Title field must be filled in. The default title is the filename of the imported image. The filename isn't always a descriptive title, so feel free to make the name more meaningful.

10. **Change the category type in the drop-down box, if necessary.**

11. **Fill in the Date, Location, and Description fields if you have this information.**

12. **If you want to attach media to additional people in your family tree, click the Attach to Another Person link and enter the person's name in the box that appears.**

    For example, if you want to attach a photograph of a family to each of the people in the photo who are included in your family tree, attach the photo to the names of the appropriate individuals.

    When you begin typing, the name begins to fill in based on the people in your family tree. You can also click the Browse List link and then select the individual from the list of individuals in the family tree.

13. **Click the Save Added Information button.**

    The photo shows up as a thumbnail image in the Media Gallery. Of course, if the media isn't a photo, you see a different icon in the Media Gallery, such as a microphone labeled Audio for an audio file.

    You can add the new media to a Fact and Event entry by clicking the Fact & Events button and then the Add Media link on the right side of the event.

Reaching out to others

At some point you might decide to make your research results available to the public. To clarify some information that you put into the database, you might want to create a comment about a particular ancestor.

It's important to know that comments placed on records of living individuals will not be viewable to the public unless you specifically give permission for others to see living individuals in your tree.

To post a comment:

1. **Display your family tree in Pedigree view, and then open the personal profile to which you want to add a comment.**

2. **Select the Comments tab.**

3. **Fill in the Subject and Comment fields.**

4. **When you're finished, click the Add Comment button.**

Hinting around about your ancestors

A special function in the online family tree is the Ancestry Hint. Ancestry Hints are designed to search through the names that you enter and match them to records available on the Ancestry.com website. Even if you don't have an Ancestry.com subscription, you can use the Hints to point you to record sets that you may be able to find in other repositories.

To see what Hints might offer for a particular ancestor, follow these steps:

1. **Display your family tree, and then open the personal profile for which you want to review Hints.**

2. **Click the Hints tab.**

    The Hints page shown in Figure 1-12 appears, listing record sources that contain a potential match with your ancestor:

    • The first column is the name of the record source.

- The second column contains information about the particular record containing your ancestor's name. Note that this column doesn't provide all the information that might be contained within the record; however, it gives you an idea of the type of information that matched the record with your ancestor.

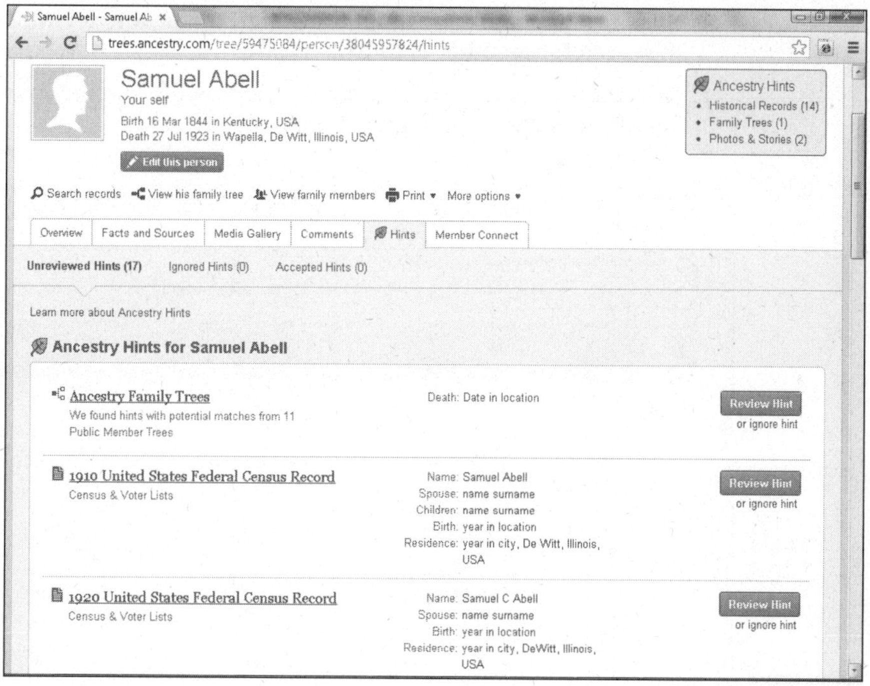

Figure 1-12: The Hints page.

3. **Click the Review Hint button to take a closer look at the record.**

   If you have a subscription to Ancestry.com, you see more information about the record. If you don't have a subscription, you see a splash page that advertises membership and explains how to start a free, two-week trial.

4. **If the Hint isn't valid for your ancestor, click the Ignore Hint link.**

TIP

Ignoring the Hint doesn't delete it from the profile. The Hint is moved to the Ignored Hints page, where you can review it again by clicking the Ignored Hints link.

Member Connect

If you decide to get a paid subscription to Ancestry.com, it gives you an additional feature of the online family tree that is worth mentioning — Member

Connect. The Member Connect feature actively looks for other people who are posting information about your ancestor on their online family trees. After finding a potential match, Member Connect lists the member's name on the tab.

To find members who are researching one of your ancestors, follow these steps:

1. **Display your family tree and then open the profile for which you want to search for member activity.**

2. **Select the Member Connect tab to see possible connections for this ancestor, as shown in Figure 1-13.**

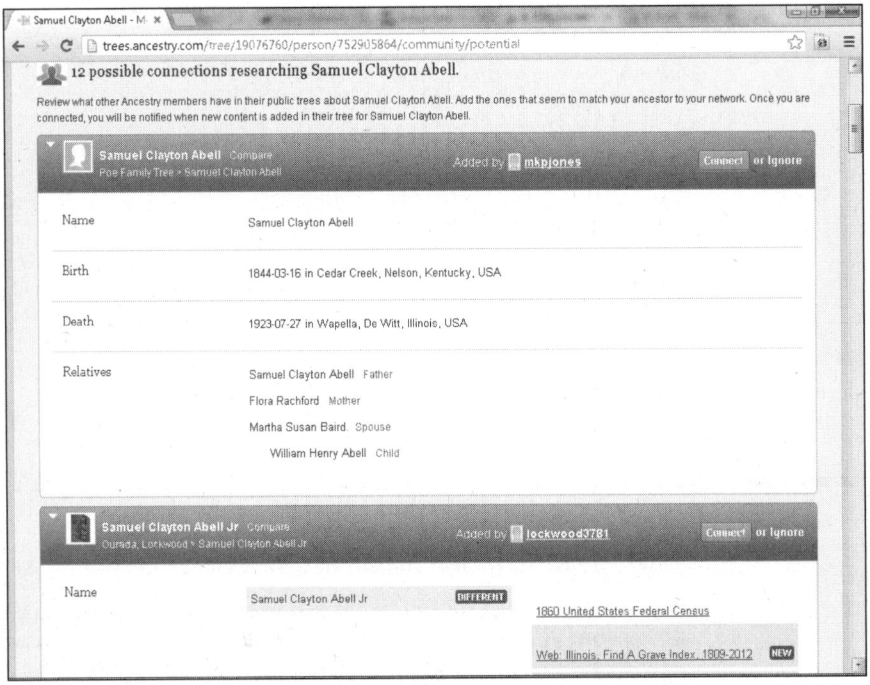

Figure 1-13:
The
Member
Connect
tab.

3. **To contact another Ancestry.com member, click the user name next to the Added By title.**

   Then click the Connect button, and type the subject and message. Clicking the Send button sends the message directly to the user. You must be a subscribing member at Ancestry.com to contact another member.

Ancestry.com subscribers see links to the family trees containing the related information about the ancestor. Nonsubscribers see only the number of records, sources, and photos available on that family tree.

Giving Your Ancestors Some Mobility

If you're one of those people who are always on the go, perhaps a better solution is to use a genealogical app instead of a standard genealogical database on your computer or an online family tree. *App* is short for *application,* and typically can run on your smartphone or tablet. Several apps on the market are free companions to genealogical software packages such as RootsMagic and Legacy Mobile, and there are some paid companion packages such as Reunion. Perhaps the most flexible is the Ancestry.com line of products that allow users to integrate the Family Tree Maker software with the Ancestry.com online family tree and the Ancestry.com mobile app.

With the free Ancestry.com mobile app, you can build a new family tree directly in the app or you can link to an online family tree that you've already started on Ancestry.com. Plus, if you're a subscriber, you can integrate the three products with the subscription content, including Ancestry.com's vast collection of digitized primary sources.

The Ancestry.com mobile app is available for iPad, iPhone, Android, and Windows 8 and Windows RT.

Follow the steps below to see how to use the Ancestry app to add information to your family tree in an iPad. Although these steps apply specifically to an iPad, using the app on another type of device is similar.

1. **Turn on your iPad and locate the Ancestry.com mobile app icon.**

   The icon has a brown background (shaped like a book) with a two green leaves against the Ancestry.com logo. If you haven't downloaded and installed the app on your iPad before, use the instructions that came with the device to find and download the app from the iTunes App Store.

2. **Tap the Ancestry.com mobile app once.**

   The first time that you access the app, a special landing page is displayed, as shown in Figure 1-14. The page contains instructions for creating a family tree beginning with yourself. Alternatively, if you started an online family tree using the steps in the previous section, you can click the Member Sign In drop-down box at the top of the screen to locate it. You need to know your user name and password to complete the login process.

3. **Tap the Add Yourself icon.**

   Let's assume you're starting a new family tree. Tapping the Add Yourself icon launches a Tell Us about Yourself pop-over box.

4. **Tap the First Name and Last Name fields and enter your name.**

   You can also tap the button for your gender and, if you're feeling adventurous, tap the photo icon to add a picture.

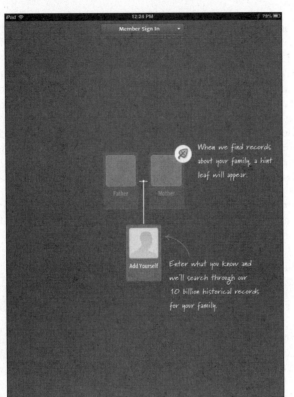

When we find records about your family, a hint leaf will appear.

Add Yourself

Enter what you know and we'll search through our 10 billion historical records for your family.

Figure 1-14:
Ancestry.
com mobile
app first-
time landing
page.

5. **Tap the Add button in the upper-right corner of the pop-over box.**

   After a few seconds of processing, a two-generation Pedigree chart appears. Your information is in the bottom box, and space for your parents is just above that. The onscreen text shows the button to tap to create an Ancestry.com account to store your family tree.

6. **Tap the Save Family Tree button.**

   The Save Family Tree pop-over box appears.

7. **To create a new account, enter your e-mail address and password.**

   If you aren't interested in receiving e-mail tips and offers, tap that box to deselect the option.

8. **Tap the Create Account button at the top-right corner of the pop-over box.**

   After a little processing time, a pop-over box should appear with your name on it.

9. **Tap the Add New Life Event button.**

   The Add Event pop-over box appears. With this box you can add information about yourself. Perhaps start with your birth.

10. **Fill in the information about the event by tapping the Choose Type, Choose Date, Choose Location, and Description buttons.**

    In our example, we tapped Type and selected Birth. Then we tapped Date and used the date wheel to set the date to March 16, 1844, and the location to Kentucky, USA. Note that when you begin typing the location, the app will try to give you standard place names to select. Each time that you complete another pop-over screen, such as the date wheel, tap the Done button.

11. **Tap the Done button.**

    The app saves the record and adds the event to the person window. When you add the event, if you entered information on someone that Ancestry.com has a match for, you see a green leaf appear in the Hints area of the window, as shown in Figure 1-15. Repeat Steps 9 through 11 to add more events.

12. **Tap the Hints button.**

    If you're interested in seeing what Ancestry.com found related to the individual, tap the Hints button. The person window is replaced with the Hints window showing any content that it believes is relevant to the person. In our case, it shows some pictures that were contributed by

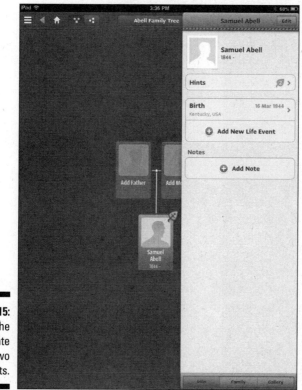

Figure 1-15:
Entering the birth date yields two hints.

other Ancestry.com users and references to digitized primary sources on the subscription site; see Figure 1-16. If you have an Ancestry.com subscription, you can select a Hint and attach it to your person, if you believe it's relevant.

13. **Tap the button containing the person's name to return to the person window.**

   The button is typically labeled as the name of the person you're viewing. It's located in the upper-left corner of the Hints window.

14. **To add information about family members, tap the Family button at the bottom of the person window.**

   Tap the Add Family Member button and a list of member types appears: Add Parent, Add Spouse, Add Child, and Add Sibling. Tap the appropriate family member type and complete the Add pop-over box.

15. **To add another person on the family tree, tap an area outside of the person window and tap the Add Father or Add Mother icon.**

   The person window slides away when you tap an area outside of the window.

Figure 1-16:
Hints
from the
Ancestry
.com mobile
app.

Chapter 2

Hunting for Sources and Ancestral Treasures

. . . .

In This Chapter

▶ Understanding primary and secondary sources

▶ Finding primary resources around the house

▶ Organizing and preserving your genealogical treasures

▶ Using research organizations

. . . .

As a genealogist, one of your goals is to prove your ancestry. Proving your family history involves gathering information from many sources. However, the most important type of documentation when proving your bloodline is the primary source.

Learning about Sources

If you're like most people, you think you know a lot about yourself. If we ask you what your birthday is, you can tell us without batting an eye. But how do you know the birth date? You were obviously there, but you weren't in a condition to be a reliable witness, given that you were a newborn and most likely not fully aware of what was going on. This is where primary sources come in handy. Most likely, witnesses were present who helped create a record of the event.

Primary sources are documents, oral accounts — if the account is made soon after the actual event and witnessed by the person who created the account — photographs, or any other items created at the time of an event. Some primary sources include birth and marriage certificates, deeds, leases, diplomas or certificates of degree, military records, and tax records.

For example, a primary source for your birth date is your birth certificate. Typically, a birth certificate is prepared within a few days of the actual event and is signed by one or more witnesses to the birth.

The timeliness and involvement of direct witnesses makes the information contained on the record (such as the time, date, and parents' names) a reliable firsthand account of the event. It's important to recognize that just because a record was prepared near the time of an event doesn't mean that every fact on the record is correct. Typographical errors can occur or incorrect information can be provided to the creator of the record. Often, these errors are not caught when the record is created. For example, in the case of a birth certificate, new parents are preoccupied with things other than government paperwork during their stay at the hospital. When our youngest child was born, the birth certificate application was created and presented to us for signature. After reading it, we discovered three pieces of incorrect data. Fortunately, we were able to correct the birth certificate before it was submitted to the county clerk — even though the hospital clerk wasn't too happy about re-creating the document multiple times. So it's always a good idea to try to find other primary records that can corroborate the information found in any record.

Secondary sources are documents, oral accounts, and records that are created some length of time after the event or for which information is supplied by someone who wasn't an eyewitness to the event. A secondary source can also be a person who was an eyewitness to the event but recalls it after significant time passes.

Some records may be considered both primary and secondary sources. For example, a death certificate contains both primary and secondary source information. The primary source information includes the death date and cause of death. These facts are primary because the certificate was prepared around the time of death, and the information is usually provided by a medical professional who pronounced the person dead. The secondary source includes the birth date and place of birth of the deceased individual. These details are secondary because the certificate was issued at a time significantly later than the birth (assuming that the birth and death dates are at least a few years apart).

Secondary sources don't have the degree of reliability of primary sources. Often secondary source information, such as birth data found on death certificates, is provided by an individual's children or descendants who may or may not know the exact date or place of birth and who may be providing information during a stressful situation. Given the lesser reliability of secondary sources, we recommend backing up your secondary sources with reliable primary sources whenever possible.

Although secondary sources are not as reliable as primary sources, that doesn't mean secondary sources are always wrong or aren't useful. A good deal of the time, the information is correct, and such records provide valuable clues to locating primary source information. For example, in the case of a birth date and birthplace on a death certificate, the information provides a place and approximate time frame you can use as a starting point when you search for a birth record.

You can familiarize yourself with primary sources by collecting some information for your own biographical profile. This is an activity we walk through in Chapter 1, so if you haven't completed it yet, you might want to flip back a few pages. Try to match primary sources for each event in your biographical sketch. If you can't locate primary source documents for each event in your life, don't fret! Your biographical sketch can serve as a primary source document because you write it about yourself.

For additional information on primary sources, see Using Primary Sources at the Library of Congress website for teachers at `www.loc.gov/teachers/usingprimarysources`.

We should also mention that you will encounter *tertiary sources*. Tertiary sources are compilations of primary and secondary sources, such as articles found online or in encyclopedias or almanacs.

For comparisons of primary, secondary, and tertiary sources and examples of each, see James Cook University's overview of primary, secondary, and tertiary sources at `http://libguides.jcu.edu.au/scholarlysources`.

Or check out William Madison Randall Library's guide for identifying primary, secondary, and tertiary sources at `http://library.uncw.edu/guides/primary_secondary_and_tertiary_sources`.

For strategies on using primary sources online, see the Reference and User Services Association (of the American Library Association) page at `www.ala.org/rusa/resources/usingprimarysources`.

Getting the 4-1-1 from Your Kinfolk

It's likely that you have some valuable but overlooked sources of genealogical gold. You may be looking right through them as they hover around the dessert table at the family reunion, reminding you about every embarrassing moment from your childhood, and overstay their welcome in your home. Yes, they are your relatives.

TIP

Good interview questions

Before you conduct a family interview, pull together a set of questions to guide the discussion. A little planning on your part makes the difference between an interview in which the family member stays focused, and a question-and-answer session that invites bouncing from one unrelated topic to another. Here are examples of some questions that you may want to ask:

✔ What is your full name, and do you know why you were named that?

✔ Where were you born and when? Do you remember any stories that your parents told you about your birth?

✔ What do you remember about your childhood? Where did you go to school? Did you finish school? If not, why? (Remember to ask about all levels of schooling.)

✔ What were your brothers and sisters like?

✔ Where and when were your parents born? What did they look like? What were their occupations? How did your parents meet?

✔ Do you remember your grandparents? Do you recall any stories about them? What did they look like? Did you hear any stories about your great-grandparents? Did you ever meet your great-grandparents?

✔ When you were a child, who was the oldest person in your family?

✔ Did any relatives (other than your immediate family) live with you?

✔ Do you remember who your neighbors were when you were a child?

✔ Did your family have any traditions or celebrate any special holidays?

✔ Do you have any items (stories, traditions, or physical items) that have been handed down through several generations of the family?

✔ When did you leave home? Where did you live?

✔ Did you join the military? If so, what branch of service were you in? What units were you a part of? Did you serve overseas?

✔ What occupations have you had? Did you have any special training?

✔ How did you meet your spouse? When and where did you get married? Did you go on a honeymoon? Where?

✔ When were your children born? Do you have any stories about their births?

✔ Do you know who in the family originally immigrated to this country? Where did they come from? Why did they leave their native land?

You can probably think of more questions that are likely to draw responses from your family. If you need additional questions, take a look at the Fifty Questions for Family History Interviews at About.com (http://genealogy.about.com/cs/oralhistory/a/interview.htm) or The Armchair Genealogist's Family History Interview Questions (www.thearmchairgenealogist.com/2010/01/family-history-interview-questions.html).

Interviewing your relatives is an important step in the research process. Relatives can provide family records and photographs, give you the proverbial dirty laundry on family members, and identify other people who might be beneficial to talk to about the family history. When talking with relatives, you want to collect the same type of information that you provide about yourself when you write your biographical sketch in Chapter 1.

Your parents, brothers, sisters, grandparents, aunts, uncles, and cousins are all good candidates for information about your family's most recent generations. Talking to relatives provides you with leads that you can use to find primary sources. (For more information on primary sources, see the preceding section.) You can complete family interviews in person or through a questionnaire. We strongly recommend that you conduct these interviews in person; it's a lot easier to ask additional questions and follow up on leads! However, if meeting your relatives in person is not feasible, by all means, drop them an e-mail, open a Skype session, or write an old-fashioned letter.

Skype is a software and service that you can use for voice and video calls. The video calling feature allows you to talk face-to-face over the Internet. For more information on Skype, check out their website (www.skype.com) or *Skype For Dummies* by Loren Abdulezer, Susan Abdulezer, and Howard Dammond.

If you're going to write an e-mail or letter to a relative, take a look at Genealogy.com's Request Genealogical Information from Family Members at www.genealogy.com/00000059.html. A nice thing about Genealogy.com's site is it offers this letter translated into other languages, including French, German, Italian, and Spanish. You can access these foreign-language versions of the letter from the Genealogy.com Census Abstracts and Form Letters page at www.genealogy.com/00000023.html.

If you prefer to write your own letter (without guidance from Genealogy. com), you can always use an online translator to convert your letter or e-mail into another language. For more information about some of these, flip to Chapter 8.

There's no easy way to say this, so please excuse us for being blunt — you may want to begin interviewing some of your older relatives as soon as possible, depending on their ages and health. If a family member passes on before you have the chance to interview him or her, you may miss the opportunity of a lifetime to find out more about his or her personal experiences and knowledge of previous generations.

Here are a few tips to remember as you plan a family interview:

- ✔ **Prepare a list of questions.** Knowing what you want to achieve during the discussion helps you get started and keeps your interview focused. (See the nearby sidebar "Good interview questions" for some ideas.) However, you also need to be flexible enough to allow the interviewee to take the conversation where he or she wants to go. Often, some of the best information comes from memories that occur while the interviewee is talking — rather than being generated strictly in response to a set of questions.

- ✔ **Bring a recorder to the interview.** Use a recorder of your choice, whether it's your phone, tablet, computer, an audiocassette recorder, or a video camera. Make sure that you get permission from each participant before you start recording. If the interviewee is agreeable and you have the equipment, we recommend you video-record the session. That way, you can see the expressions on his or her face as he or she talks.

- ✔ **Use photographs and documents to help your family members recall events.** Often, photographs can have a dramatic effect on the stories that the interviewee remembers. If you have a lull in the interview, pulling out a photo album is an excellent way to nudge things along.

- ✔ **Try to limit your interviews to two hours or less.** You don't want to be overwhelmed with information, and you don't want the interviewee to get worn out by your visit. Within two hours, you can collect a lot of information to guide your research. And remember, you can always do another interview if you want more information from the family member. Actually, we strongly encourage you to do subsequent interviews — often the first interview stimulates memories for the individual that you can cover during a later interview. Who knows? It might lead to a regularly scheduled lunch or tea time with a relative whom you genuinely enjoy visiting.

- ✔ **Be grateful and respectful.** Remember that these are people who have agreed to give you time and answers. Treat them with respect by listening attentively and speaking politely to them. And by all means, be sure to thank them when you've completed the interview.

Striking It Rich in Closets, in Basements, and under Beds

Are you a pack rat? A hoarder of sorts? You know what we mean: someone who keeps every little scrap of paper that he or she touches. If you are, you may be well suited for genealogy. In fact, if you're lucky, you descended from a whole family of pack rats who saved all those scraps from the past in their attics or basements. You may be able to share in their treasures — digging to find things that can further your genealogical research. For example, pay a visit to Grandma's attic, and you may discover an old suitcase or cigar box full of documents such as report cards, wartime ration cards, and letters. Eureka for the genealogist! These items may contain information that you can use to reconstruct part of your ancestor's past or to enhance it.

When you go through old family treasures, look for things that can serve as primary sources for facts that you want to verify. For more information on primary sources, see the earlier section of this chapter. Here's a list (although not an exhaustive one) of some specific things to look for:

- Family Bibles
- Property-related legal documents (such as mortgages, titles, and deeds)
- Insurance policies
- Wills
- Family letters
- Obituaries and newspaper articles
- Diaries
- Naturalization records
- Baptismal certificates and other church records
- Copies of vital records (such as birth, marriage, and death certificates, and divorce decrees)
- Report cards and other administrative papers from school
- Occupational or personnel records
- Membership cards or identification cards with photos

These gems that you find buried around the house contain all sorts of information: names and vital statistics of ancestors, names and addresses of friends of the family and neighbors, military units, religious affiliations, medical conditions and names of doctors or hospitals, work histories, and so many other things that can add color to your family history as well as give you place names and time frames to guide you in your subsequent research.

Dusting Off Old Photo Albums

A picture is worth a thousand words — so the saying goes. That's certainly true in genealogy. Photographs are among the most treasured documents for genealogists. Pictures show how your ancestors looked and what conditions they lived in. Sometimes the flip side of the photo is more important than the picture itself. On the back, you may find crucial information such as names, dates, and descriptions of places.

Photographs are also useful as memory-joggers for family members. Pictures can help others recollect the past and bring up long-forgotten memories. Just be forewarned — sometimes the memories are good, and sometimes they're not so good. Although you may stimulate thoughts of some great moments long ago, you may also open a can of worms when you ask Grandma about a particular person in a picture. On the plus side, she may give you the low-down on not only that person, but also every single individual in the family who has ever made her angry — this can provide lots of genealogical leads.

You may run into several types of photographs in your research. Knowing when certain kinds of photographs were produced can help you associate a time frame with a picture. Here are some examples:

- ✔ **Daguerreotypes:** Daguerreotype photos were taken from 1839 to 1860. They required a long exposure time and were taken on silver-plated copper. The photographic image appears to change from a positive to a negative when tilted.

- ✔ **Ambrotypes:** Ambrotypes used a much shorter exposure time and were produced from 1858 to 1866. The image was made on thin glass and usually had a black backing.

- ✔ **Tintypes:** Tintypes were produced from 1858 to 1910. They were made on a metal sheet, and the image was often coated with a varnish. You can usually find them in a paper cover.

- ✔ **Cartes-de-visite:** Cartes-de-visite were small paper prints mounted on a card. They were often bound together into a photo album. They were produced between 1858 and 1891.

- ✔ **Cabinet cards:** Cabinet cards were larger versions of cartes-de-visite. They sometimes included dates on the borders of the cards. The pictures themselves were usually mounted on cardboard. They were manufactured primarily between 1865 and 1906.

- ✔ **Albumen prints:** These prints were produced on thin pieces of paper that were coated with albumen and silver nitrate. They were usually mounted on cardboard. Albumen prints were used between 1858 and 1910 and were the type of photographs found in cartes-de-visite and cabinet cards.

- ✔ **Stereographic cards:** Stereographic cards were paired photographs that rendered a three-dimensional effect when used with a stereographic viewer. They were prevalent from 1850 to 1925.

> ✔ **Platinum prints:** Platinum prints have a matte surface that appears embedded in the paper. The images were often highlighted with artistic chalk. They were produced mainly between 1880 and 1930.
>
> ✔ **Glass-plate negatives:** Glass-plate negatives were used between 1848 and 1930. They were made from light-sensitive silver bromide immersed in gelatin.

When you deal with photographs, keep in mind that too much light or humidity can easily destroy them. Oil from your fingerprints isn't the greatest for old photos either, so you might want to keep a pair of light gloves in your research bag to use when handling these treasures. For more information on preserving photographs, see the section "Preserving Your Family Treasures," later in this chapter. Also, some online resources can help you identify types of pictures. See the City Gallery website at `www.city-gallery.com/learning` for information about nineteenth-century photography, and visit the Everything You Ever Wanted to Know About Your Family Photographs page at `http://genealogy.about.com/library/authors/ucmishkin1a.htm` for descriptions of several types of photographs.

Organizing Your Genealogical Finds

We bet that you've seen the stereotypical family researcher — the type who walks into a library while trying to balance a stack of binders and loose-leafed papers. This could be you! There's no way to get around it: If you get into genealogy — even online-based genealogy — you're going to collect tons of paper and photographs.

If you've been researching for a while now, you've probably used any means possible to take notes while talking with relatives about your ancestors or looking up information in the local library — from notebook paper to receipts you have in your pocket or purse to stick-on notes and paper napkins. You may have used your camera to take pictures of headstones in the cemetery where some of your ancestors are buried or of the old family homestead that's now abandoned and barely standing. And you've probably collected some original source documents, possibly the certified copy of your mother's birth certificate that Grandma gave you, the family Bible from Aunt Lola, and the old photograph of your great-great-grandfather as a child that you found while digging through the attic. Now what are you supposed to do with all these treasures? Organize, organize, organize!

Even if you decide to use genealogical software to track your research progress, you're always going to have paper records and photographs you want to keep. The following sections offer some tips to help you become well organized (genealogically, anyway).

Establishing good organizational skills

You've probably already discovered that taking notes on little scraps of paper works adequately at first, but the more notes you take, the harder it becomes to sort through them and make sense of the information on each. To avoid this situation, establish some good note-taking and organizational skills early by being consistent in how you take notes. Write the date, time, and place that you do your research, along with the names of the family members you interview, at the top of each page of your notes. Then place those notes in a binder, perhaps organized by family group. This information can help you later when you return to your notes to look for a particular fact or when you try to make sense of conflicting information.

You want to be as detailed as possible when taking notes on particular events, persons, books, and so on. Just like you were taught in grade school, you should include the who, what, where, when, why, and how. And most importantly, always cite the source of your information, keeping the following guidelines in mind:

- ✔ **Person:** If your source is a person, include that person's full name and relationship to you (if any), the information, the contact data (address, phone number, e-mail address), and the date and time that you and this person communicated. As the individual is recounting memories and family stories, be sure to ask his or her age at the time of any events that are being recalled. Also get the person's age at the time of your interview or communication. This information might help you approximate time frames when looking for documentation to support the story.

- ✔ **Record:** Include the name or type of record, record number, book number (if applicable), name and location of the record-keeping agency, and any other pertinent information.

- ✔ **Book or magazine:** Include all bibliographic information, including the name of the publication, volume number, date of issue, publisher's name, page number of the applicable article, and the repository where you found the work.

- ✔ **Microfilm or microfiche:** Include all bibliographic information, and note the document media (microfilm roll, microfiche), document number, and repository name.

- ✔ **Website or other Internet resource:** Include the name of the copyright holder for the site (or the name of the site's creator and maintainer if no copyright notice appears on it), the name of the site, the address or Uniform Resource Locator (URL) of the site, the date the information was posted or copyrighted, and any notes with traditional contact information for the site's copyright holder or creator.

It's a good idea to print or save a copy of a web page using a screen-capture utility such as Snagit (www.techsmith.com/screen-capture.asp) or HyperSnap (www.hyperionics.com). A *screen-capture utility* is software that enables you to take a picture of the computer screen and then use that screen capture as a graphic in a document, a file, or a web page. You can attach screen captures as images in your genealogical database or place the paper copies in your research files. Some websites have a tendency to disappear over time, so it's best to get documentation of the site while it exists.

You have many ways to cite sources, and even we have a difficult time remembering how to cite each different type of source consistently. Fortunately, Elizabeth Shown Mills has come to the rescue. If you need help citing almost any kind of source, check out *Evidence Explained: Citing History Sources from Artifacts to Cyberspace,* published by the Genealogical Publishing Company (www.genealogical.com). Another handy resource is *The Chicago Manual of Style Online* at www.chicagomanualofstyle.org/home.html.

Evernote: An alternative to keeping a binder filing system

In the last section, we mention taking notes on paper and placing them in a binder. Although that system works, electronic note systems are available, too. We like to use a product called Evernote (www.evernote.com/), which is a software filing cabinet. You can create a note, attach a picture, scan a document, clip a web page, and store it in the software, as shown in Figure 2-1. The software then uploads the note to a server, making the information available on any device with the Evernote software. The software supports Windows and Mac computers; iPad, iPhone, and iPod touch; and Android, BlackBerry, Palm Pre, Palm Pixi, and Windows Mobile phones.

After you place content into a *notebook* — the virtual filing cabinet — you can further organize it by placing one or more tags on each note. You can use the tags to easily find all content associated with a particular person, place, event, or any other category that you care to make. The content is fully searchable through tags or the full text of the notes.

Also, if you create a note from a mobile device, Evernote can capture your location and add that as an attribute to your note. So, if you are making notes in a cemetery and your phone supports a GPS (Global Positioning System) reading, the latitude and longitude of your current position can be attached to your note.

Figure 2-1:
A will tran-
scription
clipped from
the web and
housed in
Evernote.

Understanding genealogical charts and forms

By the time you have information on a few hundred people, it will become nearly impossible to keep all those ancestors straight. Family historians use charts and forms to organize research and make findings easier to understand and share. Allow us to give you a brief lowdown on five of the most common types of genealogical charts and reports:

- **Pedigree chart:** Flowing horizontally across a page, the *Pedigree chart* identifies a primary person by that person's name, date and place of birth, date and place of marriage, and date and place of death. The chart uses lines to show the relationship to the person's father and mother, then each of their parents, then their parents, and so on until the chart runs off the page. See Figure 2-2 for an example of a Pedigree chart.

- **Descendant chart:** A *Descendant chart* contains information about an ancestor and spouse (or spouses if more than one exists), their children and their spouses, grandchildren and spouses, and so on down the family line. The chart typically flows vertically on a page and resembles a business organizational chart. To see what a Descendant chart looks like, take a gander at Figure 2-3.

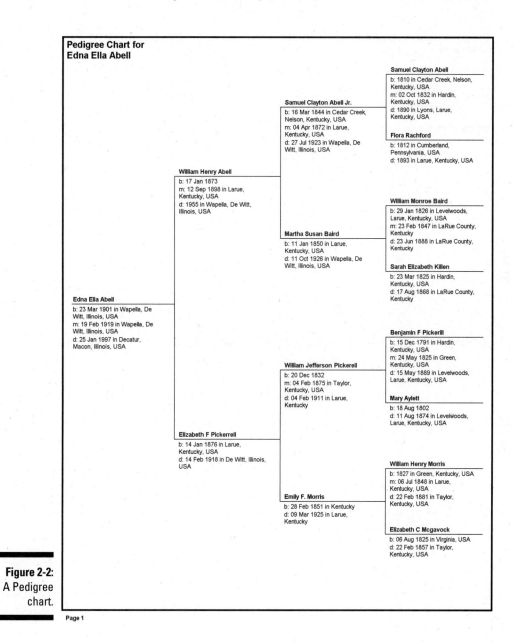

**Pedigree Chart for
Edna Ella Abell**

Samuel Clayton Abell
b: 1810 in Cedar Creek, Nelson,
Kentucky, USA
m: 02 Oct 1832 in Hardin,
Kentucky, USA
d: 1890 in Lyons, Larue,
Kentucky, USA

Samuel Clayton Abell Jr.
b: 16 Mar 1844 in Cedar Creek,
Nelson, Kentucky, USA
m: 04 Apr 1872 in Larue,
Kentucky, USA
d: 27 Jul 1923 in Wapella, De
Witt, Illinois, USA

Flora Rachford
b: 1812 in Cumberland,
Pennsylvania, USA
d: 1893 in Larue, Kentucky, USA

William Henry Abell
b: 17 Jan 1873
m: 12 Sep 1898 in Larue,
Kentucky, USA
d: 1955 in Wapella, De Witt,
Illinois, USA

William Monroe Baird
b: 29 Jan 1826 in Levelwoods,
Larue, Kentucky, USA
m: 23 Feb 1847 in LaRue County,
Kentucky
d: 23 Jun 1888 in LaRue County,
Kentucky

Martha Susan Baird
b: 11 Jan 1850 in Larue,
Kentucky, USA
d: 11 Oct 1926 in Wapella, De
Witt, Illinois, USA

Sarah Elizabeth Killen
b: 23 Mar 1825 in Hardin,
Kentucky, USA
d: 17 Aug 1868 in LaRue County,
Kentucky

Edna Ella Abell
b: 23 Mar 1901 in Wapella, De
Witt, Illinois, USA
m: 19 Feb 1919 in Wapella, De
Witt, Illinois, USA
d: 25 Jan 1997 in Decatur,
Macon, Illinois, USA

Benjamin F Pickerill
b: 15 Dec 1791 in Hardin,
Kentucky, USA
m: 24 May 1825 in Green,
Kentucky, USA
d: 15 May 1889 in Levelwoods,
Larue, Kentucky, USA

William Jefferson Pickerell
b: 20 Dec 1832
m: 04 Feb 1875 in Taylor,
Kentucky, USA
d: 04 Feb 1911 in Larue,
Kentucky

Mary Aylett
b: 18 Aug 1802
d: 11 Aug 1874 in Levelwoods,
Larue, Kentucky, USA

Elizabeth F Pickerrell
b: 14 Jan 1876 in Larue,
Kentucky, USA
d: 14 Feb 1918 in De Witt, Illinois,
USA

William Henry Morris
b: 1827 in Green, Kentucky, USA
m: 06 Jul 1848 in Larue,
Kentucky, USA
d: 22 Feb 1881 in Taylor,
Kentucky, USA

Emily F. Morris
b: 28 Feb 1851 in Kentucky
d: 09 Mar 1925 in Larue,
Kentucky

Elizabeth C Mcgavock
b: 06 Aug 1825 in Virginia, USA
d: 22 Feb 1857 in Taylor,
Kentucky, USA

Figure 2-2:
A Pedigree
chart.

Page 1

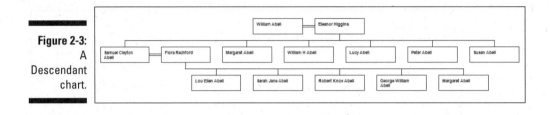

Figure 2-3:
A
Descendant
chart.

✔ **Outline report:** A family *Outline report* is a list of the descendants of a particular ancestor. The first numbered line contains the name (and sometimes the years for birth and death) of the primary ancestor. The next line shows a spouse, followed by the next numbered line, which contains the name of the ancestor and spouse's child. If that child is married and has children, the child's spouse follows, as do the names and information on each of that child and spouse's children. Each new generation within the family is indented from the last and is assigned the next number. For example, the focal ancestor is given the number 1; his or her children are all given the number 2 (for the second generation); his or her grandchildren are all given the number 3 (third generation); and so forth. After the first child's entire family is complete, the outline report lists the next child and his or her family in the same manner. See Figure 2-4 for an example of an Outline report.

✔ **Family Group Sheet:** A *Family Group Sheet* is a summary of vital information about a particular family. At the top of the page, it shows the husband, followed by the wife, and then any children of the couple, as well as biographical information (such as dates and places of birth, marriage, and death). In some contemporary Family Group Sheets, you can set the titles for the two main people if the terms *Husband* and *Wife* are not applicable. However, information on the children's spouses and children isn't included on this Family Group Sheet. That information would appear on a separate Family Group Sheet for the child's family in which the child is listed as either the husband or wife. You can get a better understanding of Family Group Sheets from Figure 2-5.

✔ **Kinship report:** A *Kinship report* is a list of family members and how they relate directly to one particular ancestor. This report includes the name of the family member, the person's relationship to the primary ancestor, and the civil and canon codes reflecting the degree of relationship between the two people. See Figure 2-6 for an example of a Kinship report.

Civil and *canon codes* explain the bloodline relationship in legal terms — in other words, they identify how many *degrees of separation* — or steps — are between two people related by blood. Civil law counts each step between two relatives as a degree, so two people who are first cousins have a degree of separation equal to four, which is the total of two steps between one cousin and the common grandparent and two steps between the other cousin and the common grandparent. Canon law counts only the number of steps from the nearest common ancestor of both relatives, so the degree of separation between two first cousins is two. Two steps separate the grandparent from each of the cousins.

Outline Descendant Report for Samuel Abell

..... 1   Samuel Abell b: 1710 in Saint Marys, Maryland, USA, d: 01 Jun 1795 in Rolling Fork, Washington, Kentucky, USA
.....   + Susanna Spalding b: 1730 in Leonardstown, Saint Marys, Maryland, USA, d: 1795 in Saint Marys, Maryland, USA
...........2   Peter Abell b: 1740 in MD, St Mary, Maryland, USA, d: 1785 in Rogers Station, Nelson, Kentucky, USA
....   + Lucy Carman b: 1745 in Saint Marys, Maryland, USA, m: 25 Oct 1769 in Saint Marys, Maryland, USA, d: 22 Jul 1814 in Wilson Creek, Nelson, Kentucky, USA
.................3   William Abell b: 1770 in Leonardtown, Saint Marys, Maryland, USA, d: 03 Nov 1838 in Cedar Creek, Nelson, Kentucky, USA
....   + Eleanor Higgins b: 1775 in Saint Marys, Maryland, USA, m: 25 Jan 1793 in Nelson, Kentucky, USA, d: 1845 in Cedar Creek, Nelson, Kentucky, USA
.......................4   Samuel Clayton Abell b: 1810 in Cedar Creek, Nelson, Kentucky, USA, d: 1890 in Lyons, Larue, Kentucky, USA
....   + Flora Rachford b: 1812 in Cumberland, Pennsylvania, USA, m: 02 Oct 1832 in Hardin, Kentucky, USA, d: 1893 in Larue, Kentucky, USA
.............................5   Samuel Clayton Abell Jr. b: 16 Mar 1844 in Cedar Creek, Nelson, Kentucky, USA, d: 27 Jul 1923 in Wapella, De Witt, Illinois, USA
....   + Martha Susan Baird b: 11 Jan 1850 in Larue, Kentucky, USA, m: 04 Apr 1872 in Larue, Kentucky, USA, d: 11 Oct 1926 in Wapella, De Witt, Illinois, USA
...................................6   William Henry Abell b: 17 Jan 1873, d: 1955 in Wapella, De Witt, Illinois, USA
....   + Elizabeth F Pickerrell b: 14 Jan 1876 in Larue, Kentucky, USA, m: 12 Sep 1898 in Larue, Kentucky, USA, d: 14 Feb 1918 in De Witt, Illinois, USA
....7   Leona Pearl Abell b: 29 Jun 1899, d: 19 Nov 1975 in Decatur, Macon, Illinois, USA
....   + Beauford Helm b: 17 Dec 1898, m: 25 Nov 1922 in Decatur, Illinois, USA, d: Jul 1972 in Tucson, Pima, Arizona, United States of America
....8   Donald L Helm b: 07 Jul 1924, d: 26 Dec 1999 in Saint Anne, Kankakee, Illinois, United States of America
....9   Living Helm
....9   Living Helm
....8   Beauford Helm b: 09 Oct 1923, d: 25 Oct 2001 in Decatur, Macon, Illinois, United States of America
....+ Ferne
....9   Living Helm
....9   Living Helm
....9   Living Helm
....9   Jeanna Helm
....8   Loretta I Helm b: 1928
....+ Living Michael b:, m:
....9   Living Michael b:
....9   Living Michael b:
....9   Living Michael b:
....9   Living Michael b:
....9   Living Michael b:
....8   Living Helm
....8   Living Helm
....8   Living Helm
....8   Living Helm
....7   Edna Ella Abell b: 23 Mar 1901 in Wapella, De Witt, Illinois, USA, d: 25 Jan 1997 in Decatur, Macon, Illinois, USA

Figure 2-4:
An Outline report.

Family Group Sheet for Peter Abell

Husband:	Peter Abell	

Birth:	1740 in MD, St Mary, Maryland, USA
Death:	1785 in Rogers Station, Nelson, Kentucky, USA
Marriage:	25 Oct 1769 in Saint Marys, Maryland, USA
Father:	Samuel Abell
Mother:	Susanna Spalding

Wife:	Lucy Carman	

Birth:	1745 in Saint Marys, Maryland, USA
Death:	22 Jul 1814 in Wilson Creek, Nelson, Kentucky, USA
Father:	
Mother:	

Children:

1 M
Name:	William Abell
Birth:	1770 in Leonardtown, Saint Marys, Maryland, USA
Death:	03 Nov 1838 in Cedar Creek, Nelson, Kentucky, USA
Marriage:	25 Jan 1793 in Nelson, Kentucky, USA
Spouse:	Eleanor Higgins

2 M
Name:	Samuel Abell
Birth:	11 Feb 1783 in Saint Marys, Maryland, USA
Death:	22 Mar 1840 in Hardin, Kentucky, USA

3 M
Name:	Ignatius Abell
Birth:	1775 in Leonardtown, Saint Marys, Maryland, USA
Death:	16 Aug 1840 in Harrison, Indiana, USA

4 F
Name:	Sarah Sally Abell
Birth:	25 Oct 1769 in Leonardstown, Saint Marys, Maryland, USA
Death:	1800 in Nelson, Kentucky, USA

5 F
Name:	Mary Polly Abell
Birth:	29 Jan 1771 in Leonardtown, Saint Marys, Maryland, USA
Death:	1850 in Newburg, Phelps, Missouri, USA

6 F
Name:	Nancy Abell
Birth:	1785 in Nelson, Kentucky, USA
Death:	Nelson, Kentucky, USA

7 F
Name:	Lucy Abell
Birth:	25 Oct 1769 in Saint Marys, Maryland, USA
Death:	Milton, Pike, Illinois, USA

8 F
Name:	Elizabeth Abell
Birth:	1784

Notes

Page 1 of 1   Tuesday, August 31, 2010 10:16:31 PM

Figure 2-5:
A Family
Group
Sheet.

Kinship Report for Peter Abell

Name:	Birth Date:	Relationship:
Mary	1698	Wife of 4th great grandfather of wife of 2nd great grandson
Abel, Margaret L	Abt. 1908	Wife of 3rd great grandson
Abell, Curtis Ray	08 Aug 1954	4th great grandson
Abell, Cuthbert	1720	Uncle
Abell, Dennis Edward	10 Aug 1922	3rd great grandson
Abell, Edmund	1760	Brother
Abell, Edna Ella	23 Mar 1901	3rd great granddaughter
Abell, Edward	1715	Uncle
Abell, Elizabeth	1750	Sister
Abell, Elizabeth	1784	Daughter
Abell, Elsie Fay	1904	3rd great granddaughter
Abell, Elvin Ray	18 Apr 1905	3rd great grandson
Abell, Enoch	1714	Uncle
Abell, Eugene Coleman	19 May 1913	3rd great grandson
Abell, George William	1848	Great grandson
Abell, Harland Vinson	10 May 1914	3rd great grandson
Abell, Henrietta	1786	Sister
Abell, Ignatius	1741	Brother
Abell, Ignatius	1775	Son
Abell, James Clayton	09 Feb 1916	3rd great grandson
Abell, James M	Abt. 1879	2nd great grandson
Abell, John	1680	Grand uncle
Abell, John	1680	Paternal grandfather
Abell, John	1711	Uncle
Abell, John Barton	1755	Brother
Abell, Joshua	1761	Brother
Abell, Leona Pearl	29 Jun 1899	3rd great granddaughter
Abell, Lillian May	17 May 1905	3rd great granddaughter
Abell, Living		4th great grandchild
Abell, Living		4th great grandchild
Abell, Living		4th great grandchild
Abell, Living		4th great grandchild
Abell, Living		4th great grandchild
Abell, Living		4th great grandchild
Abell, Lou Ellen	1842	Great granddaughter
Abell, Lucy	25 Oct 1769	Daughter
Abell, Lucy	1796	Granddaughter
Abell, Margaret	1797	Granddaughter
Abell, Margaret	1840	Great granddaughter

Page 1 of 19   Tuesday, August 31, 2010 10:17:59 PM

Figure 2-6: A Kinship report.

If you want to take a look at various genealogical charts and forms, or print some free copies to use when researching, many are available online at sites such as Genealogy Today at `www.genealogytoday.com/genealogy/enoch/forms.html`. Additionally, Chapter 11 explains how to print your own genealogical charts and reports using family history software.

The sooner you become familiar with the most common types of charts and understand how to read them, the sooner you can interpret a lot of the information you receive from other genealogists.

Assigning unique numbers to family members

If you have ancestors who share the same name, or if you've collected a lot of information on several generations of ancestors, you may have trouble distinguishing one person from another. For example, Matthew has an ancestor Samuel Abell, who had a son and two grandsons also named Samuel Abell. To avoid confusion and the problems that can arise from it, you may want to use a commonly accepted numbering system to keep everyone straight. Now genealogical numbering systems can be a bit confusing (and talking about them can be a little boring), but we'll do our best to make it as simple as possible and to give you a few examples to make it a little clearer.

The ahnentafel (Sosa-Stradonitz) system

One well-known numbering system is called *ahnentafel,* which means *ancestor* (*ahnen*) and *table* (*tafel*) in German. You may also hear the ahnentafel system referred to as the *Sosa-Stradonitz* system (the names get easier, trust us) of numbering because it was first used by a Spanish genealogist named Jerome de Sosa in 1676 and was popularized in 1896 by Stephan Kekule von Stradonitz.

The ahnentafel system is a method of numbering that shows a mathematical relationship between parents and children. Ahnentafel numbering follows this pattern:

1. **The child is assigned a particular number: *y***

    Of course, we recognize that *y* isn't really a number — it's a letter. In our mathematical (that is, algebraic) example, *y* represents a unique number for that particular person.

2. **The father of that child is assigned the number that is double the child's number: 2y**

3. **The mother of that child is assigned a number that is double the child's number plus one: 2y + 1**

4. **The father's father is assigned a number that is double the father's number: 2(2y)**

   The father's mother is assigned the number that is double the father's number plus one: 2(2y) + 1

5. **The mother's father is assigned a number that is double the mother's number: 2(2y + 1)**

   The mother's mother is assigned a number that is double the mother's number plus one: 2(2y + 1) + 1

6. **Continue this pattern through the line of ancestors.**

The mathematical relationship works the same way going forward through the generations — a child's number is one-half the father's number and one-half (minus any remainder) the mother's number.

In a list form, the ahnentafel for April's grandfather looks like the following (see Figure 2-7 for the chart):

1. John Duff Sanders, b. 10 Mar 1914 in Benjamin, Knox Co., TX; d. 15 Mar 1996 in Seymour, Baylor Co., TX; ma. 24 Dec 1939 in Sherman, Grayson Co., TX.

2. John Sanders, b. 19 Oct 1872 in Cotton Plant, Tippah Co., MS; d. 2 Mar 1962 in Morton, Cochran Co., TX; ma. 28 Sep 1902 in Boxelder, Red River Co., TX.

3. Nannie Elizabeth Clifton, b. 1 Apr 1878 in Okolona, MS; d. 27 Apr 1936 in Morton, Cochran Co., TX.

4. Harris Sanders, b. 27 Mar 1824 in Montgomery Co., NC; d. 21 Feb 1917 in Tippah Co., MS; ma. 26 June 1853.

5. Emeline Crump, b. 20 Oct 1836; d. 21 Feb 1920 in Tippah Co., MS.

6. William Clifton, b. 5 Mar 1845 in SC; d. 9 Feb 1923 in Boxelder, Red River Co., TX; ma. 5 Nov 1872 in Birmingham, AL.

7. Martha Jane Looney, b. 8 Mar 1844; d. Boxelder, Red River Co., TX.

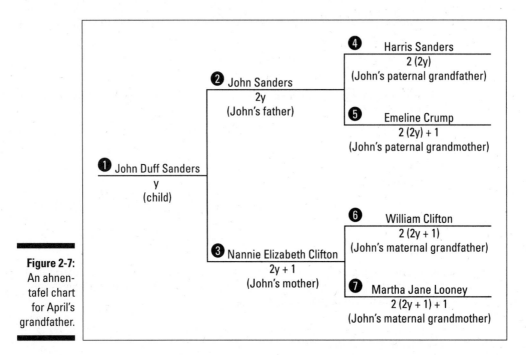

Figure 2-7:
An ahnen-
tafel chart
for April's
grandfather.

John Duff Sanders is number one because he's the base individual for the ahnentafel. His father (John Sanders) is number two (because $2 \times 1 = 2$), and his mother (Nannie Elizabeth Clifton) is number three $[(2 \times 1) + 1 = 3]$. His father's father (Harris Sanders) is four ($2 \times 2 = 4$), and his father's mother (Emeline Crump) is five $[(2 \times 2) + 1 = 5]$. John Sanders's number (2) is one-half his father's number ($4 \div 2 = 2$), or one-half minus any remainder of his mother's number ($5 \div 2 = 2.5$; 2.5 minus remainder of .5 = 2) — well, you get the idea.

As you can imagine, after a while, you begin to tire from all these calculations — especially if you do them for ten or more generations of people. So, if your genealogy software supports ahnentafel reports, we highly recommend that you run one — saving you a lot of time and trouble.

The tiny tafel system

Some people confuse ahnentafel with *tiny tafel,* which is a compact way to show the relationships within a family database. Tiny tafel provides only the Soundex code for a surname, and the dates and locations where that surname may be found according to the database. (For more on Soundex codes and how they work, check out Chapter 4.) Computer programs sometimes use tiny tafels to match the same individual in two different genealogy databases. The following example shows a tiny tafel:

C413	1845	1936	Clifton\South Carolina/Cochran Co. TX
C651	1836	1920	Crump/Mississippi
L500	1844		Looney/Red River Co. TX
S536	1824	1996	Sanders\Montgomery Co. NC/Baylor Co. TX

The Henry system

The *Henry system* is another well-known numbering system. This system assigns a particular number to the *progenitor,* or the ancestor farthest back (that you know about) in your family line. Then each of the progenitor's children is assigned a number in a sequence that starts with his number and adds the numbers 1, 2, 3, and so forth through 9. If the progenitor had more than nine children, the tenth child is assigned an X, the eleventh an A, the twelfth a B, and so on. Then the children's children are assigned the parent's number plus a number in sequence (again 1 through 9, then X, A, B, and so on). For example, if progenitor number one (1) had 12 children, his children would be 11, 12, 13,...1X, 1A, and 1B. The eleventh child's children would be assigned the numbers 1A1, 1A2, 1A3, and so on.

For example, suppose that one of your ancestors, John Jones, had 12 children. The names of these children were Joseph, Ann, Mary, Jacob, Arthur, Charles, James, Maria, Esther, Harriett, Thomas, and Sophia. Joseph had one child named Gertrude, and Thomas had three children named Lawrence, Joshua, and David. Under the standard Henry system, the children's children are numbered like this:

1   John Jones

    11   Joseph Jones

        111   Gertrude Jones

    12   Ann Jones

    13   Mary Jones

    14   Jacob Jones

    15   Arthur Jones

    16   Charles Jones

    17   James Jones

    18   Maria Jones

19   Esther Jones

1X   Harriett Jones

1A   Thomas Jones

    1A1   Lawrence Jones

    1A2   Joshua Jones

    1A3   David Jones

1B   Sophia Jones

By no means are these systems the only genealogical numbering systems. Ahnentafel and Henry are just two of the easier systems to learn. Several others have been designed to display genealogies in book form, such as the Register system (based on the style of the New England Historical and Genealogical Register) and the National Genealogical Society Quarterly system. If you're curious about some of these systems, take a look at the Numbering Systems in Genealogy page at www.saintclair.org/numbers. There you can find descriptions of each major numbering system and variations of these systems.

If you decide to use a numbering system, you can place the corresponding unique number for each individual in the file that you set up for that person in your paper record-keeping system, as well as in your genealogical software.

Making copies of source documents

You don't want to carry original records with you when you're out and about researching. You've probably gone to a lot of trouble to collect the records, and the chances of misplacing or forgetting a document are too great. You have a few options:

- ✔ You can scan the documents and store them on your laptop, or enter the information into a database. Then you can take your laptop with you. (We talk more about using computers in Chapter 1.)

- ✔ You can copy data from your computer to your *smartphone* (a mobile phone that has data capabilities) or tablet.

- ✔ You can copy data from your computer to a CD, DVD, or flash drive (see Chapter 14 for more information about flash drives). The catch here is that your research destination needs to have a computer that you can use to access the information from your CD, DVD, or flash drive.

- ✔ You can print your data from your computer or make photocopies of the documents that you must have with you for your research.

After you determine which of these solutions works best for you, you can use your past research findings while out in the field, leaving your original documents in the safest available place you can think of — a lockbox, a fireproof file cabinet or safe, or a safety-deposit box.

Deciding on a storage method

How are you going to store all that information? A filing system is in order! You can set up a good filing system in many ways, and no one system is right or wrong. Just use one that's comfortable for you.

If you're at a loss as to how to start a system, here's one we like: We prefer to have both electronic and physical components to our filing system. To establish an electronic system, enter your ancestors' names into your database. Most genealogical programs enable you to enter numbers for each individual. Use the numbers that you create in the electronic system on file folders for paper documents that you collect on each individual. Although we like to scan all our paper documents, sometimes we get behind, so we set up temporary folders in which we can store the documents until we can scan them. After we scan the documents, we transfer them to permanent folders that we keep in a fireproof container. You may consider saving your scanned images to a notebook computer's hard drive, an external hard drive, or a writable CD-ROM/DVD-ROM so that you can easily transport the images when you go on research trips.

Make backup copies of all your electronic documents as a precaution and store these backups in a location that is off-site from where the originals are stored.

Preserving Your Family Treasures

Time is going to take its toll on every artifact in your possession — whether it's a photograph or an original document. The longer you want your records and pictures to last, the better care you need to take of them now. In this section, we discuss some tips for preserving your family treasures so that you can pass them down to future generations in the best possible shape.

Storing vital records under the right conditions

Place birth certificates, marriage licenses, and other records between sheets of acid-free paper in albums. Keep these albums in a dark, dry, and temperature-consistent place: ideally, a place that is 65 to 70 degrees Fahrenheit year-round, with a relative humidity of less than 50 percent. You may consider placing these albums in a steel file cabinet (but make sure it's rust-free). Also, try to avoid using ink, staples, paper clips, glue, and tape around your documents (unless you use archival products designed for document repair).

For your precious documents (original birth certificates and family papers), rent a safety-deposit box or find another form of secure off-site storage. One of the best ways to ensure the success of your preservation efforts is to make electronic copies of your documents using a scanner, and then keep disk backups at a fire-safe, off-site location (again, a safety-deposit box is a good choice).

Protecting your photographs

Fight the urge to put all your photos of every ancestor on display because light can damage them over time. A better option is to scan the photographs and make copies or printouts to hang on the wall. Keep your most-prized pictures in a dark, dry, and temperature-consistent place. If you use a photo album for storage, make sure that it has acid-free paper or chemically safe plastic pockets, and that you affix the pictures to the pages using a safe adhesive. Other storage options include acid-free storage boxes and steel file cabinets. Store the photographs in a place that stays around 65 to 70 degrees Fahrenheit year-round, with a relative humidity of less than 50 percent. Avoid prolonged exposure of photographs to direct sunlight and fluorescent lights. And, by all means, have negatives made of those rare family photos and store them in clearly marked, acid-free envelopes (the kind without gumming or glue).

You can preserve photographs a couple of other ways. First, you can convert photographs from an earlier time to a newer and safer kind of film. A local photograph shop that specializes in preservation can do this for you. Because color photographs fade more quickly than their black-and-white counterparts, you may want to make black-and-white negatives of your color photographs. As with documents, you can preserve your photographs electronically by scanning them into your computer or by having a photo CD made by your photographic developer.

Of course, you need to store digital photos on a computer or on the camera's memory card. You should still remember to make backup copies and then store the media in a recommended manner. For more on digital media, see Chapter 14.

An electronic version of an old photograph isn't a real substitute for an original. Don't throw away the photos you scan (but you already knew that).

Here are a few websites that provide more detailed tips on preserving your family treasures:

- **Just Black and White's Tips for Preserving Your Photographs and Documents,** by David Mishkin: justblackandwhite.com/tip.htm
- **Cornell University Library's Preserving Your Family Photographs:** www.library.cornell.edu/preservation/ brochure/Family%20Photos%20Text%2001.pdf
- **Document and Photo Preservation FAQ,** by Linda Beyea: http:// loricase.com/faq.html

It's possible that some of your family videos and photos exist on film or slides. For information on preserving old 8 mm, 16 mm, and 35 mm films or slides, check out this article from *The New York Times:* "Tips on Archiving Family History, Part 2" at www.nytimes.com/2013/06/05/ booming/tips-on-preserving-family-films-and-photos. html?pagewanted=all&_r=0.

And when you're looking for some of the chemically safe archival materials that we've described in this chapter (such as albums, paper, boxes, and adhesives), head on over to

- **Archival Products** at www.archival.com
- **Light Impressions** at www.lightimpressionsdirect.com/servlet/ OnlineShopping

Even though you want to preserve everything to the best of your ability, don't be afraid to pull out your albums to show visiting relatives and friends. On the other hand, don't be embarrassed to ask these guests to use caution when looking through your albums. Depending on the age and rarity of some of your documents, you may even want to ask guests to wear latex gloves when handling the albums so that the oil from their hands doesn't get on your treasures. Upon realizing how important these items are to you, most guests won't mind using caution.

Visiting Libraries, Archives, and Historical Societies

Earlier in this chapter, we discuss getting information from living relatives. But your kinfolk aren't the only people who can help you advance your research. You don't want to forget certain institutional-type resources.

Inevitably, a time will come when you need to visit libraries in the areas where your ancestor lived. Although local history sections are not generally targeted toward genealogists, the information you can find there is quite valuable. For example, public libraries often have city directories and phone books, past issues of newspapers (good for obituary hunting), and old map collections. Libraries may also have extensive collections of local history books that can give you a flavor of what life was like for your ancestor in that area. Some libraries do have genealogy sections with all sorts of goodies to help you locate records and discover interesting stories about your family. For a list of libraries with online catalogs, see The Library Index site at www.libdex.com.

Archives are another place to find good information. They exist at three levels —national, state, and local — and have different owners — public or private. Each archive varies — some may have a large collection of certain types of documents, whereas others may contain documents from a certain geographical area. To find archives, see the Repositories of Primary Sources page at www.uidaho.edu/special-collections/Other.Repositories.html.

A third place to find information is a historical society. Generally, historical societies have nice collections of maps, documents, and local history books pertaining to the area where the society is located. They are repositories for collections of papers of people who lived in the community. Often, you can find references to your ancestors in these collections, especially if the person whose personal documents are in the collection wrote a letter or transacted some business with your ancestor. You can find links to historical societies on the Yahoo! site at http://dir.yahoo.com/arts/humanities/history/organizations/historical_societies.

Getting Involved with Genealogical Societies

At times, dealing with the many different record sets and methods of researching your family can be overwhelming. On such occasions, it's nice to be able to sit down with people who have similar experiences or more knowledge than you and discuss your research problems. One place that you can find such a group is your local genealogical society. Genealogical societies hold periodic meetings that focus on particular research methods. Some also have weekend seminars where they bring in genealogical lecturers to address topics of interest to their members.

If you have research needs in other areas of the country (or foreign countries for that matter), you might consider joining a society in that area. Although you do not live there, you can still use the resources of the society to find answers to your questions, and you can contribute to the distant organization more than you realize by sharing your findings and experiences. Most societies have people who are well versed in the records that pertain to the area where the society is located. These individuals can be a great resource as you go through the research process.

To find a genealogical society in the U.S. check out the Federation of Genealogical Societies Society Hall at `www.fgs.org/cstm_societyHall.php`.

A general search engine (such as Google) can help you find societies in other countries. In the search field, type the name of the location and the phrase *genealogical society*.

We delve into genealogical societies a bit more and explore specific ways you can become active and benefit from them in Chapter 13.

Discovering Family History Centers

If you live in a smaller community, you may be surprised to discover that your hometown has a resource specifically for local genealogical research. Sponsored by The Church of Jesus Christ of Latter-day Saints (LDS), more than 4,600 Family History Centers in 134 countries worldwide provide support for genealogical research. Microfilms that contain images of records are among the important resources found in Family History Centers.

You are not required to be a member of the LDS church to use a Family History Center; the resources they contain are available to everyone. Keep in mind that the workers at a Family History Center cannot research your genealogy for you, although they're willing to point you in the right direction. To find a Family History Center, use the FamilySearch search interface, which you can find at `https://familysearch.org/locations/centerlocator`.

Chapter 3

Searching Primary Resource Sites

. . . .

In This Chapter

▶ Selecting a good ancestor to begin your search

▶ Surveying Ancestry.com

▶ An overview of FamilySearch.org

▶ Introduction to other primary resource sites

. . . .

*B*efore the age of the Internet, searching for primary sources was like trying to find a needle in a haystack. A typical research session would begin in a crowded room containing paper indexes of census records. After searching through rows and rows of information, you would jot down some names that looked familiar along with a record's page number. Then you'd grab a roll of microfilm and scroll your way through it until you found the page number. Sometimes your potential ancestor wouldn't be on that page, requiring you to search line by line before and after the targeted page. If you still couldn't find the name for your search, you might have to read line by line through an entire county. Needless to say, it could take hours to find the individual, only to discover that it wasn't really your ancestor after all.

Fast-forward to the age of the Internet. Now you can find digitized versions of the census microfilm online; even better, many of them have indexes that link directly to the image. Although indexers still make mistakes, it takes a fraction of the time to search. Another bonus is that some sites provide links to other record sets that your ancestor may be in, which gives you even more evidence to substantiate your research. Finding primary sources is what online genealogy is all about. You can see the representation of the original record and draw your own conclusions as to what the record really indicates.

Millions of records are now available online. This chapter focuses on introducing some of the larger collections and gives you guidance on how to search for records using these sites. The searches that we conduct in this chapter are more general; for searches that focus on particular types of records, see Chapters 4 and 5.

Selecting a Person to Begin Your Search

Now that you've started collecting and organizing family documents that can help you put together your family history (if you haven't, take a quick look at Chapter 2 to get some tips), it's time to focus on one particular person and start digging deeper through the many online resources. Selecting a person sounds easy, doesn't it? Just choose your great-great-grandfather's name, and you're off to the races. But what if your great-great-grandfather's name was John Smith? You may encounter millions of sites with information on John Smith — unless you know some facts about the John Smith you're looking for, we can almost guarantee that you'll have a frustrating time online.

Trying a semi-unique name

The first time you research online, try to start with a person whose name is, for lack of a better term, semi-unique. By this we mean a person with a name that doesn't take up ten pages in your local phone book, but is still common enough that you can find some information on it the first time you conduct a search. If you're really brave, you can begin with someone with a common surname such as Smith or Jones, but you have to do a lot more groundwork up-front so that you can easily determine whether any of the multiple findings relate to your ancestor.

Also, consider variations in spelling that your ancestor's name may have. Often, you can find more information on the mainstream spelling of his or her surname than on one of its rarer variants. For example, if you research someone with the surname Helme, you may have better luck finding information under the spellings *Helm* or *Helms*. If your family members immigrated to the United States in the last two centuries, they may have *Americanized* their surname. Families often Americanized their name so that the name could be easily pronounced in English, or sometimes the surname was simply misspelled and subsequently adopted by the family.

For more information on name variations, check out the Name Variations in the United States Indexes and Records page at FamilySearch:

```
https://familysearch.org/learn/wiki/en/Name_Variations_in_
United_States_Indexes_and_Records
```

Narrowing your starting point

If you aren't sure how popular a name is, try visiting a site with surname distribution maps. The publicprofiler worldnames search site (`worldnames.publicprofiler.org`), maintained by University College London, allows you to enter a surname and find locations across the world where the surname is most prevalent. The site includes charts for the top countries, regions, and cities for the surname. Here's what to do:

1. **Open your browser and go to the publicprofiler worldnames search site (`worldnames.publicprofiler.org`).**

   The site appears with a search form at the top.

2. **Type the surname you're researching in the Map Your Surname field, type your e-mail in the My Email field, and select the appropriate gender radio button.**

   For help choosing a surname, see the preceding section.

3. **Click Search.**

   The color surname distribution map appears as in Figure 3-1. The surname is more frequent in areas colored in deep blue. The tables at the bottom of the page provide more details on the surname.

Figure 3-1: A distribution map for the surname Helm.

4. **To get a closer look at a particular area, click the country on the map and you see the regional level.**

Figure 3-2 shows the frequency of the Helm surname in Germany.

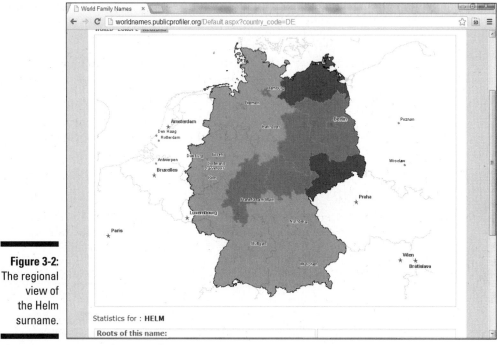

Figure 3-2:
The regional
view of
the Helm
surname.

A good reason to check out distribution maps is that you can use them to identify potential geographic areas where you can look for your family during the years covered by the site. If we hit a wall and can't find additional information online about a particular individual or the surname, we know we can start looking at records in these areas to find more clues about families with the name. We hope that by doing so, we'll find our branch.

Choosing someone you know about

In addition to choosing a person whom you're likely to have success researching, you want to use a person you already know something about. The more details that you know about a person, the more successful your initial search is likely to be.

For example, Matthew used his great-grandfather William Abell because he knew more about that side of his family. His grandmother once mentioned that her father was born in LaRue County, Kentucky, in 1876. This gives him a point of reference for judging whether a site has any relevant information on his family. A site is relevant if it contains any information on Abells who were located in or near LaRue County, Kentucky, before or around the year 1876. Try to use the same technique with your ancestor. For more information on how to extract genealogical information from your family to use in your research, see Chapter 2.

Selecting a grandparent's name

Having trouble selecting a name? Why not try one of your grandparent's names? Using a grandparent's name can have several benefits. If you find some information on an individual but you aren't sure whether it's relevant to your family, you can check with relatives to see whether they know any additional information that can help you. This may also spur interest in genealogy in other family members who can then assist you with some of your research burden or produce some family documents that you never knew existed.

With a name in hand, you're ready to see how much information is currently available on the Internet about that individual. Because this is just one step in a long journey to discover your family history, you want to begin slowly. *Don't try to examine every resource right from the start.* You're more likely to become overloaded with information if you try to find too many resources too quickly. Your best approach is to begin searching a few sites until you get the hang of how to find information about your ancestors online. And keep in mind that you can always bookmark sites in your web browser, or record the URL in a spreadsheet or your genealogical database, so that you can easily return to them later, when you're ready for more in-depth researching.

Touring Ancestry.com

A commercial site that has perhaps the most varied collection of genealogical resources is Ancestry.com. Over time, Ancestry.com has amassed its collection by acquiring several websites, genealogical software, and other data and print resources. The company, which started as a publisher of genealogical research books, now includes the Ancestry.com, Genealogy.com, MyFamily.com, RootsWeb.com, Fold3.com, and Newspapers.com websites. It owns the research company ProGenealogists and the genealogical software Family Tree Maker. Although the majority of the Ancestry.com websites require a subscription, a great deal of resources are available to use for free. This section provides an overview of the resources and shows how to use the general search function. We also refer to Ancestry.com in other portions of this book when we talk about specific types of online sources.

Trying Ancestry.com for Free

If you don't have a subscription to Ancestry.com, perhaps the first thing to do is register for a free two-week trial. Using the free trial, you can experience all the areas of the site that we cover in this book. It will also give you a chance to see if the site will fulfill your immediate research needs. To begin the free trial, do the following:

1. **Point your web browser to** `www.ancestry.com`.

   In the upper-right corner of the home page is a 14-Day Free Trial box.

2. **Click the Give Me Access link in the box.**

   The resulting page contains a table with two subscription options, as shown in Figure 3-3.

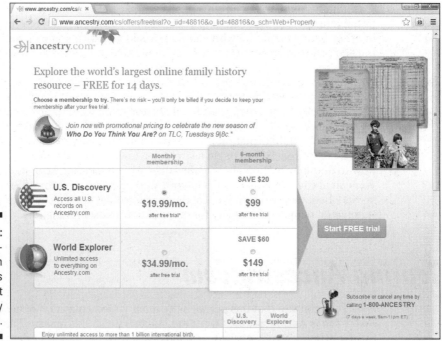

Figure 3-3:
The subscription options page at Ancestry.com.

3. **In the Monthly Membership column, click the U.S. Discovery radio button.**

   Select the monthly membership because Ancestry.com bills you after the free trial ends if you don't cancel in time (by the last day of your membership). Three-month and six-month memberships are billed in single payments, so the least amount of risk is in the monthly membership.

4. **Click the Start Free Trial button to continue.**

   The Start Free Trial button is located just to the right of the membership options. The Create Your Account page appears.

5. **If you haven't registered previously, enter your first name, last name, and e-mail address, and click the Continue button. If you're already registered, simply click the Sign In Here link.**

   Make sure that the check box next to the terms and conditions is selected.

6. **Type a password into the Password field and click the Continue button.**

   The payment details screen appears. Fill in the account information, including your street address, city, state or province, zip or postal code, country, and phone number. Also, fill in future payment information, including the card type, card number, expiration date, and security code fields.

7. **Click the Start Your Free Trial button.**

   The membership details page appears. In the right column, note the description of the 14-day free trial cancellation process so that you can use it at the end of the trial period if you decide that you don't want to continue with a subscription. Print this page and put the expiration date of the free trial on your calendar so that you remember when to cancel, if you choose to do so.

8. **Click the Get Started button at the top of the page.**

   The Search page appears, and you can start using Ancestry.com.

Searching Ancestry.com's vast collection

The most efficient way to search Ancestry.com is by using the main search form. This allows you to receive results from all collections rather than from only a single record set. Follow these steps to search for an ancestor:

1. **Point your web browser to `www.ancestry.com`, the Ancestry.com home page, and click the Search button in the toolbar at the top of the page.**

   The Search page appears.

2. **In the Search section at the top of the page, type a name into the First & Middle Name(s) and Last Name fields.**

   We entered the name Uriah Helm in these fields.

3. **Type a place where your ancestor lived in the field labeled A Place Your Ancestor May Have Lived.**

Because the field is a type-ahead field, it suggests locations as you type letters into the field. To select a location, scroll down to the location and click it to enter it into the field.

4. **If the name you're searching for is common, you may want to add optional information to distinguish one person from another. You can add life events (such as births, marriages, and deaths) by clicking the Add Life Events link.**

A new line is created when you click the link, as shown in Figure 3-4.

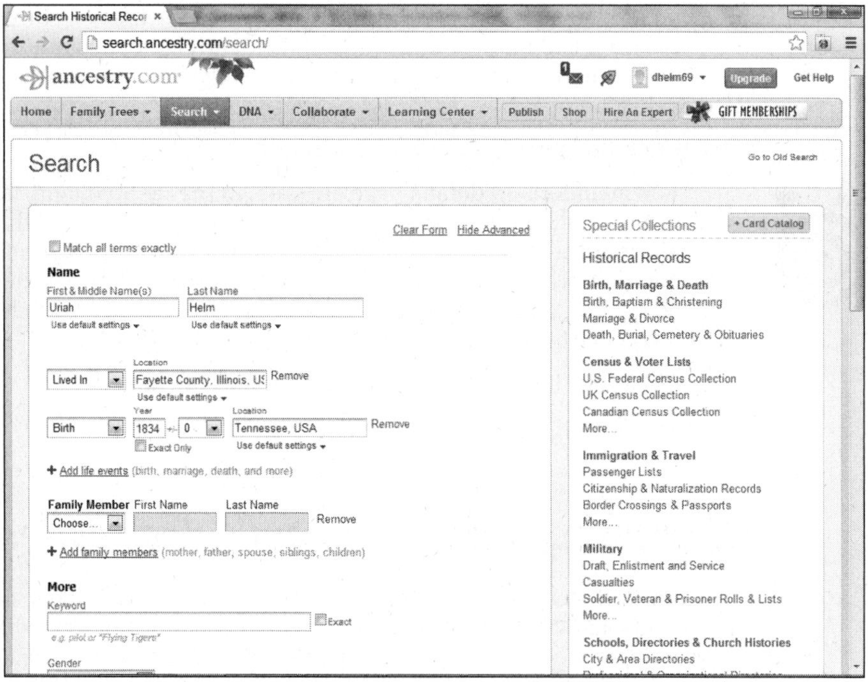

Figure 3-4:
An additional life event for birth.

5. **Click the down arrow to open the Any Event drop-down menu, and choose the appropriate event type. Enter the year and location of the event.**

You can add additional events by clicking the Add Life Events link again.

6. **If you know family members who can be found via your ancestor (such as a parent or spouse), click the optional Add Family Members link.**

Select the type of family member from the Choose drop-down menu, and complete the individual's First Name and Last Name fields. You can add additional people by clicking the Add Family Members link.

7. **To add more search criteria, fill in the other optional fields available on the form.**

8. **If you'd like, you can limit search results to the exact spelling of the name by selecting the Match All Terms Exactly check box at the top of the screen.**

Use the Match All Terms Exactly option when you know that your ancestor's name is spelled a certain way. For example, the name of Matthew's ancestor Herschel is spelled Heruhel in one record set. To find this record quickly, Matthew would use the Match All Terms Exactly option. You can also use this functionality when you're researching a name that's spelled multiple ways and you want to find records with only one spelling. For example, you might want to find only records spelled Smythe and not Smith.

9. **Click the Use Default Settings link under the First & Middle Name(s) and Last Name fields if you want to configure more search options.**

The options described in these lists restrict the search on the name (see Figure 3-5):

- *Phonetic Matches:* The Ancestry.com search engine contains algorithms that determine whether a name sounds like the name you entered into the field.

- *Names with Similar Meanings or Spellings:* This option is helpful when you search for common first names that are often shortened. For example, Richard is often shortened to Rich, Rick, or Dick.

- *Records Where Only Initials Are Recorded:* (This option isn't shown in Figure 3-5; it's under the First & Middle Name(s) Use Default Settings link.) Use this handy option when you search for people who are often referred to by their initials in records, such as A.J. rather than the full name.

- *Soundex Matches:* The Last Name field has an additional choice to restrict the result to Soundex matches — for a way of coding names according to the way their consonants sound. When we searched for Helm with this check box selected, we received matches for names with the Soundex code of H450, including Hellam and Holm, for example. Find out more about Soundex codes in Chapter 4.

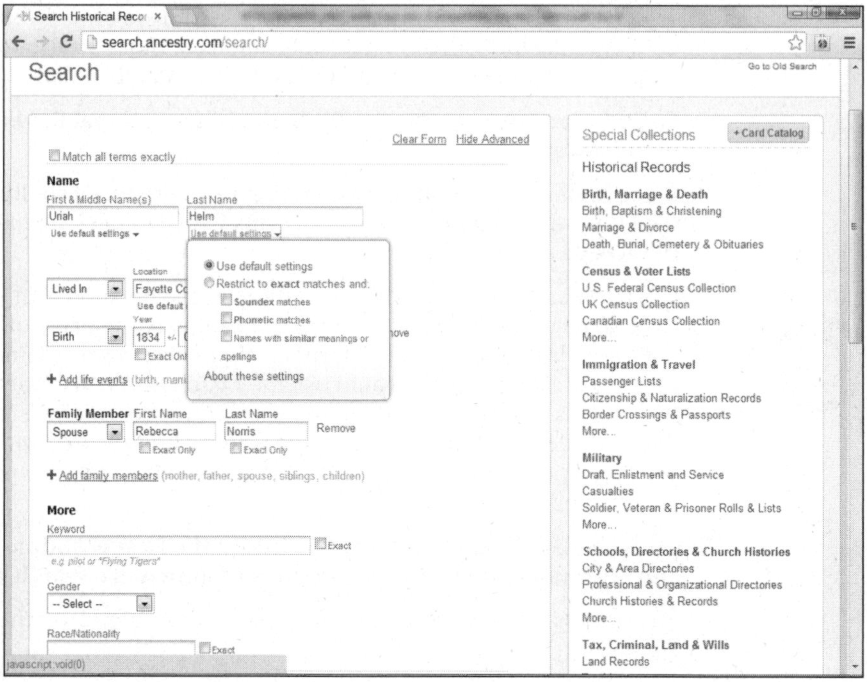

Figure 3-5:
Options
under the
Use Default
Settings
link.

10. **Click the Use Default Settings link under the Location field if you'd like to restrict the search to only the location you entered.**

    This option is helpful when you're searching for a common name and you know the location where your ancestor lived. The search then focuses on that person in the context of the location, greatly reducing the number of results.

    When you type a place-name in the field, additional choices appear, including limiting your search to the county, county/adjacent counties, state, state/adjacent states, or country. Using adjacent counties is particularly helpful when you're searching counties that were later divided into other counties. The adjacent-counties search picks up the new counties if they're adjacent to the old county.

11. **Enter a term into the Keyword field, should you want to limit your search to a specific criterion.**

    You can use a keyword to search specific items not covered in the other fields. For example, if you know that your ancestor lived near a specific post office or served in a specific regiment, you can enter that term into the field.

    You can further limit the search to the exact term by selecting the Exact check box next to the Keyword field.

12. **Click the down arrow in the Gender field and select the appropriate gender, if restricting the search this way is beneficial to you.**

Choosing the gender is useful when you're searching for an ancestor who has a name that can be either male or female, such as Kelly.

13. **Complete the Race/Nationality field if race or nationality is a helpful factor for your ancestor.**

This field is helpful when you search census records in which, depending on the census year, either race or nationality was recorded.

14. **Set the Collection Priority by clicking the arrow on its drop-down menu if you want to set preferences for some of the search criteria.**

The Collection Priority menu tells the search engine to give preference in the results to records from a particular country or ethnic group. You can use this option when an ancestor immigrated to a particular country and you want to focus the search on the new country.

15. **Use the check boxes under the Collection Priority to limit searches to only certain resource types if you desire.**

We often use the Restrict To functionality to limit searches to only historical records. This way, the results contain only records that we can use as evidence — rather than to someone's interpretation of a record in a family tree.

16. **After you finish setting all search options, click the Search button.**

The search results page appears, as shown in Figure 3-6.

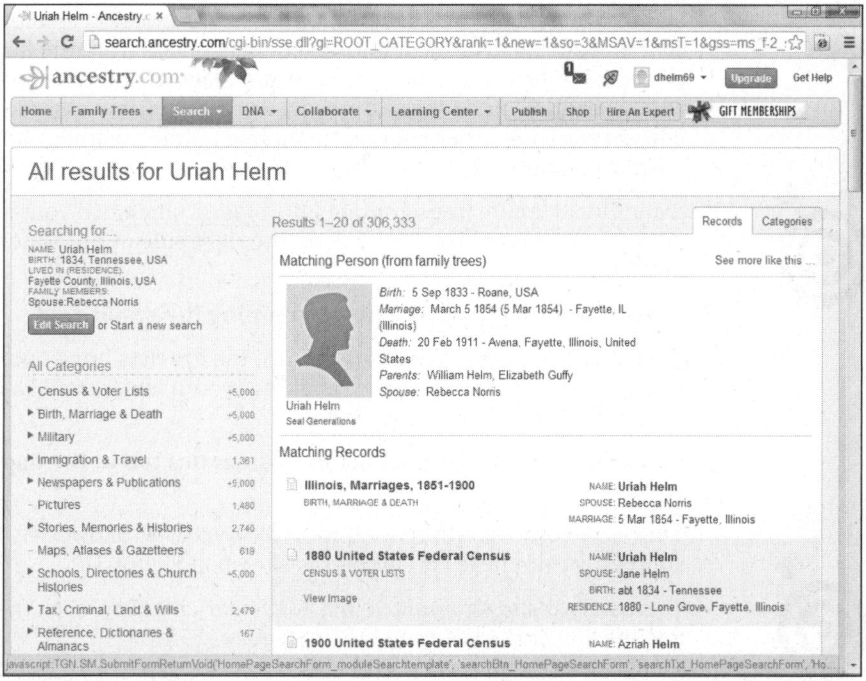

Figure 3-6: Search results from Ancestry .com.

Sifting through the results

Executing the search is only half the battle. The next part is going through the search results to find useful information on your particular ancestor. The search results page contains several sections, including

✔ **Searching For:** This section is located in the upper-left corner and lists the search criteria you used.

✔ **All Categories:** This section contains categories for displaying results.

✔ **Results:** The Results section lists the number of matches and how they're sorted along the top of the right column.

As you can see from Figure 3-6, a search that contains only a few criteria, such as birth date, residence, and spouse's name, can yield a staggering number of results — in our case more than 300,000. It's important to be able to manage the results in order to avoid spending a lot of time going through records that aren't pertinent to your research. Here are some ways to navigate and view the results:

1. **On the search results screen, take a look at the results in the right column.**

   If your search term matches a person in a family tree, that result appears first in the list. For example, in Figure 3-6, you see that a Uriah Helm with a close birth date and a spouse with the same name as our search is found in a family tree. In addition to the information similar to our search, you can also see additional details pulled from the family tree (if available), such as marriage date and place, death date and place, and parent names. Along with family tree results, you can see matching records from other sources, including public member photos and scanned documents.

   If additional family trees contain information similar to your search, click the See More Like This link on the right side of the Matching Person heading.

2. **Hover the cursor over the link containing the result name.**

   If the result is an Ancestry.com record, the Preview box appears. The Preview box shows key elements of the record and, possibly, a thumbnail of the record, if it's digitized.

3. **Sort search results by clicking the Categories tab in the upper-right corner.**

   This view contains the general record categories followed by the top five sources within these categories, as shown in Figure 3-7.

   To see all results for sources in a particular category, click the See All Results link at the bottom of the category.

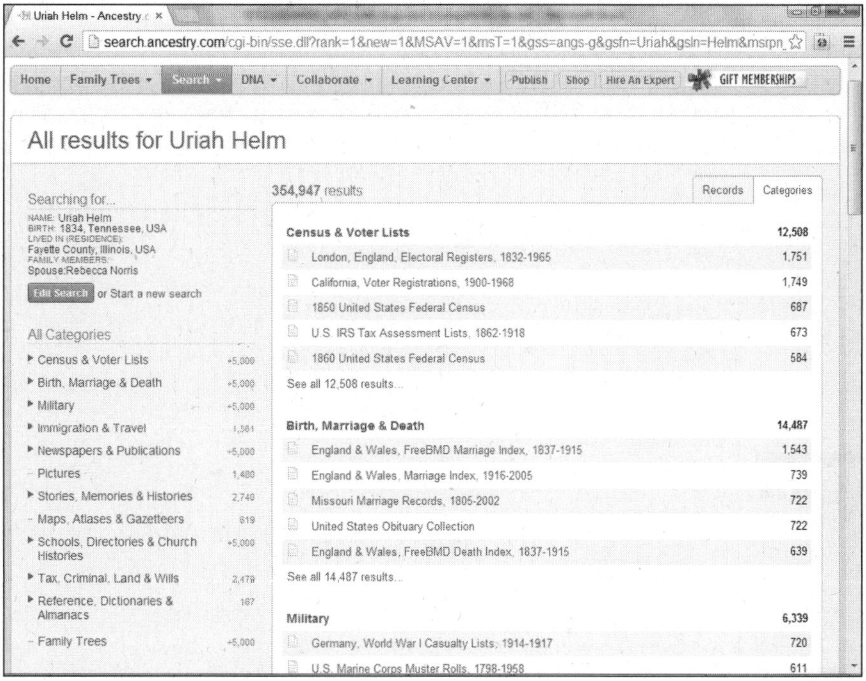

Figure 3-7:
The
Categories
view.

4. **To restrict search results to a particular type of record, click a category in the All Categories section in the left column of the page.**

   This view contains the general record categories followed by the top five sources within these categories, as shown in Figure 3-7.

   For example, if you select the Census & Voter Lists category, the results screen is filtered to include only the matches to the search that fit that category. Notice there's a list of subcategories of the census listed by year beneath the category.

5. **Click a record group in the right column that might contain records on you ancestor.**

   In our case, we clicked the 1850 United States Federal Census. A new page appears with names fitting the search criteria that are located in the record group. For example, Figure 3-8 shows a record for Mariah Helm indexed in the 1850 census. The record appears first in the results because it's the closest match to the search terms. Because this Mariah Helm has an alternate spelling of Uriah Helm, a close match to the birth date, and matches the residence and birthplace, it appears first.

Figure 3-8:
The results
for Uriah
Helm in
the 1850
census.

6. Click View Record.

If there are other details about the record, you can see them on the
Record view. In our case, the record for Mariah (Uriah) includes the
names and ages of household members, shown in Figure 3-9.

Note the box in the right column containing links to suggested records.
These are records in other groups that meet the search criteria. This can
be a shortcut to finding several records for the same individual without
executing another search.

7. If the Record view contains a thumbnail image with an orange seal labeled View Original Record, click the thumbnail.

The resulting page launches a viewer to show the digitized image of
the primary source. Figure 3-10 shows the 1850 census record for Uriah
Helm; notice that we've zoomed in on the record, so you can see the
name better.

8. Click the Tools menu to control the image.

If you need to rotate, flip, or invert the color of the image, you can use
the Tools menu.

If the handwriting is hard to read due to faded or smeared ink, sometimes you can read it easier by inverting the color of the image.

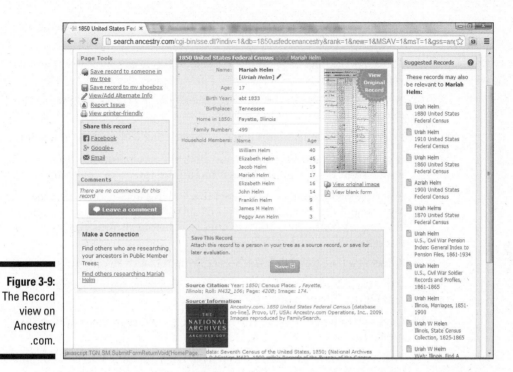

Figure 3-9:
The Record
view on
Ancestry
.com.

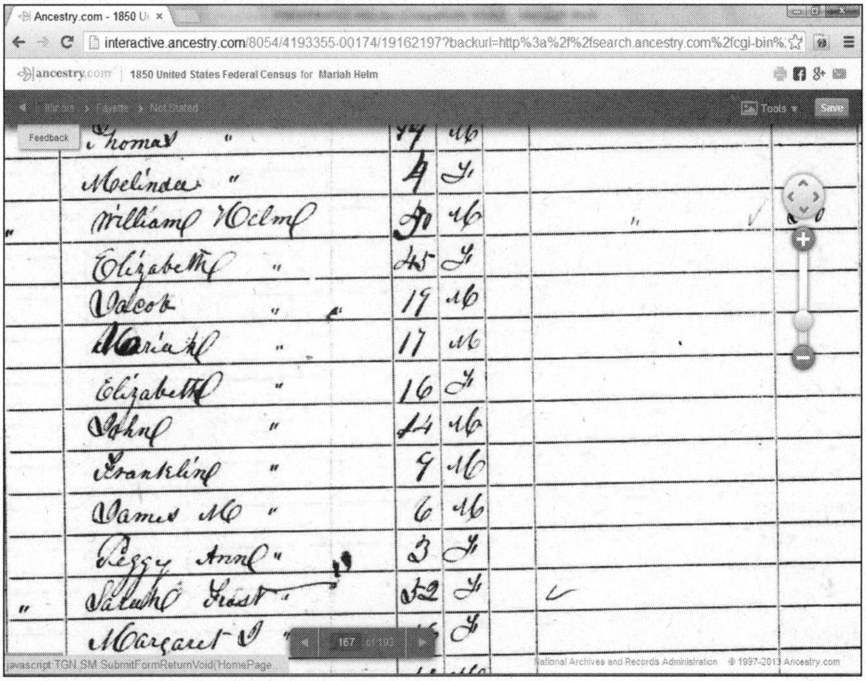

Figure 3-10:
The digitized
census
record for
Uriah Helm.

9. **To print this image, click the Print button in the top-right corner of the screen.**

   The Print Options page appears. Click Continue to send the image to your printer.

10. **To share the image, click the Facebook, Google+, or e-mail icons in the top-right corner of the screen.**

    Clicking any icon launches a new pop-over box with further instructions.

11. **If you have an online family tree, click the Save button in the upper-right corner of the screen to add the image to your tree.**

    In the dialog box that opens, select the Attach This Record to Someone in My Tree option. (See Chapter 1 for details on creating an online family tree at Ancestry.com.) The Attach Record to Someone in Your Tree pop-over box appears.

12. **Select the tree and click the Select From a List of People link.**

    The Attach Record to Someone in Your Tree page appears with a list of individuals in your family tree.

13. **Click the Select button to the left of the person you want to link the image to.**

    The Add New Information to Your Tree page appears with two columns, as shown in Figure 3-11. The left column contains information from the census record, and the right contains information from your family tree.

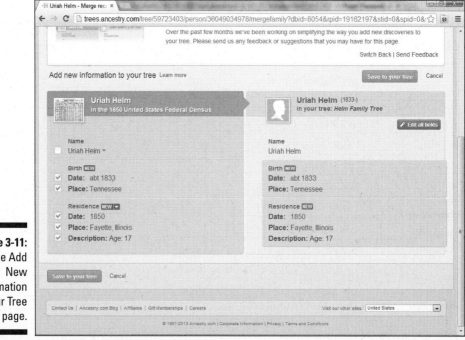

Figure 3-11:
The Add New Information to Your Tree page.

14. **Select the check boxes with the information you would like to import into your online family tree and click the Save to Your Tree button.**

   The page for the individual to which you attached the record is displayed. You can click the Facts and Sources tab to see the information added from the record.

RootsWeb.com at a Glance

RootsWeb.com is a well-established online community for genealogists. It's been around for a long time and has gone through various renditions. Several years ago, it became part of the Ancestry.com family and has remained closely associated with Ancestry. Whereas Ancestry.com relies heavily on subscriptions to keep its collection growing, RootsWeb.com relies heavily on the generosity of its users to give their time, energy, and personal resources to make free genealogical data available for all to use.

Users can contribute to RootsWeb.com by submitting transcriptions of books and records, sharing their family trees in the WorldConnect Project (a database of family trees that now has more than 700 million names in it), participating in the RootsWeb Surname List, or RSL (a registry of surnames being researched worldwide and how to contact those researching the names), and posting messages and responses to the message boards and mailing lists hosted by RootsWeb.com. RootsWeb.com also offers web hosting, where you can build your own genealogy website.

To experience RootsWeb.com, point your browser to `www.rootsweb.ancestry.com`. The directory on the home page gives you a quick and comprehensive look at what RootsWeb.com has to offer. Click any of the links to discover how you can contribute to the various RootsWeb.com projects.

Investigating FamilySearch

FamilySearch is the largest nonprofit genealogical website. It's sponsored by The Church of Jesus Christ of Latter-day Saints, but you don't have to be a member of the church to use it. The free resources available on the site include a photo collection area, an online family tree, and a collection of records containing more than 3 billion names.

Creating a free account

To make sure that you can use all the functionality of FamilySearch, it's a good idea to create a free account. To do so, follow these easy steps:

1. **Set your web browser to `www.familysearch.org`.**

   The FamilySearch home page appears.

2. **In the upper-right corner of the screen, click the Sign In link.**

   The Sign In page appears.

3. **Click the Create an Account button in the upper-right corner of the page.**

   The registration page appears. Fill out the required data including first name, last name, user name, password, e-mail, contact name, gender, country, birth date, and membership. As you complete each field a green check appears. Also, type in the letters from the CAPTCHA picture and click the check box accepting rights and privacy policies.

4. **Click the Create an Account button.**

   FamilySearch sends you an e-mail to the address you specified during registration.

5. **Check your e-mail account and click the Activate Account link in the confirmation e-mail.**

   After confirming the e-mail address, the home page for FamilySearch appears.

6. **Click the Sign In link.**

   The Sign In page appears, in which you can type your new user name and password in the form.

7. **Click the Sign In button.**

   The FamilySearch home page appears — with your name in the upper-right corner.

FamilySearching records

Here's how you search in FamilySearch:

1. **Click the Search icon below the main picture on the site or click the Search link at the top of the page.**

   The Search page appears as shown in Figure 3-12. To search for records on the site, fill in the First Names and Last Names fields. Note the check boxes next to the First Names and Last Name fields. When you select the check boxes, the search results match the name exactly.

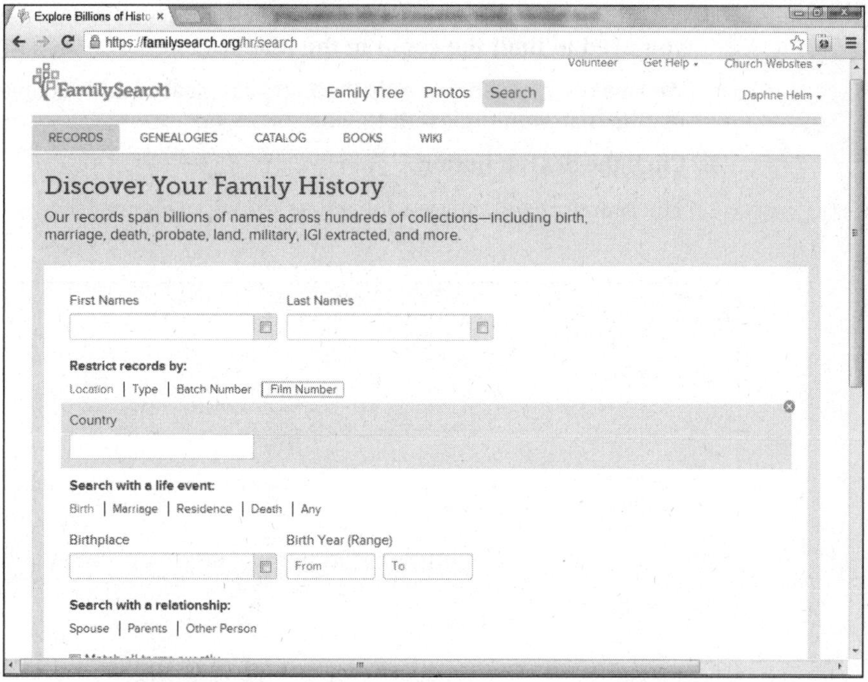

Figure 3-12:
The Family
Search
Search
page.

2. **Enter optional information in the Location, Type, Batch Number, and Film Number fields.**

   As you click the links to each of these filters, the field appears onscreen. The Batch Number and Film Number fields are for advanced searches and are useful when you have seen a reference to a particular data set on a website or in a book.

3. **Enter information in the Life Event fields.**

   As you click the links to each of these filters, the field appears onscreen. You can choose to enter information on birth, marriage, residence, death, or any place that your ancestor might be associated with. Note that you can put in a date range for the event.

   Consider using date ranges anytime that you conduct a search on FamilySearch. For example, if you know the birth date was 1833, put a date range between 1830 and 1835, just in case the date of birth or age calculation for a particular record is incorrect. That way you won't miss any records.

4. **Enter names related to your ancestor if you want the search to restrict results by associated names.**

   As you click the links to each of these filters, the field appears onscreen. You can choose to enter names for spouse, parents, or another person associated with your ancestor.

5. **Select the check box to make the search match all terms exactly, if you need to limit the count in the results.**

   We suggest you use this only if you try the search and receive too many results that aren't relevant to your ancestor.

6. **Click the Search button.**

   The search results page appears, as shown in Figure 3-13.

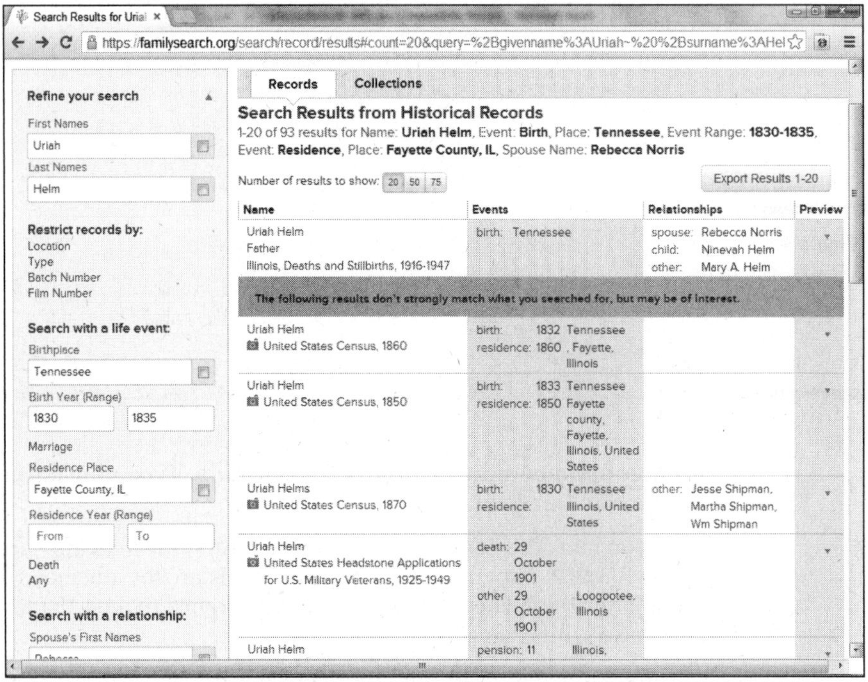

Figure 3-13:
The Family Search search results page.

Using FamilySearch results

Although you may not receive as many results in FamilySearch as in Ancestry.com, it's still important that you know how to navigate the results to save you time. The search results page is divided into two columns. The left column contains filters that you can use to limit the search results. The right column lists the results. The most relevant results appear near the top. Other records that might have relevance appear under the blue box titled "The following results don't strongly match what you searched for, but may be of interest."

Each search result is divided into four columns: Name, Events, Relationships, and Preview. The Name column includes the Name of the person and the name of the collection where the person is found. A camera icon next to the collection indicates that the collection includes images.

If your search in the previous section generated some promising leads, follow these steps to explore the results:

1. **Click the small arrow in the Preview column.**

   The Preview column expands and shows more information in the column, as shown in Figure 3-14. In our case, additional information is shown in the Relationships column about Ninevah Helm, son of Uriah Helm, who died in 1935.

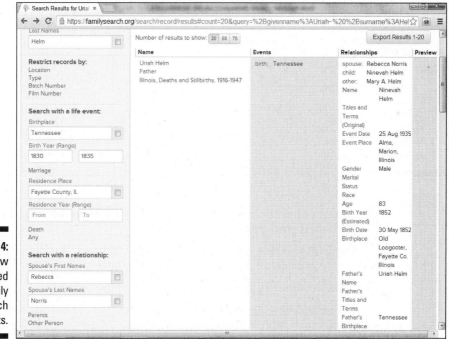

Figure 3-14: The preview is selected in the Family Search results.

2. **To sort your search results by record category, click the Collections tab.**

   The Collections view appears as shown in Figure 3-15. The top five collections are displayed under each category. You can filter multiple categories by selecting the check box to the left of each collection. The maximum number of collections that you can select is 25.

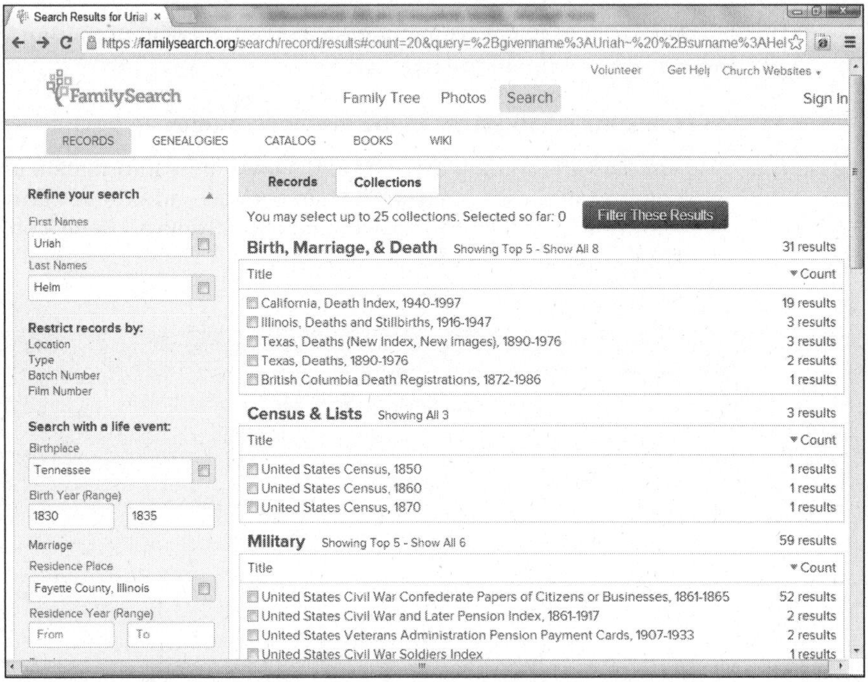

Figure 3-15:
The
Collections
view in
Family
Search
results.

3. **You can filter the results on the Records tab at the bottom of the first column, if you desire.**

   The filters include collection, birthplace, birth year, residence place, residence year, death place, death year, other place, other year, and gender.

4. **Click the name of the person under the Name column.**

   The record view appears, shown in Figure 3-16. The record view shows details such as gender, age, marital status, and publication information.

5. **If an image is available (as noted in the right column), click the View Image link.**

   The image viewer is launched, as shown in Figure 3-17. You can use the floating toolbar on the right side of the screen to zoom in and out, rotate, invert the color, save, and print the image.

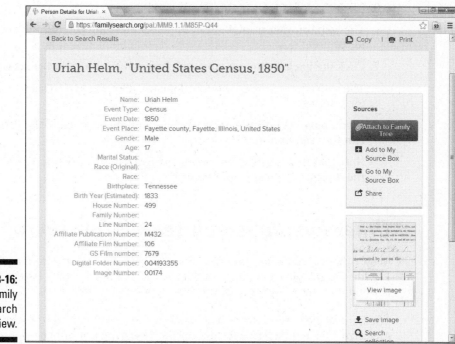

6. **Click the Print icon in the floating toolbar.**

   The web browser print window appears, allowing you to select options for printing.

7. **Click the back button on your web browser to return to the record view.**

   The web browser print window appears, allowing you to select options for printing.

8. **If you have an online family tree at FamilySearch, click the Attach to Family Tree button.**

   Note that this is a different online family tree than the one we created at the Ancestry.com site in Chapter 1.

Other FamilySearch search functions

A few other search pages on FamilySearch are well worth mentioning. These include Genealogies, Catalog, and Books. You can reach each of these by clicking their tabs at the top of the Search page; refer to Figure 3-12.

The Genealogies search page searches the entries submitted by users to the Ancestral File and Pedigree Resource File. These are not primary sources; rather, they contain information submitted by other genealogists. The information contained within them has not been vetted, and you should take extra steps to verify all information. The two files are useful in providing hints on areas to investigate and can help jump-start your research.

You can explore the catalog of genealogical materials held by the Family History Library using the Catalog search. The resources referenced in the catalog have not necessarily been digitized, but several of them have been microfilmed and can be loaned to Family History Centers (see Chapter 2 for more on Family History Centers).

The third search function is the Books search. Here you can search a focused collection of 80,000 family history publications. Note that some of the publications contained within this collection are also found on websites such as the Internet Archive (www.archive.org).

Giving Back through FamilySearch Indexing

FamilySearch Indexing is a project through which volunteers help transcribe records from all over the world and submit them for posting on the website so that others can access them for free. It's a simple process. FamilySearch obtains the records and digitizes them. You download copies of the digital images to your personal computer. Then, using special online software, you index the data in the digital records. The result — a searchable index — is made available to the public free of charge. So far, more than 1 billion records have been indexed by more than 115,000 volunteers.

For more information about the FamilySearch Indexing project, go to `https://familysearch.org/volunteer/indexing`.

Looking through Archives.com

Archives.com contains more than 2.5 billion records of interest to genealogists and family historians. The site is now owned by Ancestry.com, and there are a lot of duplicate record sets between the two sites — especially in the area of census records. One area to look at on Archives.com is the collection of vital records. The site is a subscription site, but you can get a free trial for seven days.

Creating a trial account

To see all of the content available on the Archives.com site, you must have an account. Follow these steps to set up a free account:

1. **Set your web browser to `www.archives.com`.**

   The Archives.com home page appears in your browser window.

2. **Click the Start 7-Day Free Trial button in the upper-right corner of the page.**

   The billing information screen appears.

3. **Fill out the form with your payment information and click the Begin Free Trial button.**

   The Last Step page appears.

   You can cancel your membership any time before the 7-day free trial ends, and Archives.com won't bill you.

4. **Complete the Create Your Password fields and the optional ancestor-alert information and click the Create Account button.**

   The Archives.com Welcome page opens.

5. **Click the Historical Records Search link in the right column.**

   The Search page opens, shown in Figure 3-18.

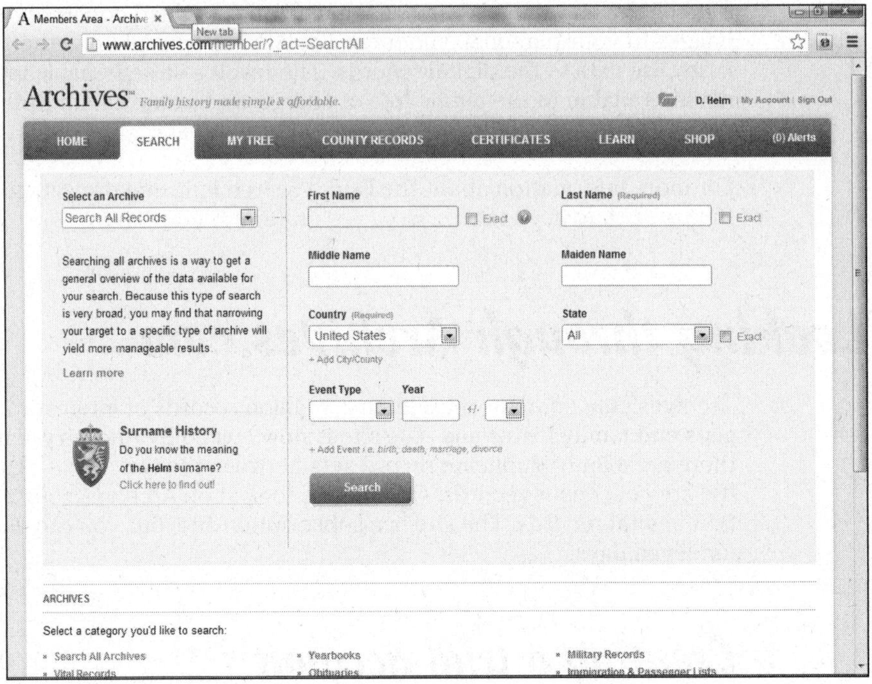

Figure 3-18:
The
Archives
.com Search
page.

Searching Archives.com

You can use the Archives.com search engine to find links to the content in each of its collections. Here are the steps for using the search function:

1. **In the Select an Archive section, set the drop-down menu to Search All Records (the default setting). Fill in the First Name, Last Name, Middle Name, Maiden Name (if applicable), Country, and State fields.**

   You can set the First Name, Last Name, or Location fields to find exact matches. If you get too few results, deselect the Exact check box.

2. **Fill in an event type, a year, and a date range, if you'd like to restrict your search with any of these criteria.**

   You can add events by clicking the Add Event link.

3. **Click the Search button.**

   The search results page appears, as shown in Figure 3-19. The results are arranged by record type. The same record is sometimes duplicated across record types.

4. **Click a record type to see its individual results.**

   For example, we clicked Census Records.

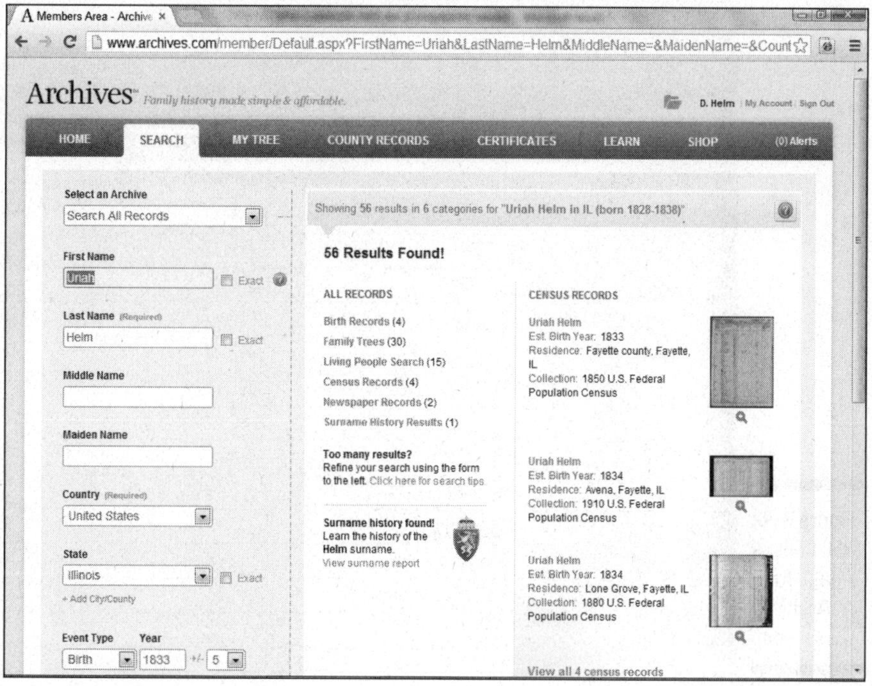

Figure 3-19:
Search
results from
Archives
.com.

5. **Click the name of the person to see the full record.**

   We clicked 1850 U.S. Federal Population Census.

6. **Click the thumbnail image just above the Image Available text on the right side of the page.**

   The record page appears with some details about the individual record, including gender, estimated birth year, birth location, and residence. The detail on this page depends on the type of record you're viewing.

   Note that some of the records contained in Archives.com are available free on other sites. For example, the 1850 census record that we viewed is actually taken from the FamilySearch site.

7. **Click the View Image button on the right side of the page.**

   The image viewer launches and displays the digitized image, as shown in Figure 3-20. For a closer look at the image, use the zoom controls in the upper-left corner of the image viewer. You can change the brightness levels and contrast or invert colors by using the controls at the top of the viewer.

8. **To download the image, click the Download button at the top of the screen.**

   A file automatically downloads to your machine.

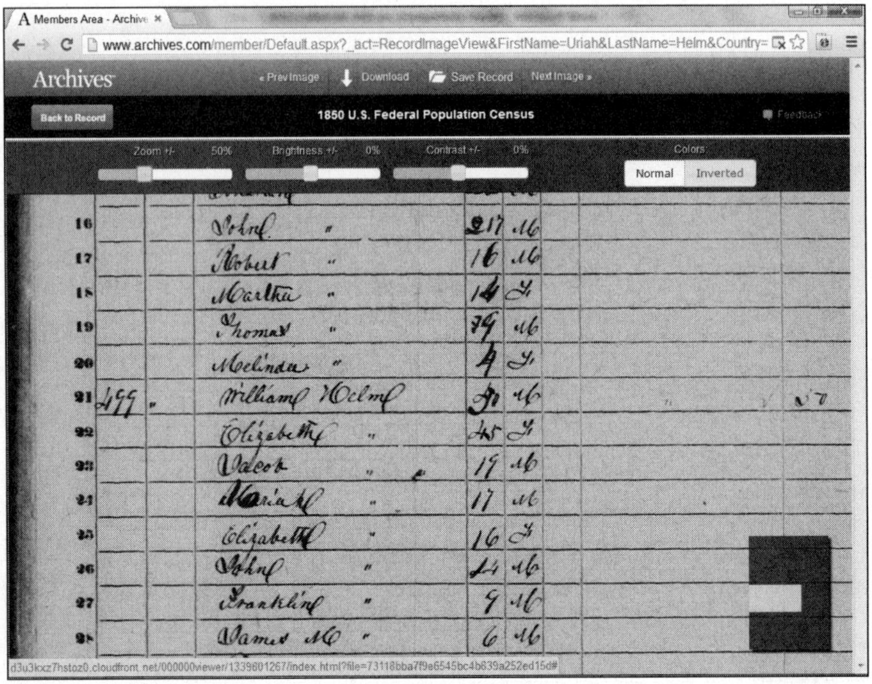

Figure 3-20:
1850 Census
image from
Archives
.com.

Saluting Fold3

Fold3 was originally named Footnote.com but was renamed shortly after being acquired by Ancestry.com. Fold3 is still run as a separate website and contains some content not found on Ancestry.com. Fold3 focuses primarily on military records, but also contains other records found on National Archives and Records Administration microfilm. In fact, the name of the site comes from the traditional flag-folding ceremony in which the third fold of the flag symbolizes the remembrance of veterans who have served in defense of the country. The site contains more than 410 million records. In addition to military records, the site has homestead records, city directories, passport applications, and census records.

Creating a trial account

Follow these steps to sign up at Fold3:

1. **Set your web browser to `www.fold3.com`.**

   The Fold3 home page appears.

2. **Click the 7-Day Free Trial button in the upper-right corner of the page.**

   The 7-Day Free Trial on Fold3 page appears.

3. **Click the Start Free Trial button in the left column.**

   The registration page appears.

4. **Fill out the e-mail address and password fields and select the I Have Read and Agree to the Fold3 Terms & Conditions check box. Then click the Continue button.**

   Be sure to click the Terms & Conditions link and read the Fold3 Terms of Use page so that you understand what you can and cannot do with the material on the Fold3 site. The page specifies what Fold3 does with information you provide as you use the site.

5. **Complete the payment information, including cardholder name, card number, expiration date, billing zip code, country, and phone number.**

   Fold3 requires credit card information to initiate the 7-day free trial, but you aren't billed until the trial periods ends. If you don't want to be billed for a subscription, don't forget to cancel the account before the 7 days have passed.

6. **After all fields are complete, click the Start Free Access button.**

   The Welcome to Your Fold3 Free Trial page appears.

7. **To continue using the Fold3 site, select the Start Searching Fold3 button.**

   The Search Fold3 page opens.

Searching at Fold3

You can search for military and other government records at Fold3 using the following steps:

1. **Go to www.fold3.com and sign in.**

   The Fold3 home page appears.

2. **Click the Advanced link located to the right of the Search form near the top of the page.**

   The advanced search form appears, as shown in Figure 3-21.

3. **Type the first name and last name of the person you're researching into the appropriate fields.**

4. **Enter a keyword or place if you want to limit your results. You can also search in specific year range or limit results to material added to the site during a particular time frame.**

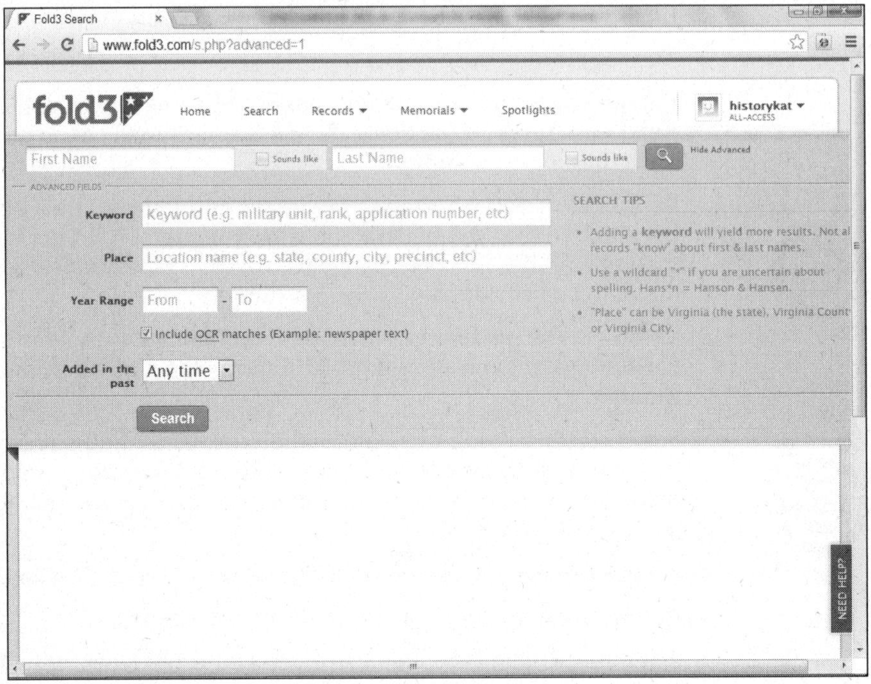

Figure 3-21:
The
advanced
search page
on Fold3.

Every piece of information you add to the search reduces the number of
results you receive. If you execute a search and receive few or no results,
omit optional search criteria to try to improve your search results. We
typed Uriah Helm, added Illinois in the Place field, and set the date range
from 1833 to 1901.

5. Click the Search button.

The search results page appears, as shown in Figure 3-22. The far
left column shows the number of results that appear in each record
category. The center column provides filters to limit your search. The
far right column shows the actual results based on the filters.

**6. To change the date range, move the sliders left or right depending on
your preferred date range and then click the Update button.**

Note that the date changes in the fields as you move the sliders. You
can omit records without dates by deselecting the Include *x* No-Date
Matches check box.

7. Select a state if you wish to limit the results by location.

You can select a state by clicking the map or by selecting the check box
next to the state name. The search results automatically update when
you add a state filter.

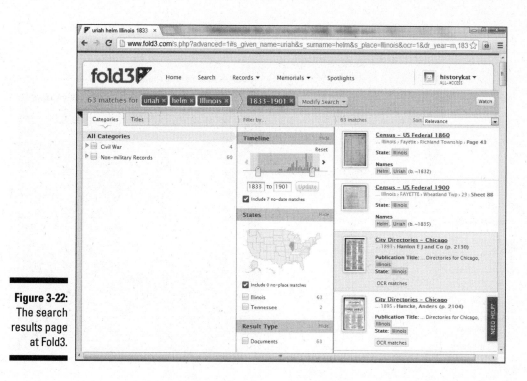

Figure 3-22: The search results page at Fold3.

8. **Select a result type or select an Added in the Past radio button.**

   The search results update as you enable filters.

9. **Click a record title.**

   The image viewer slides in from the right of the screen, displaying the digitized record, as shown in Figure 3-23.

10. **Click the View Larger button.**

    This enlarges the image viewer to full screen, as shown in Figure 3-24.

11. **If you want to perform any of the actions explained below, click the buttons below the navigation bar (in gray).**

    The buttons below the navigation bar include:

    - *About Image:* Click the About Image button to open the Image Information pane. The true value of this pane is its source information, which includes many metadata elements that you can use to record the source of the information in your genealogy database and any annotations to the record by other genealogists. Click the About Image button again to hide the Image Information pane.

    - *Like:* If you like this image or find it helpful, you can indicate so by clicking the Like button. This is just a way for Fold3 to get quick, user feedback regarding their site.

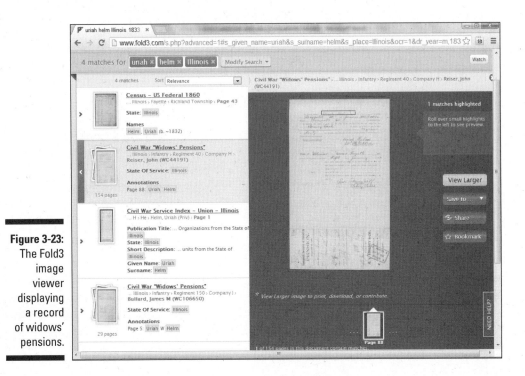

Figure 3-23:
The Fold3 image viewer displaying a record of widows' pensions.

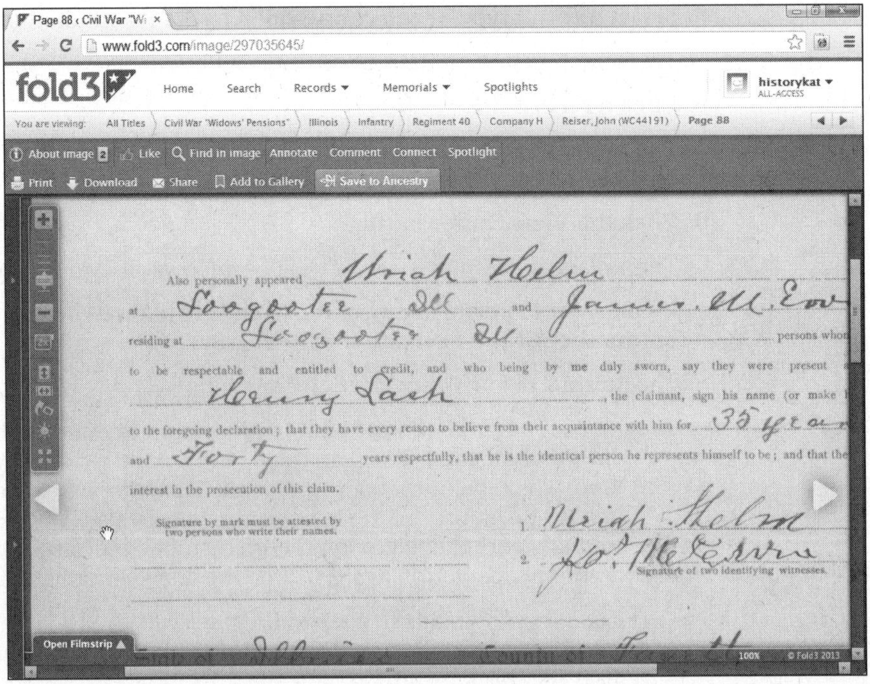

Figure 3-24:
Full-screen window in the image viewer.

- *Find in Image:* Click this button to open the Search box.

- *Annotate:* To help index the image to make it more useful for others, click the Annotate button. Underneath the new box that appears onscreen is a text box you can use to type on the record. Then click the Add button.

- *Comment:* To add a comment about the image, click the Comment button and enter your text in the Comment field. Then click the Save button.

- *Connect:* The Connect button allows users to connect an image with another image or with a particular page on Fold3.

- *Spotlight:* This feature allows Fold3 users to create stories attached to particular parts of a record.

- *Print:* To print the image, click the Print button. In the menu that pops up, choose whether you want to print the entire image or select a portion of it.

- *Download:* To save a copy of the image, click the Download button. A pop-up box opens and lets you save the entire image or a portion of it. If you select the entire image, another box opens and asks you for a location in which to save the file. The file is saved in .jpg format. If you select a portion of an image, you must size the rectangle around the portion that you want to save and then click the Download button.

- *Share:* To share an image, click the Share button. In the dialog box that opens, choose whether to e-mail the page or post it to Facebook, Twitter, Google Bookmarks, or Delicious. Click the More link to see additional services you can post to.

- *Add to Gallery:* Click the Add to Gallery button to add a link to the image in your personal gallery. The page doesn't show that the image has been added to the gallery; however, you can view the gallery by clicking your user name in the upper-right corner of the page and selecting Your Gallery. You can then link other images to this image to create a personal collection. You can even upload your own images into the gallery and link them to this image.

- *Save to Ancestry:* If you have an Ancestry.com online family tree, you can save the record to it by clicking this button. Simply select the Tree, type in the person's name, and click the Save button.

   12. **Click the buttons on the toolbar on the left of the image to change the
       view of the image.**

       • *Zoom In/Zoom Out:* To see the image more closely (to zoom in),
         click the plus sign (+) on the vertical bar on the left side of the
         image. Click the minus sign (–) to zoom out.

         To see the full context of the information you're viewing, zoom out
         of the image when you first open it. Then zoom in closer to see ele-
         ments more clearly. If the image is too high or too low onscreen
         when you zoom in and out of it, click the scroll bar on the far right
         side of the screen to reposition the image.

       • *Show Magnifier:* When the standard zoom control doesn't let you
         look closely enough or it loses the context of the document, use
         the Show Magnifier to display a magnifying lens onscreen. You can
         increase the zoom by clicking the plus-sign button to the right of
         the magnifier.

       • *Fit to Height:* See the image at its full height onscreen.

       • *Fill the Width:* See the document at its full width onscreen.

       • *Rotate:* Move the image 90 degrees clockwise. This button shows a
         curved arrow next to a tilted rectangle.

       • *Adjust Image:* Change the brightness and contrast of the image. You
         can also invert the color of the image by selecting the Invert check
         box. The button is a shining sun icon.

       • *Full Screen:* View the image at its maximum size onscreen. Press
         the Esc key on your keyboard or click the Full Screen button again
         to exit Full Screen mode.

   13. **Move to another image in the collection.**

       There are two methods to do this:

       • *Click the large arrow* on the right side of the image to move to the
         next image in the collection. When you place the cursor over the
         arrow, a small thumbnail of the next image appears onscreen.

       • *Click the Open Filmstrip link* at the bottom of the page to open a
         window showing the few images on either side of the image you're
         looking at; see Figure 3-25. Click any thumbnail image to view the
         full image. To see more images in either direction, click the arrow
         on either side of the filmstrip.

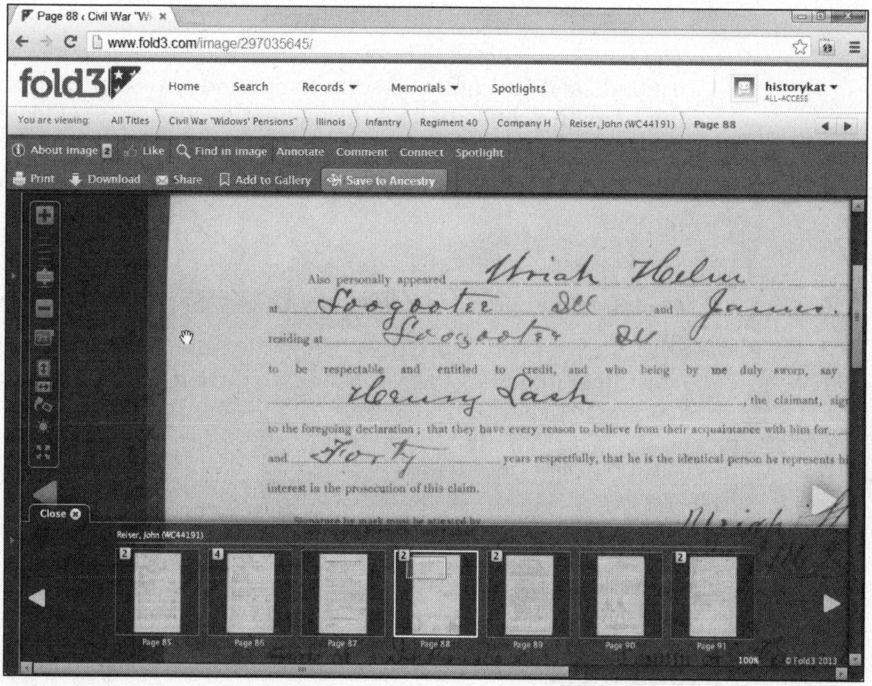

Figure 3-25:
The Filmstrip
view in
Fold3.

Finding Your Past

Findmypast.com is one of a few sites owned by brightsolid online publishing. It focuses on records from the United States, United Kingdom, Ireland, Australia, and New Zealand. You can find census records, census substitutes, vital records, newspapers, military records, and some passenger lists. Some of the record sets are just textual, and others are a digitized image.

You can get a 14-day free trial by following these steps:

1. **Set your web browser to `www.findmypast.com`.**

    The findmypast.com home page appears.

2. **Click the Sign Up Today 14-Day Free Trial button.**

    The button is located in the upper-right corner of the home page. A subscription page appears with two tabs: one for a World subscription, and the other for a U.S. subscription. Select the appropriate tab for the records that interest you.

3. **Click the Start Free Trial button.**

   The button is located in the three columns that contain the 1 month, 6 month, and 12 month subscription periods. We suggest that you select the 1 month column to limit the amount of charges, should you forget to cancel the subscription during the free-trial period.

4. **Fill out the registration form and click the Register to Start Free Trial button.**

   The Payment Details page appears.

5. **Complete the payment details fields and then click the Continue button.**

   The Congratulations Page appears. On the left is a search form that you can use to begin your first search on the site; see Figure 3-26.

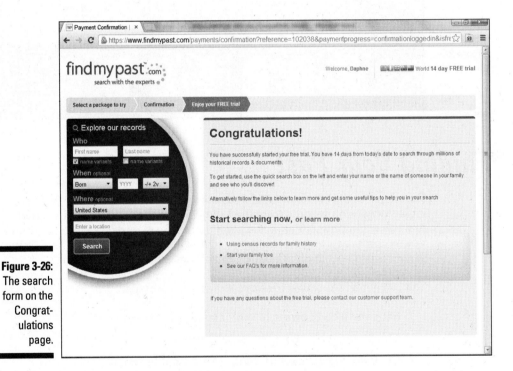

Figure 3-26:
The search form on the Congrat-ulations page.

6. **Complete the First Name and Last Name fields.**

7. **If you want to limit the results based on time and location, complete the When and Where fields.**

   The When field has a drop-down menu that contains Born, Died, and Other event choices. You can also add a date range from the field next to the year field. It defaults to the -/+ 2yrs setting. The Where field has a drop-down menu in which you can choose one of four countries, or you can broaden your search and choose the World. To further refine your results, you can type in a location.

8. Click the Search button.

The search results page appears as seen in Figure 3-27. The left column contains filters that you can use to focus the results. The right column lists the search results.

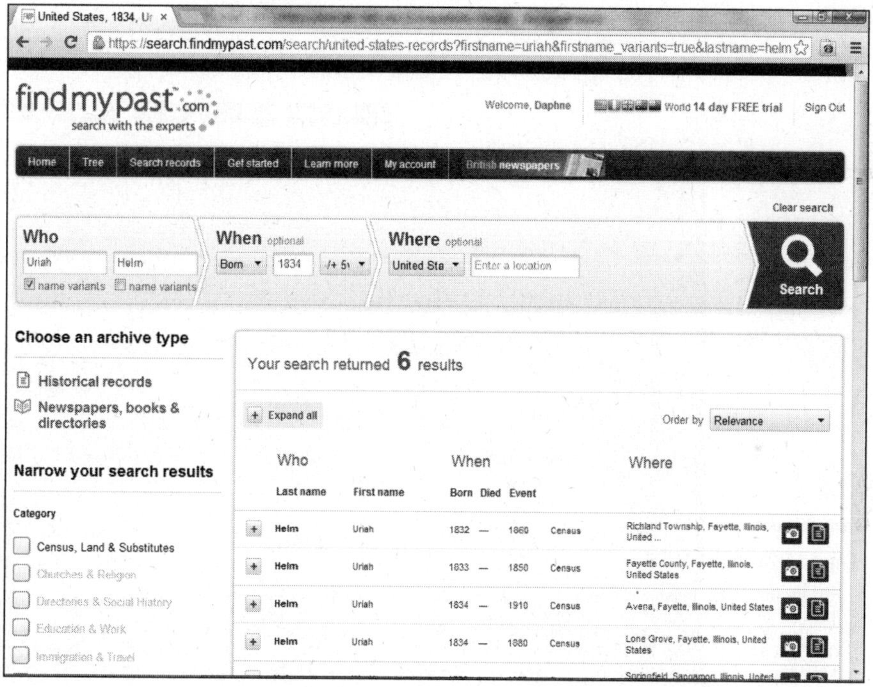

Figure 3-27:
The search results page for findmypast .com.

9. To filter the results, click a category (or categories) in the left column.

Details about the specific record appear beneath the search result. You can create filters on country, state, county, city/township, census year, other household member, record collection, record set, optional keywords, and race.

10. Click the plus sign next to the name of the person in the search result.

Details about the specific record appear beneath the search result.

11. **Click the Transcription icon (blue paper icon) or the Image icon (camera icon).**

    If you click the Transcription icon, the transcription page containing textual information taken from the record displays.

    If you click the Image icon, the he image viewer appears, as shown in Figure 3-28. For our example, we click the Image icon.

12. **Click the Download Image button.**

    Your web browser downloads the image as a .jpg file.

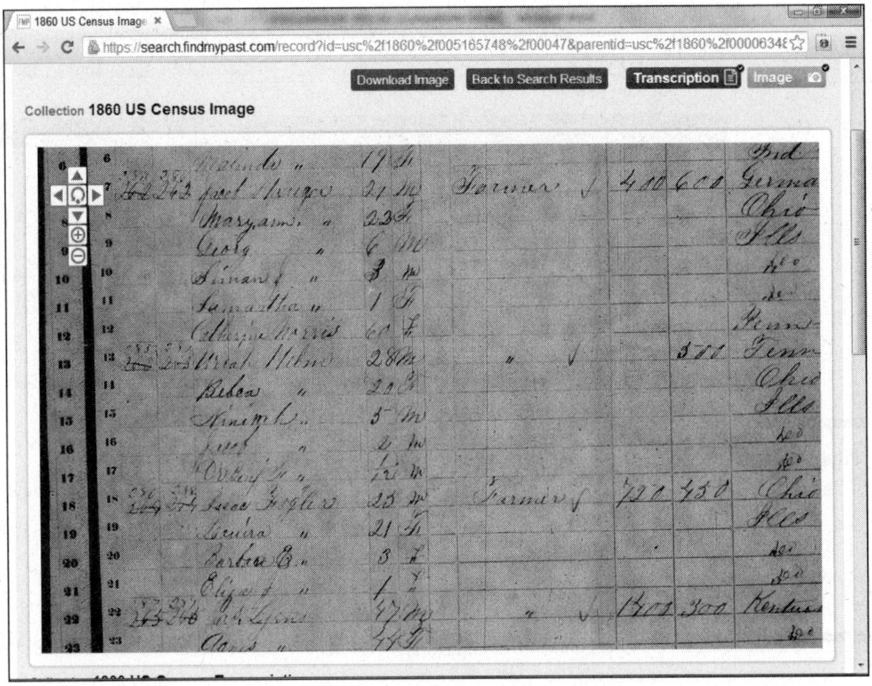

Figure 3-28:
The image
viewer on
findmypast
.com.

Chapter 4

Using All of Your Censuses

*A*lthough some people believe that the census is a nuisance every ten years, genealogists and family historians believe it's one of the most important sources of information. Not so many years ago, only bits and pieces of transcribed censuses were online. Now, several sites contain digitized and indexed census records, not only for the United States, but also for other countries. The quality of both the digitization and indexing varies among the sites, making it worthwhile to look at more than one site when multiples are available.

In this chapter, we show you what census records are currently available and describe some of the major projects that you can use as keys for unlocking government treasure chests of genealogical information.

Coming to Your Census

We like to think of researching census records like tracking a submarine. Every so often the submarine emerges, submerges, and then resurfaces. You don't really know the direct path the submarine took between the two points, but at least you can guess the general direction its moving based on where it started and where it ended. Census records are similar in that you can use one census record as a starting point and a second census record (in a different year) as an ending point. Then you can look at common migration paths to predict the path your ancestor might have taken to get to his or her final destination.

To effectively use census records, it's important to understand what information they include and why they were created. *Census records* are periodic counts of a population by a government or organization. These counts can be conducted at regular intervals (such as every ten years) or special one-time counts made for a specific reason.

Census records are valuable for tying a person to a place and for discovering relationships between individuals. For example, suppose you have a great-great-great-grandfather by the name of Nimrod Sanders. You're not sure who his father was, but you do know that he was born in North Carolina. By using a census index, you may be able to find a Nimrod Sanders listed in a North Carolina census index as a member of someone's household. If the information about Nimrod in that record (age, location, and siblings' names) fits what you know from family legend, you may have found one or more generations to add to your genealogy. You can use the name of the head of household and his or her spouse as a lead to investigate in identifying Nimrod's parents.

Often a census includes information such as a person's age, sex, occupation, birthplace, and relationship to the head of the household. Sometimes the *enumerators* — the people who conduct the census — add comments to the census record (such as a comment on the physical condition of an individual or an indication of the person's wealth) that may give you further insight into the person's life.

United States census schedules

Federal census records in the United States have been around since 1790. Censuses are conducted every ten years to count the population for a couple of reasons — to correctly divide the number of seats in the U.S. House of Representatives and to assess federal taxes. Although census collections are still performed, privacy restrictions prevent the release of any detailed census information on individuals for 72 years. Currently, you can find federal census data on individuals for the census years 1790 to 1940. However, practically all of the 1890 census was destroyed due to actions taken after a fire in the Commerce Building in 1921 — for more on this, see "First in the Path of the Firemen," The Fate of the 1890 Population Census, at

```
www.archives.gov/publications/prologue/1996/spring/1890-
census-1.html.
```

Federal census records are valuable because you can use them to take historical snapshots of your ancestors in ten-year increments. These snapshots enable you to track your ancestors as they moved from county to county or state to state, and to identify the names of parents and siblings of your ancestors who you may not have previously known. Also, by paying attention to neighbors listed in the census, you may be able to determine families that later intermarried with your ancestor's family or discover why a family member was given a particular first name. For example, a child's first name might have been named after a close neighbor's last name.

Each census year contains a different amount of information, with more modern census returns (also called *schedules*) containing the most information. Schedules from 1790 to 1840 list only the head of household for each family, along with the number of people living in the household broken down by age classifications. Schedules from 1850 on have the names and ages of all members of the household, and each subsequent census year's schedules contain additional information on members of the household.

Using American Soundex to search U.S. census records

For the censuses conducted from 1880 to 1920, you can use microfilmed indexes organized under the American Soundex system. Figure 4-1 shows an example of a Soundex card prepared for the 1920 census available on the Internet Archive (www.archive.org).

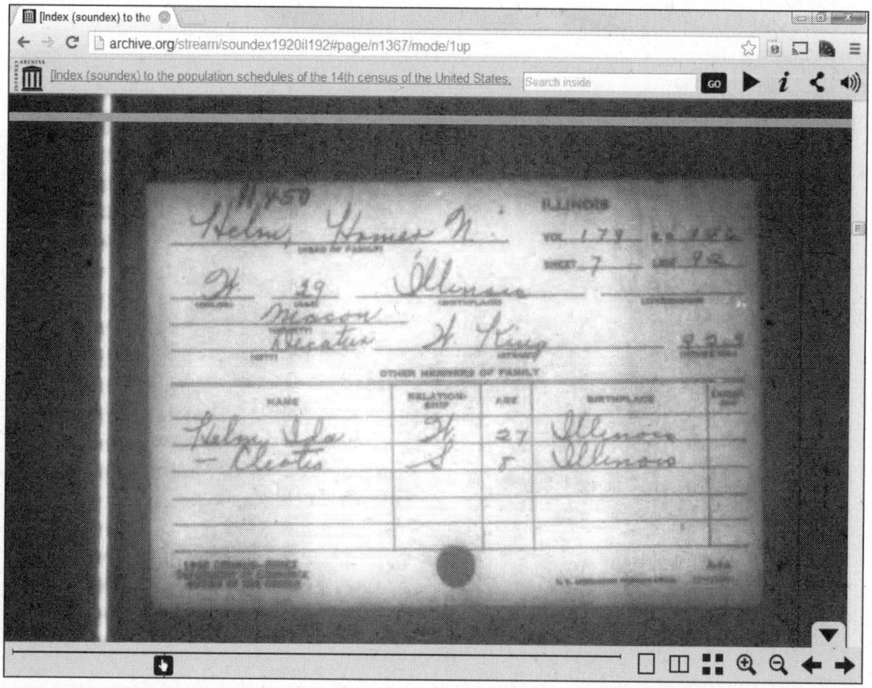

Figure 4-1:
A Soundex card for the 1920 census.

The American Soundex system is an indexing method that groups names that are pronounced in a similar way but are spelled differently. This indexing procedure allows you to find ancestors who may have changed the spelling of their names over the years. For example, you find names such as Helm, Helme, Holm, and Holme grouped in the American Soundex.

Soundex improvements

Many of you have heard of Soundex —especially if you've worked with the U.S. census in the past, if you live in a state that uses Soundex as part of your driver's license number, or if you're just a nut for indexing systems. However, you might not realize that more than one Soundex system exists. The American Soundex, which is the one used for the U.S. census and the one most widely recognized, is not the only one, nor was it the first system developed.

The Russell Soundex system: Robert C. Russell patented the first Soundex system in 1918. The Russell Soundex system categorizes the alphabet phonetically and assigns numbers to the categories. You find eight categories and four other rules to follow. The odd-looking terms that refer to parts of the mouth are technical descriptions of how to make the sounds; just try making the sounds of the letters shown with each one, and you'll get the idea. Here's what they look (and sound) like:

Categories:

1. Vowels or oral resonants: *a, e, i, o, u, y*

2. Labials and labio-dentals: *b, f, p, v*

3. Gutturals and sibilants: *c, g, k, s, x, z*

4. Dental-mutes: *d, t*

5. Palatal-fricative: *l*

6. Labio-nasal: *m*

7. Dento- or lingua-nasal: *n*

8. Dental-fricative: *r*

Other rules:

- The code always begins with the first letter of the word.

- If you have two letters in a row that are the same, they are represented in the code as one letter (for example, *rr* is represented as *r*).

- If the word ends in *gh, s,* or *z*, those letters are ignored.

- Vowels are considered only the first time they appear.

The American Soundex system: The American Soundex system, the system with which most people are familiar, modified the Russell Soundex system. The changes include these:

- The code disregards vowels altogether, unless the first letter of the word is a vowel.

- The letters *m* and *n* are categorized together and represented by the same number.

- Words ending in *gh, s,* and *z* are treated the same as other words, and those letters are assigned values.

The American Soundex code begins with the first letter of the word and has three numbers following. Zeros are added to the code to ensure that it has three numbers. You can see the categories of letters and numbers assigned to them in the section "Using American Soundex to search U.S. census records," in this chapter.

The Daitch-Mokotoff Soundex system: The Daitch-Mokotoff Soundex system builds on the Russell and American Soundex systems and addresses difficulties in categorizing many Germanic and Slavic names that the other two systems encounter. The major points of this system are as follows:

- The code is made up of six numbers.

- The first letter of the word is also represented by a number. If the first letter is a vowel, it has the code 0.

- Some double-letter combinations that sound like single letters are coded as single.

- If a letter or letter combination can have two sounds, it is coded twice.

If you want more detailed information about the various Soundex systems, take a gander at the Soundexing and Genealogy website at `www.avotaynu.com/soundex.html`.

The Beider-Morse Phonetic Matching system: A problem with the various Soundex systems is that they often match names that are not really closely related. The goal of Phonetic Matching is to remove the irrelevant name matches, while not losing matches that are closely related. The features of the system include the following:

- Because the pronunciation of a name depends on the language that the name comes from, the system includes pronunciation tables for several languages, including Catalan, Czech, Dutch, English, French, German, Greek, Hebrew, Hungarian, Italian, Polish, Portuguese, Romanian, Russian, Spanish, and Turkish.

- After the language of the name is known, the name is converted to a sequence of phonetic tokens that are compared with other names that have been converted to tokens.

- Some double-letter combinations that sound like single letters are coded as single.

You can find more details on phonetic matching on the Phonetic Matching: A Better Soundex page at `http://stevemorse.org/phonetics/bmpm2.htm`.

And if you want to run some names through the American Soundex, Daitch-Mokotoff Soundex, and Beider-Morse Phonetic Matching systems at the same time, visit the Generating Soundex Codes and Phonetic Tokens in One Step converter at `http://stevemorse.org/census/soundex.html`.

The American Soundex code for a name consists of a letter and then three numbers. Double letters count for only one number, and if your surname is short or has a lot of vowels in it, you use zeros on the end to bring the total number to three. To convert your surname to American Soundex, use the first letter of your surname as the first letter of the American Soundex code and then substitute numbers for the next three consonants according to the following list. For example, the American Soundex code for the surname *Helm* is H450.

1. B, P, F, V
2. C, S, K, G, J, Q, X, Z
3. D, T
4. L
5. M, N
6. R

That explanation probably sounds confusing, so just follow these steps to convert your surname to an American Soundex code:

1. **Write down your surname on a piece of paper.**

   As an example, we'll convert the surname *Abell.*

2. **Keep the first letter of the surname, and then cross out any remaining vowels (A, E, I, O, U) and the letters *W, Y,* and *H.***

   If your surname begins with a vowel, keep the first vowel. If your surname does not begin with a vowel, cross out all the vowels in the surname. So, in the surname *Abell,* we keep the letters *A, B, L,* and *L.*

3. **If the surname has double letters, cross out the second letter.**

   For example, the surname Abell has a double *L,* so we cross out the second *L,* which leaves us with the letters *A, B,* and *L.*

4. **Convert your letters to the American Soundex code numbers according to the preceding list.**

   Because *A* is the first letter of the surname, it remains an *A.* The *B* converts to the number 1 and the *L* to the number 4. That leaves us with A14.

5. **Cross out the second occurrence of any repeated numbers that are side by side, including a number that repeats the value that the letter at the beginning would have.**

   The remaining numbers of the Abell (A14) surname do not have the same numerical code next to each other. But it could happen with a name such as Schaefer. Ordinarily, the name Schaefer would have the American Soundex code of S216. However, because the *S* and the *C* would both have the code of 2 and are side by side, you would eliminate the second 2, resulting in an American Soundex code of S160.

6. **If you do not have three numbers remaining, fill in the rest with zeros.**

   Only two numbers remain in the Abell surname after we cross out the vowels and double letters. Because the American Soundex system requires a total of three numbers to complete the code, we fill in the remaining numerical spot with a 0. Thus, our result for Abell is A140.

If you're like we are, you want the most efficient way to do things. Although figuring out an American Soundex is not overly complicated, it can be a little time-consuming if you have several names to calculate. Fortunately, some free online sites are available to calculate American Soundex codes. Here are a few:

- ✔ **Yet Another Soundex Converter:** www.bradandkathy.com/ genealogy/yasc.html

- ✔ **RootsWeb's Soundex Converter:** http://resources.rootsweb. ancestry.com/cgi-bin/soundexconverter

- ✔ **Surname to Soundex Calculator:** www.searchforancestors.com/ soundex.html

American Soundex indexes are subject to human error and, in some cases, are incomplete. For example, the 1880 federal census American Soundex primarily focused on indexing those households with children age ten years or younger. And those who carried out the actual indexing did not always handle American Soundex codes correctly or consistently. So the indexer may have made a coding error or failed to include some information. Therefore, if you're relatively certain that an ancestor *should* show up in a particular county in a census that uses American Soundex, but the American Soundex microfilm doesn't reflect that person, you may want to go through the census microfilm for that county anyway and look line by line for your ancestor. This process may seem tedious, but the results can be worthwhile.

Regular population schedules were not the only product of the federal censuses. Special schedules, including census returns for particular populations such as slaves, mortality, agriculture, manufacturing, and veterans, were also conducted. Each type of special schedule contains information pertaining to a specific group or occupation. In the case of slave schedules (used in the 1850 and 1860 censuses), slaves were listed under the names of the slave owner, and information was provided on the age, gender, and race of the slave. If the slave was more than 100 years old, his or her name was listed on the schedule. Note, though, that enumerators may have included names for other slaves if he or she felt inclined to list them. Although the slave schedules do not contain a lot of information, they can be used as a starting point for further research. Figure 4-2 shows an example of a slave schedule from the 1850 census.

Mortality schedules (used in 1850, 1860, 1870, and 1880) include information on people who died in the 12 months previous to the start of the census. For example, the 1860 schedule contains details such as name, age, sex, color, free or slave, married or widowed, place of birth, month of death, profession, cause of death, and number of days ill. Figure 4-3 shows a page from the 1860 schedule.

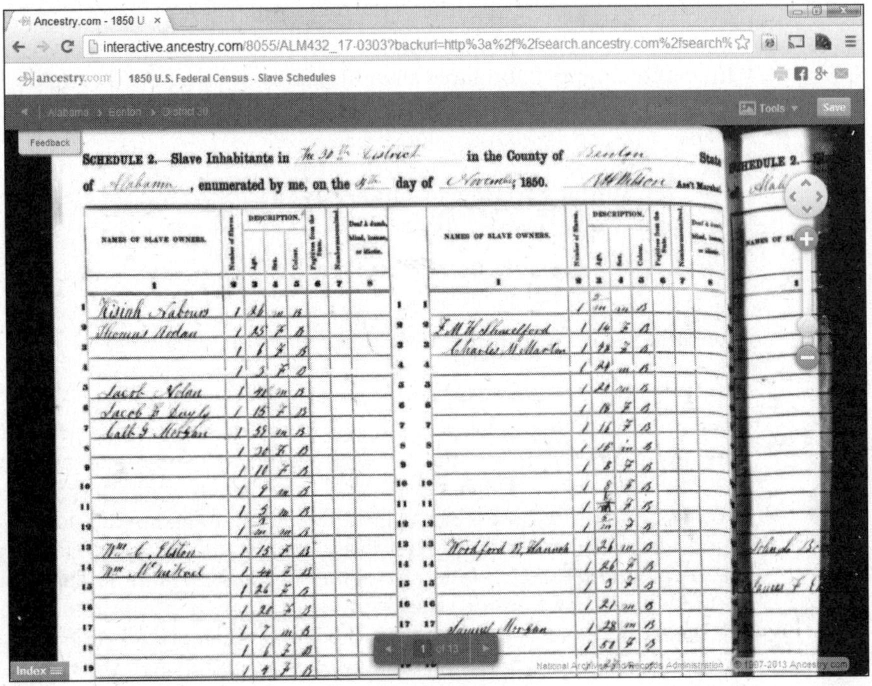

Figure 4-2:
1850 slave
schedule
for Benton
County,
Alabama.

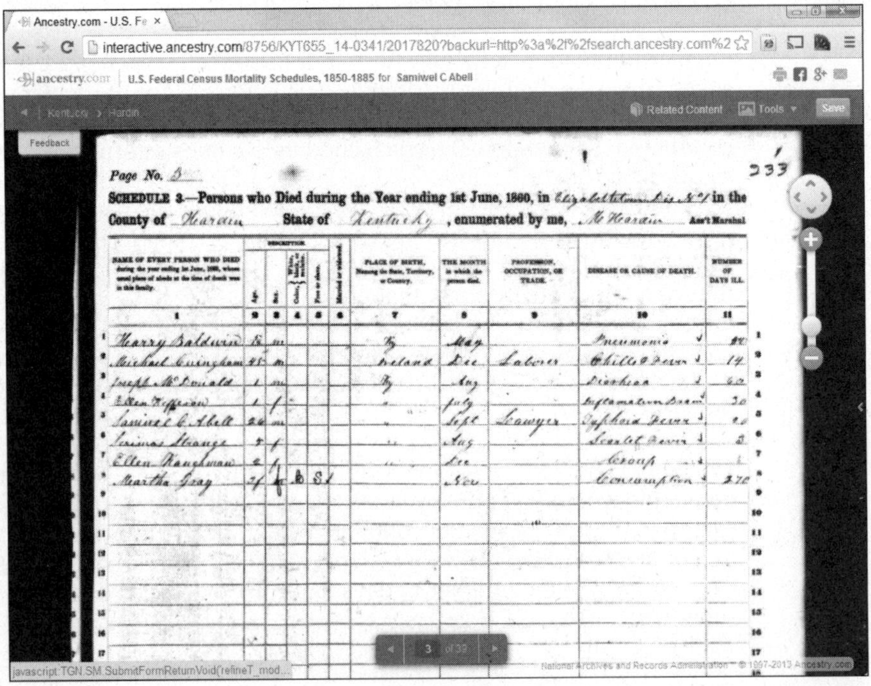

Figure 4-3:
1860
mortality
schedule
for Hardin
County,
Kentucky.

Agricultural schedules were used between 1840 and 1910. However, only the schedules from 1840 to 1880 survive. They contain detailed demographic and financial information on farm owners. Information contained on the schedules includes name of owner or manager of the farm, acres of land, cash value of the farm, value of implements and machinery, number and value of livestock, value of produce, and value of animals slaughtered; see Figure 4-4.

Manufacturing schedules (taken infrequently between 1810 and 1880) contain information on business owners and their business interests. Details included on the 1850 schedule included the name of the company, product manufactured, capital invested, raw material used, kind of power used, average number of people employed, wages paid, and annual product produced; see Figure 4-5.

Veteran schedules include the Revolutionary War pensioner census, which was taken as part of the 1840 census, and the special census for Union veterans and their widows (taken in 1890). Information found on the 1890 special census includes rank, company, regiment or vessel, date of enlistment, date of discharge, and length of service. The remarks section includes information on disability and other comments the enumerator felt compelled to make. Figure 4-6 contains an example of the 1890 special schedule, including surviving soldiers, sailors, marines, and widows.

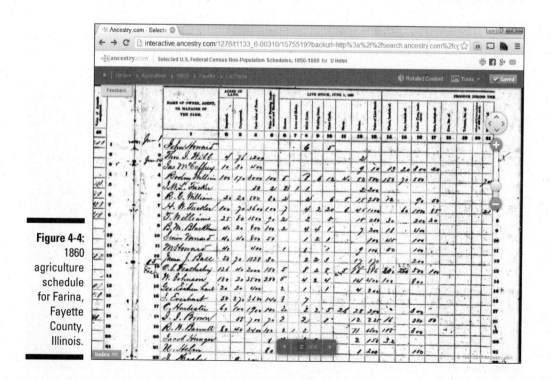

Figure 4-4: 1860 agriculture schedule for Farina, Fayette County, Illinois.

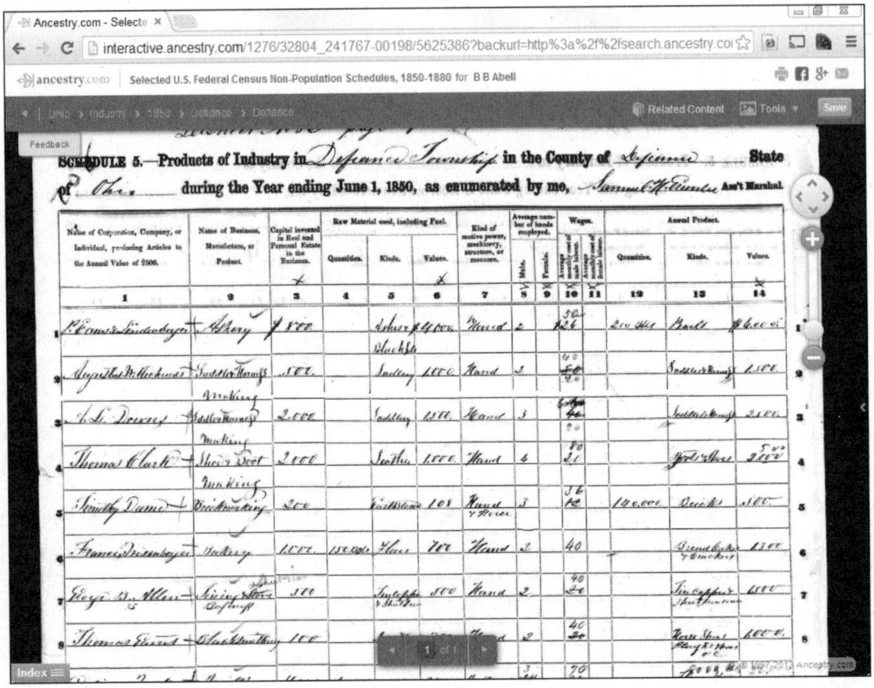

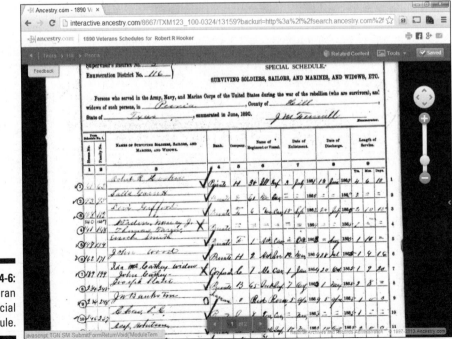

Figure 4-5:
1850 manu-
facturing
schedule
for Defiance
County,
Ohio.

Figure 4-6:
1890 veteran
special
schedule.

State, territorial, and other census records

Federal census records are not the only population enumerations you can find for ancestors in the United States. You may also find census records at the state, territorial, and local level for certain areas of the United States.

Several state and territorial censuses have become available online. Ancestry.com (www.ancestry.com) has, within its subscription collection, state and territorial censuses for Alabama (1820–1866), California (1852), Colorado (1885), Florida (1867–1945), Illinois (1825–1865), Iowa (1836–1925), Kansas (1855–1925), Michigan (1894); Minnesota (1849–1905), Mississippi (1792–1866), Missouri (1844–1881), Nebraska (1860–1885), Nevada (1875), New Jersey (1895), New York (1880, 1892, 1905), North Carolina (1784–1787), North Dakota (1915, 1925), Oklahoma (1890, 1907), Rhode Island (1865–1935), South Dakota (1895),Washington (1857–1892), and Wisconsin (1895, 1905), as well as a host of other census records, including images of the U.S. Indian census schedules from 1885 to 1940.

Another source for state and territorial census images is at the free site HistoryKat (www.historykat.com). HistoryKat has images for Colorado (1885), Florida (1885), Illinois (1820–1865), Iowa (1836), Minnesota (1857), New Mexico (1885), Oklahoma (1890, 1907), and Wisconsin (1836–1847). Figure 4-7 shows an image from the 1820 Illinois state census for Franklin County.

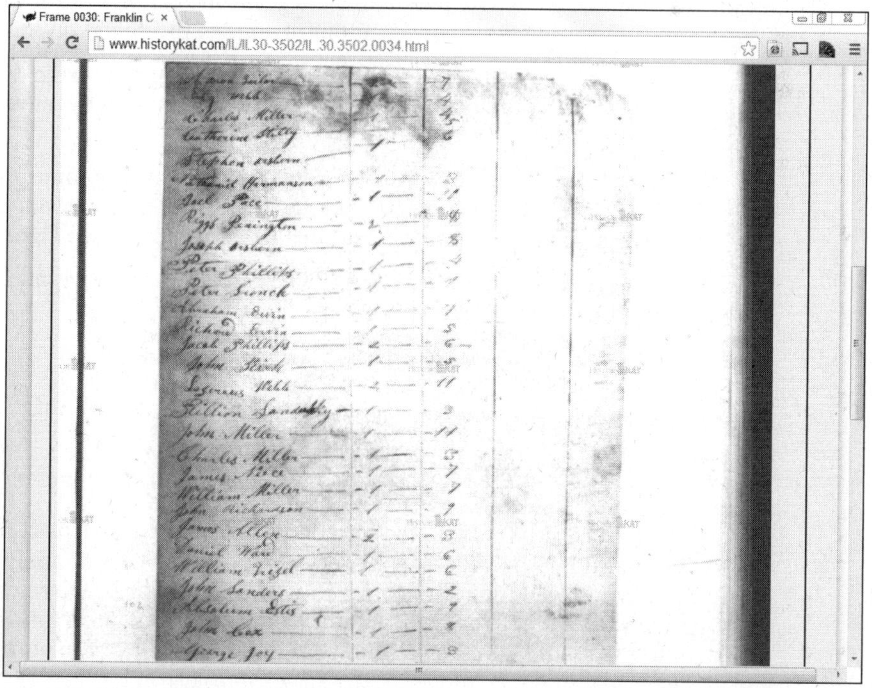

Figure 4-7: The 1820 Illinois state census for Franklin County.

Indexes and some images for state and territorial censuses are also found at no charge on FamilySearch (www.familysearch.org). Locations available on the site include Alabama (1855, 1866), California (1852), Colorado (1885), Florida (1885, 1935, 1945), Illinois (1855, 1865), Iowa (1885, 1895, 1905), Massachusetts (1855, 1865), Michigan (1894), Minnesota (1865–1905), New Jersey (1885, 1905), New York (1855–1925), Rhode Island (1885–1935), and South Dakota 1905–1945).

Special census records can often help you piece together your ancestors' migration patterns, account for ancestors who may not have been enumerated in the federal censuses, or provide greater details on ancestors who were members of a specific population. Some examples of special censuses available at Ancestry.com (www.ancestry.com) include

- **Census of merchant seamen, 1930:** Contains name, age, date of admission and discharge, habits, education, names and addresses of relatives and friends, questions on extended family, and questions on tendency toward self-sufficiency or dependence

- **New York census of inmates in almshouses and poorhouses, 1830–1920:** Contains name, age, date of admission and discharge, habits, education, names and addresses of relatives and friends, questions on extended family, and questions on tendency toward self-sufficiency or dependence

- **Puerto Rico, special censuses, agricultural schedules, 1935:** Lists the names of owners and managers of farms, acreage, farm value, machinery, livestock, and amount of staples produced on the farm

- **U.S. special census on deaf family marriages and hearing relatives, 1888–1895:** Contains information on how the person became deaf and other relatives that might also be deaf

- **U.S. special census of Indians, 1880:** Includes Indian name, English translation of the name, whether a chief, whether full-blooded, number of years on the reservation, and health information; see Figure 4-8

- **U.S. Indian census rolls, 1885-1940:** A collection of several censuses performed on Indian reservations

Finding your ancestors in U.S. census records

Imagine that you're ready to look for your ancestors in census records. You hop in the car and drive to the nearest library, archives, or Family History Center. On arrival, you find the microfilm roll for the area where you believe your ancestors lived. You then go into a dimly lit room, insert the microfilm into the reader, and begin your search. After a few hours of rolling the

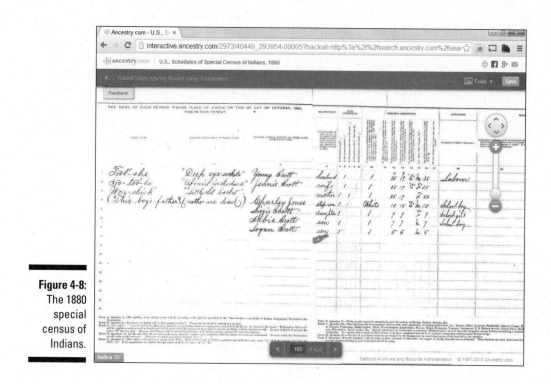

Figure 4-8:
The 1880 special census of Indians.

microfilm, the back pain begins to set in, cramping in your hands becomes more severe, and the handwritten census documents become blurry as your eyes strain from reading each entry line by line. You come to the end of the roll and still haven't found your elusive ancestor. At this point, you begin to wonder if a better way exists.

Fortunately, a better way *does* exist for U.S. census records: census indexes. A *census index* contains a listing of the people who are included in particular census records, along with references indicating where you can find the actual census record. Back in the day, these indexes were in book form, but you can now find these indexes online. Although no single website contains indexes of all available census records for all countries (at least not yet), some sites contain substantial collections of census indexes.

So how do you find these online indexes? Well, you have a few ways, depending on whether you want to use a free site or a subscription site. The easiest way, if you have the financial means, is to subscribe to a site that has indexed census records that link to images of the census microfilm. These sites include Ancestry.com (www.ancestry.com), Archives.com (www.archives.com), FamilyLink.com (www.familylink.com), findmypast.com (www.findmypast.com), and MyHeritage (www.myheritage.com). These sites are at various stages in indexing, so you want to make sure that you look on the site to determine whether the year you're looking for is available.

If you don't want to pay a fee to access census indexes online, you can use a combination of sites to locate your ancestor in a census index and then find the matching digitized copy of the record. It may take longer to find information on your ancestor, but you can use the census indexes at FamilySearch (www.familysearch.org) to determine what page and film number your ancestor is on, and then use the free site Internet Archive (www.archive.org) to view the digitized record.

Say you want to find Samuel Abell (Matthew's sixth great-grandfather), who lived in St. Mary's County, Maryland, in 1790. Your first step is to visit FamilySearch:

1. **Point your web browser to https://familysearch.org.**

2. **Click Search at the top of the page.**

   The Discover Your Family History search page appears. Under the First Names and Last Names fields is a list of links to restrict the records searched.

3. **Click the Type link under the Restrict Records By section.**

   Several check boxes appear under the Type heading.

4. **Select the Census, Residence, and Lists check box.**

   A check mark appears next to your selection.

5. **Type your ancestor's name in the First Names and Last Names fields.**

   We typed **Samuel** in the First Names field and **Abell** in the Last Names field.

6. **To refine your search, type a country into the Country field.**

   We typed United States. A State or Province field appears.

7. **Type a state into the State or Province field.**

   We typed Maryland.

8. **Under Search With a Life Event, click the Any link.**

   A new row appears with an Any Place heading.

9. **Under the Any Year (Range) heading, type a year in the From field and in the To field. Then click the Search button.**

   We typed 1790 and 1800, respectively. The search criteria yielded 48 results, with the most relevant near the top of the page, as shown in Figure 4-9.

10. **Click a name that interests you.**

   We selected Samuel Abell in the United States Census, 1790 in St. Marys, Maryland. The record page appears; see Figure 4-10.

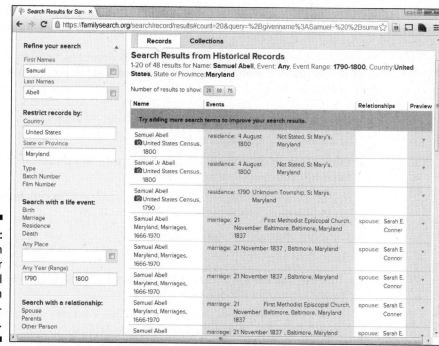

Figure 4-9:
Search
results for
Samuel
Abell in
Family-
Search.

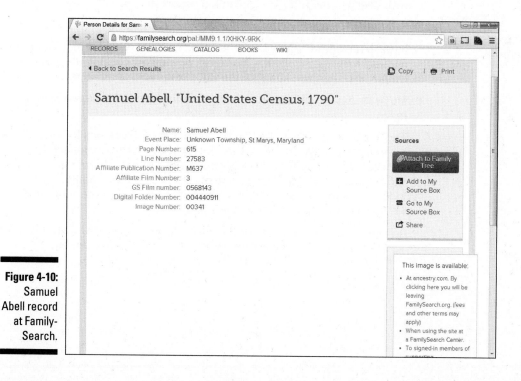

Figure 4-10:
Samuel
Abell record
at Family-
Search.

> **11. Record the information in the Event Place, Page Number, Affiliate Publication Number, Affiliate Film Number, and Image Number fields.**

The information from the FamilySearch record should be enough to find the digitized record at the Internet Archive site. To find the record on Internet Archive, follow these steps:

1. **Point your web browser to `http://archive.org/details/us_census`.**

   The United States Census page loads.

2. **Click a link to the census year that interests you under the Sub-Collections section.**

   Because we were looking for Samuel Abell in the 1790 census, we clicked 1st Population Census of the United States - 1790.

3. **Click the appropriate state link.**

   We clicked Maryland.

4. **Click the link for the reel number that contains the Affiliate Film Number from the FamilySearch index.**

   In our case, there's only one link, but for other census years there could be multiple reels for each state. The Affiliate Number from the FamilySearch index (refer to Figure 4-10) was 3. So, we selected the link with Reel 3 in the title. The collection page appears.

5. **Select the format for viewing the digitized image.**

   In the left column, under View the Book, you can choose different formats for viewing the digitized images. We suggest clicking the Read Online link. Digitized images from the census microfilm appear.

6. **Move the image slider to the Image Number from the FamilySearch index.**

   The image slider is a white hand icon on a small black box located at the bottom of the page. To move the slider, click the white hand and drag the slider to the right. Note that a black box appears to the right of the slider telling you what page you're on. In our case, the FamilySearch index listed the Image Number as 00341. So, we moved the slider until we saw 341/577 appear in the black box.

   An alternative to the image slider is to go page by page through the schedule by clicking the arrows in the lower right of the screen.

7. Locate your ancestor in the image.

The FamilySearch index showed that Samuel Abell was located on Image Number 341 and Page Number 615. When we placed the slider on 341, an image appears with four pages. At the top of the digital image on each page is a page number. In our case, we found page 615 and scrolled down the page looking for Samuel Abell (see Figure 4-11). To zoom in the image, click the magnifying glass icon with the plus sign.

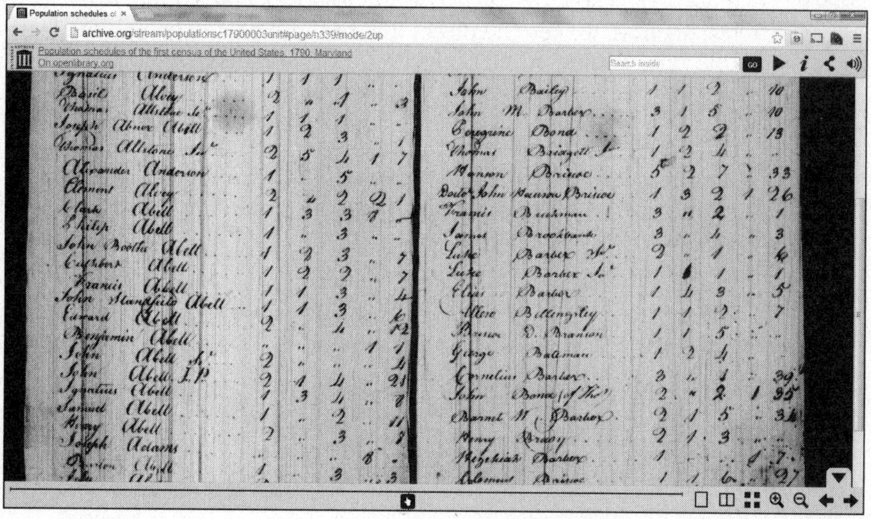

Figure 4-11:
Samuel Abell in the digitized image on the Internet Archive.

One thing to keep in mind is that the index could contain an error. For example, the FamilySearch index said that Samuel Abell is located on page 615 of the census record. Actually, he's located on page 614. So, if you can't find your ancestor on the page specified in the index, try looking on the previous or next page. Either way, the index will point you to the part of the digitized record where your ancestor can be found.

Finding individuals in subscription indexes

WARNING!

A number of subscription sites contain indexes that are linked to the corresponding digital images. We mention a few of them in the "Finding your ancestors in U.S. census records" section. Be careful when using these indexes. Not all indexes include every person in the census. Some are merely head-of-household indexes. So, it's a good idea to read the description that comes with the index to see how complete it is. Also, the same quality control may not be there for every census year, even within the same index-producing company. If you do not find your ancestor in one of these indexes, don't automatically assume that he or she is not in the census. Also remember that many indexes were created outside the United States by people who were not native English speakers and who were under time constraints. It's quite possible that the indexer was incorrect in indexing a particular entry — possibly the person you're searching for.

If we do a search on Ancestry.com for the same Samuel Abell as we did in the last section, we see the direct link to the digitized image; see Figure 4-12. In this case, Samuel Abell ranks first based on his name and his location in St. Mary's County, Maryland. From this same search results page, you can view a textual record of the individual, as well as a link to see a digital image of the census record. In addition to presenting results based on your search criteria, this search mechanism displays other results that are similar — such as individuals with the same last name or people who have a name that sounds similar to the search criteria.

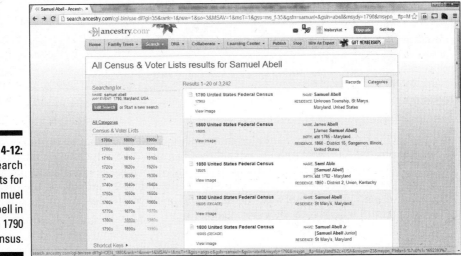

Figure 4-12:
Search results for Samuel Abell in the 1790 census.

If you click the 1790 United States Federal Census link, you'll see the textual record for Samuel Abell. In the right column, you'll see suggested records that may match Samuel Abell — making it easier to find additional records without executing multiple searches; see Figure 4-13.

Figure 4-13:
The Suggested Records column for Samuel Abell.

Using a transcribed online census

If you can't find your ancestor in one of the census indexes, another option might be to look for a transcribed census record. Sometimes individuals who transcribe records may enter comments about name variations that will assist you in locating a hard-to-find ancestor. Keep in mind that most of the free online transcriptions cover only a portion of a census area, deal with a particular family, or are complete transcriptions for a county.

As with any transcribed record, you should always verify your findings with a digitized or microfilm copy of the original record. Often, census records are difficult to read because of their age, the quality of the handwriting, and so on — so mistakes do occur in the transcription process.

Finding transcribed records on the Internet is similar to finding census indexes. You can try one of the comprehensive genealogical sites under a geographical category or a search engine.

Census records in the United States are a mainstay of genealogists, so most transcribed censuses you see on the Internet come from the United States (although that doesn't mean censuses from other countries aren't online — as we explain later in the chapter). A couple of projects are undertaken by USGenWeb volunteers to systematically transcribe census records. You can find the USGenWeb Archives Census Project at `www.rootsweb.com/~usgenweb/census` and the USGenWeb Census Project On-Line

Inventory of Transcribed Censuses at `www.us-census.org/inventory/inventory.htm`. Individuals simply transcribed those censuses that they were interested in or those associated with a geographical area they're researching. This fact doesn't diminish the importance of these efforts; it only explains why you may see a census record for one county but not for the county right next to it.

Here's a sample search on the USGenWeb Archives Census Project site:

1. **Go to the USGenWeb Census Project site (`www.rootsweb.com/~census/states.htm`).**

    You see a page with a map and a list of states and territories for which census transcriptions are available.

2. **Select a state for your search by clicking the state on the map or its link in the list.**

    For our example, we're looking for census information on Isaac Metcalf, who lived in Baylor County, Texas around 1880, so we select Texas. A list of available census schedules for the state appears.

3. **Click a year or type of schedule that interests you.**

    We select 1880. The resulting page contains a table listing the location, roll number, status of the project, and transcriber's name.

4. **Scroll through the list and click the available census link (Online, Images, Index, or Archives) in the Links column next to the County name.**

    We choose the transcription for Baylor County by clicking the Online link, which takes us to the Information on Baylor County web page.

5. **Scroll down and click the 1880 Baylor County Federal Census link.**

    A page of transcribed census entries is displayed, and we can scroll down to an individual named Isaac Metcalf. You can also use your browser's Find in Page option to find the name you're looking for.

The transcriptions on this site are the works of volunteers; you might find errors here and there. Typographical errors may crop up, some censuses may not be indexed, or the status of the project for a particular county may be incorrect.

The most plentiful type of transcribed census records you're likely to encounter is what we refer to as the *plain-text census,* which is a web page or text file that's simply a transcription of the actual census record without any kind of search function. You either have to skim the page or use your web browser's Find in Page option to find the person you're looking for. The 1850 census for Stark County, Illinois, at `http://us-census.org/pub/usgenweb/census/il/stark/1850/pg0195a.txt`, is an example of this type of census return, as shown in Figure 4-14. For each individual, the record includes the line number (LN), house number (HN), family number (FN), last name, first name, age, sex, race, occupation, value (VAL), and birthplace. This site is also typical of smaller census sites in its focus on the records of one county (actually, one township in one county).

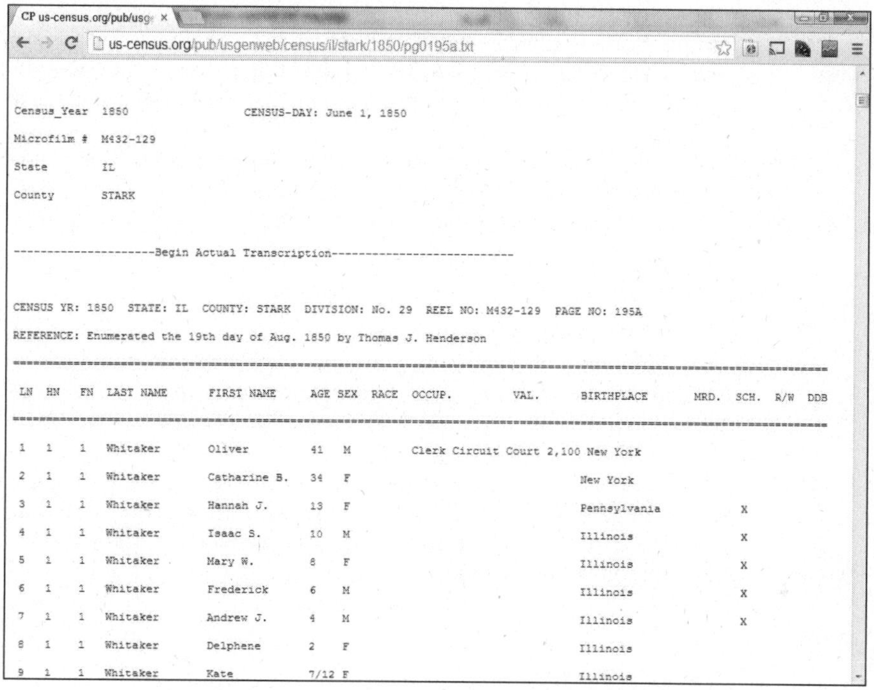

Figure 4-14:
A plain-text census page for Stark County, Illinois.

Some sites contain collections of several census returns for a specific geographic area (over an extended period of time). A good example of this type of site is the Transcribed Census Records for Vernon County, Missouri, at `http://freepages.genealogy.rootsweb.ancestry.com/~jrbakerjr/census/census1.htm`, which has several transcribed census returns for the county from 1860 to 1930.

Census Records from Afar

Of course, the U.S. isn't the only country to carry out census enumerations. Several countries around the world have taken periodic snapshots of the population. The frequency of these enumerations wasn't always every ten years and wasn't always for the same purposes as in the U.S. In the next few pages, we cover some examples of the censuses available online.

Australia

Although Australia has taken a census every ten years since 1901, the first Australia-wide census was conducted in 1911. Now for some bad news — every return has been destroyed, in accordance with law. You can substitute other records for census returns in the form of convict returns and musters and post office directories. These returns are available for some states for the years 1788, 1792, 1796, 1800, 1801, 1805, 1806, 1811, 1814, 1816, 1817–1823, 1825, 1826, and 1837. Some of these records can be found at these locations:

✔ The New South Wales Government, Department of Commerce, State Records Authority of New South Wales site, at www.records.nsw.gov.au/state-archives/indexes-online

✔ LINC Tasmania at http://portal.archives.tas.gov.au/menu.aspx?search=10

✔ The Public Records Office of Victoria at www.prov.vic.gov.au

An index to the 1841 census is maintained by the New South Wales Government at www.records.nsw.gov.au/state-archives/indexes-online/census-records/index-to-the-1841-census/index-to-the-1841-census/?searchterm=1841%20census. The index contains only the name of the head of household and has a little more than 9,000 entries. For more information on locating census returns, see the Census in Australia page at www.jaunay.com/auscensus.html.

Argentina

FamilySearch has added images of census records for the following years:

1855 – https://familysearch.org/search/collection/1469065 (Buenos Aires)

1869 – https://familysearch.org/search/collection/1462401

1895 – https://familysearch.org/search/collection/1410078

Austria

Austrian censuses were taken in the years 1857, 1869, 1880, 1890, 1900, and 1910. The first census that listed individuals by name was the 1869 census. These returns include surname, sex, year of birth, place of birth, district, religion, marital status, language, occupation, literacy, mental and physical defects, residence, and whether the household had farm animals. Some general information is available on the content of the Galicia censuses and is contained in two articles on the Federation of East European Family History Societies site: Austrian Census Returns from 1869 to 1890 (www.feefhs.org/links/galicia/shea.html) and Austrian Census for Galicia (www.feefhs.org/links/galicia/1880-gal.html).

FamilySearch has posted more than 5,000 images from census records for Wels, Upper Austria at https://familysearch.org/search/collection/2046771.

Canada

Canadian census returns are available for the years 1851, 1861, 1871, 1881, 1891, and 1901. The returns from 1851 to 1891 contain the individual's name, age, sex, province or country of birth, religion, race, occupation, marital status, and education. The returns for 1901 also include birth date, year of immigration, and address. For more information on data elements in the 1901 census, see the Description of Columns on the 1901 Census Schedule page at http://freepages.genealogy.rootsweb.ancestry.com/~wjmartin/census.htm.

Library and Archives Canada maintains information on the 1825, 1831, 1842, 1851, 1861, 1870, 1871, 1881, 1891, 1901, 1906, 1911, and 1916 censuses online at www.bac-lac.gc.ca/eng/census/Pages/census.aspx.

Automated Genealogy (http://automatedgenealogy.com) has indexes to the 1851, 1852, 1901, 1906 (a special census that included only the provinces of Alberta, Saskatchewan, and Manitoba), and 1911 censuses.

FamilySearch (https://familysearch.org) contains indexes to the 1851, 1871, 1881, 1891, 1901, 1906, and 1916 censuses.

Ancestry.ca (www.ancestry.ca) contains name indexes and images for the 1851, 1861, 1871, 1881, 1891, 1901, 1911, and 1921 censuses as well as the 1906 and 1916 censuses of Manitoba, Saskatchewan, and Alberta. It also contains indexes to various censuses conducted in Ontario and Nova Scotia from 1800 to 1842 and the 1770 census of Nova Scotia.

You might be interested in presenting some context to your research by using statistical information from past censuses. For example, you may want to include in your research how many people lived in a particular province during a given census year. You can find this kind of information in the Historical Statistics of Canada at the Statistics Canada site (www.statcan.gc.ca).

Czech Republic

The South Bohemian Census 1857–1921 contains digitized images from the 1857, 1869, 1880, 1890, 1900, 1910, and 1921 censuses. You can find the images at http://digi.ceskearchivy.cz/DA?lang=en&menu=0&doctree=1t &id=5.

FamilySearch has placed more than 1.7 million images of census records from 1843-1921 at https://familysearch.org/search/ collection/1930345.

Denmark

The Danish Archives has census returns for the years 1787, 1801, 1834, 1840, 1845, 1850, 1855, 1860, 1870, 1880, 1890, 1901, 1906, 1911, 1916, 1921, 1925, and 1930. You can find information from these censuses at the Statens Arkiver site (www.sa.dk/content/dk/ao-forside/find_folketal linger) and the Dansk Demografisk Database (http://ddd.dda.dk/ kiplink_en.htm). The returns contain name, age, occupation, and relationship for each individual in the household. After 1845, census returns include information on the individual's place of birth. Census returns for Denmark are available after 80 years. The Dansk Demografisk Database also includes censuses and lists of emigrants and immigrants for Denmark.

Estonia

FamilySearch has placed almost 600,000 images of population registers from Estonia (https://familysearch.org/search/collection/1983333). Years covered include 1918 through 1944.

Ghana

FamilySearch has added images of census records from 1982 to 1984. You can browse the images at https://familysearch.org/search/ collection/1615258.

Guatemala

FamilySearch contains the Cuidad de Guatemala Census of 1877 at https:// familysearch.org/search/collection/1648736.

Germany

The German central government held censuses in 1871, 1880, 1885, 1890, 1895, 1900, 1905, 1910, 1919, 1925, 1933, and 1939. Unfortunately, these census returns do not have much genealogical value because they were statistical in nature. Some local censuses are available. The collection at Ancestry.de (`www.ancestry.de`) contains the Mecklenburg-Schwerin censuses of 1819, 1867, 1890, and 1900.

FamilySearch (`https://familysearch.org`) has also posted the Mecklenburg-Schwerin censuses of 1867, 1890, and 1900, as well as the Westfalen, Minden Citizen Lists from 1574 to 1902.

Ireland

Countrywide census enumerations have been conducted every ten years since 1821. Unfortunately, the census returns from 1821 to 1851 were largely destroyed in a fire at the Public Record Office in 1922. Fragments of these census returns are available at the National Archives of Ireland.

The government destroyed the returns from 1861 and 1871. Returns for 1901 and 1911 still survive and are available at the National Archives of Ireland. The 1901 and 1911 censuses are available online at `www.nationalarchives.ie`. See Figure 4-15 for an example.

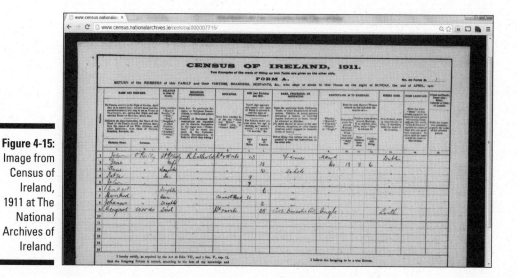

Figure 4-15: Image from Census of Ireland, 1911 at The National Archives of Ireland.

Historical statistics for Irish censuses can be found on the census page maintained by the Central Statistics Office of Ireland at www.cso.ie/census. No names are included in the publications, but the data can be used to gain some historical perspective on a particular area.

Findmypast.com (www.findmypast.com) has some Irish census returns on its site, including:

- Dublin City Census 1901: Rotunda Ward
- Census of Elphin, 1749
- Index to the Dublin City Census, 1851

Italy

FamilySearch holds images of the census of Mantova from 1750 to 1900 at https://familysearch.org/search/collection/2212671.

Ivory Coast

FamilySearch has posted images from the 1975 census at https://familysearch.org/search/collection/1779107.

Luxembourg

FamilySearch has uploaded 1.1 million images of census records from 1843 to 1900 at https://familysearch.org/search/collection/2037957.

Mexico

The Mexican government attempted censuses in 1868 and 1878. However, the population refused to participate. A census was taken in 1895, and from 1900 on, the census has been performed every ten years. The 1930 federal census is the only census available for public viewing.

You can search the free index of the 1930 census at FamilySearch, as well as view digitized images of the enumerations; see Figure 4-16. Ancestry.com also has the 1930 census as part of its subscription service.

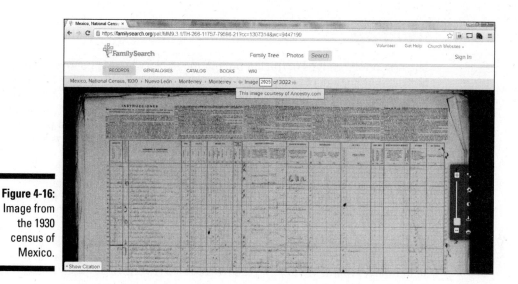

Figure 4-16:
Image from the 1930 census of Mexico.

Transcribed records are also available on sites that focus on Hispanic ancestors. For example, you can view transcribed records from the 1750 and 1753 censuses of the village of Guerrero at www.hispanicgs.com/census. html.

Moldova

FamilySearch has placed online poll tax censuses and census lists from 1796 to 1917 at https://familysearch.org/search/collection/1985804.

Netherlands

Censuses for parts of the Netherlands were taken in 1714, 1744, 1748, 1749, and 1795. A decennial census was enumerated from 1829 to 1930. Modern censuses were taken in 1947, 1960, and 1971.

FamilySearch houses census and population registers from 1645 to 1940 (https://familysearch.org/search/collection/2018408) and Noord-Brabant Province population registers from 1820 to 1930 (https://familysearch.org/search/collection/1392827).

Norway

The first public census of the full population in Norway was conducted in 1769, and statistical censuses were also conducted in 1815, 1835, 1845, and 1855. Censuses by name were conducted in 1801, 1865, 1870, 1875, 1885, 1891, and 1900. Censuses by name were also taken in 1910, 1920, 1930, 1946, and 1950 — but research on these can be performed only for statistical purposes, due to privacy restrictions. Each census after 1865 contained information such as name, sex, age, relationship.

Tap to head of household, civil status, occupation, religion, and place of birth. For more details on the censuses, see the Documenting the Norwegian Censuses page at www.rhd.uit.no/nhdc/census.html.

Table 4-1 lists what's available at the National Archives of Norway's Digitalarkivet site. For a detailed description of the collection and a main search page, visit http://digitalarkivet.uib.no/cgi-win/WebMeta.exe?slag=vismeny&fylkenr=&knr=&katnr=1&emnenr=&dagens=&aar=17&alle=true.

Table 4-1	Census Resources from the National Archives of Norway	
Year	*Web Address*	*Form*
1664–1666	www.arkivverket.no/eng/content/view/full/5462	Census images
1701	www.arkivverket.no/eng/Digitalarkivet/About-the-Digital-Archives/Source-Information/Realistisk-ordnet-avdeling/The-1701-Census	Census images
1801	http://digitalarkivet.arkivverket.no/ft/sok/1801	Online searchable index
1865	http://digitalarkivet.arkivverket.no/ft/sok/1865	Online searchable index
1875	http://digitalarkivet.no/cgi-win/WebMeta.exe?slag=vismeny&katnr=1&emnenr=4	Online searchable index
1885	http://digitalarkivet.arkivverket.no/ft/sok/1885	Online searchable index

Year	Web Address	Form

1891	`www.arkivverket.no/`
	`arkivverket/Digitalarkivet/`
	`Om-Digitalarkivet/`
	`Om-kjeldene/`
	`Folketellingen-1891`
		Online searchable index

1900	`http://digitalarkivet.no/cgi-`
	`win/WebMeta.exe?slag=vismeny&`
	`katnr=1&emnenr=5`
		Online searchable index

1910	`http://digitalarkivet.` `arkivverket.no/ft/sok/1910`	Online searchable index

The 1865, 1875, 1900, and 1910 censuses of Norway are also available from the Norwegian Historical Data Centre. Some parish registers are also available on the site (`www.rhd.uit.no/indexeng.html`).

Russia

FamilySearch contains poll tax census records for Tartarstan between 1719 and 1859 at `https://familysearch.org/search/collection/1931807`.

Spain

FamilySearch houses the Catastro de Ensenada, 1749–1756 at `https://familysearch.org/search/collection/1851392`. The collection contains census records from Andalucía, Asturias, Cantabria, Castilla-La Mancha, Castilla y León, Extremadura, Galicia, La Rioja, Madrid, and Murcia.

Slovakia

Censuses under Hungary occurred in 1784 through 1785, 1808, 1828, 1848 (Jews only), 1850, 1857, 1869, 1880, 1890, 1900, and 1910. Under Czechoslovakia, censuses were conducted in 1921, 1930, 1940, 1950, 1961, 1970, 1980, and 1991.

FamilySearch has posted images of the 1869 census at `https://familysearch.org/search/collection/1986782`.

Switzerland

FamilySearch (https://familysearch.org) contains census enumerations from Fribourg for the years 1811, 1818, 1831, 1834, 1836, 1839, 1842, 1845, 1850, 1860, 1870, and 1880.

United Kingdom

Since 1801, censuses have been taken in England and Wales every ten years (except 1941). Most of the returns from 1801 to 1831 were statistical and did not contain names, making them of little use for genealogists. Beginning in 1841, the administration of the census became the responsibility of the Registrar General and the Superintendent Registrars, who were responsible for recording civil registrations (vital records). This changed the focus of the census from the size of the population to details on individuals and families. The National Archives releases information in the census after 100 years.

For general information on census records, see the National Archives Census page at www.nationalarchives.gov.uk/records/looking-for-person/recordscensus.htm.

You can find online versions of the following censuses:

- ✔ **Images** of the 1841 through 1911 censuses are available at 1901CensusOnline.com (www.1901censusonline.com), Ancestry.uk (www.ancestry.co.uk), FindMyPast.co.uk (www.findmypast.co.uk), and Genes Reunited (www.genesreunited.co.uk). British Origins (www.britishorigins.com) contains images of the 1841, 1861, and 1871 censuses.

- ✔ **Transcriptions** are sporadic for the 1841 through 1891 censuses at the FreeCEN site (http://freecen.rootsweb.com). Also, partial transcriptions are available at TheGenealogist.co.uk (www.thegenealogist.co.uk).

- ✔ **Indexes** for the 1841 through 1911 censuses are available at the FamilySearch site (www.familysearch.org).

- ✔ **Maps** of the registration districts for the 1871 census are available at the Cassini site (www.cassinimaps.co.uk/shop/tnal.asp?id=166&page=ce).

ScotlandsPeople (www.scotlandspeople.gov.uk) contains the 1841 through 1911 censuses for Scotland. It also contains street indexes for some of the areas covered by the censuses.

Part II
Bringing Your Ancestor to Life

Explore migration to the United States and potentially identify areas to look for your ancestors at www.dummies.com/extras/genealogyonline.

In this part...

- Discover effective ways to search for your ancestor using search engines.
- Learn the power of geographic resources to provide context to the life of your ancestors.
- Locate online resources for locations outside of the United States, as well as ethnic-specific sites.

Chapter 5

Digging Deeper into Your Ancestors' Lives

As we all know, governments love paper. Sometimes it seems that government workers can't do anything without a form. Luckily for genealogists, governments have been this way for a number of years — otherwise, it might be next to impossible to conduct family history research. In fact, the number of useful government records available online has exploded in the past decade. Not only have government entities been placing records and indexes online — private companies have put great effort into digitizing and indexing government records for online use.

In this chapter, we show you what kinds of records are available and describe some of the major projects that you can use as keys for unlocking government treasure chests of genealogical information.

These Records Are Vital

It seems that some kind of government record accompanies every major event in our lives. One is generated when we are born, another when we get married (as well as get divorced), another when we have a child, and still another when we pass on. *Vital records* is the collective name for records of these events. Traditionally, these records have been kept at the local level — in the county, parish, or in some cases, the town where the event occurred. However, over time, some state-level government agencies began making an effort to collect and centralize the holdings of vital records.

Reading vital records

Vital records are among the first sets of primary sources typically used by genealogists (for more on primary sources, see Chapter 2). These records contain key and usually reliable information because they were produced near the time that the event occurred, and a witness to the event provided the information. (Outside the United States, vital records are often called *civil registrations*.) You explore the four types of vital records in this section.

Birth records

Birth records are good primary sources for verifying the date of birth, birthplace, and names of an individual's parents. Depending on the information requirements for a particular birth certificate, you may also discover the birthplace of the parents, their ages, occupations, addresses at the time of the birth, whether the mother had given birth previously, date of marriage of the parents, and the names and ages of any previous children.

Sometimes, instead of a birth certificate, you may find another record in the family's possession that verifies the existence of the birth record. For example, instead of having a certified copy of a birth certificate, Matthew's grandmother had a Certificate of Record of Birth. This certificate attests to the fact that the county has a certificate of birth and notes its location. These certificates were used primarily before photocopiers became commonplace, and it became easier to get a certified copy of the original record.

Birth records were less formal in earlier times. Before modern record-keeping, a simple handwritten entry in a book sufficed as an official record of an individual's birth. So be very specific when citing a birth record in your genealogical notes. Include any numbers you find in the record and where the record is located (including not only the physical location of the building, but also the book number and page number of the information, and even the record number if one is present).

Marriage records

Marriage records come in several forms. Early marriage records may include the following:

- **Marriage bonds:** Financial guarantees that a marriage was going to take place

- **Marriage banns:** Proclamations of the intent to marry someone in front of a church congregation

- **Marriage licenses:** Documents granting permission to marry

- **Marriage records or certificates:** Documents certifying the union of two people

These records usually contain the groom's name, the bride's name, and the location of the ceremony. They may also contain occupation information, birthplaces of the bride and groom, parents' names and birthplaces, names of witnesses, and information on previous marriages.

When using marriage records, don't confuse the date of the marriage with the date of the marriage bond, bann, or license. The latter records were often filed anywhere from a few days to several weeks *before* the actual marriage date. Also, don't assume that because you found a bond, bann, or license, a marriage took place. Some people got cold feet then (as they do today) and backed out of the marriage at the last minute.

If you have trouble finding a marriage record in the area where your ancestors lived, try looking in surrounding counties or parishes or possibly even states. Like today, destination weddings did occur! Lucky for those of us researching in the twenty-first century — most of our ancestors' destinations were nearby towns instead of exotic, far-off places. Typically, the reason some ancestors traveled to another location was to have the wedding at a particular relative's house or church. So if the record isn't in the location you expect, be sure to look in the areas where the parents of the ancestors lived.

Divorce records

One type of vital record that may be easy to overlook is a divorce decree. Later generations may not be aware that an early ancestor was divorced, and the records recounting the event can be difficult to find. However, divorce records can be valuable. They contain many important facts, including the age of the petitioners, birthplace, address, occupations, names and ages of children, property, and the grounds for the divorce.

Death records

Death records are excellent resources for verifying the date of death but are less reliable for other data elements such as birth date and birthplace because people who were not witnesses to the birth often supply that information. However, information on the death record can point you in the right direction for records to verify other events. More recent death records include the name of the individual, place of death, residence, parents' names, spouse's name, occupation, and cause of death. Early death records may contain only the date of death, cause, and residence.

Gauging vitals online

Historically, researchers were required to contact the county, parish, or town clerk to receive a copy of a vital record. This meant either traveling to the location where the record was housed or ordering the record through the mail. With the advent of online research, most sites covering vital records are geared toward providing addresses of repositories, rather than information on the vital records of particular individuals. The reason for this is the traditional sensitivity of vital records — and the reluctance of repositories to place vital records online due to identity theft and privacy concerns.

A few years ago, the number of resources containing information about specific vital records, including indexes and digitized records, began to greatly increase. Today, the vast majority of resources are indexes to vital records, but digitized records are starting to appear more frequently.

To get a better idea of how to search for vital records, we use members of Matthew's family as examples as we look at the different types of records that you will encounter online.

Vital record indexes

A good first place to start in your quest for vital records is to search for a vital records index for the place where you suspect your ancestor was born, married, or died. Vital record indexes point to the locations of original records. You can use indexes to confirm that an ancestor's vital records are available prior to submitting a request for the record. Or, in some cases, you can use the index to lead you to a digitized copy of the record (typically on subscription sites). And knowing the exact location of the record can often make retrieval of the record a lot easier.

Although the majority of indexes are on subscription sites, sometimes you can find them on free genealogy project sites. To find these sites, you can conduct a search in a search engine for the locality, and then use the site search engine to find the individual you're looking for.

For example, Matthew is interested in acquiring a copy of the death certificate for his great-grandfather, William Henry Abell, who died in Kentucky. According to his headstone, William was born in 1873 and died in 1955. With this information, Matthew can begin to search for a vital records index.

To find an online index, you can use a search engine such as Google (www.google.com). For example, to find a death index for Kentucky, type the following search into Google:

> +death index+Kentucky

At the top of the results list is a link to RootsWeb Presents Kentucky Death Records 1911–2000. To find information on William Henry Abell, we go through the following steps:

1. **Go to the Kentucky Death Records site (http://vitals.rootsweb. ancestry.com/ky/death/search.cgi).**

   You see search fields in the middle of the page.

2. **In the Last Name field, type the surname of your ancestor. In the First Name field, type his or her given name.**

   Sticking with the example, we type **Abell** and **William**.

3. **If you want to restrict your search to a particular place of death, residence, or year, type those values in the appropriate fields.**

   For our example, we restrict the search by Year (of death) by entering **1955**.

4. **Click Search.**

   Wait for the results to return.

5. **Scan the results of your query.**

   In our case, the results page contained one individual named William H. Abell, as shown in Figure 5-1. The death date — September 7, 1955 — and the age, 82, is consistent with the information on the gravestone. The database also supplies us with the record volume number and certificate number, which we can use to obtain a copy of the certificate.

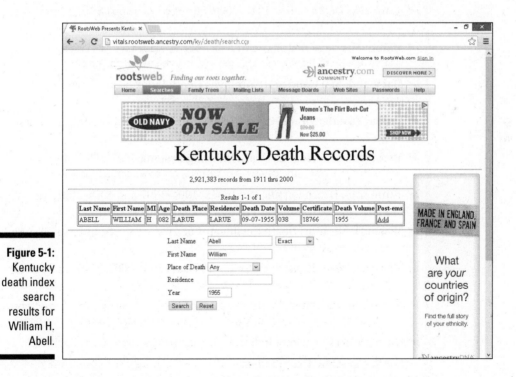

Figure 5-1: Kentucky death index search results for William H. Abell.

Now that you know how to use the Kentucky death index online, here are some other free sites containing state-wide vital records indexes:

- **California:** Death Records, 1940–1997, at `http://vitals.rootsweb.com/ca/death/search.cgi`

- **Colorado:** Marriage and Divorce Records at `http://coloradoc2.prod.acquia-sites.com/archives/archives-search`

- **Idaho:** Death Index, 1911–1956, at `http://abish.byui.edu/specialCollections/famhist/Death/searchForm.cfm`

- **Illinois:** Statewide Marriage Index, 1763–1900, at `www.cyberdriveillinois.com/departments/archives/databases/marriage.html`

- **Illinois:** Death Certificates, 1916–1950, at `www.cyberdriveillinois.com/departments/archives/databases/idphdeathindex.html`

- **Kansas:** Kansas Marriage Index, 1854–1861, at `www.kshs.org/p/kansas-marriage-index-1854-1861/11315`

- **Kentucky:** Death Index, 1911–2000, at `http://vitals.rootsweb.com/ky/death/search.cgi`

- **Maine:** Marriage History Search at `http://portal.maine.gov/marriage/archdev.marriage_archive.search_form`

- **Maryland:** Maryland State Archives Death Indexes, at `http://mdvitalrec.net/cfm/dsp_search.cfm`

- **Massachusetts:** Vital Records, 1600–1850, at `www.ma-vitalrecords.org`

- **Michigan:** Genealogical Death Indexing System, 1867–1897, at `www.mdch.state.mi.us/pha/osr/gendisx/search2.htm`

- **Minnesota:** Death Certificates Index, 1904–1907 and 1955–2001, at `http://people.mnhs.org/dci/Search.cfm?bhcp=1`

- **Missouri:** Missouri Death Certificates at `www.sos.mo.gov/archives/resources/deathcertificates`

- **Montana:** Death Registry Index, pre-1954 and 1954–2002, at `www.rootsweb.ancestry.com/~mtmsgs/death_records.htm`

- **North Dakota:** Public Death Index, 1881–present, at `https://secure.apps.state.nd.us/doh/certificates/deathCertSearch.htm`

- **Ohio:** Death Certificate Index at `www.ohiohistory.org/dindex`

- **South Carolina:** Death Indexes, 1915–1962, at `www.scdhec.net/administration/vr/vrdi.htm`

- **South Dakota:** Birth Record Search Site for South Dakota Birth Records with Birth Dates Over 100 Years, at `http://apps.sd.gov/applications/PH14Over100BirthRec/index.asp`

✔ **Tennessee:** Index to Tennessee Death Records, 1908–1912, at `www.tennessee.gov/tsla/history/vital/death2.htm`

✔ **Tennessee:** Index to Tennessee Death Records, 1914–1933, at `www.tennessee.gov/tsla/history/vital/tndeath.htm`

✔ **Texas:** Texas Death Records, 1964–1998, at `http://vitals.rootsweb.com/tx/death/search.cgi`

✔ **Virginia:** Death Records Index, 1853–1896, at `http://lva1.hosted.exlibrisgroup.com/F/?func=file&file_name=find-b-clas29&local_base=clas29`

✔ **Wisconsin:** Wisconsin Genealogy Index, pre-1907 birth, death, and marriage records, at `www.wisconsinhistory.org/vitalrecords`

✔ **Western States:** Western States Marriage Indexes at `http://abish.byui.edu/specialCollections/westernStates/search.cfm`

A number of free vital records indexes are available on the FamilySearch.org Records Search site at `https://familysearch.org/search`.

Digital images of vital records

Digitization of vital records has boomed over the past few years. Initially, archives that house vital records were reluctant to digitize them due to privacy concerns. However, as more and more requests came in for vital records, these archives have allowed companies to place those records that fall outside the provisions of the privacy act online. And finding these digitized vital records gets easier and easier as time goes on.

Through family interviews, Matthew knows that John C. Martin, his great-great grandfather on his mother's side of the family, was married to Emma Temperance Gardiner in Missouri. Let's suppose that you too are interested in finding a copy of the record documenting the marriage. (It's more likely that you just want to learn the method for finding such a record for one of your ancestors.) To find digitized vital records, try this:

1. **Go to the search engine Bing (`www.bing.com`) and type the search term** Missouri Marriage Records.

   You might prefer to use a different state name, depending on whether your ancestor was from Missouri or somewhere else.

2. **Click the Missouri Marriage Records, 1805–2002 — Ancestry.com link.**

   The resulting screen includes a search form requesting name, spouse, and marriage information.

3. **Type** John Martin **in the name field and** Emma Gardiner **in the spouse field, and then click the Search button; see Figure 5-2.**

   Again, you might want to substitute your own ancestors' names. If so, your results will vary a bit. A table containing search results is displayed. The top two results contain a record for John C. Martin who married an Emma Gardiner. Both records have the marriage occurring in Lafayette County. The difference is Emma's middle initial.

Figure 5-2:
The search form for the Missouri Marriage Records collection at Ancestry .com.

4. **Click the icon on the far right of the row in the View Images column.**

   A page appears with subscription information. If you already have a subscription, you can log in to your account at the upper-right corner of the screen. If not, you have to follow the prompts to get a free 14-day trial. We fill in the login information and click the Sign In button. After the login, the page displays the image of the marriage record.

5. **After the image pops up, click the Zoom In button to see the image more clearly.**

   Figure 5-3 shows the image of the marriage record. In the search results, we have two entries in the index because Emma's middle initial is not entirely clear. It could have been either a *T* or an *S*. From the image, we can see that William C. Dawson married John and Emma on August 27, 1868.

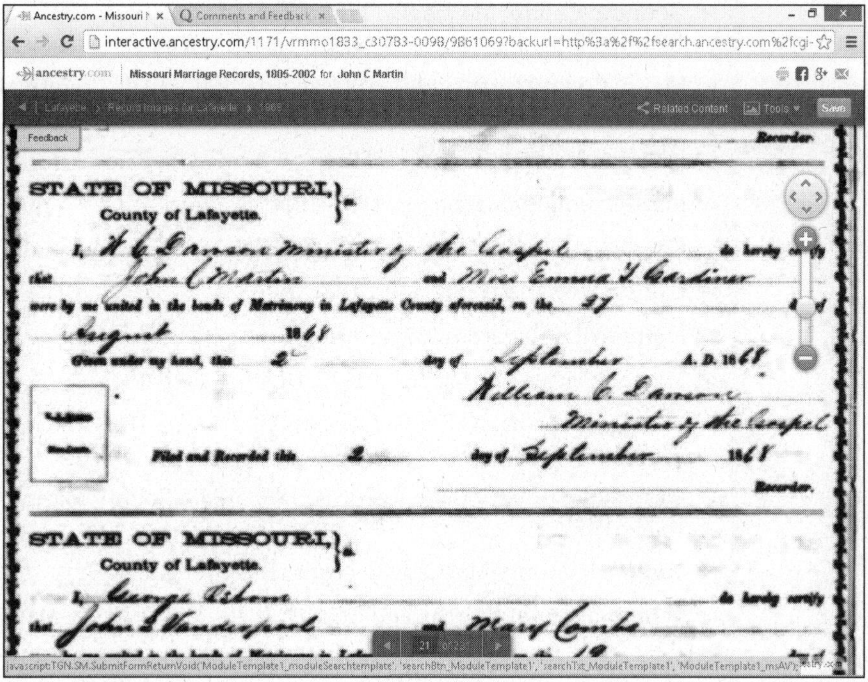

Figure 5-3: Image recording the marriage of John C. Martin to Emma T. Gardiner.

The FamilySearch.org Records Search site (`https://familysearch.org/search/collection/list#page=1&region=UNITED_STATES`), which we explore in the preceding section, has a nice selection of digitized images of vital records by location:

- **Alabama:** County Marriages, 1809–1950
- **Arizona:** Deaths, 1870–1951
- **Arkansas:** County Marriages, 1837–1957
- **California:** County Birth and Death Records, 1849–1994; County Marriages, 1850–1952; Death Index, 1905–1939
- **Colorado:** County Marriages, 1864–1995; Statewide Divorce Index, 1900–1939; Statewide Marriage Index, 1853–2006
- **Delaware:** Deaths Records, 1855–1961; Marriage Records, 1913–1954, State Birth Records, 1861–1922
- **District of Columbia:** Deaths, 1874–1959; Marriages, 1811–1950; Birth Returns, 1874–1897
- **Florida:** Marriages, 1830–1993

✔ **Georgia:** County Marriages, 1785–1950; Deaths, 1914–1927; Deaths, 1928–1930

✔ **Idaho:** County Birth and Death Records, 1907–1920; County Marriages, 1864–1950; Death Certificates, 1911–1937

✔ **Indiana:** Marriages, 1811–1959

✔ **Kansas:** County Marriages, 1855–1911

✔ **Kentucky:** County Marriages, 1797–1954

✔ **Louisiana:** Parish Marriages, 1837–1957

✔ **Maine:** Vital Records, 1670–1907

✔ **Massachusetts:** Births, 1841–1915; Deaths, 1841–1915

✔ **Michigan:** Births, 1867–1902; County Marriages, 1820–1935, Deaths, 1867–1897; Marriages, 1868–1925

✔ **Minnesota:** County Birth Records, 1863–1983; County Marriages, 1860–1949

✔ **Missouri:** County Marriage Records, 1819–1969

✔ **Montana:** County Births and Deaths, 1840–2004; County Marriages, 1865–1950

✔ **Nevada:** County Birth and Death Records, 1871–1992; County Marriages, 1862–1993

✔ **New Hampshire:** Birth Records, Early to 1900; Death Records, 1654– 1947; Marriage Records, 1637–1947

✔ **New Jersey:** County Marriages, 1682–1956

✔ **New Mexico:** County Death Records, 1907–1952, County Marriages, 1885–1954

✔ **New York:** County Marriages, 1908–1935

✔ **North Carolina:** County Marriages, 1762–1979; Deaths, 1906–1930

✔ **Ohio:** County Births, 1841–2003; County Marriages, 1789–1994; Deaths, 1908–1953

✔ **Oklahoma:** County Marriages, 1890–1995

✔ **Oregon:** County Marriages, 1851–1975

✔ **Pennsylvania:** County Marriages, 1885–1950

✔ **Tennessee:** County Marriages, 1790–1950; Death Records, 1914–1955

✔ **Texas:** Birth Certificates, 1903–1935; County Marriage Records, 1837–1977; Deaths, 1890–1976; Deaths, 1977–1986

✔ **Utah:** Death Certificates, 1904–1956

✔ **Vermont:** Vital Records, 1760–2003

- ✔ **Washington:** County Deaths, 1891–1907; County Divorce Records, 1852–1950, County Marriages, 1855–2008

- ✔ **West Virginia:** Births, 1853–1930; Deaths, 1804–1999; Marriages, 1853–1970

In addition to U.S.-based vital records, this site has an assortment of international vital records or civil registrations. Australia, Belgium, Brazil, the Czech Republic, France, Iceland, Italy, Mexico, Wales, and Zimbabwe are just a sample of the countries for which you can find indexes and some online images here. For more on researching international ancestors, take a gander at Chapter 8.

Other sites offer vital records online, too. Here is a list of examples:

- ✔ **Arizona:** Arizona Genealogy Birth and Death Certificates (births 1855–1937; deaths 1861–1962) at `http://genealogy.az.gov`

- ✔ **Colorado:** Arapahoe County (includes City of Denver) Marriages 1861–1868 at `www.colorado.gov/dpa/doit/archives/DenMarriage/denver_and_arapahoe_county_marri.htm`

- ✔ **Kentucky:** Death Records, 1852–1953 (subscription site), at `http://search.ancestry.com/search/db.aspx?htx=List&dbid=1222&offerid=0%3a7858%3a0`

- ✔ **Michigan:** Death Records at `http://seekingmichigan.org/` — to search the records at this site, you need to use the Advanced Search function, which you can access through the link at the top-right of the home page

- ✔ **Missouri:** Death Certificates at `www.sos.mo.gov/archives/resources/deathcertificates/#searchdeat`

- ✔ **Utah:** Death Certificates, 1904–1961, at `http://archives.utah.gov/research/indexes/20842.htm`

- ✔ **West Virginia:** Birth, Death, and Marriage Certificates at `www.wvculture.org/vrr/va_select.aspx`

General information sites

If you've had only a little luck finding a digitized vital record or index (or you need a record that falls within the range of the privacy act), your next step might be to visit a general information site. If you're looking for information on how to order vital records in the U.S., you can choose among a few sites. Several commercial sites have addresses for vital records repositories. Unfortunately, some of them are full of advertisements for subscription sites, making it difficult to determine which links will lead you to useful information and what is going to lead you to a third-party site that wants to make a sale.

One site that contains useful information without the advertisements is the Where to Write for Vital Records page on the Centers for Disease Control and Prevention site (`www.cdc.gov/nchs/w2w.htm`). To locate information, simply click a state and you see a table listing details on how to order records from state-level repositories.

Investigating Immigration and Naturalization Records

You may have heard the old stories about your great-great-grandparents who left their homeland in search of a more prosperous life. Some of these stories may include details about where they were born and how they arrived at their new home. Although these are interesting and often entertaining stories, as a genealogist, you want to verify this information with documentation.

Often the document you're looking for is an immigration or naturalization record. *Immigration records* are documents that show when a person moved to a particular country to reside. They include passenger lists and port-entry records for ships, and border-crossing papers for land entry into a country. *Naturalization records* are documents showing that a person became a citizen of a country without being born in that country. Sometimes an immigrant will reside in a country without becoming a naturalized citizen, and you can find paperwork on him or her, too. You can look for alien registration paperwork and visas. A *visa* is a document permitting a noncitizen to live or travel in a country.

Immigration and naturalization documents can prove challenging to find, especially if you don't know where to begin looking. Unless you have some evidence in your attic or have a reliable family account of the immigration, you may need a record or something else to point you in the right direction. Census records are useful. (For more information about census records, see Chapter 4.) Depending on the year your ancestors immigrated, census records may contain the location of birth and tell you the year of immigration and the year of naturalization of your immigrant ancestor.

Emigration records — documents that reflect when a person moved out of a particular country to take up residence elsewhere — are also useful to researchers. You find these records in the country your ancestor left. They can often help when you can't find immigration or naturalization records in the new country.

To find more information on research using immigration records in the U.S., we recommend taking a look at the National Archives: Immigration Records (Ship Passenger Arrival Records) site at `www.archives.gov/research/immigration/index.html`. This site provides general information on using immigration records and also identifies the types of immigration records held by the National Archives. The Olive Tree Genealogy: NaturalizationRecords. com site (www.naturalizationrecords.com) provides an overview of what you might glean from naturalization records in the U.S. and Canada.

You can also check out Chapter 9: "Immigration Records," written by Loretto Dennis Szucs, Kory L. Meyerink, and Marian L. Smith, in *The Source: A Guidebook of American Genealogy,* Third Edition, edited by Szucs and Sandra Hargreaves Luebking (Ancestry Publishing, Inc.). Other sources to refer to include *They Became Americans: Finding Naturalization Records and Ethnic Origins,* written by Loretto Dennis Szucs (Ancestry Publishing), and *They Came in Ships: Finding Your Immigrant Ancestor's Arrival Record,* Third Edition, written by John Philip Colletta (Ancestry Publishing). All of these selections provide more information about immigration and naturalization within the U.S.

Although locating immigration, emigration, and naturalization records online has been challenging in the past, it's a growing field and more is available than ever. Common types of records that genealogists use to locate immigrants — passenger lists, immigration papers, and emigration records — have increased in availability on the Internet over the past decade and will likely continue to increase in numbers. A good starting point for determining an ancestor's homeland is to look at census records. (Again, for more information about census records, see Chapter 4.) Because a great deal of early immigration and naturalization processing occurred at the local level, census records may give you an indication of where to look for immigration records.

Some examples of online records, indexes, and databases include the following:

- ✔ **McLean County Circuit Clerk:** McLean County, Illinois, Immigration Records (www.mcleancountyil.gov/index.aspx?NID=161)

- ✔ **New Mexico Genealogical Society:** Passport Records, 1828–1836: Mexican Records from the Port of Entry at Santa Fe, New Mexico Territory (www.nmgs.org/artpass.htm)

- ✔ **MayflowerHistory.com:** Mayflower Passenger List (http://mayflowerhistory.com/mayflower-passenger-list/)

- ✔ **Iron Range Research Center:** 1918 Minnesota Alien Registration Records (www.ironrangeresearchcenter.org/genealogy/collections/alienregistration/index.htm)

Although the number of websites offering immigration and naturalization records has grown substantially, it's still kind of hit and miss whether you'll find an independent site that has what you need. You're more likely to have success at one of the major subscription sites, like Ancestry.com.

Ancestry.com's Immigration and Travel records are sorted into the following categories:

- Passenger Lists
- Crew Lists
- Border Crossings & Passports
- Citizenship & Naturalization
- Immigration & Emigration Books
- Ship Pictures & Descriptions
- Other Records

In the next two sections, you explore passenger lists and naturalization records in a little more detail. But you can use the steps that follow for searching Ancestry.com's Immigration and Travel collection to look for both types of records. Ancestry.com's collection contains information on millions of names and immigration records from more than 100 countries. Highlights of the collection include

- U.S. passport applications, 1795–1925
- Passenger lists from several U.S. cities (including Boston, Philadelphia, New Orleans, Seattle, and Honolulu), as well as countries (such as Australia, Wales, Germany, Canada, and Latvia)
- Naturalization records, 1700s–1900s

For our example, we'll search the Ancestry.com Immigration and Travel collection for any immigration records relating to April's ancestor, Absolom Looney. Here are the steps:

1. **Go to Ancestry.com (`www.ancestry.com`).**

2. **In the navigation bar at the top, hover your mouse over the Search button, and select Immigration & Travel from the drop-down menu.**

   The Immigration & Travel search form appears.

3. **Click the Show Advanced button at the top of the page to see the check box. Check the Match All Terms Exactly check box at the top of the Search form if you want this search to match names, dates, and locations exactly.**

4. **Enter the name of your ancestor in the First and Middle Name(s) and Last Name fields.**

   For our example, we enter Absolom in the First and Middle Name(s) field, and Looney in the Last Name field; see Figure 5-4. Of course, you may wish to use your own ancestor's name.

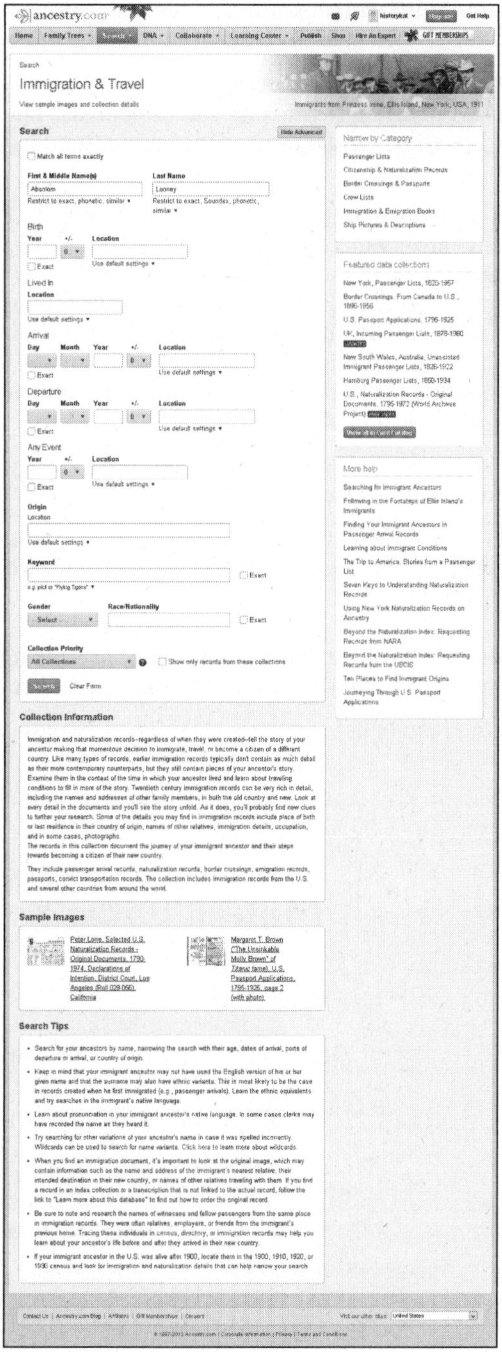

Figure 5-4:
The
Immigration
& Travel
search form
at Ancestry
.com.

5. **If you know additional information about your ancestor and wish to use it to limit the results of your search, enter it in the appropriate field(s).**

   The optional fields include: Birth Date, Birth Location, Lived In Location, Arrival Date, Arrival Location, Departure Date, Departure Location, Event Year, Event Location, Origin, Keyword search, Gender, and Race/Nationality.

   In our case, we don't know much about Absolom Looney, but we do know his name may have been spelled different ways. So we set the Exact Match criteria for the First and Last Names by clicking the links under each field and selecting the check boxes that fit our needs. In this case, we set the first name matching on phonetic names and names with similar spellings or meanings, and we set the last name matching on these two criteria plus Soundex. For more information about how Soundex codes work, take a peek at Chapter 4.

6. **Near the bottom of the Search form, set the Search Priority. The default is to set to search All Collections.**

   If you do not wish to search All Collections, select a different option from the drop-down list. The choices are locale or ethnicity based.

7. **Click the Search button.**

8. **Scroll through the results and click any that look promising to see more information about that record and the digitized document.**

   Figure 5-5 shows the results list from our search on Absolom Looney.

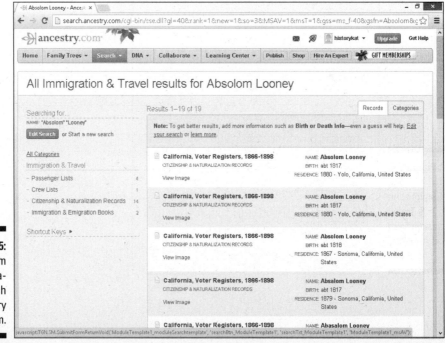

Figure 5-5:
Results from an immigration search at Ancestry.com.

Passenger lists

One type of immigration record that you can find on the web is passenger lists. Passenger lists are manifests of who traveled on a particular ship. You can use passenger lists not only to see who immigrated on a particular ship, but you can also see citizens of the U.S. who were merely traveling by ship (perhaps coming back from vacation in Europe).

To find passenger lists, you can try using a general search engine or a genealogically focused search engine. This is a particularly good strategy if you don't know what the name of the ship was or the year that your ancestors immigrated. If you do know the name of the ship, a comprehensive genealogical index may be more appropriate.

As an example, suppose family legend says that Martin Saunders immigrated to America on a ship called *Planter* sometime in the first part of the 17th century. The following steps show you how to search for a passenger list to confirm the legend:

1. **Go to the Ask.com search engine (**`www.ask.com`**).**

   The search box is located at the top of the home page.

2. **In the search field, type your search terms and then click Find Answers.**

   For this example, we type **Martin Saunders on the ship Planter.**

3. **Click a promising link from the list of results.**

   The results page shows the first 10 links of more than 2,000 links found for these search terms. One of the top links goes to a transcription of the passengers on the *Planter,* which sailed on April 6, 1635 — the first on the list being "Martin Saunders, aged 40 years." Another link on the results page reads "Ships Passenger List — PLANTER of London for Boston Massachusetts." In the abstract that you access by clicking the link, you see that a Martin Saunders, age 40, sailed on the *Planter.*

Another source for passenger lists is the Immigrant Ships Transcribers Guild passenger-list transcription project (`www.immigrantships.net`). Currently, the Guild has transcribed more than 14,000 passenger manifests. The passenger lists are organized by date, ship's name, port of departure, port of arrival, passenger's surname, and captain's name. You can also search the site to find the person or ship that interests you. Other pages containing links to passenger lists include:

- ✔ **Rootsweb.com Passenger Lists:** `http://userdb.rootsweb.com/ passenger`
- ✔ **Olive Tree Genealogy:** `www.olivetreegenealogy.com/ships/ index.shtml`
- ✔ **Castle Garden (the precursor to Ellis Island):** `www.castlegarden.org`

- **Famine Irish Passenger Record Data File:** `http://aad.archives.gov/aad/fielded-search.jsp?dt=180&tf=F&cat=SB302&bc=sb,sl`

- **Ship Passenger List Index for New Netherlands:** `www.rootsweb.com/~nycoloni/nnimmdex.html`

- **Boston Passenger Manifests (1848–1891):** `www.sec.state.ma.us/arc/arcsrch/PassengerManifestSearchContents.html`

- **Maine Passenger Lists:** `www.mainegenealogy.net/passenger_search.asp`

- **Partial Transcription of Inward Slave Manifests:** `www.afrigeneas.com/slavedata/manifests.html`

- **Maritime Heritage Project: San Francisco:** `www.maritimeheritage.org/log.htm`

- **Galveston Immigration Database:** `www.galvestonhistory.org/Galveston_Immigration_Database.asp`

If you know (or even suspect) that your family came through Ellis Island, one of your first stops should be the Ellis Island Foundation site. The site contains a collection of 25 million passengers, along with ship manifests and images of certain ships.

To illustrate how the Ellis Island Foundation site works, look for Harry Houdini, who passed through the port a few times. Use these steps to search for Harry Houdini and see the results:

1. **Go to the Ellis Island site at** `www.ellisisland.org/default.asp`.

   The search box is located just under the main header.

2. **Type the passenger's name in the search boxes and click Start Search.**

   You should see a results box with the name of the passenger, residence (if stated), arrival year, age, and some links to the passenger record, ship manifest, and the ship's image (if available).

   For our example, we type Harry in the Passenger's First Name field, and Houdini in the Passenger's Last Name field. When we click Start Search, we get a list of three results — entries for travel in 1911, 1914, and 1920.

3. **Click the ship manifest link for the 1920 record.**

   When you click the link to see the ship manifest, the Ellis Island site advises that you must be a registered user.

4. **If you're already a member, follow the prompts to sign in, and then go to Step 6. If you're not yet a member, click the Register Now link and go to Step 5.**

   Registration is free and takes only a few minutes.

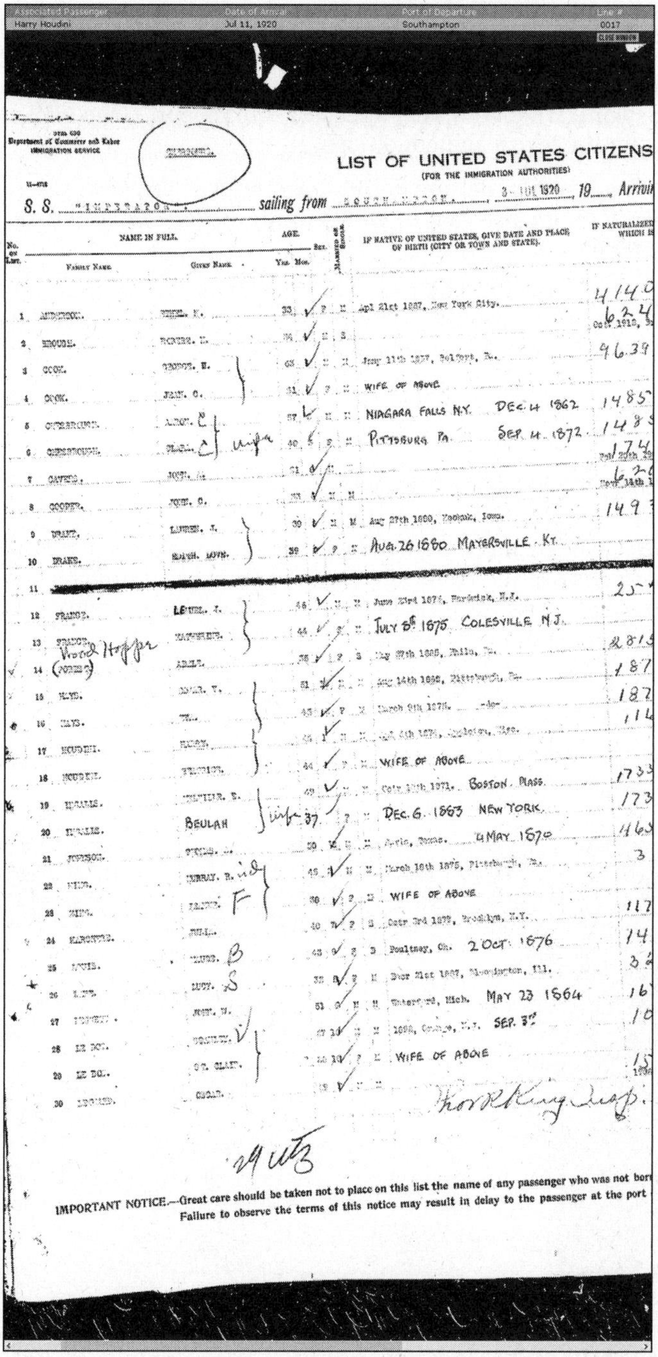

Figure 5-6:
Harry Houdini's entry in a passenger list at the Ellis Island site.

5. **Click on the Yes, I am new to this site link. Complete the online membership registration form, then Click Submit.**

   You must provide your first name, last name, e-mail address, user name, password (which has very specific requirements), and click the check box for the terms and conditions.

6. **Review the information about this manifest and click the thumbnail picture of the manifest to enlarge and explore the digitized copy of the record.**

   Figure 5-6 shows the manifest for the ship *Imperator* that sailed from Southampton on July 3, 1920 and arrived on July 11, 1920. If you scroll through the manifest online, you can see that Harry was traveling with his wife.

Naturalization records

The road to citizenship was paved with paper, which is a good thing for researchers. On the Fold3 site (www.fold3.com), you can find naturalization records housed in the National Archives online. Figure 5-7 shows a naturalization record from Fold3.

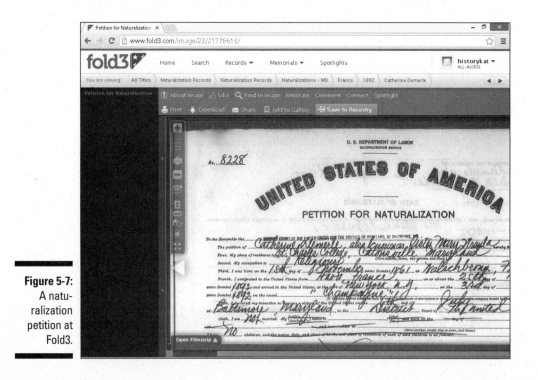

Figure 5-7: A naturalization petition at Fold3.

Fold3 has more than 7.6 million naturalization records that you can search or browse by location and last name. Some of the collections include

- ✔ Naturalization Petitions for the Southern District of California, 1887–1940

- ✔ Records of the U.S. Circuit Court for the Eastern District of Louisiana, New Orleans Division: Petitions, 1838–1861

- ✔ Petitions and Records of Naturalizations of the U.S. District and Circuit Courts of the District of Massachusetts, 1906–1929

- ✔ Naturalization Petitions of the U.S. District Court for the District of Maryland, 1906–1930

- ✔ Naturalization Petitions for the Eastern District of Pennsylvania, 1795–1930

- ✔ Naturalization Petitions of the U.S. Circuit and District Courts for the Middle District of Pennsylvania, 1906–1930

- ✔ Naturalization Petitions of the U.S. District Court, 1820–1930, and Circuit Court, 1820–1911, for the Western District of Pennsylvania

- ✔ Index to Naturalizations of World War I Soldiers, 1918

For more about Fold3 and all its records, flip back to Chapter 3.

You can also find some database indexes of naturalizations online. Here are some examples:

- ✔ **Arkansas:** Arkansas Naturalization Records Index, 1809–1906, at `www.naturalizationrecords.com/usa/ar_natrecind-a.shtml`

- ✔ **California:** Index to Naturalization Records in Sonoma County, California, 1841–1906, at `www.rootsweb.com/~cascgs/nat.htm`

- ✔ **California:** Index to Naturalization Records in Sonoma County, California, Volume II, 1906–1930, at `www.rootsweb.com/~cascgs/nat2.htm`

- ✔ **Colorado:** Colorado State Archives Naturalization Records at `www.colorado.gov/dpa/doit/archives/natural.html`

- ✔ **Delaware:** Naturalization Records Database at `http://archives.delaware.gov/collections/natrlzndb/nat-index.shtml`

- ✔ **Indiana:** Indiana Commission on Public Records Naturalization Index at `www.state.in.us/serv/icpr_naturalization`

- ✔ **Kansas:** Index of the Petitions for Naturalization at the Osage County Courthouse at `http://skyways.lib.ks.us/towns/Lyndon/genealogy/natindex1.htm`

✔ **Missouri:** Naturalization Records, 1816–1955, at `www.sos.mo.gov/ archives/naturalization`

✔ **New York:** Eastern District Court of New York Naturalization Project at `www.italiangen.org/records-search/naturalizations.php`

✔ **North Dakota:** North Dakota Naturalization Records Index at `http:// library.ndsu.edu/db/naturalization`

✔ **Ohio:** Miami County Naturalization Papers, 1860–1872, at `www. thetroyhistoricalsociety.org/m-county/natural.htm`

✔ **Pennsylvania:** Centre County Naturalization Records, 1802–1929, (includes images of the records) at `http://co.centre.pa.us/ centreco/hrip/natrecs/default.asp`

✔ **Washington:** Digital Archives at `www.digitalarchives.wa.gov/ default.aspx`

Land Ho! Researching Land Records

In the past, an individual's success was often measured by the ownership of land. The more land your ancestors possessed, the more powerful and wealthy they were. This concept encouraged people to migrate to new countries in the quest to obtain land.

In addition to giving you information about the property your ancestor owned, land records may tell you where your ancestor lived before purchasing the land, the spouse's name, and the names of children, grandchildren, parents, or siblings. To use land records effectively, however, you need to have a general idea of where your ancestors lived and possess a little background information on the history of the areas in which they lived. Land records are especially useful for tracking the migration of families in the U.S. before the 1790 census.

Most land records are maintained at the local level — in the town, county, or parish where the property was located. Getting a foundation in the history of land records before conducting a lot of research is a good idea because the practices of land transfers differed by location and time period. A good place to begin your research is at the Land Record Reference page at `www. directlinesoftware.com/landref.htm`. This page contains links to articles on patents and grants, bounty lands, the Homestead Act, property description methods, and how land transactions were conducted. For a more general treatment of land records, see "Land Records," by Sandra Hargreaves Luebking, in *The Source: A Guidebook of American Genealogy,* Third Edition, edited by Loretto Dennis Szucs and Luebking (Ancestry Publishing, Inc.).

Surveying land lovers in the U.S.

Land resources are among the most plentiful sources of information on your ancestors in the U.S. Although a census would have occurred only once every ten years on average, land transactions may have taken place multiple times during that decade, depending on how much land your ancestor possessed. These records don't always contain a great deal of demographic information, but they do place your ancestor in a time and location, and sometimes in a historical context as well. For example, you may discover that your ancestors were granted military bounty lands. This discovery may tell you where and when your ancestors acquired the land, as well as what war they fought in. You may also find out how litigious your ancestors were by the number of lawsuits they filed or had filed against them as a result of land claims.

Your ancestors may have received land in the early U.S. in several ways. Knowing more about the ways in which people acquired land historically can aid you in your research.

Your ancestor may have purchased land or received a grant of land in the public domain — often called *bounty lands* — in exchange for military service or some other service for the country. Either way, the process probably started when your ancestor petitioned (or submitted an application) for the land. Your ancestor may have also laid claim to the land, rather than petitioning for it.

If the application was approved, your ancestor was given a *warrant* — a certificate that allowed him or her to receive an amount of land. (Sometimes a warrant was called a *right*.) After your ancestor presented the warrant to a land office, an individual was appointed to make a *survey* — a detailed drawing and legal description of the boundaries — of the land. The land office then recorded your ancestor's name and information from the survey into a *tract book* (a book describing the lots within a township or other geographic area) and on a *plat map* (a map of lots within a tract).

After the land was recorded in the tract book, your ancestors may have been required to meet certain conditions, such as living on the land for a certain period of time or making payments on the land. After they met the requirements, they were eligible for a *patent* — a document that conveyed title of the land to the new owner.

If your ancestors received bounty lands in the U.S., you might be in luck. The Bureau of Land Management (BLM), General Land Office Records (www. glorecords.blm.gov) holds more than 5 million federal land title records issued between 1820 and the present, and images of survey plats and field notes from 1810.

Follow these steps to search the records on this site:

1. **Go to the Official Federal Land Records Site (www.glorecords.blm. gov).**

2. **In the green bar at the top of the page, click Search Documents.**

   This brings you to a search form that you can fill out to search all of the contents at the BLM site. Matthew's interest, for example, is in finding land that one of his ancestors, Jacob Helm, owned in Illinois.

3. **Click the Search Documents By Type tab on the top of the form.**

   The other tabs are Search Document By Location and Search Documents By Identifier.

4. **Click Patents on the left side of the form.**

   The other options are Surveys, LSR (Land Status Records), and CDI (Control Document Index).

5. **In the Locations section of the form, use the drop-down list to select a state and, if desired, a county.**

   For our example, we select Illinois for the State field, and use the default Any County in the County field.

6. **In the Names section of the form, type a last name and first name in the appropriate fields.**

   We type **Helm** in the Last Name field and **Jacob** in the First Name field. See Figure 5-8.

Figure 5-8: A search for land records for Jacob Helm in Illinois.

7. **If you have other criteria for your search that fits in the Land Description or Miscellaneous sections, you can enter it now.**

   For our example, we don't know much else than the state and name, so we don't provide any other search criteria.

8. **Click the Search Patents button at the bottom of the form.**

   The results list generates.

9. **Scroll through the results and choose one that looks promising. If you want to go directly to the image of the document, click the Image icon. But if you want additional information about the record, click the Accession link.**

   We want as much information about the record as possible, so we click the Accession link for the single result for Jacob Helm in Illinois. This opens a page with three tabs: Patent Details, Patent Image, and Related Documents.

10. **The view defaults to the Patent Details tab. Review the information provided.**

    Depending on the specific record, this detailed entry provides information such as name on the patent, the land office involved, mineral rights, military rank, document numbers, survey data, and a land description.

11. **Click the Patent Image tab to view a digitized copy of the patent.**

    You can view the document as a PDF within the frame. We can then save the copy of the document on your computer. Figure 5-9 shows the patent for Jacob Helm.

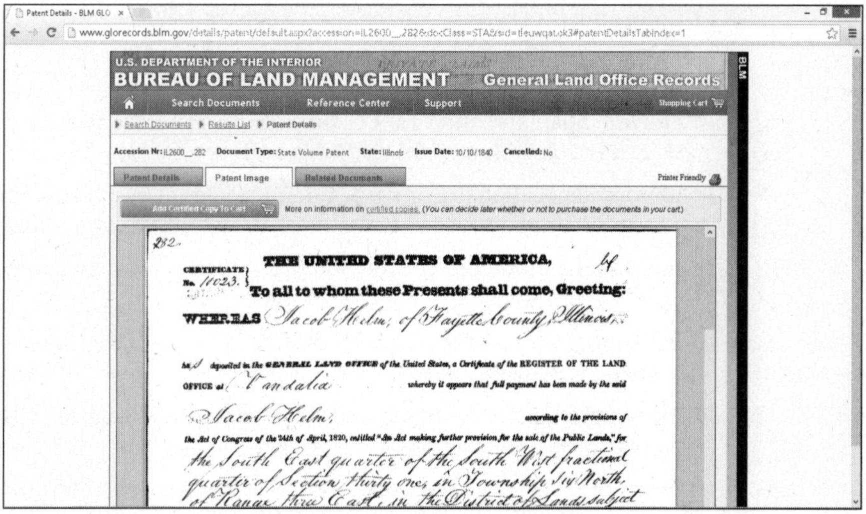

Figure 5-9:
The land patent for Jacob Helm at the General Land Office site.

12. **If you're interested in learning about your ancestor's neighbors, click the Related Documents tab.**

    A list of other documents with the same land description — township, range, and section — generates. You can use this list to see who your ancestor's neighbors were and learn more about them.

For secondary land transactions (those made after the original grant of land), you probably need to contact the recorder of deeds for the county in which the land was held. Several online sites contain indexes to land transactions in the U.S. Some of these are free, and other broader collections require a subscription. The easiest way to find these sites is to consult a comprehensive genealogical index site and look under the appropriate geographical area. In a land index, you're likely to encounter the name of the purchaser or warrantee, the name of the buyer (if applicable), the location of the land, the number of acres, and the date of the land transfer. In some cases, you may see the residence of the person who acquired the land.

Here are some websites with information on land records:

- **Legal Land Descriptions in the USA:** `http://illinois.outfitters.com/genealogy/land/`
- **Alabama:** Land Records at `www.sos.state.al.us/govtrecords/land.aspx`
- **Arkansas:** Land Records at `http://searches.rootsweb.com/cgi-bin/arkland/arkland.pl`
- **California:** Early Sonoma County, California, Land Grants, 1846–1850, at `www.rootsweb.com/~cascgs/intro.htm`
- **Colorado:** Kit Carson County Land Registration Receipts 1913–1919 at `www.colorado.gov/dpa/doit/archives/land/kit_carson_land_index.html`
- **Florida:** Spanish Land Grant Claims at `www.floridamemory.com/Collections/SpanishLandGrants`
- **Illinois:** Illinois Public Domain Land Tract Sales at `www.cyberdriveillinois.com/departments/archives/databases/data_lan.html`
- **Indiana:** Land Records at the State Archives at `www.in.gov/icpr/2585.htm`
- **Louisiana:** Office of State Lands at `www.doa.la.gov/SLO/DocumentAccess.htm%20`
- **Maryland:** Land Records in Maryland at `http://guide.mdsa.net/viewer.cfm?page=mdlandrecords`
- **New York:** Ulster County Deed Books 1, 2 & 3 Index at `http://archives.co.ulster.ny.us/deedsearchscreen.htm`

- ✔ **North Carolina:** Alamance County Land Grant Recipients at `www.rootsweb.com/~ncacgs/ala_nc_land_grants.html`

- ✔ **Ohio:** Introduction to Ohio Land History at `www.directlinesoftware.com/ohio.htm`

- ✔ **Oregon:** Oregon State Archives Land Records at `http://arcweb.sos.state.or.us/land.html`

- ✔ **Texas:** Texas General Land Office Archives at `www.glo.texas.gov/`

- ✔ **Wisconsin:** Wisconsin Public Land Survey Records: Original Field Notes and Plat Maps at `http://digicoll.library.wisc.edu/SurveyNotes`

In addition to the methods we mention in this section, you may want to check out geography-related resources, such as The USGenWeb Project (`www.usgenweb.org`) or the WorldGenWeb Project (`www.worldgenweb.org`). These sites organize their resources by location (country, state, county, or all three, depending on which you use). Of course, if your attempts to find land records and information through comprehensive sites and geography-related sites don't prove as fruitful as you'd like, you can always turn to a search engine such as Yahoo! (`search.yahoo.com`) or Google (`www.google.com`).

Using HistoryGeo.com to map your ancestor's land

HistoryGeo.com is an interesting subscription site that enables you to see public land-related information on a map with functionality to show you how the land changed over time. Until recently, the site contained only land information from two publications — Arphax Publishing's *Family Maps* and *Texas Land Survey Maps* — including 2.4 million people seen through thousands of maps. But in August 2013, HistoryGeo.com released the First Landowners Project.

The First Landowners Project allows users to see more than 7 million landowners' names and information on one master map. Initially, this new and improved HistoryGeo.com site contains data for 17 states. Over the next few months, HistoryGeo.com plans to release data for all 23 western states, so this number will grow substantially.

The First Landowners Project is available only to subscribers, but the legacy functionality of the HistoryGeo.com site is available through a free demonstration account.

Before we can take a look at HistoryGeo.com, you need to register for a free demonstration account. (Of course, if you already have a subscription to HistoryGeo.com, you can skip this registration process.) Follow these steps to register for a demo account:

1. **Go to HistoryGeo.com (`www.historygeo.com`).**

2. **Click the Register Your Demo Account link at the top of the page.**

3. **Complete the online form, providing your e-mail address; your password (which you confirm by typing a second time); first, middle, and last names; name of your hometown and state; and your gender.**

4. **Click the Terms of Use link to review the terms for using the site. After reading it, select the check box indicating you agree to the terms.**

5. **Click Submit.**

The free account allows you to view HistoryGeo.com videos in the training library and access how-to articles.

Exploring HistoryGeo.com through the legacy viewer

The free demonstration account allows you to use the original map viewer available at HistoryGeo.com. To get started from the welcome page, follow these steps:

1. **Click the Original HistoryGeo Viewer (Legacy) link.**

2. **If you get a pop-up message indicating that some functionality has been disabled as a result of HistoryGeo's move to the new version of the site, click OK.**

   The original viewer launches, showing a map of the U.S., as shown in Figure 5-10. You can navigate the map using the up, down, left, and right arrows on the right of the map, and you can zoom in or out using buttons just below the arrows.

3. **Click the Map Chooser button at the top of the screen.**

   A list of the maps, which are available for use, pops up; see Figure 5-11.

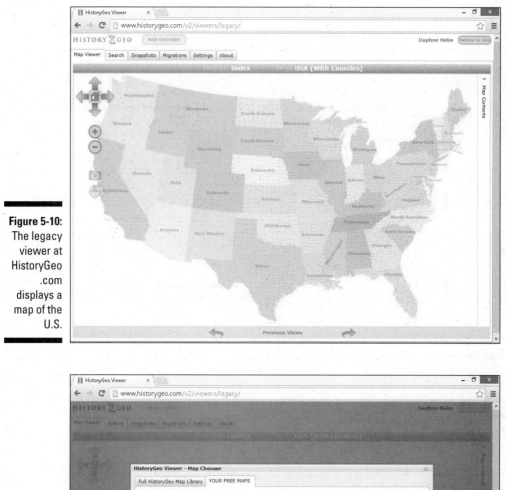

Figure 5-10:
The legacy
viewer at
HistoryGeo
.com
displays a
map of the
U.S.

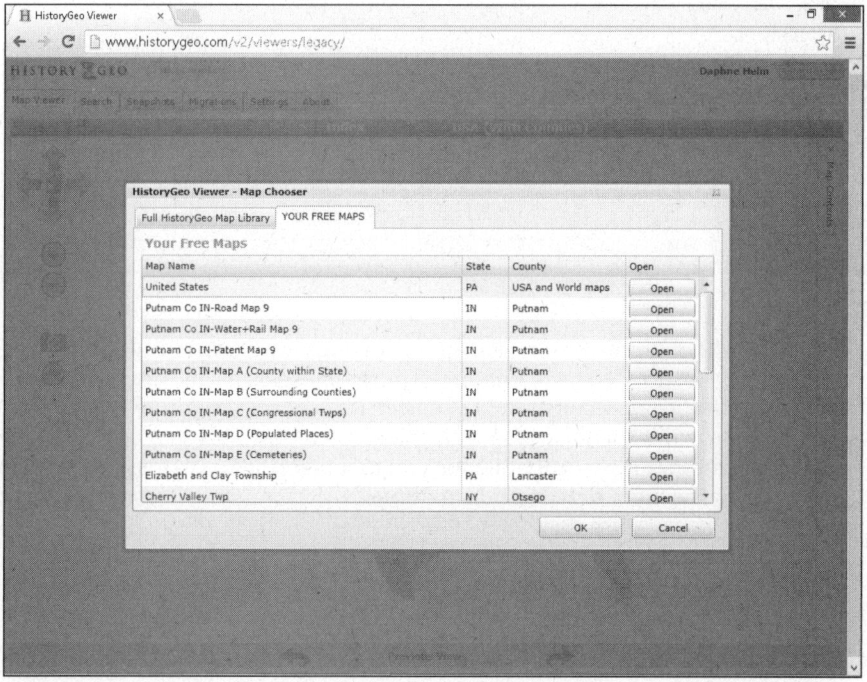

Figure 5-11:
A list of
maps
available for
viewing with
a free demo
account at
HistoryGeo
.com.

4. **Highlight a map in the list, and then click Open.**

For our example, we select Cooke Co TX-Map E (Cemeteries). This brings up a cemetery map for this county, which you can see in Figure 5-12.

A message pops up informing us that this is a survey map, and a link in the message navigates to a website with more information about the Texas Land Survey Maps. We click the close (X) button on the pop-up message.

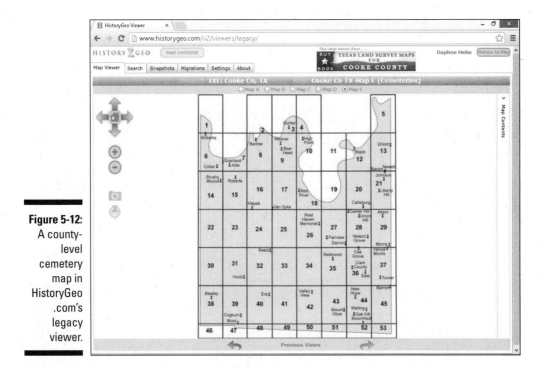

Figure 5-12: A county-level cemetery map in HistoryGeo.com's legacy viewer.

Although the free registration won't allow you to see all of the maps in the collection, you can conduct a surname search (on the Search tab) to see how many results you'll generate for a surname you're researching. The list provides the locations with the map names. This may give you an indication whether it's worthwhile for you to subscribe to HistoryGeo.com to get access to the more detailed information.

Expanding options with the First Landowners Project

The new version of the HistoryGeo.com viewer — known as the First
Landowners Project — is available only to subscribers. The functionality is
quite handy though, so we think it warrants a closer look.

The First Landowners Project enables you to search by surname the original
owners of public lands in the U.S. You can also restrict the search by state
and county, if desired. In examining this site, we search for Matthew's ancestor, Jacob Helm, in Illinois. The results contain numerous Helms, but we
know Jacob lived in Fayette County, so we home in on him and his brother
rather quickly; see Figure 5-13. Then, by clicking the green person icon, we
see details about the land parcel and even connect to an image of the original
Bureau of Land Management document.

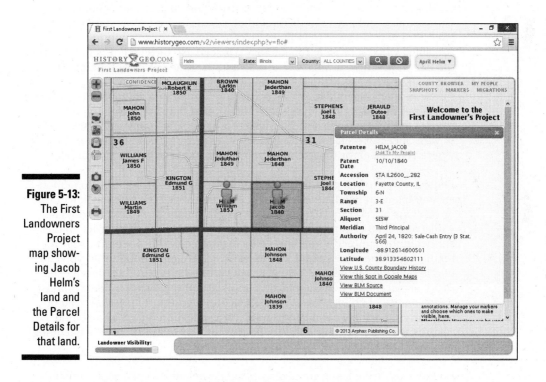

Figure 5-13:
The First
Landowners
Project
map show-
ing Jacob
Helm's
land and
the Parcel
Details for
that land.

In addition to being able to see information about the piece of land, you can
add markers on the map to indicate events in your ancestors' lives, save
people to your list of favorites, and plot migration patterns for multiple
ancestors or families at a time.

Marching to a Different Drummer: Searching for Military Records

Although your ancestors may not have marched to a different drummer, at least one of them probably kept pace with a military beat at some point. Military records contain a variety of information. The major types of records that you're likely to find are service, pension, and bounty land records. Draft or conscription records may also surface in your exploration.

Service records chronicle the military career of an individual. They often contain details about where your ancestors lived, when they enlisted or were *drafted* (or *conscripted,* enrolled for compulsory service), their ages, their discharge dates, and in some instances, their birthplaces and occupations. You may also find pay records (including muster records that state when your ancestors had to report to military units) and notes on any injuries that they sustained while serving in the military. You can use these records to determine the unit in which your ancestor served and the time periods of their service.

This information can lead you to pension records that can contain significant genealogical information because of the level of detail required to prove service to receive a pension. Service records can give you an appreciation of your ancestor's place within history — especially the dates and places where your ancestor fought or served as a member of the armed forces.

Pensions were often granted to veterans who were disabled or who demonstrated financial need after service in a particular war or campaign; widows or orphans of veterans also may have received benefits. These records are valuable because, to receive pensions, your ancestors had to prove that they served in the military. Proof entailed a discharge certificate or the sworn testimony of the veteran and witnesses. Pieces of information that you can find in pension records include your ancestor's rank, period of service, unit, residence at the time of the pension application, age, marriage date, spouse's name, names of children, and the nature of the veteran's financial need or disability. If a widow submitted a pension application, you may also find records verifying her marriage to the veteran and death records (depending on when the veteran ancestor died).

Bounty lands were lands granted by the government in exchange for military service that occurred between 1775 and 1855. Wars covered during this period include the American Revolution, War of 1812, Old Indian Wars, and the Mexican Wars. To receive bounty lands, soldiers were required to file an application. These applications often contain information useful to genealogical researchers.

If you're new to researching U.S. military records, take a look at the Research in Military Records page at the National Archives site (`www.archives.gov/research/military/index.html`). It contains information on the types of military records held by the archives, how you can use them in your research, and information on records for specific wars. Also, for the historical context of the time period that your ancestor served, see the U.S. Army Center of Military History Research Material page at `www.history.army.mil/html/bookshelves/resmat/index.html`. This site contains links to chapters from *American Military History,* which covers military actions from the Colonial period through the war on terrorism.

The largest collections for military records are currently housed in subscription sites. Here we give you a quick rundown on what several subscription sites have within their collections.

Fold3 (`www.fold3.com`) partnered with the National Archives to place digitized images of microfilm (held by the archives) online. As a result, most of the military records on Fold3 are federal. Here are some examples of available record sets:

- Navy Casualty Reports, 1776–1941
- Service Records of Volunteers, 1784–1811
- Revolutionary War Service and Imprisonment Cards
- War of 1812 Pension Files
- War of 1812 Society Applications
- Letters Received by the Adjutant General, 1822–1860
- Mexican War Service Records
- Civil War and Later Veterans Pension Index
- Confederate Amnesty Papers
- Spanish-American War Service Record Index
- Confidential Correspondence of the Navy, 1919–1927
- Foreign Burial of American War Dead
- Naturalization Index — WWI Soldiers
- Military Intelligence Division — Negro Subversion
- Missing Air Crew Reports, WWII
- WWII War Diaries
- Korean War Casualties

- Navy Cruise Books, 1918–2009
- Vietnam Service Awards

Ancestry.com (www.ancestry.com) has more than 1,100 collections of military records. Its collections include records for servicemen from the U.S. and several other countries. These military collections include

- World War I Draft Registration Cards, 1917–1918
- Sons of the American Revolution Membership Applications, 1889–1970
- U.S. Revolutionary War Miscellaneous Records (Manuscript File), 1775–1790s
- U.S. Civil War Soldiers, 1861–1865
- Confederate Service Records, 1861–1865
- Civil War Prisoner of War Records, 1861–1865
- U.S. Colored Troops Military Service Records, 1861–1865
- U.S. Marine Corps Muster Rolls, 1798–1958
- World War I Draft Registration Cards, 1917–1918
- U.S. World War II Army Enlistment Records, 1938–1946
- British Army WWI Service Records, 1914–1920
- British Army WWI Medal Rolls Index Cards, 1914–1920
- British Army WWI Pension Records, 1914–1920
- Germany & Austria Directories of Military and Marine Officers, 1500–1939
- Canada War Graves Registers (Circumstances of Casualty), 1914–1948
- Canada Loyalist Claims, 1776–1835
- New Zealand Army WWII Nominal Rolls, 1939–1948

At WorldVitalRecords.com (http://worldvitalrecords.com), you can find some different military collections, including:

- List of Officials, Civil, Military, and Ecclesiastical of Connecticut Colony, 1636–1677
- Spanish American War Volunteers — Colorado
- Korean War Casualties
- Army Casualties 1956–2003
- Muster Rolls of the Soldiers of the War of 1812: Detached from the Militia of North Carolina in 1812 and 1814

And, if the big military collections don't quite meet your needs, here is a sampling of the different records that are available on free sites:

- **Muster Rolls and Other Records of Service of Maryland Troops in the American Revolution:** www.msa.md.gov/megafile/msa/speccol/ sc2900/sc2908/000001/000018/html/index.html

- **Ohio Historical Society War of 1812 Roster of Ohio Soldiers:** www.ohiohistory.org/resource/database/rosters.html

- **Illinois Black Hawk War Veterans Database:** www.cyberdrive illinois.com/departments/archives/databases/blkhawk.html

- **South Carolina Records of Confederate Veterans 1909–1973:** www.archivesindex.sc.gov

- **Colorado Volunteers in the Spanish American War (1898):** www.colorado.gov/dpa/doit/archives/military/span_am_war

- **National World War II Memorial Registry:** www.wwiimemorial.com/ default.asp?page=registry.asp&subpage=intro

Another set of valuable resources for researching an ancestor that participated in a war is information provided by a lineage society. Some examples include:

- **Daughters of the American Revolution** (www.dar.org)

- **Sons of the American Revolution** (www.sar.org)

- **Society of the Cincinnati** (www.societyofthecincinnati.org)

- **United Empire Loyalists' Association of Canada** (www.uelac.org)

- **National Society United States Daughters of 1812** (www.usdaughters1812.org)

- **Daughters of Union Veterans of the Civil War** (www.duvcw.org)

- **Sons of Confederate Veterans** (www.scv.org)

One interesting collection of military records at a free site is the Civil War Soldiers and Sailors System (CWSS). The CWSS site (www.itd.nps.gov/cwss) is a joint project of the National Park Service, the Genealogical Society of Utah, and the Federation of Genealogical Societies. The site contains an index of more than 6.3 million soldier records of both Union and Confederate soldiers. Also available at the site are regimental histories and descriptions of 384 battles.

Follow these steps to search the records on this site:

1. **Point your browser to the Civil War Soldier and Sailors System (`www.nps.gov/civilwar/soldiers-and-sailors-database.htm`).**

   On the left side of the screen are links to information on the site, including links to Soldiers, Sailors, Regiments, Cemeteries, Battles, Prisoners, Medals of Honor, and Monuments.

2. **Click the appropriate link for the person you're looking for.**

   We're looking for a soldier who served, so we click the Soldier link.

3. **Type the name of the soldier or sailor in the appropriate field and click Show Results.**

   If you know additional details, you can select the side on which your ancestor fought, the state they were from, and rank. We typed **Helm** in the Last Name field, **Uriah** in the First Name field, selected the **Union** radio button, and **Illinois** in the By State field. One search result appeared with that information.

4. **Review your results and click the name of the soldier or sailor to see the Detailed Soldier Record.**

   The soldier details show that Uriah served in Company G, 7th Illinois Cavalry; see Figure 5-14. He entered and left the service as a private. His information is located on National Archives series M539 microfilm, roll 39.

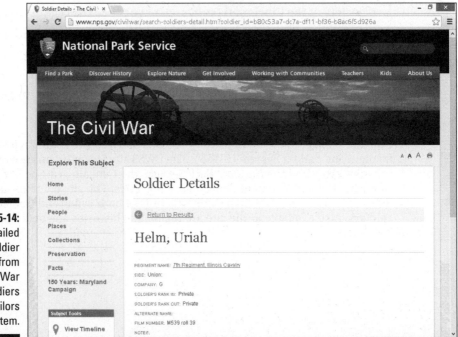

Figure 5-14: Detailed soldier record from the Civil War Soldiers and Sailors System.

Taxation with Notation

Some of the oldest records available for research are tax records — including property and inheritance records. Although some local governments have placed tax records online, these records are usually very recent documents rather than historical tax records. Most early tax records you encounter were likely collected locally (that is, at the county level). However, many local tax records have since been turned over to state or county archives — some of which now make tax records available on microfilm, as do Family History Centers. (If you have a Family History Center in your area, you may be able to save yourself a trip, call, or letter to the state archives — check with the Family History Center to see whether it keeps copies of tax records for the area in which you're interested.) And a few maintainers of tax records — including archives and Family History Centers — are starting to make information about their holdings available online. Generally, either indexes or transcriptions of these microfilm records are what you find online.

Additionally, both Ancestry.com and FamilySearch have some tax records available through their sites. We explore how to use both of these sites in Chapter 3.

Here are just a few examples of the types of resources that you can find pertaining to tax records:

- ✔ **Tax List:** 1790 and 1800 County Tax Lists of Virginia at `www.binnsgenealogy.com/VirginiaTaxListCensuses`

- ✔ **Tax List:** Territory of Colorado Tax Assessment Lists, 1862–1866, at `http://digital.denverlibrary.org/cdm/ref/collection/p16079coll15/id/1976`

- ✔ **Land and Poll Tax:** Benton County, Tennessee 1836 Land and Poll Tax List at `www.tngenweb.org/benton/databas2.htm`

If you're locating records in the U.S., try USGenWeb for the state or county. Here's what to do:

1. **Go to the USGenWeb site (`www.usgenweb.org`).**

2. **Click a state in the left column.**

   We click the Pennsylvania link because we're looking for tax records in Lancaster County.

   As a shortcut, you can always get to any USGenWeb state page by substituting the two-letter state code for the 'us' in `www.usgenweb.org`. For example, for Pennsylvania, you could type **`www.pagenweb.org`**.

3. **From the USGenWeb state page (for the state that you choose), find a link to the county in which you're interested.**

   On the Pennsylvania Counties page, we click the Lancaster link to get to the Lancaster County GenWeb site.

4. **Scroll through the main page for the state you've selected and click any tax-related links that look promising.**

   We click the link for Proprietary and State Tax Lists of the County of Lancaster for the Years 1771, 1772, 1773, 1779, and 1782; edited by William Henry Egle, M.D. (1898) under the Documents section.

The state and county websites in the USGenWeb Project vary immensely. Some have more information available than the Pennsylvania and Lancaster County pages, while others have less. The amount of information that's available at a particular USGenWeb site affects the number of links you have to click through to find what you're looking for. Don't be afraid to take a little time to explore and become familiar with the sites for the states and counties in which your ancestors lived.

One other strategy for finding tax assessment information is to search local newspapers for the time period in which your ancestor lived. A tax list was published on a yearly basis in some localities. To find out more about searching newspapers online, see Chapter 7.

Trial and Error at the Courthouse

Do you have an ancestor who was on the wrong side of the law? If so, you may find some colorful information at the courthouse in the civil and criminal court records. Even if you don't have an ancestor with a law-breaking past, you can find valuable genealogical records at your local courthouse, given that even upstanding citizens may have civil records on file or may have been called as witnesses. Typical records you can find there include land deeds, birth and death certificates, divorce decrees, wills and probate records, tax records, and some military records (provided the ancestors who were veterans deposited their records locally).

Court cases and trials aren't just a phenomenon of today's world. Your ancestor may have participated in the judicial system as a plaintiff, defendant, or witness. Some court records can provide a glimpse into the character of your ancestors — whether they were frequently on trial for misbehavior or called as character witnesses. You can also find a lot of information on your ancestors if they were involved in land disputes — a common problem in some areas where land transferred hands often. Again, your ancestor may not have been directly involved in a dispute but may have been called as a witness. Another type of court record that may involve your ancestor is a probate case. Often, members of families contested wills or were called upon as executors or witnesses, and the resulting file of testimonies and rulings can be found in a probate record. Court records may also reflect appointments of ancestors to positions of public trust such as sheriff, inspector of tobacco, and justice of the peace.

Finding court records online can be tricky. They can be found using a subscription database service or a general search engine, such as Bing (www. bing.com). Note, however, that good data can also be tucked away inside free databases that are not indexed by search engines. In this case, you will have to search on a general term such as *Berks County wills* or *Berks County court records*. Here is an example:

1. **Go to the Bing search engine site (www.bing.com).**

    The search box is near the top of the page.

2. **Type your search terms in the search box and click the Search icon (magnifying glass) or press Enter.**

    The results page is displayed. We type *Berks County wills* and received 249,000 results. Please note that this number changes often as new sites are added to the database. If the number of results you get is too large to reasonably sort through, you can narrow your search with additional terms, such as specific years or town names.

3. **Click a link that looks relevant to your search.**

    We select the link to the Berks County Register of Wills at www. co.berks.pa.us/rwills/site/default.asp. This site contains a database where you can search more than 1 million records covering a variety of areas, including birth, death, marriage, and estate.

Here are some sites to give you an idea of court records that you can find online:

- ✔ **Missouri's Judicial Records:** www.sos.mo.gov/archives/mojudicial/

- ✔ **Atlantic County Library System's Historic Resources – Wills, Orphans Court, Guardianship and Letters of Administration:** www.atlantic library.org/historical_resources

- ✔ **Earl K. Long Library, The University of New Orleans Historical Archives of the Supreme Court of Louisiana:** http://libweb.uno. edu/jspui/handle/123456789/1

- ✔ **The Proceedings of the Old Bailey: London's Central Criminal Court, 1674 to 1913:** www.oldbaileyonline.org

Chapter 6

Searching for that Elusive Ancestor

As a genealogist, you may experience sleepless nights trying to figure out all the important things in life — the maiden name of your great-great-grandmother, whether great-grandpa was really the scoundrel that other relatives say he was, and just how you're related to Daniel Boone. (Well, isn't everyone?) Okay, so you may not have sleepless nights, but you undoubtedly spend a significant amount of time thinking about and trying to find resources that can give you answers to these crucial questions.

In the past, finding information on individual ancestors online was compared with finding a needle in a haystack. You browsed through long lists of links in hopes of finding a site that contained a nugget of information to aid your search. But looking for your ancestors online has become easier than ever. Instead of merely browsing links, you can use search engines and online databases to pinpoint information on your ancestors.

This chapter covers the basics of searching for an ancestor by name, presents some good surname resource sites, and shows you how to combine several Internet resources to successfully find information on your family.

Letting Your Computer Do the Walking: Using Search Engines

Finding information on an ancestor on the web can be a challenge. In the past, it was sometimes difficult to find any kind of information about a given individual because online collections were just beginning to grow and become accessible. Now, with the myriad resources available, the challenge is sorting through all the nonrelevant information to find data that can help progress your research. One of the key online resources that you can use to help locate and filter some of the online data is a search engine.

Search engines are programs that examine huge indexes of information generated by web robots, or simply bots. *Bots* are programs that travel throughout the Internet and collect information on the sites and resources that they find. You can access the information contained in search engines through an interface, usually through a form on a web page.

The real strength of search engines is that they allow you to search the full text of web pages instead of just the title or a brief abstract of the site. This is particularly valuable in a family history because a researcher may be looking for someone who is one of thousands who descended from a particular individual — for whom the web page may be named. For example, many genealogy websites are named for the progenitor of the family. In Matthew's case, the progenitor for his branch of the Helm family was Georg Helm. A web page might be named something like The Georg and Dorothea Helm Family. If Matthew is looking for one of Georg's great-great-great grandsons, Uriah Helm, he might not know to look under the Georg Helm website to find him. Some genealogy programs create websites with thousands of pages of information, but only one of which might pertain to Uriah. If a search engine bot happens to index all the pages of the site, Uriah's name becomes visible through the search results.

Although search engines offer a lot of coverage of the web, to find what you're looking for is sometimes more of an art than a science. In the following pages, we look at search strategies as well as the different kinds of search engines that are available to aid your search.

Diving into general Internet search engines

General search engines (such as Google or Bing) send out bots to catalog the Internet as a whole, regardless of the subject(s) of the site's content. Therefore, on any given search, you're likely to receive a lot of hits, perhaps only a few of which hold any genealogical value — that is, unless you refine your search terms to give you a better chance at receiving relevant results.

You can conduct several types of searches with most search engines. Looking at the Help link for any search engine to see the most effective way to search is always a good idea. Also, search engines often have two search interfaces — a simple search and an advanced search. With the *simple search,* you normally just type your query and click the Submit button. With an *advanced search,* you can use a variety of options to refine your search. These options can be in the form of check boxes, or they can be the manner that you format the search terms. The best way to become familiar with using a search engine is to experiment and see what kinds of results you get.

To demonstrate various strategies for using a search engine, we run through some searches using Google for Matthew's ancestor Georg. Before we begin the search, it's a good idea to have some useful facts at hand to help define our search terms. From previous research, Matthew knows that Georg's name is spelled *Georg* on his gravestone — but *George* in land records. He also knows that Georg was born in 1723 and died in 1769 and that he owned land in Winchester, Frederick County, Virginia. He was married to a woman named Dorothea.

Not all search terms are equal

When first using a search engine, a number of people simply type the name of an ancestor, expecting the search engine to take care of the rest. Although search engines do have some default ways of searching, these ways aren't always the best for genealogical searches. The following table lists the number of results that we received with different search criteria.

Search Criteria	*Number of Results*
Georg Helm	2,660,000
George Helm	20,200,000
Georg OR George Helm	22,700,000

The first search, using *Georg Helm,* produces millions of results because it looks for any content containing the words *Georg* and *Helm.* The results include not only pages that contain the name Helm but also pages containing the common word *helm.* Some search engines also expand the search to include variations on the spelling of the word. (This practice is common in search engines and is referred to as *stemming.*) The search for *George Helm* yields more results because the addition of the letter *e* in George forms a more popular first name. The third search demonstrates the capability of Google to search for multiple conditions within a single set of search terms. Placing the OR modifier in the search terms allows both Georg and George to be searched and ranked into one set of results. Searching with these dual terms generates a list that includes all the results from the first *(Georg Helm)* and second *(George Helm)* searches.

Although each of these searches produces millions of results, only a tiny fraction has anything to do with the Georg Helm that we're looking for. So, we need to refine our search method to get a better selection of more appropriate results.

Searching with phrases

Using quotation marks in Google searches helps you specify the exact form of the word to search. Placing *"Georg Helm"* in quotation marks means that you want Google to search words that exactly match *Georg Helm*. Using parentheses indicates the search engine should look for multiple words in conjunction with other words, allowing you to search more efficiently. For example, putting parentheses around both first names with the conjunction OR tells the search engine to look for either of those first names when they appear with that last name.

Even with these modifiers on the first names, you can see that the results for "Georg" Helm and "George" Helm in the following table still number in the tens of thousands because the search engine is looking for any content that contains both the words *Georg* and *Helm or George and Helm*.

Search Criteria	Number of Results
(Georg OR George) Helm	22,700,000
"(Georg OR George) Helm"	45,500

Performing targeted searches

The search strategies we mention earlier in this chapter are fine for getting a general idea of what's available for a particular name or for searching for a unique name, but they're not necessarily the most efficient for finding information on a specific person. The best strategies involve using specific search terms that include geographic information or other family members associated with the individual.

Using the same example from earlier — searching for information about Georg Helm — we can find more targeted information on Georg Helm by including geographical terms in the search. The following search term yields 516 results:

"(Georg OR George) Helm" (Winchester OR "Frederick County") + Virginia

The search term requires that the online content contain the following:

✔ The words *Georg Helm* or *George Helm*

✔ The word(s) *Winchester* or *Frederick County*

✔ The word *Virginia*

Of these results, less than a quarter of the results have anything to do with the Georg Helm who is the ancestor of Matthew.

Because other George Helms are associated with Frederick County, Virginia, we can further clarify the search terms to include Georg's wife's name — Dorothea. The following search term generates 261 results:

> "(Georg OR George) Helm" (Winchester OR "Frederick County") + Virginia Dorothea

You can also use targeted searches to meet specific research goals. For example, if Matthew is looking for the will of Georg Helm, he could use the following search terms:

> "(Georg OR George) Helm" (Winchester OR "Frederick County") + Virginia Dorothea + will

The eighth search result is the transcription of Georg's will on the USGenWeb Archives site.

A few other Google hints

To get the most relevant content to meet your research goals, you have a few other ways to control the results presented by Google. The first is to exclude certain results by using the – (minus) sign. In the case of Matthew's search for George Helm, several of the results that he received in his previous searches dealt with another George Helm who was born in Frederick County, Virginia, and who is unrelated to Matthew's Georg. This second George was married to Sarah Jackman and later moved to Cumberland County, Kentucky. To avoid seeing results for the second George, we can modify our search terms to the following:

> "(Georg OR George) Helm" (Winchester OR "Frederick County") + Virginia –Jackman –"Cumberland County"

Sometimes searching on a phrase can be too exact. If the person you're researching is listed with a middle name, you might not find the content with a phrase search. One way around this is to use the * wildcard term. A search term such as *Georg * Helm* would pick up content containing the name Georg Smith Helm, as well as content containing Georg and Dorothea Helm.

You can also use number ranges within your search terms to push more relevant search results to the top of your results list. When searching within Google, you can specify number ranges by placing two periods between the range of numbers. So, if you want to search on a range of numbers from 1723 to 1769, place two periods between 1723 and 1769. For example, you could use the following search terms:

> "(Georg OR George) Helm" 1723..1769

This term searches for content with Georg Helm or George Helm with a number between 1723 and 1769. In our example, this search would yield pages related to Georg Helm who died in 1769, as well as his son who was born in 1751.

Google offers a few other useful features for limiting results. If you're searching for a relatively common name, you can try to focus your search on the page titles of content to keep from being overwhelmed by millions of results. To do this, use `intitle` or `allintitle` in your search terms. (Yes, you are seeing those correctly — do not put spaces in the phrases `intitle` [for in title] or `allintitle` [for all in title] when using them in the search term. Google knows how to interpret them without the spaces.) For example, the search term *intitle:Georg Helm Dorothea* looks for sites that have Georg, Helm, or Dorothea in the page title. However, the search includes even the sites that don't have all the search terms in the title (although it scores sites that contain all three words higher than those that don't). To do that, use the `allintitle` function — *allintitle:Georg Helm Dorothea.*

Similarly, you can use the `intext` function to limit the results to search terms that appear in the text of the page. By using the search term *intext: Georg Helm Dorothea* (or if you want all search terms to appear — *allintext: Georg Helm Dorothea*), you can search for sites with those specific words in the text of the web page. If you remember that you found a link on a page that is important to your research but can't remember where you found the link, you can use the `inanchor` function. A search such as *inanchor: Georg Helm* looks for Georg Helm in links within a page. The search modifier `allinanchor` looks for all the search terms within the link. And finally, if you want to look for search terms within a Uniform Resource Locator, use the `inurl` and `allinurl` search modifiers (such as *inurl: Georg Helm*).

Using the advanced search form

Perhaps you don't want to use the search syntax for the search engine. Fortunately for you, most search engines offer an advanced search form, which makes your search easier. Try the following steps to use the Google advanced search:

1. **Point your web browser to `www.google.com/advanced_search`.**

   The Advanced Search page opens with several fields that you can use to limit the search results.

2. **Type your ancestor's name (or other search term) in one of the fields in the Find pages with section.**

   You can put your search terms in one of the following fields. We've given you some hints as to when you might use each field:

   - *All These Words:* When the words can appear in any order or context

   - *This Exact Wording or Phrase:* When you're typing a name or location that needs to match the exact order

   - *Any of These Words:* When you want Google to look for any site that might have one of many words (such as location names within a state or county)

3. **Enter unwanted search terms into the field marked None of These Words.**

   You might want to enter terms in this field when you want to differentiate your ancestor from someone else with the same name.

4. **Add information into other fields to limit your results in the Narrow Your Results By section.**

   On the first search, you might not want to limit your results, but the fields are there in case you do.

5. **Click the Advanced Search button.**

   A Google results page appears.

Looking at general Internet metasearch engines

Wouldn't it be nice if you never had to visit multiple sites to search the Internet? This burning question led directly to the creation of *metasearch engines,* which use a single interface (or form) to execute searches using multiple search engines. They then return the results of all the individual search engines to a single page that you can use to view the results. The number of results from metasearch engines can be overwhelming, so it's important to have a good search term and to know something substantial about the person you're researching. That way, you can quickly determine whether a result is relevant to your search. You also need to have patience because you may have to trudge through several sets of results before you find something useful. One metasearch engine to experiment with is Dogpile (`www.dogpile.com`). Dogpile uses results from the Google, Yahoo!, and Yandex search engines.

1. **Open your web browser and go to `www.dogpile.com`.**

   The Dogpile home page contains a search form. Just below the search form is a link to the advanced search.

2. **Click the Advanced Search link.**

   The default search form turns gray, and a new set of search fields are presented.

3. **Type your search terms in the appropriate fields and click the Go Fetch button.**

   Dogpile formats your search terms and executes the search, as shown in Figure 6-1.

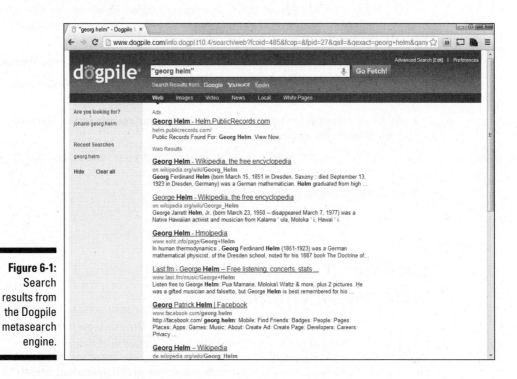

Figure 6-1:
Search results from the Dogpile metasearch engine.

Other metasearch engines include the following:

- **Ixquick:** http://ixquick.com
- **Mamma:** www.mamma.com
- **MetaCrawler:** www.metacrawler.com
- **Search.com:** www.search.com

Flying with Genealogy Vertical Search Engines

If you have used a general Internet search engine, you know that you can receive a lot of extraneous results that are unrelated to genealogy or local history. Even searching for Georg Helm produces hundreds of links about the mathematical theories of the German mathematician, Georg Helm. Although those theories might be interesting, we have only so much time to dedicate to research, and we want to use that time wisely.

One way to maximize your research time is to use a vertical genealogy search engine. A *vertical search engine* is a site that indexes content about a specific topic rather than attempting to index the entire web. So, in theory, the results from a genealogy vertical search engine should contain things that pertain to genealogy and local history. The challenge for the owners of vertical search engines is to ensure that the content that is indexed by the bot is consistent with the topic. That means that the maintainers of the search engine must screen the sites that are included in the index, either through the technology or by indexing only particular sites. Two vertical search engines to look at for genealogy and local history are Mocavo (`www.mocavo.com`) and the Genealogy Toolbox (`www.genealogytoolbox.com`). (In the spirit of full disclosure, we maintain the Genealogy Toolbox search engine.)

Mocavo

Mocavo launched in 2010 as a free vertical search engine. Over time, it has increased its services to include subscription databases and alert features. To use the free search engine, follow these steps:

1. **Point your web browser to `www.mocavo.com`.**

   The Mocavo home page appears with a box to complete if you wish to create a free account.

2. **Click the Search link at the top of the page.**

   The search box appears.

3. **Type the ancestor's first and last names in the appropriate text boxes.**

   If you want to fine-tune the results, try placing a location where your ancestor lived in the Keywords text box.

4. **Click the Search button.**

   You may have to click the *X* on an advertisement for the Mocavo subscription services before you can see the results. The results page should appear. (See Figure 6-2.)

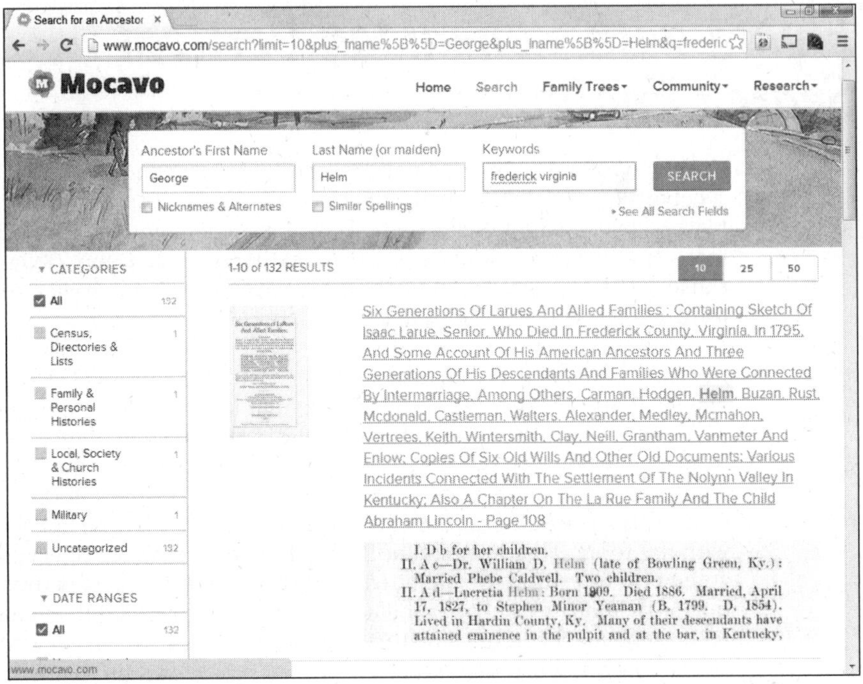

Figure 6-2:
Mocavo
search
results.

The Mocavo results are a mixture of results from its subscription content and content on the web at large. So, some links lead to a subscription pop-up box, and others go to a site on the web. As of the time this book was written, a lot of the subscription content is freely available online at locations such as the Internet Archive (www.archive.org). The value-add at Mocavo is the better search interface and results that are more genealogically related. If you don't want to pay for the subscription searches, you could use Mocavo to discover the record that your ancestor is mentioned in, note the page number, and find the corresponding record on the Internet Archive.

Genealogy Toolbox

The Genealogy Toolbox has been around since 1994. It began as a list of links to genealogy and local-history resources and added a search engine in 1998. Today, the focus of the free site is on the search engine and in preformatted searches.

1. **Navigate to www.genealogytoolbox.com.**

   The Genealogy Toolbox home page appears. Under the section labeled Genealogy Toolbox Full-Text Search is a search box.

2. Type your search terms in the search box and click the Search button.

For hints on search syntax read the information located above the search box. The search results appear, as shown in Figure 6-3.

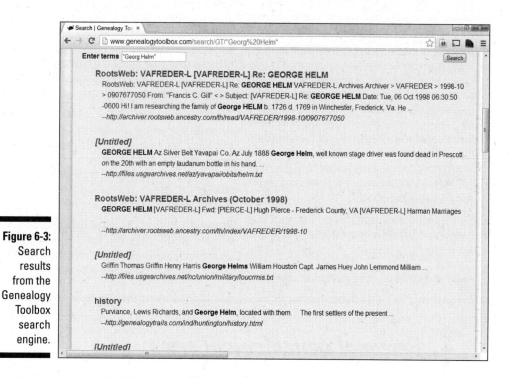

Figure 6-3:
Search
results
from the
Genealogy
Toolbox
search
engine.

3. Click on a link that interests you.

You can also use the preformatted searches located on the home page to reduce the amount of time spent searching. These preformatted searches appear as links in the Search Categories text box located just below the search form.

Finding the Site That's Best for You

Your dream as an online genealogist is to find a website that contains all the information that you ever wanted to know about your family. Unfortunately, these sites simply don't exist. However, during your search, you may discover a variety of sites that vary greatly in the amount and quality of genealogical information. Before you get too deep into your research, it's a good idea to look at the type of sites that you're likely to encounter.

What about blogs?

Since previous editions of this book were published, the Internet has been inundated by blogging. A *blog* is an online, personal journal of sorts — a site where an individual or even a group of people with a common interest can record their daily, weekly, monthly, or whatever-timed-interval thoughts and experiences. The field of genealogy is no exception! Many genealogy blogs are now available, and they can't be categorized under just one of the groupings we've covered so far in this chapter. In other words, they don't all fit into personal genealogical sites, nor do they all fit into family associations or organizations.

One example of a blog that is genealogical and geographic in nature is the Texas History and Genealogy Blog (`http://texashistory blog.blogspot.com`). As you might imagine, it covers a variety of topics relating to Texas. At irregular intervals, the host of the blog posts various types of information ranging from cemetery transcriptions, to information about upcoming conferences, to historical markers, to things to see when driving through Texas, to other websites or articles that she thinks will interest readers.

There are also blogs that recount the research pursuits of particular individuals and there are blogs that focus on events in the genealogy world. You can find a list of blogs on the Genealogy Blog Roll page at the GeneaBloggers website (`http://geneabloggers.com/ genealogy-blogs`).

When you're ready to share your knowledge with the world, you might consider setting up your own genealogical blog. We provide the specific steps for doing so in Chapter 11.

Personal genealogical sites

The majority of non-subscription pages that you encounter on the web are maintained by an individual who is interested in researching a particular person or family line. These pages usually contain information on the site maintainer's ancestry or on particular branches of several different families rather than on a surname as a whole. That doesn't mean valuable information isn't present on these sites — it's just that they have a more personal focus.

You can find a wide variety of information on personal genealogical sites. Some pages list only a few surnames that the maintainer is researching; others contain extensive online genealogical databases and narratives. A site's content depends on the amount of research, time, and computer skills the maintainer possesses. Some common items that you see on most sites include a list of surnames, an online genealogical database, pedigree and descendant charts, family photographs, research blogs, and the obligatory list of the maintainer's favorite genealogical Internet links.

Personal genealogical sites vary not only in content but also in presentation. Some sites are neatly constructed and use plain backgrounds and aesthetically pleasing colors. Other sites, however, require you to bring out your sunglasses to tone down the fluorescent colors, or they use lots of moving graphics and banner advertisements that take up valuable space and make it difficult to navigate through the site. You should also be aware that the JavaScript, music players, and animated icons that some personal sites use can significantly increase your download times.

An example of a personal genealogical site is the Rubi-Lopez Genealogy Page (`http://rubifamilygen.com`), shown in Figure 6-4. The Rubi-Lopez page contains articles on different lines of the family, a photo gallery, and links to other family websites.

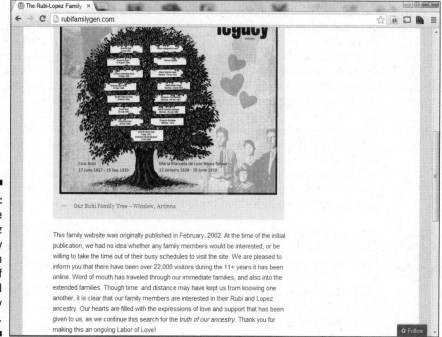

Figure 6-4:
The Rubi-Lopez Genealogy Page is an example of a personal genealogy site.

After you find a site that contains useful information, write down the maintainer's name and e-mail address and contact him or her *as soon as possible* if you have any questions or want to exchange information. Personal genealogical sites have a way of disappearing without a trace because individuals frequently switch Internet service providers or stop maintaining sites.

One-name study sites

If you're looking for a wide range of information on one particular surname, a one-name study site may be worth your while. These sites usually focus on one surname regardless of the geographic location where the surname appears. In other words, they welcome information about people with the surname worldwide. These sites are quite helpful because they contain all sorts of information about the surname, even if they don't have specific information about your branch of a family with that surname. Frequently they have information on the variations in spelling, origins, history, DNA, and heraldry of the surname. One-name studies have some of the same resources you find in personal genealogical sites, including online genealogy databases and narratives.

Although one-name study sites welcome all surname information regardless of geographic location, the information presented at one-name study sites is often organized around geographic lines. For example, a one-name study site may categorize all the information about people with the surname by continent or country — such as Helms in the United States, England, Canada, Europe, and Africa. Or, the site may be even more specific and categorize information by state, province, county, or parish. So, you're better off if you have a general idea of where your family originated or migrated from. But if you don't know, browsing through the site may lead to some useful information.

The Bowes Surname website (www.bowesonenamestudy.com) is a one-name study site with several resources for the Bowe, Bows, Bow, Boe, and De Bowes surnames. From the home page (see Figure 6-5), you can choose to view news on recent additions to the site, articles on current discoveries, results of the surname DNA project, research in different countries, and information on how to join a mailing list of the surnames.

The maintainers of one-name study sites welcome any information you have on the surname. These sites are often a good place to join research groups that can be instrumental in assisting your personal genealogical effort.

To find one-name study sites pertaining to the surnames you're researching, you have to go elsewhere. Where, you ask? One site that can help you is the Guild of One-Name Studies (www.one-name.org).

Gee, we bet you can't figure out what the Guild of One-Name Studies is! It's exactly as it sounds — an online organization of registered sites, each of which focuses on one particular surname. The Guild has information about more than 8,400 surnames. Follow these steps to find out whether any of the Guild's members focus on the surname of the person you're researching:

1. **Open your web browser and go to www.one-name.org.**

   The home page appears with a search field just below the title of the site.

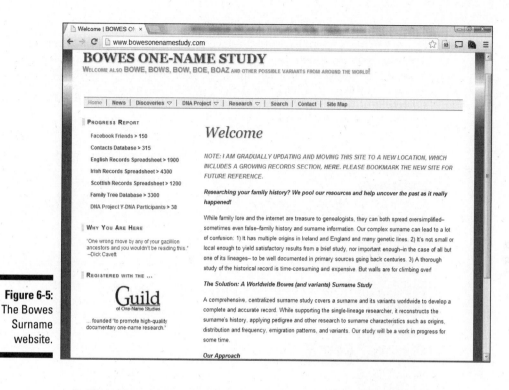

Figure 6-5:
The Bowes
Surname
website.

2. **Type the surname you're researching in the field entitled Is Your Surname Registered?**

3. **Click the Search button.**

   If a registered one-name study is available, you see a box entitled See a Profile of This One-Name Study.

4. **Click the box to find more information about the one-name study.**

   The profile contains information such as a website address and e-mail address of the maintainer of the one-name study.

Family associations and organizations

Family association sites are similar to one-name study sites in terms of content, but they usually have an organizational structure (such as a formal association, society, or club) backing them. The association may focus on the surname as a whole or just one branch of a family. The goals for the family association site may differ from those for a one-name study. The maintainers may be creating a family history in book form or a database of all individuals descended from a particular person. Some sites may require you to join the association before you can fully participate in their activities, but this is usually at a minimal cost or free.

The Wingfield Family Society site (www.wingfield.org), shown in Figure 6-6, has several items that are common to family association sites. The site's contents include a family history, newsletter subscription details, a membership form, queries, mailing list information, results of a DNA project, and a directory of the society's members who are online. Some of the resources at the Wingfield Family Society site require you to be a member of the society to access them.

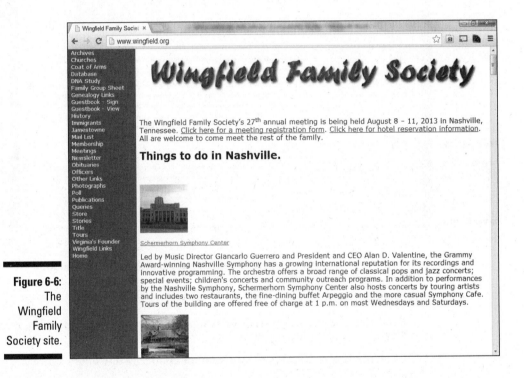

Figure 6-6:
The
Wingfield
Family
Society site.

To find a family association website, your best bet is to use a search engine. For more on search engines, see the section "Diving into general Internet search engines," earlier in this chapter. Be sure to use search terms that include the surname you're interested in researching and one of these keywords: *society, association, group,* or *organization.*

Surnames connected to events or places

Another place where you may discover surnames is a site that has a collection of names connected with a particular event or geographic location. The level of information available on these sites varies greatly among sites and among surnames on the same site. Often, the maintainers of such sites include more information on their personal research interests than other surnames, simply because they have more information on their own lines.

Typically, you need to know events that your ancestors were involved in or geographic areas where they lived to use these sites effectively. Also, you benefit from the site simply because you have a general, historical interest in the particular event or location, even if the website contains nothing on your surname. Finding websites about events is easiest if you use a search engine, a comprehensive website, or a subscription database. Because we devote an entire chapter to researching geographic locations (Chapter 7), we won't delve into that here.

Taking the Plunge

After you've decided on a particular person to research (for more on selecting a good research candidate, see Chapter 3), it's time to research online. As we've mentioned frequently in this book, it's a good idea to arm yourself with some facts about the individual before venturing online.

Perhaps Matthew wants to research his paternal grandfather's line. His grandfather was Herschel Helm, who lived in Macon County, Illinois. From memory and supported by a copy of a death certificate for Herschel, Matthew knows that his grandfather died in 1985 — information that can be used to distinguish him from another Herschel Helm found online.

Due to privacy laws, the amount of information online on people in the United States after 1940 is limited. However, one source that does provide information on deceased individuals during this time period is the Social Security Death Index (SSDI), also called the Social Security Death Master file — a good place to get your feet wet.

As of 2013, the SSDI contained more than 92 million records of deaths of individuals having a Social Security Number. The vast majority of these records deal with individuals who died after 1962 — although a few scattered records predate that year. Each entry includes the following:

- ✔ Name of deceased
- ✔ Birth date
- ✔ Death date
- ✔ Last residence
- ✔ Last benefit received
- ✔ Social Security Number
- ✔ State where person lived when Social Security card was issued

Several places exist online where the SSDI can be searched. The most up-to-date version is found at the GenealogyBank.com site at `www.genealogy bank.com/gbnk/ssdi.html`. However, a membership is required for access.

For free access to the SSDI, try visiting `http://search.ancestry.com/search/db.aspx?dbid=3693`.

To search the SSDI, do the following:

1. **Point your browser to** `http://search.ancestry.com/search/db.aspx?dbid=3693`.

   The Social Security Death Index Interactive Search page at Ancestry.com appears, with a search form in the middle of the page.

2. **Type the last name and first name of the individual and click Submit.**

   You can search for an exact match on the surname or use a phonetic match for the search by clicking on the Use Default Settings link. (For more information about Soundex, flip back to Chapter 4.) These sound-based equivalents can be used to find names that are not spelled exactly as you expect them to be. In our case, we type *Helm* in the Last Name field and *Herschel* in the First Name field.

3. **Browse the results page for the appropriate individual.**

   The results are presented in a table with six columns. Our search yielded eight close matches, and only one of those has the last residence of Macon County and a death date of 1985.

If you find an ancestor in the database, you can order the original Social Security application (Form SS-5) from the Social Security Administration. The order form for the SS-5 is available online at `https://secure.ssa.gov/apps9/eFOIA-FEWeb/internet/main.jsp`.

Family Trees Ripe for the Picking: Finding Compiled Resources

Using online databases to pick pieces of genealogical fruit is wonderful. But you want more, right? Not satisfied with just having Social Security information on his grandfather, Matthew is eager to know more — in particular, he'd like to know who Herschel's grandfather was. You have a few research tactics to explore at this point. Perhaps the first is to see whether someone has already completed some research on Herschel and his ancestors.

When someone publishes his or her genealogical findings (whether online or in print), the resulting work is called a *compiled genealogy.*

Compiled genealogies can give you a lot of information about your ancestors in a nice, neat format. When you find one with information relevant to your family, you get an overwhelming feeling of instantaneous gratification. Wait! Don't get too excited yet! When you use compiled genealogies, it's important to remember that you need to verify any information in them that you're adding to your own findings. Even when sources are cited, it's wise to get your own copies of the actual sources to ensure that the author's interpretation of the sources was correct and that no other errors occurred in the publication of the compiled genealogy.

Compiled genealogies take two shapes online. One is the traditional narrative format — the kind of thing that you typically see in a book at the library. The second is in the form of information exported from an individual's genealogical database and posted online in a lineage-linked format (*lineage-linked* means that the database is organized by the relationships between people).

Narrative compiled genealogies

Narrative compiled genealogies usually have more substance than their exported database counterparts. Authors sometimes add color to the narratives by including local history and other text and facts that can help researchers get an idea of the time in which the ancestor lived. An excellent example of a narrative genealogy is found at The Carpenters of Carpenter's Station, Kentucky, at `http://freepages.genealogy.rootsweb.ancestry.com/~carpenter`.

The site maintainer, Kathleen Carpenter, has posted a copy of her mother's historical manuscript on the Carpenter family, as well as some photos and a map of Carpenter's Station. You can view the documents directly through the web or download PDF copies.

To locate narrative genealogies, try using a search engine or comprehensive genealogical index. (For more information on using these resources, see the sections later in this chapter.) Often, compiled genealogies are part of a personal or family association website.

You can also find a collection of family histories at the Family History Books portion of FamilySearch (`https://books.familysearch.org/primo_library/libweb/action/search.do?dscnt=1&vid=FHD_PUBLIC&`). Just type the name that interests you in the search form to see whether a compiled genealogy has been placed online.

Compiled genealogical databases

Although many people don't think of lineage-linked, online genealogical databases as compiled genealogies, these databases serve the same role as narrative compiled genealogies — they show the results of someone's research in a neatly organized, printed format.

For example, the Simpson History site (`http://simpsonhistory.com/_main_page.html`) is a personal site that contains a compiled genealogical database providing information on John "The Scotsman" Simpson and his descendants. You can navigate through descendant charts and family group sheets, clicking particular individuals to access more information about them.

Finding information in compiled genealogical databases can sometimes be tough. There isn't a grand database that indexes all the individual databases available online. Although general Internet search engines have indexed quite a few, some very large collections are still accessible only through a database search — something that general Internet search engines don't normally do.

In the preceding section, we conducted a search on Matthew's grandfather, Herschel Helm. Now we want to find out more about his ancestry. We can jump-start our research by using a lineage-linked database in hopes of finding some information compiled from other researchers that can help us discover who his ancestors were (perhaps even several generations' worth). From documents such as his birth and death certificates, we find out that Herschel's father was named Emanuel Helm. And from interviews with family members, we also learn that Emanuel was born in Fayette County, Illinois, in the early 1860s. Armed with this information, we can search a compiled genealogical database.

The FamilySearch Internet Genealogy Service (`www.familysearch.org`) is the official research site for the Church of Jesus Christ of Latter-day Saints (LDS). This free website allows you to search several LDS databases including the Ancestral File, International Genealogical Index, Pedigree Resource File, vital records index, census records, and a collection of abstracted websites — all of which are free. The two resources that function much like lineage-linked databases are the Ancestral File and the Pedigree Resource File. Fortunately, you don't have to search each of these resources separately. A master search is available that allows you to search all seven resources on the site at once. See Chapter 3 for more on how to use the FamilySearch site.

You can find several other lineage-linked collections that may contain useful information. The following list gives you details on some of the better-known collections:

- ✔ **Ancestry World Tree:** The Ancestry.com site (`http://trees. ancestry.com/Default.aspx?req=tree`) contains a free area where researchers can contribute GEDCOM files from their individual databases, as well as search through the files of other researchers.

- ✔ **WorldConnect:** The WorldConnect Project (`http://wc.rootsweb. ancestry.com/`) is part of the RootsWeb.com site. The Project has more than 640 million names in its database.

- ✔ **MyTrees.com:** MyTrees.com (`www.mytrees.com`) is a site maintained by Kindred Konnections. The site has a lineage-linked database available only by subscription.

- ✔ **OneGreatFamily.com:** OneGreatFamily.com (`www.onegreatfamily. com/Home.aspx`) hosts a subscription-based, lineage-linked database.

- ✔ **GenCircles:** GenCircles (`www.gencircles.com`) is a free, lineage-linked database site with a twist. Its SmartMatching feature compares individuals from different files and attempts to match them together. Thus, a researcher who contributes to GenCircles can get in contact with another who may be working on the same family lines.

Online Subscription Databases: Goldmines of Genealogy?

Some of your ancestors may have been prospectors. You know the type — they roamed from place to place in search of the mother lode. Often, they may have found a small nugget here or there, but they never seemed to locate that one mine that provided a lifetime supply of gold. When searching on the Internet, you become the prospector. You pan through results from search engines only to find small nuggets of information here and there. However, don't lose hope. There may be some gold mines waiting for you if you can only stumble upon the right site to dig — and the right site may be in the form of an online subscription database.

Online subscription databases are repositories of information that you can retrieve by paying a monthly, quarterly, or yearly fee. Most online subscription databases are searchable and allow you to type your ancestor's name and execute a search to determine whether any information stored in the database relates to that particular name. Databases can be large or small;

they can focus on a small geographic area or have a broad scope that encompasses many different areas. Each database may also have its own unique search method and present information in its own format. The online subscription database sites vary in the types of content they offer and the amounts and quality of background or historical information they provide about each of the databases within their collections.

You can find online subscription databases in many ways. You can locate references to them through search engines, comprehensive genealogical indexes, and links that appear on personal and geographic-specific websites. For examples of the types of data available on subscription sites, see Chapters 1 and 3.

Browsing Comprehensive Genealogical Indexes

If you're unable to find information on your ancestor through a search engine or online database, or if you're looking for additional information, another resource to try is a comprehensive genealogical index. A *comprehensive genealogical index* is a site that contains a categorized listing of links to online resources for family history research. Comprehensive genealogical indexes can be organized in a variety of ways, including by subject, alphabetically, or by resource type. No matter how the links are organized, they usually appear hierarchically — you click your way down from category to subcategory until you find the link for which you're looking.

Some examples of comprehensive genealogical indexes include the following:

✔ **Cyndi's List of Genealogy Sites on the Internet:** www.cyndislist.com

✔ **Linkpendium:** www.linkpendium.com

To give you an idea of how comprehensive genealogical indexes work, try the following example:

1. **Fire up your browser and go to Linkpendium (www.linkpendium. com).**

   This step launches the home page for Linkpendium.

2. **Scroll down to the portion of the main page with the links to surnames.**

3. **Click a link with a letter for your surname.**

   For example, we're looking for Helm, so we click the H surnames link.

4. **Click the link that contains the first three letters of the surname you're researching.**

   We click the link entitled Hel Families: Surname Genealogy, Family History, Family Tree, Family Crest.

5. **Click the link to your surname.**

   We click the Helm Family: Surname Genealogy, Family History, Family Tree, Family Crest link. Figure 6-7 shows the links for the Helm surname.

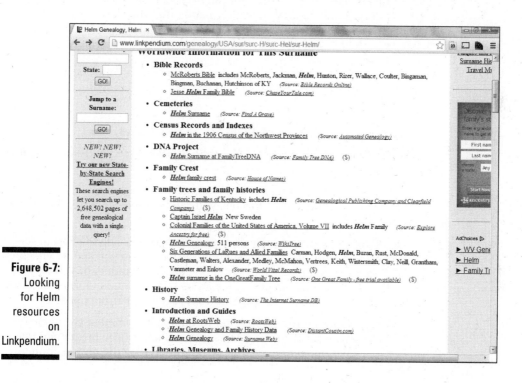

Figure 6-7:
Looking for Helm resources on Linkpendium.

One drawback to comprehensive genealogical indexes is that they can be time-consuming to browse. It sometimes takes several clicks to get down to the area where you believe links that interest you may be located. And, after several clicks, you may find that no relevant links are in that area. This lack may be because the maintainer of the site has not yet indexed a relevant site or the site may be listed somewhere else in the index.

Query for One: Seeking Answers to Your Surname Questions

Even if you can't find any surname-specific sites on your particular family, you still have hope! This hope comes in the form of queries. *Queries* are research questions that you post to a particular website, mailing list, or newsgroup so that other researchers can help you solve your research problems. Other researchers may have information that they haven't yet made available about a family, or they may have seen some information on your family, even though it isn't a branch that they're actively researching.

One of the quickest ways to reach a wide audience with your query is through a query site on the web. For an example of a query site, try GenForum:

1. **Open your web browser and go to www.genforum.com.**

2. **In the field below Forum Finder, type the surname you're looking for and click Find.**

    We entered *Helm*. But feel free to enter a surname that interests you. If you feel like browsing the forums, you can also select a letter below the word *Surnames*.

    Don't worry if your surname doesn't have a forum. The GenForum section is constantly growing and adding surnames, so you should check back every so often to see whether one has been added, or you may consider requesting that a new forum be added for your surname. (Look for the Add Forum link near the bottom of the GenForum pages.)

    You may also want to search other forums to see whether the name is included in a variant spelling or whether someone else mentioned the name in a passing reference in another forum. (See the next section for details.)

3. **After you find a forum, read a message by clicking its link.**

    As soon as your browser loads the message board page, you should see a list of bulleted messages to choose from, as shown in Figure 6-8. You can also navigate to other pages of the message board if the messages don't fit on a single page. If you don't want to read all the messages, you have the option to see only the latest messages, only today's messages, or any messages posted in the last seven days. These options are available at the top of the list of posted messages.

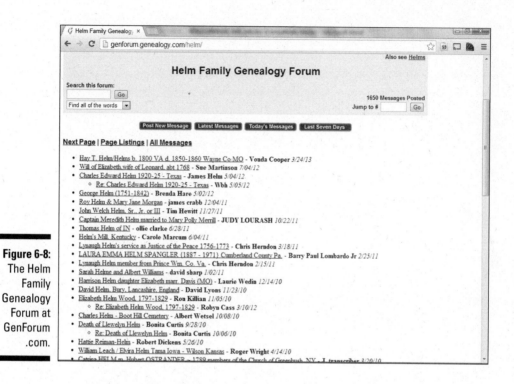

Figure 6-8:
The Helm
Family
Genealogy
Forum at
GenForum
.com.

4. **To post a new query, click Post New Message at the top of the list of posted messages.**

   If you're not already a registered user of GenForum, you see a page with instructions on registering.

   If you're already a registered user or after you become one, a page containing the fields that generate your message pops up. This page includes the name of the forum to which you're posting, your name and e-mail address, the subject of the posting, and a free-form text field where you can enter your message.

5. **Fill out the appropriate fields and then click Preview Message.**

   Make sure that your message contains enough information for other researchers to determine whether they can assist you. Include full names, birth and death dates, places (if known), and geographic locations where your ancestors lived (if known).

   Clicking the Preview Message button is an important step because you can see how the message will look when it's posted. This option can prevent you from posting a message filled with those embarrassing typos.

6. **When you're satisfied with the way the message looks, click Post Message.**

Chapter 7

Mapping the Past

· ·

In This Chapter

▶ Identifying where your ancestors lived

▶ Locating places on maps and in history

▶ Using maps in your research

▶ Getting information from local sources

· ·

Say you dig up an old letter addressed to your great-great-great-grandfather in Winchester, Virginia. But where is Winchester? What was the town like? Where exactly did he live in the town? What was life like when he lived there? To answer these questions, you need to go a little further than just retrieving documents — you need to look at the life of your ancestor within the context of where he lived.

Geography played a major role in the lives of our ancestors. It often determined where they lived, worked, and migrated. (Early settlers typically migrated to lands that were similar to their home state or country.) It can also play a major role in how you research your ancestor. Concentrating on where your ancestor lived can point you to area-specific record sets or offer clues about where to research next.

A number of tools and technologies can assist you in meeting your research goals. These tools include geographic information system applications, geocoding, and geographic applications specific to genealogy. In this chapter, we look at several ways to use geographical resources to provide a boost to your family history research.

Are We There Yet? Researching Where "There" Was to Your Ancestors

What did "there" mean for your ancestors? You have to answer this question to know where to look for genealogical information. These days, a family that lives in the same general area for more than two or three generations is rare. If you're a member of such a family, you may be in luck when it comes to researching. However, if you come from a family that moved around at least every few generations (or not all members of the family remained in the same location), you may be in for a challenge.

How do you find out where your ancestors lived? In this section, we look at several resources you can use to establish locations: using known records, interviewing relatives, consulting gazetteers, looking at maps, using GPS devices, and charting locations by using geographical software. As we go through these resources, we use a real-life example to show how the resources can be used together to solve a research problem — finding the location of the final resting place of Matthew's great-great-grandfather.

Using documents that you already possess

When you attempt to locate your ancestors geographically, start by using any copies of records or online data that you or someone else has already collected. Sift through all those photocopies and original documents from the attic and printouts from online sites — those details can help you determine places to look for additional information about your ancestors. Pay particular attention to any material that provides definite whereabouts during a specific time period. You can use these details as a springboard for your geographical search.

For example, Matthew's great-great-grandfather, Uriah Helm, is found in a record from the United States Headstone Applications for U.S. Military Veterans, 1925–1949. This collection is available on FamilySearch. (For more on FamilySearch, see Chapter 3.) The record (see Figure 7-1) shows that the headstone was going to be installed at the German Reform Cemetery, in or near Loogootee, Illinois. The record provides the further clues that the headstone was to be shipped to the post office located in Brownstown, Fayette County, presumably a post office close to the cemetery. The mention of Fayette County, Illinois, gives Matthew some context to begin the search.

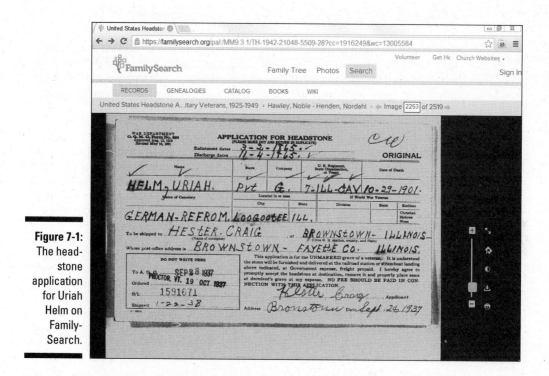

Figure 7-1:
The head-
stone
application
for Uriah
Helm on
Family-
Search.

Grilling your relatives

If you don't have records to guide your search, check out your notes from
interviews with family members or from other resources you've found on
your ancestors. Your notes may contain some information about locations
where the family lived and, we hope, the approximate time frames.

Chances are good that you have at least some notes with statements such as,
"Uncle Zeke recalled stories about the old homestead in Red River County,
Texas." Of course, whether he recalled firsthand stories (those that he lived
through or participated in) or stories he heard from his ancestors affects the
time frames within which you look for records in Red River County. Either
way, these stories give you a starting point.

For details on interviewing your family members, see Chapter 2.

Where is Llandrindod, anyway?

At some point during your research, you're bound to run across something that says an ancestor lived in a particular town or county or was associated with a specific place, but your resource contains no details of where that place was — no state or province or other identifiers. How do you find out where that place was located?

A *gazetteer,* or geographical dictionary, provides information about places. By looking up the name of the town, county, or some other kind of place, you can narrow your search for your ancestor. The gazetteer identifies every place by a particular name and provides varying information (depending on the gazetteer) about each. Typically, gazetteers provide at least the name of the principal region where the place is located. Many contemporary gazetteers available online also provide the latitude and longitude of the place.

By adding the information you get from the online gazetteer to the other pieces of your puzzle, you can reduce the list of places with the same name to just those you think are plausible for your ancestors. By pinpointing the location of a place, you can look for more records to prove whether your ancestors really lived there and even visit the location to get pictures of burial plots or old properties.

For research in the United States, a first stop is the U.S. Geological Survey's Geographic Names Information System (GNIS) website. The GNIS site contains information on more than 2 million places within the United States and its territories (the site also includes data for Antarctica).

To find the precise location of the cemetery where Uriah Helm is buried, we decided to use the Geographic Names Information System (GNIS) site. Follow these steps:

1. **Start your web browser and head to the U.S. Geological Survey's Geographic Names Information System (GNIS):**

   `http://geonames.usgs.gov/pls/gnispublic`

   This page contains the search form for the United States and its territories, as shown in Figure 7-2.

2. **Enter any information that you have, tabbing or clicking to move between fields.**

   We're looking for the cemetery in Illinois where we believe Uriah Helm is buried. Remember that we found the name of a cemetery in the headstone record mentioned in the previous section, so we entered *German Reform* in the Feature Name field and selected Illinois from the state drop-down list. To target your search, you can select a Feature Class to the right of the Feature Name field. In our case, we selected Cemetery as the feature class.

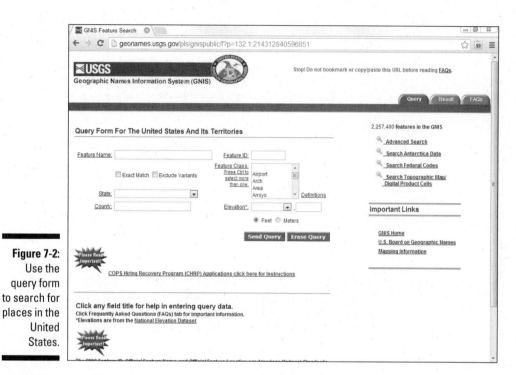

Figure 7-2:
Use the
query form
to search for
places in the
United
States.

If you're not sure what a particular field asks for but you think you may want to enter something in it, click the title of the field for an explanation.

3. **When you're finished, click Send Query.**

The result of the search shows a German Reformed Cemetery in Fayette County, Illinois. The cemetery is located at latitude of 38 degrees, 55 minutes, 58 seconds north and longitude of 88 degrees, 54 minutes, 18 seconds west and is found on the Brownstown map. We're fairly certain that this is the right cemetery because the cemetery name, county, and map name all match items on the headstone record. Next, we can use an online map to plot the longitude and latitude to see the actual location of the cemetery.

In addition to using the GNIS database, you might want to review some online gazetteers that identify places in other countries as well as places in the United States. One that builds on worldwide data available through Google Maps is Maplandia.com: Google Maps World Gazetteer. To use this gazetteer, follow these steps:

1. **Using your web browser, go to Maplandia.com at** `www.maplandia.com`.

You see the welcome page, which has search fields to look for locations by place-name or region.

2. **In the World Places field, type the name of the place you're trying to locate.**

   If you're trying to identify an entire region, you may prefer to use the World Regions field instead.

   We entered the *Llandrindod* place-name.

3. **Click Search.**

   Figure 7-3 shows the results of the search. The only result for our example was a place called Llandrindod Wells in Powys, Wales, in the United Kingdom. Clicking the result takes us to a page that contains the longitude and latitude of Llandrindod Wells and a map of the town.

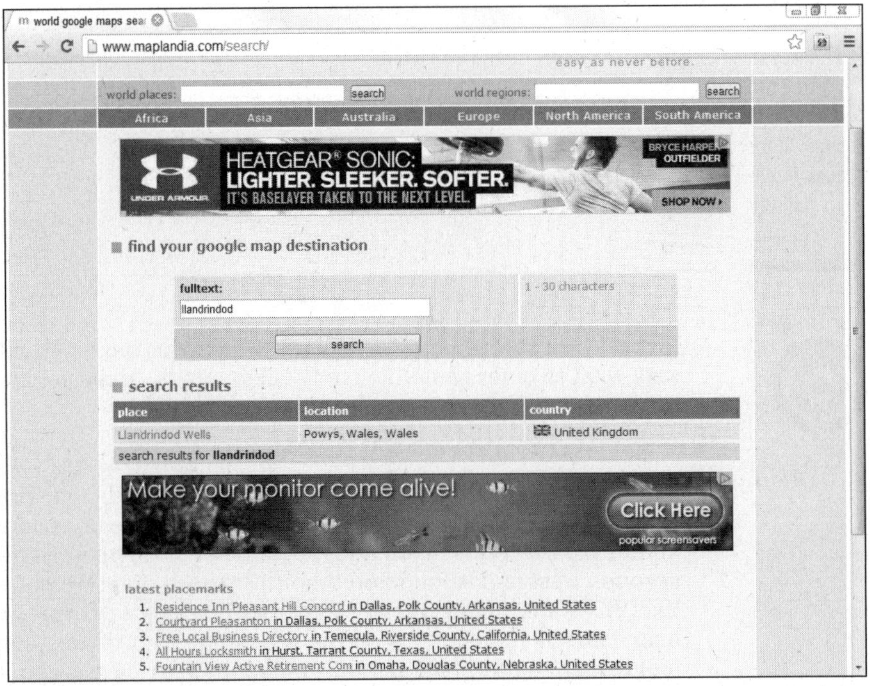

Figure 7-3:
Results for a search on Llandrindod at Maplandia .com.

Following are some gazetteer sites for you to check out. You can use some for worldwide searches; others are country specific:

✔ **Alexandria Digital Library Gazetteer Server**

   www.alexandria.ucsb.edu

   This site has a worldwide focus.

✔ **Directory of Cities, Towns, and Regions in Belgium**

   www.fallingrain.com/world/BE

✔ **Geoscience Australia Place Name Search**

www.ga.gov.au/map/names/

✔ **Canada's Geographical Names**

www4.rncan.gc.ca/search-place-names/name.php

✔ **China Historical GIS**

www.fas.harvard.edu/~chgis

✔ **Gazetteer of Australia Place Name Search**

www.ga.gov.au/place-names

✔ **Gazetteer for Scotland**

www.scottish-places.info

✔ **Gazetteer of British Place Names**

www.gazetteer.co.uk

✔ **GENUKI Gazetteer**

www.genuki.org.uk/big/Gazetteer

The gazetteer covers England, Ireland, Wales, Scotland, and the Isle of Man.

✔ **German Historic Gazetteer (in German)**

http://gov.genealogy.net

✔ **Institut Géographique National (in French)**

www.ign.fr

✔ **IreAtlas Townland Data Base (Ireland)**

www.seanruad.com

✔ **Metatopos.org (in Dutch)**

www.metatopos.org

✔ **National Gazetteer of Wales**

http://homepage.ntlworld.com/geogdata/ngw/home.htm

✔ **Land Information New Zealand (LINZ)**

www.linz.govt.nz/placenames/find-names/nz-gazetteer-official-names.

✔ **KNAB, the Place Names Database of EKI (in Estonian and English)**

www.eki.ee/knab/knab.htm

✔ **Registro de Nombres Geograficos (in Spanish)**

http://mapserver.inegi.gob.mx/rnng

✔ **Statens Kartverk (in Norwegian)**

`http://kart.statkart.no/adaptive2/default.aspx?gui=1&lang=2`

This site is in Norwegian; however, if you'd like to see an English version, just click the English Bokmal Nynorsk link in the upper-left corner.

✔ **Swedish Gazetteer**

`www.sna.se/gazetteer.html`

✔ **World Gazetteer**

`http://world-gazetteer.com`

✔ **GPS Data Team: Coordinate Finder**

`www.gps-data-team.com/map`

Most online gazetteers are organized on a national level and provide information about all the places (towns, cities, counties, landmarks, and so on) within that country. However, you find some exceptions. Some unique gazetteers list information about places within one state or province. One such example is the Kentucky Atlas and Gazetteer (`www.kyatlas.com`), which has information only about places within — you guessed it — Kentucky. For each place, it provides the name of the place, county, type of the place (civil division, school, cemetery, airport, and so on), source of information, an identification number, topoquad (topographic-map quadrangle that contains the feature), latitude, longitude, elevation, population (if applicable), area (if applicable), date of establishment, and the URL for a map showing you the location of the place. The name of the place is typically a link that goes directly to the map.

If you can't find a location in current gazetteers, you may need to consult a historical gazetteer. A couple of examples of these include A Vision of Britain through Time (British), available at `www.visionofbritain.org.uk`, and the Digital Gazetteer of the Song Dynasty, at `http://songgis.ucmerced.edu`. One way to find a historical gazetteer is to visit a general search engine (such as Google, at `www.google.com`) and search the place-name plus the words *historical gazetteer*. Another option is to visit a thesaurus, such as the Getty Thesaurus of Geographic Names Online at `www.getty.edu/research/tools/vocabularies/tgn`. You can type a name into the thesaurus, and it will provide a list of place types that contain the name, including the latitude and longitude and the former names of the place.

Mapping your ancestor's way

After you determine where a place is located, it's time to dig out the maps. Maps can be an invaluable resource in your genealogical research. Not only do maps help you track your ancestors' locations at various points in their lives, but they also enhance your published genealogy by illustrating some of your findings.

Different types of online sites have maps that may be useful in your genealogical research.

- ✔ **Historical maps:** Several websites contain scanned or digitized images of historic maps. In a lot of cases, you can download or print copies of these maps. Such sites include the following:

    - David Rumsey Map Collection: `www.davidrumsey.com`

    - Perry-Castañeda Library Map Collection, University of Texas at Austin: `www.lib.utexas.edu/maps/index.html`

    - American Memory Map Collections of the Library of Congress: `http://memory.loc.gov/ammem/gmdhtml/gmdhome.html`

    You can also find local collections of maps at several university and historical society sites. Here are a few examples:

    - Cartography: Historical Maps of New Jersey (Rutgers University): `http://mapmaker.rutgers.edu/MAPS.html`

    - Ohio Historical Maps (The Ohio State University): `http://library.osu.edu/find/subjects/maps/ohio-historical-maps`

    - Massachusetts Maps (The Massachusetts Historical Society): `www.masshist.org/online/massmaps`

- ✔ **Digitized historical atlases:** In addition to map sites, individuals have scanned portions or the entire contents of atlases, particularly those from the 19th century. Examples include the following:

    - *Countrywide atlases:* An example is the 1895 U.S. Atlas at `www.livgenmi.com/1895`.

    - *County atlases:* The 1904 Maps from the New Century Atlas of Cayuga County, New York, are a good example at `www.rootsweb.com/~nycayuga/maps/1904`.

- *Specialty atlases:* An occupational example is the 1948 U.S. Railroad Atlas at `http://trains.rockycrater.org/pfmsig/atlas.php`.

✔ **Interactive map sites:** A few sites have interactive maps that you can use to find and zoom in on areas. When you have the view you want of the location, you can print a copy of the map to keep with your genealogical records. Here are some examples:

- *Google Maps:* `http://maps.google.com`

- *MapQuest:* `www.mapquest.com`

- *Bing Maps:* `www.bing.com/maps`

- *National Geographic MapMachine:* `http://maps.nationalgeo-graphic.com/maps`

- *The U.K. Street Map Page:* `www.streetmap.co.uk`

Interactive maps are especially helpful when you're trying to pinpoint the location of a cemetery or town you plan to visit for your genealogical research, but they're limited in their historical helpfulness because they typically offer only current information about places.

Zeroing in

We've looked at a few types of maps, but the real promise of mapping technology is the ability to use different maps together to see the whole picture of where your ancestors lived. One of the ways of doing this is by using mapping layers.

A good example of mapping layers is the Google Earth technology. Google Earth (`www.google.com/earth/index.html`) is a downloadable program that combines Google searches with geographic information. When you launch the program, you see the Earth represented as a globe. Enter a place-name or a longitude and latitude coordinate, and the system maps it for you. Then you can add more map layers to see other information about that particular place.

Here's an example of how the layering works: In the cemetery example used in the previous sections, we know two pieces of information about where that cemetery is located. The headstone record states that the cemetery is in Fayette, Illinois; the GNIS tells us that the cemetery is in Fayette County, Illinois, at a specific latitude and longitude. Because Matthew wants to see the gravestone for himself, we can use Google Earth to locate the cemetery and get an idea of what that area looked like at the time his ancestors lived there.

Here is how to generate a Google Earth map by latitude and longitude (you need to download the Google Earth program from `www.google.com/earth/index.html` to your computer before following these steps):

1. **Open the Google Earth program.**

   When Google Earth launches, you see the Earth as viewed from space, as shown in Figure 7-4. In the upper-left corner of the screen is the Search area, where you can enter coordinates for latitude and longitude.

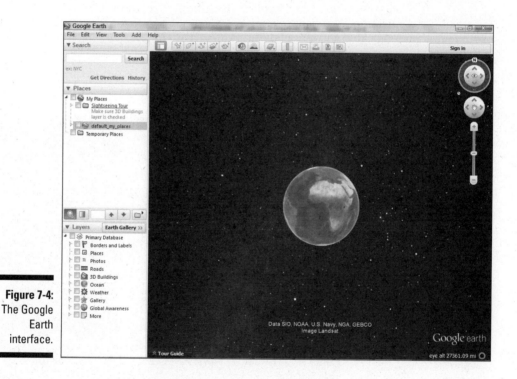

Figure 7-4: The Google Earth interface.

2. **Enter the latitude and longitude of the location and click the Search button.**

   We entered the latitude and longitude from the GNIS entry for the cemetery — 38 55.58 N, 088 54.18 W. The Google Earth application "flies" to the location on the map.

   The location is marked with a pushpin, and the latitude and longitude label appears to the right. If the map zooms in too far, you can use the scale in the upper-right corner of the map to zoom out. Just move your cursor to the area containing the circle with the *N*. Using your cursor on the *N* moves the map in a circle. Clicking in the circle below it moves the map up, down, right, and left so that you can see different areas. Below the compass is a scale with plus and minus signs — clicking the plus and minus signs allows you to zoom the map in and out.

3. **Add a place mark to label the location.**

   Move your cursor to the top of the screen and click the Placemark icon (the yellow pushpin). When you click the icon, a dialog box appears, allowing you to title the place mark, add a description, and change attributes of the place mark. We entered *Uriah Helm's Grave* in the Name field and a brief description on the Description tab. The resulting image is shown in Figure 7-5.

Figure 7-5:
The location of Uriah Helm's grave in Fayette County, Illinois.

4. **Overlay the Roads layer.**

   The bottom area in the left column contains a list of available layers. We clicked the Roads layer. From this layer, we can see that Illinois Route 185 runs past the cemetery.

5. **Add the Rumsey Historical Maps layer, located under the Gallery directory of the Layers section.**

   Visiting the Layers area again, we clicked the Gallery item and then clicked the small arrow next to the Gallery label. A list of items appeared and we scrolled down the Rumsey Historical Maps and checked it. There may be several other layers already checked. You may want to uncheck those to concentrate only on the Rumsey Historical Maps layer. To add a map, you need to click the MapFinder option, activating it. Zoom out (using the zooming tools explained in Step 2) until you see compass roses (little sun-looking icons) all over the map. Each compass rose represents a historical map that you can select to overlay your location. After selecting one, you can zoom in again to see your location up close.

Using the Rumsey Historical Maps layer, we selected the United States 1833 layer — the compass rose is near Columbus, Ohio, when we zoomed out on the map of the United States. The 1833 map of the United States appears; then we zoomed in again to Uriah's gravesite. Although Uriah Helm lived several decades after the map was made, his grandfather moved into the area around 1840 — so we can see roughly what the area looked like when the family arrived, as shown in Figure 7-6.

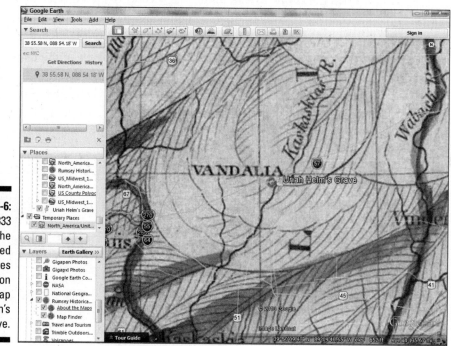

Figure 7-6: The 1833 map of the United States overlaid on the map of Uriah's grave.

Although interactive maps are good for getting a general idea of the location of a place, more specific maps are sometimes necessary for feature types such as creeks or ridges. Topographic maps are an especially good set to use for these purposes; they contain not only place-names but also information on features of the terrain (such as watercourses, elevation, vegetation density, and, yes, even cemeteries). At the USGS National Map site (http://nationalmap.gov), you can view a variety of map layers, including topographical maps.

To view a topographic map at the National Map, follow these steps:

1. **Direct your browser to** `http://nationalmap.gov/viewers.html`.

2. **Scroll down and click the link labeled** *Click here to go to The National Map Viewer and Download Platform!*

   After a few moments, a map of the United States appears.

3. **At the top of the page, type a place or longitude and latitude and click Search.**

   We typed *German Reformed Cemetery* and clicked the Search button. A Tasks/Results pane appeared on the left, with six results — the second result was the German Reformed Cemetery in Illinois. The map opened automatically to an overview map showing the location of each result. You can close the Tasks/Results pane by clicking the arrow to the right of the Cart tab.

4. **Click the Zoom To link under the second German Reformed Cemetery link.**

   The map zooms to the selected area.

5. **Click on the zoom slider on the upper-left corner of the map to zoom into the map.**

   The topographic map appears on the screen, as shown in Figure 7-7.

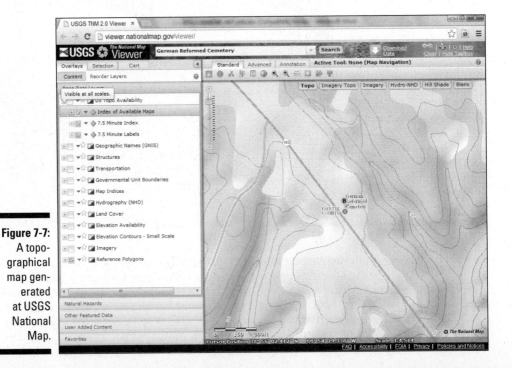

Figure 7-7:
A topo-graphical map gen-erated at USGS National Map.

Crossing the line

Just as maps help you track your ancestors' movements and where they lived, they can also help you track when your ancestors *didn't* really move. Boundaries for towns, districts, and even states have changed over time. Additionally, towns and counties sometimes change names. Knowing whether your ancestors really moved or just appeared to move because a boundary or town name changed is important when you try to locate records for them.

To determine whether a town or county changed names at some point, check a gazetteer or historical text on the area. (Gazetteers are discussed earlier in this chapter, in the "Where is Llandrindod, anyway?" section.) Finding boundary changes can be a little more challenging, but resources are available to help you. For example, historical atlases illustrate land and boundary changes. You can also use online sites that have maps for the same areas over time, and a few sites deal specifically with boundary changes in particular locations. Here are a few examples:

- ✔ **NationalAtlas.gov:** `www.nationalatlas.gov/index.html`
- ✔ **Atlas of Historical County Boundaries:** `http://publications.newberry.org/ahcbp`
- ✔ **The Counties of England, Wales, and Scotland Prior to the 1974 Boundary Changes:** `www.genuki.org.uk/big/Britain.html`

You can also use software designed to show boundary changes over time. Programs like these can help you find places that have disappeared altogether:

- ✔ **The Centennial Historical Atlas** tracks boundary changes in Europe. Its website is `www.clockwk.com`.
- ✔ **AniMap Plus** tracks boundary changes in the United States. Its website is `www.goldbug.com/AniMap.html`.

The following is a quick walkthrough using the Atlas of Historical County Boundaries to see how some counties have changed over time:

1. **Point your web browser to** `http://publications.newberry.org/ahcbp`.

   The homepage for the atlas appears. You can choose to look at data at a national level or the county level. Continuing with the earlier example, we are interested in finding more information about Fayette County, Illinois.

2. **Click the state that interests you.**

   We clicked on Illinois. A page appears with links to view an interactive map, an index of counties, a chronology of state and county boundaries, individual county chronologies, a bibliography, historical commentary, and downloadable geographic information system (GIS) files.

3. **Click the View Interactive Map heading.**

A map of the state appears, as shown in Figure 7-8. You can use the toolbar on the left side of the screen to zoom in or out of the map, measure distances, create a query, and print the map.

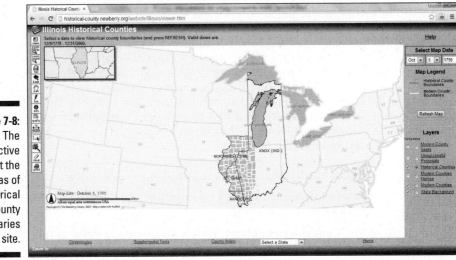

Figure 7-8:
The interactive map at the Atlas of Historical County Boundaries site.

4. **Under Select Map Date (in the upper-right corner of the screen), type in the date that interests you.**

We typed in *Dec 31 1840*.

5. **Click the Refresh Map button.**

The county boundaries change based upon the date that you entered.

6. **Use the Zoom In button on the toolbar to see the county boundaries more clearly.**

The county boundaries change based upon the date that you entered.

Positioning your family: Using global positioning systems

After discovering the location of the final resting place of great-great-great-grandpa, you just might get the notion to travel to the cemetery. Now, finding the cemetery on the map is one thing, but often finding the cemetery on the ground is a completely different thing. That is where global positioning systems come into play.

A *Global Positioning System* (GPS) is a device that uses satellites to determine the exact location of the user. The technology is sophisticated, but in simple terms, satellites send out radio signals that are collected by the GPS receiver — the device that you use to determine your location. The receiver then calculates the distances between the satellites and the receiver to determine your location. Receivers can come in many forms, ranging from vehicle-mounted receivers to those that fit in your hand. (We frequently use a GPS receiver mounted inside Matthew's cell phone for quick readings.)

While on research trips, we use GPS receivers not only to locate a particular place but also to document the location of a specific object within that place. For example, when we visit a cemetery, we take GPS readings of the gravesites of ancestors and then enter those readings into our genealogical databases. That way, if the marker is ever destroyed, we still have a way to locate the grave. As a final step, we take that information and plot the specific location of the sites on a map, using geographical information systems software. (See the following section for more details on geographical information systems.)

If you don't want to lug around a separate GPS device, many smartphones contain GPS capability beyond just simple location services. For example, although not made specifically for genealogy, the iPhone app MotionX-GPS (www.motionx.com) contains a variety of tools that are useful for the genealogist in the field. It can show your position on the street, topographic maps, and satellite maps. You can also set the application to track your movements and set waypoints as you go. The application even has a built-in compass and the capability to take a picture and automatically associate it with a latitude and longitude.

Plotting against the family

Although finding the location where your ancestors lived on a map is interesting, it's even more exciting to create maps specific to your family history. One way genealogists produce their own maps is by plotting land records: They take the legal description of the land from a record and place it into land-plotting software, which then creates a map showing the land boundaries. A couple of programs for plotting boundaries are DeedMapper, by Direct Line Software (www.directlinesoftware.com/deedmapper_42), and Metes and Bounds, by Sandy Knoll Software (www.tabberer.com/sandyknoll/more/metesandbounds/metes.html). And a subscription site called HistoryGeo.com has lands already plotted and searchable for original land-owners of public states. For more information on HistoryGeo.com, flip to Chapter 5. You can also find a number of commercial plotting programs by using a search engine such as Google (www.google.com).

Another way to create custom maps is through geographical information systems (GIS) software. GIS software allows you to create maps based on layers of information. For example, you may start with a map that is just an outline of a county. Then you might add a second layer that shows the township sections of the county as they were originally platted. A third layer might show the location of your ancestor's homestead based on the legal description of a land record. A fourth layer might show watercourses or other terrain features within the area. The resulting map can give you a great appreciation of the environment in which your ancestor lived.

To begin using GIS resources, you first have to acquire a GIS data viewer. This software comes in many forms, including free software and commercial packages. One popular piece of free software is ArcReader, which is available on the ESRI site at `www.esri.com/software/arcgis/arcreader/download.html`. Then you download (or create) geographical data to use with the viewer. A number of sites contain data, both free and commercial. Starting points for finding data include ArcGIS Online (`www.arcgis.com/home`), GIS Data Depot (`http://data.geocomm.com`), and the geospatial portion of Data.gov (`http://catalog.data.gov/dataset?metadata_type=geospatial`). For more information on GIS software, see GIS.com at `www.esri.com/what-is-gis`.

You can also use maps from other sources and integrate them into a GIS map. When visiting cemeteries, we like to use GIS resources to generate an aerial photograph of the cemetery and plot the location of the grave markers on it. When we get back home, we use the aerial photograph as the base template and then overlay the grave locations on it electronically to show their exact positions.

For example, when grave hunting for the German Reformed Cemetery (discussed earlier in the chapter), we generated an aerial view of the area at Bing.com (`www.bing.com/maps`). In the search field, we entered the place-name (German Reformed Cemetery Illinois) and then clicked on the arrow next to Bird's Eye on the menu bar and selected Aerial.

Figure 7-9 shows the photograph at its maximum zoom. The cemetery is the slightly lighter, triangular gray area near the center of the photograph. (It's bordered on the west by the highway and on the east by a grove of trees.) This view of the cemetery helps a lot when we try to find it on the ground.

From the map, we know that the cemetery is right off the highway, between two farms, and not far from a small lake (although we have to keep in mind that the aerial photograph may have been taken long ago — some things might have changed since then).

After plotting the gravestone locations based on GPS readings at the cemetery, we can store that picture in our genealogical database so that it's easy to find gravestones at that cemetery should we (or anyone else) want to visit it in the future.

Figure 7-9:
An aerial
map at
Bing.com.

There's No Place Like Home: Using Local Resources

A time will come (possibly early in your research) when you need information that's maintained on a local level — say, a copy of a record stored in a local courthouse, confirmation that an ancestor is buried in a particular cemetery, or just a photo of the old homestead. So how can you find and get what you need?

Finding this information is relatively easy if you live in or near the county where the information is maintained — you decide what you need, find out where it's stored, and then go get a copy. Getting locally held information isn't quite as easy, however, if you live in another county, state, or country. Although you can determine what information you need and where it may be stored, finding out whether the information is truly kept where you think it is and then getting a copy is another thing. Of course, if this situation weren't such a common occurrence for genealogists, you could just make a vacation out of it — travel to the location to finish researching there and get the copy you need while sightseeing along the way. But unfortunately, needing records from distant places is a common occurrence, and most of us can't afford to pack our bags and hit the road every time we need a record or item from a faraway place — which is why it's nice to know that resources are available to help.

A lot of resources are available to help you locate local documents and obtain copies, such as these:

✔ Geographic-specific websites

✔ Local genealogical and historical societies

> ✔ Libraries with research services
>
> ✔ Individuals who are willing to do lookups in public records
>
> ✔ Directories and newspapers
>
> ✔ Localizing searches

Some resources are free, but others may charge you a fee for their time, and still others will bill you only for copying or other direct costs.

Geographic-specific websites

Geographic-specific websites are those pages that contain information only about a particular town, county, state, country, or other locality. They typically provide information about local resources, such as genealogical and historical societies, government agencies and courthouses, cemeteries, and civic organizations. Some sites have local histories and biographies of prominent residents online. Often they list and have links to other web pages that have resources for the area. Sometimes they even have a place where you can post *queries* (or questions) about the area or families from there in the hope that someone who reads your query will have some answers for you.

You can find several good examples of general geographic-specific websites:

> ✔ **The USGenWeb Project** (www.usgenweb.org) conveys information about the United States. The USGenWeb Project is an all-volunteer online effort to provide a central genealogical resource for information (records and reference materials) pertaining to counties within each state. (See the sidebar "The USGenWeb Project" for more information.)
>
> ✔ **GENUKI: UK + Ireland Genealogy** (www.genuki.org.uk) is an online reference site that contains primary historical and genealogical information in the United Kingdom and Ireland. It links to sites containing indexes, transcriptions, or digitized images of actual records. All the information is categorized by locality — by country, then county, then parish.
>
> ✔ **The American Local History Network** (www.alhn.org) organizes its resources by state and by topic.
>
> ✔ **National Library of Australia** (www.nla.gov.au/family-history/ genealogy-selected-websites) has a listing of all sorts of state and territory resources in Australia, including archives, libraries, societies, and cemeteries. It also has links directly to indexes and records at some local levels.
>
> ✔ **The WorldGenWeb Project** (www.worldgenweb.org) attempts the same type of undertaking as USGenWeb, only on a global scale.

The USGenWeb Project

The USGenWeb Project provides a central resource for genealogical information (records and reference materials) pertaining to counties within each state. USGenWeb offers state-level pages for each state within the United States that has links to pages for each county, as well as links to other online resources about the state. At the county level, the pages have links to resources about the county.

In addition to links to other websites with genealogical resources that are geographic-specific, most of the county-level pages have histories of the county or places within that county and a query section where you can post or read queries about researching in that county. Some of the county-level pages offer other services in addition to the query section, such as online records (transcribed or digitized), information about ongoing projects for that county, a surname registry for anyone researching in the county, and a lookup section that identifies people who are willing to look up information for others.

Although some states have uniform-looking county pages with the same standard resources for each county, other states don't. The content and look of USGenWeb state and county pages vary tremendously from state to state.

In addition to state- and county-level pages, the USGenWeb Project includes special projects that cross state and county lines. Some of these projects include the following:

- A project to collect and transcribe tombstone inscriptions so that genealogists can access the information online

- An undertaking to transcribe all federal census data for the United States and make it available online

- The Pension project — an attempt to transcribe pensions for all wars before 1900

- The Digital Map Library project, which provides free, high-quality digital maps to researchers

- A Census image project to place free versions of images online

- Transcriptions of marriage records at the Marriage Project

The various pages and projects that make up the USGenWeb Project are designed and maintained by volunteers. If you're interested in becoming involved, visit the USGenWeb home page at www.usgenweb.org.

Genealogical and historical societies

Most genealogical and historical societies exist on a local level and attempt to preserve documents and history for the area in which they are located. Genealogical societies also have another purpose — to help their members research their ancestors whether they lived in the local area or elsewhere. (Granted, some surname-based genealogical societies, and even a few virtual societies, are exceptions because they aren't specific to one particular place.) Although historical societies usually don't have a stated purpose of aiding their members in genealogical research, they are helpful to genealogists anyway. Often, if you don't live in the area from which you need a record or information, you can contact a local genealogical or historical society to get help. Help varies from lookup services in books and documents the society maintains in its library to volunteers who actually locate records for you and get copies to send you. Before you contact a local genealogical or historical society for help, be sure you know what services it offers.

Many local genealogical and historical societies have web pages and identify exactly which services they offer to members and nonmembers online. To find a society in an area you're researching, you can try a search in a search engine, such as the following:

Frederick County Virginia society genealogy OR historical

Or, you can find an index of genealogical and historical societies — such as the Society Hill Directory (www.daddezio.com/society) or the Federation of Genealogical Societies directory (www.fgs.org/cstm_societyHall. php). You might try this if a search engine search yields nothing — because some societies still don't maintain web pages. The Society Hill Directory contains directories for societies in the United States, Canada, and Australia. To find a society in the directory, try this:

1. **Using your web browser, go to Society Hill Directory at www.daddezio.com/society.**

2. **Click the link to the country where the society resides.**

   We clicked United States Historical & Genealogical Societies.

3. **Click a state.**

   You have two ways to search after you're on the state page. You can use the search form to search by a society name, or you can browse through the alphabetical listings.

4. **Type a name in the search box and click Go.**

   We typed *Frederick*. The results page contained a link to the Winchester-Frederick County Historical Society.

Libraries and archives

Often, the holdings in local libraries and archives can be of great value to you — even if you can't physically visit the library or archive to do your research. If the library or archive has an Internet site, go online to determine whether that repository has the book or document you need. (Most libraries and archives have web pages with their card catalogs or another listing of their holdings.) After seeing whether the repository has what you need, you can contact it to borrow the book or document (if it participates in an inter-library loan program) or to get a copy of what you need. (Most libraries and archives have services to copy information for people at a minimal cost.)

To find online catalogs for libraries in particular places, follow these steps:

1. **Using your web browser, go to LibDex: The Library Index at www.libdex.com.**

2. **Scroll down to the bottom of the page and click the Browse by Country link.**

   A geographic index of links sorted by country is displayed. For example, you can look for the National Library of Australia to see whether its collection has books that would help your Australian research.

3. **Scroll down and click the link for Australia.**

   Clicking the link for Australia takes you to a page that lists regions in Australia.

4. **Click a region and browse through the list to find a library of interest.**

   Depending on the link you select, you're taken to a page for that particular location. For example, clicking the Tasmania link leads to the Geographic: Countries: Australia: Tasmania page, where you can scroll through a list of catalogs.

5. **Click the State Library of Tasmania link.**

   Selecting the State Library of Tasmania link takes you to a description page with a link to the State Library's catalog online. From this point, follow the site's instructions to search for books of interest and applicability to your particular research.

Professional researchers

Professional researchers are people who research your genealogy — or particular family lines — for a fee. If you're looking for someone to do all the research necessary to put together a complete family history, some do so. If you're just looking for records in a particular area to substantiate claims in your genealogy, professional researchers can usually locate the records for you and get you copies. Their services, rates, experience, and reputations vary, so be careful when selecting a professional researcher to help you. Look for someone who has quite a bit of experience in the area in which you need help. Asking for references or a list of satisfied customers isn't out of the question. (That way, you know who you're dealing with before you send the researcher money.) To find a researcher in a particular location, you can do a search by geographic specialty on the Association of Professional Genealogists website at

```
www.apgen.org/directory/search.html?type=geo_specialty&new_search=true
```

Looking at directories and newspapers

If you have a general idea of where your family lived at a particular time but no conclusive proof, city and county directories and newspapers from the area may help. (Census records, which we discuss in Chapter 4, are quite helpful for this purpose, too.) Directories and newspapers can help you confirm whether your ancestors indeed lived in a particular area, and in some cases, they can provide even more information than you expect. A friend of ours has a great story — morbid as it is — that illustrates just this point. He was looking through newspapers for an obituary about one of his great-uncles. He knew when his great-uncle died but couldn't find mention of it in the obituary section of the newspaper. As he set the newspaper down (probably in despair), he glanced at the front page — only to find a graphic description of how a local man had been killed in a freak elevator accident. And guess who that local man was? That's right! He was our friend's great-uncle. The newspaper not only confirmed for him that his great-uncle lived there but also gave our friend a lot more information than he ever expected.

Directories

Like today's telephone books, the directories of yesteryear contained basic information about the persons who lived in particular areas, whether the areas were towns, cities, districts, or counties. Typically, the directory identified at least the head of the household and the location of the house. Some directories also included the names and ages of everyone in the household and occupations of any members of the household who were employed.

When looking for a city directory, make your first stop the City Directories of the United States of America at www.uscitydirectories.com. The intent of this site is to identify repositories of city directories online and offline and to guide you to them. Other sites can lead you to directories for particular geographic areas too. You can find a list of city directories available on microfilm at the Library of Congress for nearly 700 American towns and states through the U.S. City Directories on Microfilm in the Microform Reading Room web page (www.loc.gov/rr/microform/uscity). If you're looking for city directories for England and Wales, look at the Historical Directories site (http://cdm16445.contentdm.oclc.org/cdm/landingpage/collection/p16445coll14). The site contains digitized directories from 1750 to 1919. You can also often find lists of city directories on the websites of local and state libraries.

Some individuals have posted city directories in their areas. An example of this is the Fredericksburg, Virginia, City Directory 1938 page at http://resources.umwhisp.org/Fredericksburg/1938directory.htm.

Additionally, a commercial effort from Ancestry.com is re-creating the 1890 Census through city directories. For more information on this subscription-based site, see Chapter 1 or jump on over to the Ancestry.com website at

http://search.ancestry.com/group/1890census/1890_Census_
Substitute.aspx. Be sure to check out other subscription genealogy sites
to see what directories they may house.

For tips on using city directories, see the YouTube video produced by
Ancestry.com, at www.youtube.com/watch?v=8I5wDy_y4M4.

You can find a directory of sites housing historical directories at the Online
Historical Directories website at https://sites.google.com/site/
onlinedirectorysite.

Also, some genealogical and historical societies and associations have made a
commitment to post the contents of directories for their areas or at least an
index of what their libraries hold online so that you know before you contact
them whether they have something useful to you. Check out the section
"Genealogical and historical societies," earlier in this chapter, for more
information on how to find these organizations.

Newspapers

Unlike directories that list almost everyone in a community, newspapers are
helpful only if your ancestors did something newsworthy — but you'd be surprised at what was considered newsworthy in the past. Your ancestor didn't
necessarily have to be a politician or a criminal to get his or her picture and
story in the paper. Just like today, obituaries, birth and marriage announcements, public records of land transactions, advertisements, and gossip sections were all relatively common in newspapers of the past.

Historical newspapers are now finding their way online. Most of these sites
contain just partial collections of newspapers, but they may just have the
issue that contains information on your ancestor. The following are some of
the larger national collections:

- ✔ **Chronicling America** (http://chroniclingamerica.loc.gov), a
  free searchable site containing newspapers from 1836 to 1922

- ✔ **GenealogyBank** (www.genealogybank.com), a subscription site
  containing over 6,500 newspapers

- ✔ **Google News Newspapers** (http://news.google.com/newspapers),
  a free collection of newspapers from the United States and Canada

- ✔ **NewspaperArchive.com** (http://newspaperarchive.com), a
  subscription site with over 5,000 titles from the United States, Canada,
  and the United Kingdom

- ✔ **Newspapers.com** (www.newspapers.com), a subscription site containing
  digitized copies of over 1,700 newspapers from the United States

- ✔ **NewspapersSG** (http://newspapers.nl.sg), 200 Singapore and
  Malaya newspapers from 1831 to 2009

✔ **Papers Past** (`http://paperspast.natlib.govt.nz`), two million pages of New Zealand newspapers from 1839 to 1945

✔ **Trove** (`http://trove.nla.gov.au/newspaper`), a free site from the National Library of Australia that has digitized over ten million pages of newspapers

There are also some state collections, such as the following:

✔ **Arizona Digital Newspaper Program,** `http://adnp.azlibrary.gov`

✔ **California Digital Newspaper Collection,** `http://cdnc.ucr.edu/cgi-bin/cdnc`

✔ **Historic Oregon Newspapers,** `http://oregonnews.uoregon.edu`

✔ **Library of Virginia,** `http://virginiachronicle.com`

✔ **Missouri Digital Newspaper Project,** `http://shs.umsystem.edu/newspaper/mdnp`

✔ **New York Heritage Digital Collections,** `www.nyheritage.org/newspapers`

✔ **North Carolina Newspaper Digitization Project,** `www.archives.ncdcr.gov/newspaper/index.html`

✔ **Utah Digital Newspapers,** `http://digitalnewspapers.org`

✔ **Washington Historic Newspapers,** `www.sos.wa.gov/history/newspapers.aspx`

There is even a search engine that you can use to find items in digitized newspapers around the world. Elephind.com (`www.elephind.com`) indexes over 1,300 newspaper titles from Australia, New Zealand, Singapore, and the United States. Figure 7-10 shows a search result for "George Helm" on the site.

Localizing your search

To find a lot of detail about a specific area and what it was like during a particular timeframe, local histories are the answer. Local histories often contain information about when and how a particular place was settled and may have biographical information on earlier settlers or principal people within the community who sponsored the creation of the history.

Figure 7-10: Search results from Elephind .com.

Online local histories can be tucked away in geographically specific websites, historical society pages, library sites, and web-based bookstores. You can also find a few sites that feature local histories:

- ✔ Ancestry.com (`www.ancestry.com`) features several thousand works in its Stories, Memories, and Histories collection.

- ✔ A collection of Canadian local histories is available at Our Roots/Nos Racines (`www.ourroots.ca`).

- ✔ You can search by location and find a growing collection of local histories on Google Books (`http://books.google.com`).

- ✔ FamilySearch Family History Books collection (`https://books.familysearch.org`) contains local histories digitized from seven libraries.

- ✔ The Internet Archive (`http://archive.org`) contains digitized versions of thousands of local histories.

- ✔ The digital library at Hathi Trust (`www.hathitrust.org`) contains a vast collection of local histories. (See Figure 7-11.)

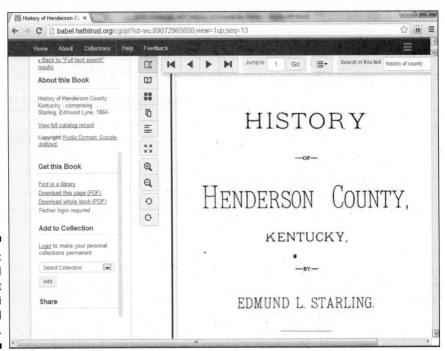

Figure 7-11:
A local
history at
the Hathi
Trust Digital
Library.

Chapter 8

Going Beyond Borders: International and Ethnic Records

At some point in your research, you'll encounter an ancestor who was born outside the United States (or before the U.S. was a country) or who is associated with a particular ethnicity that requires you to use a specific set of sources. These records often have characteristics that make them different from the typical records found in the U.S. Even if you can't find the actual records online (a lot of international records have been placed online over the past few years), certain sites can help identify what records are available in archives and how to use them to benefit your research. In this chapter, we look at strategies to find these resources online as well as provide links to some key sites to consult.

Fishing for International and Ethnic Sources

You can use a number of strategies when attempting to locate international and ethnic resources online. These strategies range from using genealogical wikis to search engines and comprehensive genealogical indexes.

Wiki-ing for answers

When beginning to research in a new geographical area, we always like to start by seeing what's available in that area at the FamilySearch Research Wiki (`https://familysearch.org/learn/wiki/en/Main_Page`). You can type the country or locality in the search box at the top of the page, or you can browse articles by country by clicking the links in the Find Records by Place box. Some of the topics contained in the articles are Getting Started with Research, Jurisdictions, Research Tools, Help Wanted (ways that users can contribute what they know about the country), Featured Content, and Did You Know? Embedded in the left-side navigation of an article are links to other articles that might be relevant to the country or geographical area, as shown in Figure 8-1.

Figure 8-1: The Netherlands topic on the FamilySearch Research Wiki.

You can also search for ethnic entries in the FamilySearch Research Wiki through the search box. Topics on ethnic articles might include Records and Databases, Related Web Sites, Help Near You, presentations regarding the ethnic group, Helpful Guides, FamilySearch Forums, Research Aids, Forms, FamilySearch Indexing Projects, and LDS Church Service Resources.

Surveying sites with comprehensive genealogy indexes

To get an idea of what's generally available online, a comprehensive genealogy index is always a good start. These indexes have the benefit of being genealogically focused, so you don't have to wade through a lot of links that aren't relevant to genealogy or history. Typically, these sites also categorize the links in such a way that you can get to what you're looking for in a few clicks.

For example, if you're interested in researching an ancestor who lived in the Netherlands, you could visit Cyndi's List (www.cyndislist.com), click "N" under Browse Categories, and select the Netherlands/Nederland link, and see links organized into 23 groups.

Using search engines

If you haven't found what you're looking for in a comprehensive genealogy index, your next stop should be a general search engine. Similar to searches for information on particular individuals, you need to ensure that your search criteria are fairly specific, or you risk receiving too many search results — most of which might be irrelevant to your search. For example, when we type the search term *Belgium genealogy,* we receive 3,520,000 results in Google and 852,000 results in Bing.

Search engines are a good resource when you're looking for information on records in a specific locality. So, instead of *Belgium genealogy,* if we use the search criteria *Hainaut baptism records,* we receive a fraction of the results.

WorldGenWeb

The WorldGenWeb Project (www.worldgenweb.org) contains links to websites for countries and areas in the world. To find a specific country, follow these steps:

1. **Go to the WorldGenWeb Project site (www.worldgenweb.org).**

   You see a page with a map and a list of resources along the left side of the page (below the map).

2. **Click the link to the Country Index under the Main Menu column.**

   For our example, we're looking for information on civil registrations in Jamaica.

3. **Click the link in the WorldGenWeb Region column for your target country.**

   We click the CaribbeanGenWeb link next to the entry for Jamaica. This link takes us to the region project page. In our case, the CaribbeanGenWeb page has three versions — in English, French, and Spanish. We choose the English version.

4. **From the region page, find a link to the countries represented in the project.**

   On the CaribbeanGenWeb page, we click the Island Links link located near the top of the page in the second column. If you didn't choose the same region, you have to find the appropriate link on your particular region page.

5. **Select the link to your country.**

   We click the Jamaica link, which takes us to the Genealogy of Jamaica page.

6. **Choose a link to a resource that interests you.**

   On the Genealogy of Jamaica home page, we find a list of available resources. We click the Civil Registration link, which displays the Civil Registrations of Jamaicans page, as shown in Figure 8-2.

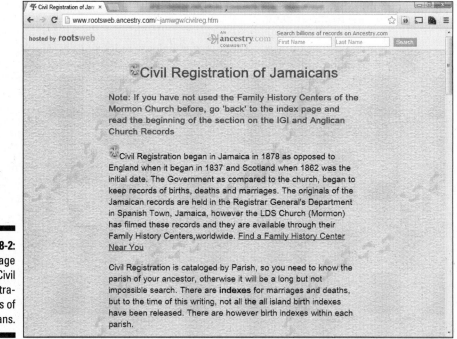

Figure 8-2:
Page
for Civil
Registra-
tions of
Jamaicans.

When researching your European roots, keep in mind that due to the number of European countries, no single European GenWeb Project site exists. Instead, you find the following four European region sites:

- **Ireland & United KingdomGenWeb** (www.iukgenweb.org/) contains projects for British Overseas Territories, Channel Islands, England, Ireland, Isle of Man, Northern Ireland, Scotland, and Wales.

- **CenEuroGenWeb** (www.worldgenweb.org/ceneurogenweb/) lists pages for Belgium, Denmark, Greenland, Germany, Iceland, Latvia, Liechtenstein, Lithuania, Luxembourg, Netherlands, Norway, Poland, Sweden, and Switzerland.

- **EastEuropeGenWeb** (www.rootsweb.ancestry.com/~easeurgw) contains sites for Albania, Austria, Belarus, Bosnia-Herzegovina, Bulgaria, Croatia, Czech Republic, Estonia, Finland, Hungary, Macedonia, Moldova, Montenegro, Romania, Russia, Serbia, Slovak Republic, Slovenia, Ukraine, and Yugoslavia.

- **MediterraneanGenWeb** (https://sites.google.com/site/mediterraneangenweb/) has project pages for Andorra, Azores, France, Gibraltar, Greece, Italy, Madeira, Malta, Monaco, Portugal, San Marino, Spain, and Vatican City.

Translating sites

Within this chapter (and when you search online), you'll encounter several sites in languages other than English. Due to advancements in translation websites and web browser translators, the fact that the site is in a different language doesn't mean that it's not useful in your research. The translation site Google Translate, at http://translate.google.com/, has the capability to translate a block of text, or you can enter a URL to translate an entire web page.

Rather than going to the Google Translate page each time we encounter a site in a foreign language, we prefer to have that functionality built into our browser. The Google Chrome browser (www.google.com/chrome/intl/en/landing_chrome.html?hl=en) has the Google Translate functionality built in. When you reach a site in a foreign language, the Translate toolbar appears and suggests the language that the site is authored in. It then asks whether you want the site translated. If you say yes, the page is translated — that is, the text that's not part of a graphic is translated. Although the translation isn't perfect, it's usually good enough to give you a good idea of the text's meaning.

Records from the English-Speaking World

Currently, the most prolific number of records available on the web are from countries with English as their native language. In the following sections, we look at records in the United Kingdom, Ireland, and Canada. For information specifically on census records for these countries, see Chapter 4.

Gathering information from England and Wales

To become familiar with records in England and Wales, visit the National Archives site (www.nationalarchives.gov.uk). By clicking the red circle entitled Menu at the top of the page, you can find a link to the Catalogues and Online Records page (under the Records column, about two-thirds of the way down the list), where you find links to the following resources:

- **Discovery — Our Catalogue** (formerly PROCAT) contains descriptions of 20 million documents generated by the government.

- **Digital microfilm** includes downloadable documents digitized by the National Archives, such as wills and medal index cards.

- **Library Catalogue** lists the works contained in the National Archives research library.

- **Taxation records** contains descriptions of documents that relate to medieval and early-modern tax records.

- **Trafalgar Ancestors database** includes records of everyone who served on the British side in the Battle of Trafalgar.

Birth, marriage, and death records

A number of online sources are available for transcribed and digitized documents. BMD Registers (www.bmdregisters.co.uk) features images of birth, baptism, marriage, and death records taken from nonparish sources from 1534 to 1865. You can conduct a search of its database; however, you must purchase credits before being able to view an image of the digitized document. The Genealogist (www.thegenealogist.co.uk), a subscription site, has a complete index of birth, marriage, and death records for England and Wales. If you're looking for free birth, marriage, and death records, see the FreeBMD project at www.freebmd.org.uk. This volunteer effort has transcribed more than 230 million records — although the collection is still not complete.

The subscription sites 1901CensusOnline.com (www.1901censusonline. com), Ancestry.uk (www.ancestry.co.uk), FindMyPast.co.uk (www. findmypast.co.uk), and Genes Reunited (www.genesreunited.co.uk) also have birth, marriage, and death records. For links to subscription and free birth, marriage, and death resources online, see the UK BMD site (www.ukbmd.org.uk).

Other records

A number of records (and pointers to records housed in archives) are available on both subscription and government sites. These sites include the following:

- ✔ **Access to Archives** (www.nationalarchives.gov.uk/a2a/) is a consortium of archives in England and Wales. The Access to Archives site features a database with descriptions of the holdings of 418 record offices and repositories.

- ✔ **British Origins** (www.britishorigins.com) includes the Dorset Marriage Index, a marriage license allegation index, wills indexes, probate indexes, apprenticeship records, court records, burial records, militia records, and passenger lists.

- ✔ **British Library — India Office Family History Search** (http:// indiafamily.bl.uk/UI) holds records of the government of pre-1949 India. The site features a bibliographical index that contains more than 300,000 entries.

- ✔ **Commonwealth War Graves Commission** (www.cwgc.org) is responsible for maintaining the 1.7 million graves of those who died in the two world wars. The CWGC website includes a searchable database under the Find War Dead menu, which provides basic information on those covered by the Commission.

- ✔ **General Register Office** (https://www.gov.uk/browse/births-deaths-marriages/register-offices) holds birth, marriage, and death records in England and Wales from July 1, 1837, up to one year ago. The GRO website details how to get copies of certificates and has some basic guides on researching genealogy.

- ✔ **Imperial War Museums** (www.iwm.org.uk) chronicles the wars of the twentieth century from 1914. Its website contains fact sheets on tracing ancestors who served in the armed forces and an inventory of war memorials.

- ✔ **National Library of Wales/Llyfrgell Genedlaethol Cymru** (www. llgc.org.uk/index.php?id=2) holds documents such as electoral lists, marriage bonds, probate and estate records, and tithe maps. The library's website contains a list of independent researchers, and you can search databases including an index to the gaol files (*gaol* is the British word for *jail*), applicants for marriage licenses, and descriptions of the library's archival holdings.

FamilySearch

The Historical Records Collections on the FamilySearch site (https://familysearch.org/search/collection/list#page=1&region=UNITED_KINGDOM_IRELAND) contains a variety of record sets for the Channel Islands, England, Isle of Man, and Wales. Some examples include

- Channel Islands, Births and Baptisms, 1820–1907
- England and Wales censuses
- English parish registers, probate records, tax assessments, and manorial documents
- Isle of Man, Marriages, 1849–1911

Ancestry.co.uk

Ancestry.co.uk (www.ancestry.co.uk) contains more than 1,500 databases related to records for the Channel Islands, England, Isle of Man, and Wales. The record groups are divided into

- Census and electoral rolls
- Birth, marriage, and death, including parish
- Military
- Immigration and Travel
- Newspapers and periodicals
- Pictures
- Stories, memories, and histories
- Maps, atlases, and gazetteers
- Schools, directories, and church histories
- Tax, criminal, land, and wills
- Reference, dictionaries, and almanacs
- Family trees

Finding help

To contact other genealogists interested in British genealogical research, see the Society of Genealogists (www.sog.org.uk). The site includes information on membership, publications, and the Society's online library catalog.

For societies at a local level, consult the list of members of the Federation of Family History Societies (www.ffhs.org.uk). The Federation's site includes information on its current projects and on upcoming events, as well as a set of subscription databases.

If you're not finding what you're looking for in one of the previously mentioned sites, your next stop should be the GENUKI: United Kingdom and Ireland Genealogy site, at `www.genuki.org.uk`. The GENUKI site is similar to the GenWeb sites (in fact, several of the GenWeb sites point to GENUKI content) in that it contains subsites for the various counties. You can find a variety of guides, transcribed records, and other useful data on the GENUKI sites.

If you need professional help, you can find a list of professional researchers at the Association of Genealogists and Researchers in Archives site at `www.agra.org.uk`. You can search for researchers by area of expertise, alphabetically, or by region where they are based.

A lot more than haggis — finding Scottish records

The ScotlandsPeople site (`www.scotlandspeople.gov.uk`) is the official government site for Scottish records. The subscription site contains statutory registers of births (1855–1910), marriages (1855–1937), and deaths (1855–1960); old parish registers of births and baptisms (1553–1854) and banns and marriages (1553–1854); census records (1841–1911); and wills and testaments (1513–1925).

Other sites that can assist you in tracking down Scottish ancestors follow:

- **General Register Office for Scotland** (`www.gro-scotland.gov.uk`) holds birth, marriage, divorce, adoption, and death records in Scotland from 1855. The GROS is also responsible for the periodic censuses for Scotland.

- **National Archives of Scotland** (`www.nas.gov.uk`) contains records of when Scotland was its own kingdom as well as those of modern Scotland. Records housed there include land transfers, records of the Church of Scotland parishes, estate papers, court papers, and taxation lists. Both the National Archives of Scotland and the General Register Office for Scotland merged to form the National Records of Scotland. You can find the site for the merged organization at `www.nrscotland.gov.uk`.

- **Scottish Archive Network** (`www.scan.org.uk`) is a joint project between the National Archives of Scotland, the Heritage Lottery Fund, and the Genealogical Society of Utah. The project has placed the holdings of 52 Scottish archives into an online catalog and has digitized more than 2 million records.

✔ **Scottish Genealogy Society** (www.scotsgenealogy.com) provides assistance for individuals researching their Scottish roots. The website contains information on the Society's library, classes, and annual conference.

✔ **Scottish Register of Tartans** (www.tartanregister.gov.uk), part of the National Archives of Scotland, houses a repository of tartans. On the website, you can search for tartans by name and view an image of the material.

Researching the north o' Ireland

If you're looking for ancestors in Northern Ireland (specifically, the counties of Antrim, Armagh, Down, Fermanagh, Londonderry, and Tyrone), you have a few places to check. The Public Record Office of Northern Ireland, or PRONI (www.proni.gov.uk), holds items such as estate, church, business, valuation and tithe, school, and wills records. The website includes online databases that contain signatories to the Ulster Covenant, freeholders records, street directories, and will calendars. You can also find guides to some of the more popular collections at PRONI on its Online Guides and Indexes page at www.proni.gov.uk/index/research_and_records_held/catalogues_guides_indexes_and_leaflets/online_guides_and_indexes.htm.

The General Register Office for Northern Ireland (www.nidirect.gov.uk/gro) maintains registrations of births, stillbirths, adoptions, deaths, marriages, and civil partnerships. The website contains summaries of these record types and a family history guide that can assist you with your research in Northern Ireland at www.nidirect.gov.uk/news-aug13-researching-your-family-history-online.

Also, take a look at the North of Ireland Family History Society site (www.nifhs.org). The site contains details on the Society's Research Centre, branches, publications, and meeting calendar. For books on genealogy in Northern Ireland and for research services, see the web page for the Ulster Historical Foundation at www.ancestryireland.com. This site also contains pay-per-view and members-only online databases, including indexes to birth, marriage, and death records for County Antrim and County Down, index to the 1796 Flaxgrowers Bounty List, directories, sporadic census and education records, emigration records, wills, election records, and estate records.

Emerald Ancestors (www.emeraldancestors.com) maintains subscription databases on more than 1 million ancestors from Northern Ireland, including birth, marriage, death, and census records. For free resources, see the

Northern IrelandGenWeb site at www.rootsweb.ancestry.com/~nirwgw. The site contains a resource listing and links to a variety of helpful online resources. The Ireland page on GENUKI also contains links to resources in the counties of Northern Ireland at www.genuki.org.uk/big/irl. To find a professional genealogist, consult the Society of Genealogists Northern Ireland website at www.sgni.net.

Because some of the resources overlap between Northern Ireland and Ireland, you might also look at some of the resources described in the following section.

Traversing the Emerald Isle

As we mention in the previous section, the GENUKI site (www.genuki.org.uk) contains information on a variety of geographic areas in the United Kingdom and Ireland. You see pages for all 32 counties of Ireland, and you can find brief articles on a variety of topics, including cemeteries, censuses, church records, civil registrations, court records, emigration and immigration, land and property, newspapers, probate records, and taxation. You can also find county pages at the Genealogy Projects in Ireland site (http://irelandgenealogyprojects.rootsweb.ancestry.com) and the Ireland Genealogy Project and Ireland Genealogy Project Archives at www.igp-web.com.

To get an overview of Irish genealogy, take a look at the Directory of Irish Genealogy at http://homepage.eircom.net/~seanjmurphy/dir. In particular, look at A Primer in Irish Genealogy, available as a link at the top of the site's home page. You can also find information on genealogy courses and articles on Irish genealogy on this site. On the parent page to this site, the Centre for Irish Genealogical and Historical Studies (http://homepage.tinet.ie/~seanjmurphy), you find guides to the National Archives of Ireland and the General Register Office of Ireland. Ancestry.co.uk also contains some records for Ireland. See the previous section for more on the types of records available on the site.

Other Irish genealogy resources

A few sites contain databases and transcriptions of Irish records of interest to genealogists. Irish Family Research (www.irishfamilyresearch.co.uk) contains both free and subscription content, including a directory of headstones, electoral registers, city directories, Griffith's Valuation, hearth rolls, school records, and a variety of other sources. The Department of Arts, Heritage, and the Gaeltacht sponsors the Irish Genealogy site (www.irishgenealogy.ie/en/), which contains an index of church records and provides tips for planning a research trip to Ireland.

In addition to census records, the National Archives of Ireland (`www.nationalarchives.ie`) houses other records of interest to researchers, including Tithe Applotment Books and Griffith's Valuation, wills, estate records, private source records, parish records and marriage licenses, and Crown and Peace records. Tithe Applotment Books for the years 1823 to 1837 are available online at `http://titheapplotmentbooks.nationalarchives.ie/search/tab/home.jsp`.

If you're looking for maps, check out Past Homes (`www.pasthomes.com`), which has a subscription site with Irish townland maps. The maps on the site were surveyed between 1829 and 1843. The Irish Family History Foundation hosts an online database of 20 million records, including birth, marriage, and death records, at its RootsIreland.ie site (`www.rootsireland.ie`). The Foundation also provides research services for a fee. Additional online databases can be found at the Irish Origins site (`www.irishorigins.com`). The site includes census, electoral register, marriage, will, burial, military, passenger list, and directory records.

At some point, you may need help with a specific area in Ireland. One site that may help is Ireland Roots at `www.irelandroots.com`. The site features message boards for each Irish county, where you can post queries about your family or questions about research in that particular county. If you need professional assistance, take a look at the Association of Professional Genealogists in Ireland site at `www.apgi.ie`. The Association establishes standards for its members to help ensure quality research. The website includes a member directory listing its areas of specialization.

Heading north for Canadian records

So you want to research your ancestors from Canada, eh? Well, a place to start is the Genealogy and Family History page (`www.collectionscanada.gc.ca/genealogy/index-e.html`), maintained by Library and Archives Canada. The site contains information for beginners, including what to do first and search strategies for a variety of record types.

In the Guides section, see the online version of the Tracing Your Ancestors in Canada brochure (`www.collectionscanada.gc.ca/genealogy/022-607.001-e.html`), if you're new to Canadian resources. Also, at the top of the Genealogy on Family History web page, you can find a search engine that provides results for the databases maintained by Library and Archives Canada.

To get an idea of what online resources are available for Canadian research, some genealogical link sites specialize in Canada. These include CanGenealogy (`www.cangenealogy.com`) and Canadian Genealogy Resources (`www.canadiangenealogy.net`).

Local resources

For resources on a more local basis, go to the CanadaGenWeb Project site at
www.rootsweb.ancestry.com/~canwgw. The project site includes links
to genealogical sites, research queries, lookups, and a timeline. You also
find a branch of the site oriented to kids at www.rootsweb.ancestry.
com/~cangwkid. The following provinces also have a GenWeb Project page:

- ✔ **Alberta:** www.rootsweb.ancestry.com/~canab/

- ✔ **British Columbia:** www.rootsweb.ancestry.com/~canbc

- ✔ **Manitoba:** www.rootsweb.ancestry.com/~canmb/index.htm

- ✔ **New Brunswick:** www.rootsweb.ancestry.com/~cannb

- ✔ **Newfoundland/Labrador:** www.rootsweb.ancestry.com/~cannf/
  index.html

- ✔ **Nova Scotia:** www.rootsweb.ancestry.com/~canns/index.html

- ✔ **Northwest Territories and Nunavut:** www.rootsweb.ancestry.
  com/~cannt

- ✔ **Ontario:** www.geneofun.on.ca/ongenweb

- ✔ **Québec:** www.rootsweb.ancestry.com/~canqc/index.htm

- ✔ **Saskatchewan:** www.rootsweb.ancestry.com/~cansk/

- ✔ **Yukon:** www.rootsweb.ancestry.com/~canyk

Although Acadia is not a province, you can also find an Acadian GenWeb site
at http://acadian-genweb.acadian-home.org/frames.html.

Other records and resources

The Library and Archives Canada site (www.collectionscanada.gc.ca/
genealogy/index-e.html) not only has images of census records, but
also houses images of the following records:

- ✔ Chinese Immigration Registers, 1887–1908

- ✔ Canadians in the South African War, 1899–1902

- ✔ Attestation Papers of Soldiers of the First World War, 1914–1918

- ✔ Upper Canada and Canada West Naturalization Records, 1828–1850

- ✔ Ward Chipman, Muster Master's Office, 1777–1785 (Loyalist registers)

- ✔ Immigrants from the Russian Empire

- ✔ Canadian Patents, 1869–1894

- ✔ Passenger Lists, 1865–1935

The Ancestry.ca subscription site maintains a variety of record sets, including census and voter lists; birth, marriage, and death records; military records; newspapers; maps and gazetteers; school and church histories; tax records; and wills.

When it comes time to do some on-site research, you can look at the directory of archives at the Canadian Council of Archives. The website search interface (`www.cdncouncilarchives.ca/directory_adv.html`) allows you to search by an archive name or by province. The information on the site includes an overview of the collections of each archive along with its hours of operation. To get more detailed information on the holdings in various archives across Canada, consult the ArchivesCanada.ca site (`www. archivescanada.ca/english/index.html`) — part of the Canadian Archival Information Network (CAIN). You can use a single search form to search by keyword for descriptions of collections, or you can use a separate form to find online exhibits. For published items held in the Library and Archives Canada and more than 1,300 other Canadian libraries, you can search the AMICUS national catalog at `http://amicus.collectionscanada. gc.ca/aaweb/aalogine.htm`. To make things even easier to find, the Library and Archives Canada has created a search engine that brings together several resources to make searching for genealogical data easier. The That's My Family site (`www.thatsmyfamily.info`) features a search form that allows you to specify what resources you want to search (either federal or by individual provinces) by keyword. Figure 8-3 shows the results page for a search on the surname Helm.

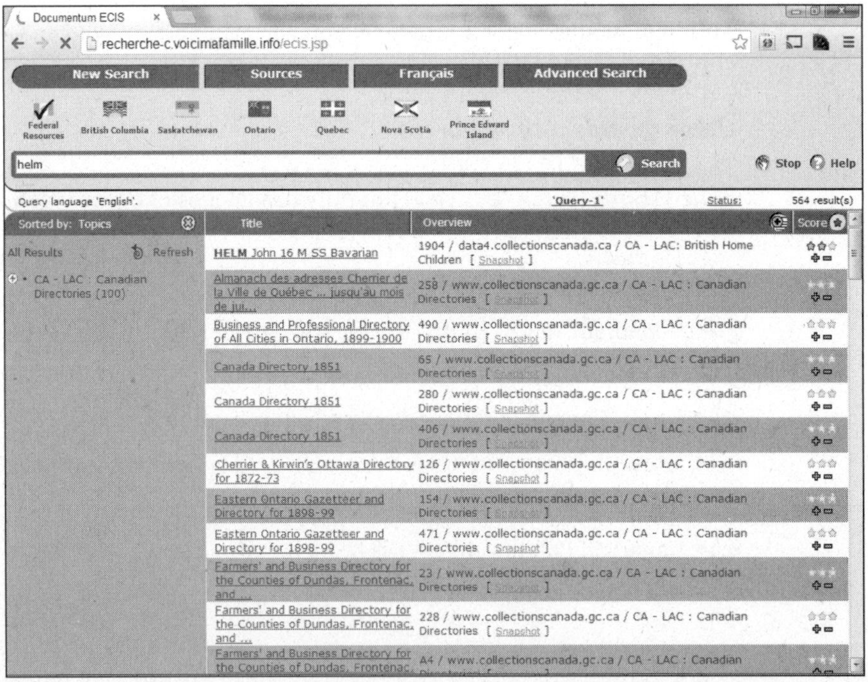

Figure 8-3:
The search results for Helm at That's My Family.

A number of sites contain abstracts of Canadian records. Olive Tree Genealogy (`www.olivetreegenealogy.com`) has free databases of ship and passenger lists, civil registrations, and cemetery records. For pointers to military records, you can search the catalog of the Canadian War Museum at `http://catalogue.warmuseum.ca/musvw/Vubis.csp?Profile=Profile`. This catalog contains entries (and in some cases abstracts) for textual and photographic records.

FamilySearch has a freely searchable International Genealogical Index (`https://familysearch.org/search/collection/igi`) that contains data extracted from various original records — such as birth, christening, death, burial, and marriage dates. The Search page contains indexes to many collections, including the following:

- British Columbia Birth, Marriage, and Death Registrations
- Canada Births and Baptisms, 1661–1959
- Canada Marriages, 1661–1949
- New Brunswick Census, 1861
- Nova Scotia Antigonish Catholic Diocese, 1823–1905
- Quebec Catholic Parish Registers, 1621–1979 (browsable images only)

If your family immigrated to Canada between 1928 and 1971, take a look at the Pier 21 Immigration Museum site (`www.pier21.ca`). The site gives a brief overview of the function of Pier 21 and information on the research services available on the site. It also has a ship arrivals database that covers the years 1928 to 1971. From 1869 to 1948, more than 100,000 British children were sent to Canada as laborers until they reached the age of 21. A site dedicated to these children is the Canadian Centre for Home Children, at `www.canadianhomechildren.ca`. A searchable database of Home Children is on the Library and Archives Canada site at `www.collectionscanada.gc.ca/databases/home-children/001015-100.01-e.php`.

Not able to travel to a distant cemetery in Canada to see the headstone of your ancestor? Then visit the Canadian Headstone Photo Project (`www.canadianheadstones.com`) to see whether someone has already snapped a photo or transcribed the headstone. This site currently boasts more than 716,000 photos from across Canada.

While searching through records, you may run into a place name that you don't recognize. The Atlas of Canada (`http://atlas.nrcan.gc.ca/site/english/index.html`) at the Natural Resources Canada site contains a variety of geographical resources including a place-name finder, satellite maps, and topographical maps. For a searchable database of Canadian geographical names, see the Canadian Geographical Names Data Base page at `www4.rncan.gc.ca/search-place-names/name.php`. If you want a historical perspective on the geography of Canada, look at the Historical Atlas of Canada project at `www.historicalatlas.ca/website/hacolp`.

Getting help

If you're looking for local genealogical experts, you can turn to a number of genealogical societies in Canada. An example is the Alberta Family Histories Society (www.afhs.ab.ca). The site includes the monthly schedule of meetings, publications for sale, document transcriptions, research aids, queries, and information about the society library.

Because Canada has a history of immigration of a number of different ethnicities, you might also check to see whether a site is dedicated to the ethnic group that you're researching. For example, the Chinese-Canadian Genealogy site (www.vpl.ca/ccg), maintained by the Vancouver Public Library, contains information on the early Chinese immigrations, Chinese name characteristics, biographic resources, and a survey of the types of record sets associated with the Canadian Chinese population.

Accessing Australian sources

The Australian Family History Compendium (http://afhc.cohsoft.com.au/) offers information on societies, archives, and a wider range of record types, as well as maps and a glossary.

A transcription of the convicts on Australia's first three fleets and the Irish convicts that came to New South Wales from 1788 to 1849 is located at http://members.pcug.org.au/~pdownes.

The Heraldry and Genealogy Society of Canberra maintains a database of Australian memorials of Australians in the Boer War (1899–1902) at www.hagsoc.org.au/sagraves/abwmdb/abwm-search.php. The Metropolitan Cemeteries Board of Western Australia has a database of internments in five cemeteries at http://www2.mcb.wa.gov.au/NameSearch/search.php.

The Donegal Relief Fund site (http://freepages.genealogy.rootsweb.ancestry.com/~donegal/relief.htm) includes a description of the background of the relief fund, passenger lists, and subscription lists for those who donated to the fund. A searchable index of birth, marriage, and death records for New South Wales is available at www.bdm.nsw.gov.au/.

Ancestry.com.au (www.ancestry.com.au) features more than 150 databases of use in Australian research. Examples of databases on the site include

- ✔ Australia, Electoral Rolls, 1903–1980
- ✔ Victoria, Australia, Assisted and Unassisted Passenger Lists, 1839–1923
- ✔ Sands Directories: Sydney and New South Wales, Australia, 1858–1933
- ✔ Rockingham, Western Australia, School Indexes, 1830–1970

Hispanic and Portuguese Roots

A growing number of genealogists are researching their Hispanic and Portuguese roots. If you have these ancestors, you can use several types of records to pursue your genealogy, depending on when your ancestor immigrated.

If your ancestor immigrated in the nineteenth or twentieth century, look for vital records, military records, photographs, passports, church records, passenger lists, naturalization papers, diaries, or other items that can give you an idea of the birthplace of your ancestor. For those ancestors who immigrated before the nineteenth century, you may want to consult Spanish or Portuguese Colonial records after you exhaust any local records in the region where your ancestor lived.

If you're interested in general conversation on Hispanic genealogy, see the Hispanic Genealogy blog at hispanicgenealogy.blogspot.com.

For more information on researching Hispanic records, see the following:

- ✔ *The Source: A Guidebook of American Genealogy,* Third Edition, edited by Loretto Dennis Szucs and Sandra Hargreaves Luebking (Ancestry, Inc.). In particular, see Chapter 17, "Hispanic Research," written by George R. Ryskamp. You can find this online at www.ancestry.com/wiki/index.php?title=Overview_of_Hispanic_Research.

- ✔ *Hispanic Family History Research in a L.D.S. Family History Center,* written by George R. Ryskamp (Hispanic Family History Research).

Within the United States

Individuals of Hispanic descent have been in the present-day U.S. since St. Augustine was founded in 1565. Consult some of the following helpful resources when conducting research on your Spanish-speaking ancestors:

- ✔ **Hispanic Genealogy Center** (www.hispanicgenealogy.com): Maintained by the Hispanic Genealogical Society of New York, the site contains information on Society events and publications, including the newsletter *Nuestra Herencia* and the Hispanic Genealogy Workbook.

- ✔ **Hispanic Genealogical Society of Houston** (www.hispanicgs.org): The Society maintains a list of online resources for Hispanic research.

- **Hispanic Genealogical Research Center of New Mexico** (`www.hgrc-nm.org`)**:** The Center maintains the Great New Mexico Pedigree Database and publishes the journal *Herencia*.

- **Society of Hispanic Historical and Ancestral Research** (`http://shhar.net`)**:** The Society is based in Orange County, California, and publishes the online newsletter *Somos Primos*.

- **Puerto Rican/Hispanic Genealogical Society** (`www.rootsweb.ancestry.com/~prhgs`)**:** The site contains a transcription of the 1935 Census of Puerto Rico and a query page.

- **Colorado Society of Hispanic Genealogy** (`www.hispanicgen.org`)**:** The Society hosts a list of links and information in its publication *Colorado Hispanic Genealogist*.

- **La Genealogia de Puerto Rico** (`www.rootsweb.ancestry.com/~prwgw/index.html`)**:** The site contains a number of resources, including message boards, surname databases, links to personal pages, microfilm index, and a partial transcription of the 1910 census.

If you are going to Puerto Rico for research, you might consider visiting the websites of the Archivo General de Puerto Rico and the Biblioteca Nacional (`www.puertadetierra.info/edificios/archivo/archivo.htm`) for information on their holdings.

Exploring south of the border: Mexican sources

To get your feet wet with resources from Mexico, take a look at the FamilySearch Research Wiki at `https://wiki.familysearch.org/en/Mexico`. You can find a primer on tracing your ancestors on the Mexico Genealogy 101 page at the About.com genealogy site (`http://genealogy.about.com/od/mexico/a/records.htm`).

The following are some sites related to genealogy in Mexico:

- **Baja California:** `www.californiagenealogy.org/labaja`

- **Durango:** `www.rootsweb.ancestry.com/~mexdur/Durango.html`

- **Morelos:** `www.rootsweb.ancestry.com/~mexmorel/Morelos.html`

- **San Luis Potosí:** `www.rootsweb.ancestry.com/~mexsanlu`

- **Sonora:** `homepages.rootsweb.ancestry.com/~windmill/sonora`

- **Tabasco:** `www.rootsweb.ancestry.com/~mextab`

The Genealogy of Mexico site (http://garyfelix.tripod.com/index1.htm) features several sets of transcribed records, including lists of individuals who accompanied Cortez, early entrants into New Spain, surnames contained in literature on Mexico, and a DNA project.

FamilySearch (https://familysearch.org/search/collection/list#page=1&region=MEXICO) has also begun placing online records related to Mexico, including the following:

- Baja California and Baja California Sur, Catholic Church Records, 1750–1984
- Mexico, Colima, Civil Registration, 1860–1997
- Mexico, National Census, 1930
- Mexico, San Luis Potosí, Miscellaneous Records, 1570–1876

Transcribed records are also available on sites that focus on Hispanic ancestors. For example, you can view transcribed records from the 1750 and 1753 censuses of the village of Guerrero at www.hispanicgs.com/census.html.

Continental resources

Eventually, your research may take you across the Atlantic, back to the Iberian Peninsula to Spain or Portugal. If you're researching Spain, stop by the Genealogía Española–España GenWeb site at www.genealogia-es.com. The site contains an introduction to research, links to surname databases, and links to provincial web pages. The Asociación de Genealogía Hispana (www.hispagen.es) also maintains a website dedicated to helping those who are researching their Spanish roots.

For official records, point your web browser to the Portal de Archivos Españoles site at http://pares.mcu.es. The portal is designed to point to resources housed in many different national and local archives. A large project housed on the site is the Ibero-American Migratory Movements Portal (http://pares.mcu.es/MovimientosMigratorios/staticContent.form?viewName=presentacion). The goal of the project is to provide access to information on individuals who emigrated from Spain to Central America in modern times. The project is a partnership between the Archivo General de la Administración de España, Archivo General de la Nación de México, Archivo General de la Nación de la República Dominicana, and Archivo Nacional de la República de Cuba.

FamilySearch (https://familysearch.org/search/collection/list#page=1&countryId=1927167) has placed online 40 collections of records relating to Spain. Some of these collections include digitized images. Examples from the collection are

- ✔ Catholic Church Records, 1500–1930

- ✔ Consular Records of Emigrants, 1808–1960

- ✔ Province of Cádiz, Passports, 1810–1866

- ✔ Province of León, Municipal Records, 1642–1897

Portuguese official records are housed in a network of national and 16 regional archives coordinated by the Direção Geral de Arquivos (`http://dgarq.gov.pt`). The organizations are cooperating in the construction of the Portal Português de Arquivos at `http://portal.arquivos.pt`. The Portal is designed to allow keyword searches of all the collections of the participating archives. Another resource to check out is the Biblioteca Nacional de Portugal (`www.bnportugal.pt`). For a more focused search on genealogy, you may want to search the catalogs on the Biblioteca Genealogica de Lisboa website, at `www.biblioteca-genealogica-lisboa.org`.

FamilySearch (`https://familysearch.org/search/collection/list#page=1&countryId=1927058`) contains more than 30 collections of databases and digitized records relating to Portugal. Some sample collections include

- ✔ Aveiro, Passport Registers, 1882–1965

- ✔ Braga, Priest Application Files (Genere et Moribus), 1596–1911

- ✔ Coimbra, Civil Registration, 1893–1980

- ✔ Vila Real, Diocesan Records, 1575–1992

Those with Basque ancestors may find the resources at the Basque Genealogy Homepage (`http://home.earthlink.net/~fybarra/index.html`) useful. You find a list of surnames contained within the author's database and information on fee-based research services.

Central and South American research

Research in Central and South America has been a rapidly growing area recently. The following resources, broken down by country, should help you along your way:

- ✔ **Argentina:** The Archivo General de la Nación (`www.mininterior.gov.ar/archivo/archivo.php?idName=arc&idNameSubMenu=&idNameSubMenuDer=`) and the Instituto de Estudios Genealógicos y Heráldicos de la

Provincia de Buenos Aires (`www.genproba.com.ar`) are places to get an idea of records available for Argentina. FamilySearch (`https://familysearch.org/search/collection/list#page=1&countryId=1927135`) offers a growing collection of records from Argentina including Catholic Church records, national censuses, and marriage records.

✔ **Brazil:** BrazilGenWeb (`www.rootsweb.ancestry.com/~brawgw`) has a how-to guide and links to individual Brazilian states. To see records available in Brazil, visit the Arquivo Nacional website (`www.arquivonacional.gov.br`). FamilySearch (`https://familysearch.org/search/collection/list#page=1&countryId=1927159`) hosts nearly 30 collections including Catholic Church records, civil registrations, immigration cards, and burial records.

✔ **Belize:** The BelizeGenWeb page (`www.worldgenweb.org/index.php/north-america/belize`) has a few links to general resources. The website for the Belize Archives and Records Service, at `www.archives.gov.bz/`, contains some general information on accessing records.

✔ **Bolivia:** You can get general information on the national archives at the Archivo y Biblioteca Nacionales site at `www.archivoybibliotecanacionales.org.bo/abnb/index.php`. A few collections exist for Bolivia at FamilySearch (`https://familysearch.org/search/collection/list#page=1&countryId=1927158`). Records include baptism, Catholic Church records, deaths, and marriages.

✔ **Chile:** A site with several compiled genealogies of Chilean families is the Genealogía de Chile site, at `http://genealog.cl`. See the web page for the Archivos y Museos (`www.dibam.cl/Vistas_Publicas/publicHome/homePublic.aspx?idInstitucion=67`) for Chilean records. A small number of Chilean records are available at FamilySearch (`https://familysearch.org/search/collection/list#page=1&countryId=1927143`) including baptism, civil registration, death, marriage, and cemetery records.

✔ **Columbia:** The website for the Columbian Archivo General de la Nación is located at `www.archivogeneral.gov.co`. The site explains the system of archives both at the national and local level and has a catalog of its holdings. Columbian records are available on FamilySearch at `https://familysearch.org/search/collection/list#page=1&countryId=1927162`. The collections include baptism, Catholic Church records, death, marriage, and military records.

✔ **Costa Rica:** The GenWeb page for Costa Rica is located at `www.worldgenweb.org/index.php/north-america/costa-rica`, and the web page for the Archivo Nacional de Costa Rica is at `www.archivonacional.go.cr`. Costa Rican records are available on FamilySearch at `https://familysearch.org/search/collection/list#page=1&countryId=1927128`.

✔ **Cuba:** You can find links to Cuban genealogical resources at the CubaGenWeb.org website (`www.cubagenweb.org`). The site contains a passenger list database and links to personal sites on the web with Cuban family trees. To find records in Cuba, see the website for the Archivo Nacional de la República de Cuba (`www.arnac.cu`).

✔ **Dominican Republic:** República Dominicana en el proyecto CaribbeanGenWeb (`www.rootsweb.ancestry.com/~domwgw/mhhbcgw.htm`) contains a few links to resources for the Dominican Republic. Records for the country are held at the Archivo General de la Nación (`http://agn.gov.do`). FamilySearch (`https://familysearch.org/search/collection/list#page=1&countryId=1927011`) contains some databases related to the Dominican Republic. The collections include baptism, Catholic Church records, death, marriage, and civil registration records.

✔ **Ecuador:** Discover more about records in Ecuador at the Archivo Nacional de Ecuador site, at `www.ane.gob.ec/`. Records from Ecuador are available on FamilySearch at `https://familysearch.org/search/collection/list#page=1&countryId=1927138`.

✔ **El Salvador:** El Salvadoran records are available on FamilySearch.org at `https://familysearch.org/search/collection/list#page=1&countryId=1927124`.

✔ **Guatemala:** See the Archivo General de Centro América page (`www.archivogeneraldecentroamerica.com`) for general information on available records. Guatemalan records are available on FamilySearch.org at `https://familysearch.org/search/collection/list#page=1&countryId=1927125`. In addition to baptism, church, marriage, and death records, you can also find the Guatemala City census of 1877 at the site.

✔ **Haiti:** The Généalogie d'Haiti et de Saint-Domingue, at `www.rootsweb.ancestry.com/~htiwgw`, contains information on the history and geography of the country. It also has links to other Haiti resources. For further information, see L'Association de Généalogie d'Haïti (`www.agh.qc.ca`). FamilySearch has some digital images of civil registrations available at `https://familysearch.org/search/collection/list#page=1&countryId=1927183`.

✔ **Honduras:** Some basic information is available on the HondurasGenWeb project page at `www.worldgenweb.org/index.php/north-america/honduras`. You can find baptism and marriage records as well as digital images of civil registrations on the FamilySearch.org site at `https://familysearch.org/search/collection/list#page=1&countryId=1927126`.

✔ **Nicaragua:** The GenWeb page for Nicaragua is at `www.rootsweb.ancestry.com/~nicwgw`. A brief description of the Archivo General de la Nación can be found at `www.inc.gob.ni/index.php?option=com_content&task=view&id=14&Itemid=29`. Nicaraguan records such as civil registrations and digital images of Catholic Church records are available on FamilySearch at `https://familysearch.org/search/collection/list#page=1&countryId=1927127`.

✔ **Panama:** Some brief information on the National Archives is available at the Archivo Nacional de Panamá site, at `www.archivonacional.gob.pa/arte.htm`. You can find records for baptisms, deaths, marriages, and digital images of Catholic Church records on FamilySearch at `https://familysearch.org/search/collection/list#page=1&countryId=1927175`.

✔ **Paraguay:** Information on the holdings of the Archivo Nacional de Asunción is available at `http://archivonacionaldeasuncion.org/Bienvenida.html`. Records for baptisms and marriages, plus digital images of cemetery records and Catholic Church records are available on FamilySearch at `https://familysearch.org/search/collection/list#page=1&countryId=1927141`.

✔ **Peru:** For records regarding Peru, see the Archivo General de la Nación site, at `www.agn.gob.pe/portal/`. Thirteen Peruvian record collections are available on FamilySearch (`https://familysearch.org/search/collection/list#page=1&countryId=1927168`) including digital images of civil registrations and Catholic Church records.

✔ **Uruguay:** You can find an overview of records for Uruguay at the Archivo General de la Nación page (`www.agn.gub.uy`). Baptism and marriage records are available on FamilySearch at `https://familysearch.org/search/collection/list#page=1&countryId=1927142`.

✔ **Venezuela:** Information on the Archivo General de la Nación can be found at `http://agn.gob.ve`. FamilySearch contains some digital images of Catholic Church records and civil registrations at `https://familysearch.org/search/collection/list#page=1&countryId=1927137`.

Swimming through Caribbean genealogy

To be successful in researching Caribbean genealogy, you have to be aware of the history of the particular island that you're researching. Some islands have a variety of record sets that may differ significantly depending on what country was in control of the island.

A place to start your research is the CaribbeanGenWeb Project page, at `www.rootsweb.ancestry.com/~caribgw`. The project is an umbrella site for each of the individual islands that have their own project pages. The site contains a list of the transcribed data sets held within the CaribbeanGenWeb Archives portion of the project, along with a global search engine for searching those data sets, descriptions of the mailing lists available for each island, links to surname resources, and some research tips. The individual island pages include

- ✔ **Antigua and Barbuda:** www.rootsweb.ancestry.com/~atgwgw
- ✔ **Bahamas:** www.rootsweb.ancestry.com/~bhswgw
- ✔ **Bermuda:** www.rootsweb.ancestry.com/~bmuwgw/bermuda.htm
- ✔ **Jamaica:** www.rootsweb.ancestry.com/~jamwgw/index.htm
- ✔ **St. Kitts and Nevis:** www.tc.umn.edu/~terre011/genhome.html
- ✔ **St. Vincent & the Grenadines:** www.rootsweb.ancestry.com/~vctwgw
- ✔ **Trinidad and Tobago:** www.rootsweb.ancestry.com/~ttowgw
- ✔ **U.S. Virgin Islands:** www.rootsweb.ancestry.com/~usvi

You can also find information on some islands on the GenWeb Project page of the mother country. For example, Guadeloupe and Martinique genealogical data can be found on the FranceGenWeb Project page at www.francegenweb.org/~sitesdgw/outremer. Another resource for the French islands is the Généalogie et Histoire de la Caraïbe (www.ghcaraibe.org). The site contains some transcribed records and articles on the history of the area.

If you have a question about a specific individual, you can post a query on the Caribbean Surname Index (CARSURDEX) at www.candoo.com/surnames/index.php. The site has message boards based on the first letter of the surname and has research specialty boards for the French West Indies, Dutch West Indies, and Spanish West Indies.

FamilySearch (www.familysearch.org/search/collection/list#page=1&region=CENTRAL_SOUTH_AMERICA) also has some records for use in tracing Caribbean lines.

Auchtung! Using Sites for the German-Speaking World

As German-speaking peoples have migrated to several places in Europe, as well as to the U.S., you could very well encounter an ancestor of German descent. German Roots (www.germanroots.com) contains a variety of information to help you get started in researching your German roots. It contains a directory of websites, a basic research guide, and links to articles on record sets that are useful in completing your research.

To get a bird's-eye view of available German genealogical sites, a good place to start is Genealogy.net (`www.genealogy.net/genealogy.html`). The site includes home pages for German genealogical societies, general information on research, a gazetteer, a ships database, a passenger database, and a list of links to websites. Ahnenforschung.net (`http://ahnenforschung.net`) is a German-language site containing tips for genealogists and discussion forums on a number of topics.

Along the beautiful Danube: Austrian roots

A place to begin your Austrian journey is the Austrian Genealogy Pages (`www.rootsweb.ancestry.com/~autwgw`). The site contains some general information on Austria as well as links to Austrian resources. From the home page of this site, you can access links to the provinces of Austria. These links are divided into two types — provinces of modern Austria (since 1918) and areas of the Austrian Empire and Austro-Hungarian Empire (until 1918). Areas listed under the second group are covered in other GenWeb projects, such as KüstenlandGenWeb, CzechGenWeb, RomanianGenWeb, UkraineGenWeb, SloveniaGenWeb, CroatiaGenWeb, PolishGenWeb, ItalianGenWeb, and FranceGenWeb.

If you're looking for help with your Austrian research, check out the Familia Austria website (`www.familia-austria.at`) maintained by the Österreichische Gesellschaft für Genealogie und Geschichte. The site contains links to a variety of Austrian resources, including maps, cemetery databases, and a wiki covering many topics related to individual provinces. It also has databases developed by the Association, including a family name finder; a birth, marriage, and death index for Wiener Zeitung; a marriage index before 1784; and directories of individuals holding particular occupations.

To get information on records available in the national archives, see the Austrian State Archives page, at `www.oesta.gv.at/DesktopDefault.aspx?alias=oestaen&init`. Another site to visit is the Österreichische Nationalbibliothek (National Library), at `www.onb.ac.at/ev/index.php`. If you need professional help, you might look at the Historiker Kanzlei research firm (`www.historiker.at`), which specializes in Austrian research.

FamilySearch (`https://familysearch.org/search/collection/list#page=1&countryId=1927070`) contains more than a dozen collections centered on Austria. These include digital images of military records, Lutheran Church records, citizen rolls, death certificates, and Jewish registers of births, marriages, and deaths.

Consulting German resources

The Germany GenWeb Project site (www.rootsweb.ancestry.com/
~wggerman) has a few resources such as maps and links to other sites.
The German Genealogy Group (www.germangenealogygroup.com) was
formed to help individuals research their German roots. The website contains
descriptions on the various databases that the Group maintains and some
presentations on research in Germany.

The German Emigrants Database (www.dad-recherche.de/hmb/index.
html), maintained by the Historisches Museum Bremerhaven, contains information on emigrants who left Europe for the U.S. from German ports between 1820
and 1939. At the time this book was written, the database contained more than
5 million emigrants. The site allows users to search an index of individuals and
order records for a fee based on the results. For more information on emigrants
from the port of Hamburg, see Ballinstadt Hamburg (www.ballinstadt.net/
BallinStadt_emigration_museum_Hamburg/english_BallinStadt_
das_Auswanderermuseum_Hamburg_besonderes_Ausflugsziel_
Ausflugsort_Erlebnisort_Freizeit_leisureworkgroup_
Geschaeftsfuehrer_Jens_Nitschke_Berater_Museen_Fachmann_
Entwicklung_Konzeption_Design_Erlebniswelt_Erlebnismuseum.
html), a site that describes the emigrant experience at the Hamburg port.

An important group of records in German research are church records. The
Association of Church Archives created the Kirchenbuchportal site (www.
kirchenbuchportal.de) to post detailed inventories of parish registers in
their collections.

Ancestry.com has a subscription site for German genealogy at www.ances-
try.de. Ancestry.de provides access to more than 1,800 databases, including census records; birth, marriage, and death records; military records;
immigration and emigration records; and local and family histories. Examples
of databases are the Hamburg Passenger lists (1850–1934), Bremen sailor
registers (1837–1873), and Bremen ship lists (1821–1873). For descriptions of
records held in archives, see the Bundesarchiv site at www.bundesarchiv.
de/index.html.en.

FamilySearch https://familysearch.org/search/collection/
list#page=1&countryId=1927074 houses more than 50 collections
of German records, many of them digital images. Examples of collections
include

✔ Brandenburg, Berlin, Probate Records, 1796–1853

✔ Hesse-Nassau, Civil Registers and Church Books, 1701–1875

✔ Prussia, East Prussia, Königsberg, Index to Funeral Sermons and
Memorials, 1700–1900

You can find resources for other Germanic areas on the Federation of East European Family History Societies site at `http://feefhs.org` and on the following sites:

- **Liechtenstein:** LiechGenWeb Project (`www.rootsweb.ancestry.com/~liewgw`) and FamilySearch (`https://familysearch.org/search/collection/list#page=1&countryId=1927121`)

- **Luxembourg:** Luxembourg home page (`www.rootsweb.ancestry.com/~luxwgw`) and FamilySearch (`https://familysearch.org/search/collection/list#page=1&countryId=1927075`)

- **Swiss:** Swiss Genealogy on the Internet (`www.eye.ch/swissgen/gener-e.htm`), Swiss Roots Genealogy (`www.theswisscenter.org/swissroots/genealogy/`), and FamilySearch (`https://familysearch.org/search/collection/list#page=1&countryId=1927039`)

Focusing on French Resources

For an overview of genealogy in French-speaking regions, drop by the FrancoGene site, at `www.francogene.com/genealogy`. The site features resources for Quebec, Acadia, the U.S., France, Belgium, Switzerland, and Italy. If you're not familiar with French surnames, you might want to see how common a surname is in France. At Geopatronyme.com (`www.geopatronyme.com`), you can view the surname distribution of more than 1.3 million names.

GeneaBank (`www.geneabank.org`) contains transcribed records created by French genealogical societies. To access the information in the site's databases, you must be a member of a society participating in the project. GeneaNet (`www.geneanet.org`) is a fee-based site that has transcriptions of some civil registers. The Lecture et Informatisation des Sources Archivistiques site (`www.lisa90.org`) contains a database with more than 360,000 transcribed parish records covering the eighteenth and nineteenth centuries, and Migranet (`www.francegenweb.org/~migranet/accueil.php`) houses a database of more than 45,000 French marriages where one of the participants was listed as a migrant.

Ancestry.fr (`www.ancestry.fr`) has a collection of more than 500 subscription databases. This collection includes birth, marriage, death, military, and immigration and emigration records as well as maps.

FamilySearch also has a few French digital image record sets at `https://familysearch.org/search/collection/list#page=1&countryId=1927089`.

Scanning Scandinavian Countries

For a general overview of Scandinavian research, see the Scandinavia portal at the FamilySearch Research Wiki (`https://familysearch.org/learn/wiki/en/Scandinavia`). The following sections cover available resources for the Scandinavian countries.

Denmark

An article to launch your Danish research is Genealogy Research in Denmark (`www.progenealogists.com/denmark`), found on the ProGenealogists website. It offers a brief introduction to every major record type that you might use during your research. MyDanishRoots.com (`www.mydanishroots.com`) contains articles on vital records, census lists, place names, emigration, and Danish history.

DIS-Danmark (`www.dis-danmark.dk`) is a group of genealogists using computing in their research. The website includes information on the districts and parishes of Denmark, data on indexed church books, and a database of Danish online records. The Statens Arkiver is also digitizing church books and placing them online at `www.sa.dk/content/dk/ao-forside`.

Finding another researcher who is researching the same family as you can make your research life a lot easier. Sending a GEDCOM file to the GEDCOMP site, at www.lklundin.dk/gedcomp/english.php, allows it to be compared with other researchers' files to see where overlaps exist. Other members of GEDCOMP can then contact you for further research.

If you're planning a research trip to Denmark, you may want to visit the collection at the Statens Arkiver (State Archives). You can find a list of resources available, as well as descriptions of records that are critical to Danish research, at `www.sa.dk/content/us`. FamilySearch houses a few Danish record sets including some digital images at `https://familysearch.org/search/collection/list#page=1&countryId=1927025`.

Finland

The Finland GenWeb site (`www.rootsweb.ancestry.com/~finwgw`) has a small number of biographies, some transcribed U.S. census records of individuals of Finnish descent, a few obituaries of people who were born in Finland and died in the U.S., and links to web pages of those interested in Finnish research.

The Genealogical Society of Finland site (www.genealogia.fi/indexgb. html) contains some advice on getting started in your research, membership information, blogs, and links to member pages.

You can find transcriptions of passport lists for the Åland Islands in Finland at the Transcription of the Borough Administrator's Passport List 1882–1903 (www.genealogia.fi/emi/magistrat/indexe.htm) and Sheriff's Passport List 1863–1916 (www.genealogia.fi/emi/krono/indexe.htm) sites. The database at DISBYT Finland (www.dis.se) contains more than 160,000 individuals who lived in Finland prior to 1913. The Genealogy Society of Finland maintains a list of christenings, marriages, burials, and moves as part of its HisKi project at http://hiski.genealogia.fi/historia/indexe.htm.

The Institute of Migration/Siirtolaisuusinstituutti (www.migrationinstitute. fi/index_e.php) maintains a database of more than 550,000 emigrants from Finland.

FamilySearch contains a few collections at https://familysearch.org/ search/collection/list#page=1&countryId=1927095.

Keep in mind that up to 1809, Finland was a part of Sweden. So, you may need to consult Swedish records to get a complete picture of your ancestors.

Norway

For help with your Norwegian ancestors, see the article "Basics of Norwegian Research," www.rootsweb.ancestry.com/~wgnorway/list-basics. htm. Another useful guide, "How to Trace Your Ancestors in Norway" (http://digitalarkivet.uib.no/sab/howto.html), is housed on the site for the National Archives of Norway. The Velkommen to Norway Genealogy site (http://www.rootsweb.ancestry.com/~wgnorway/), part of the WorldGenWeb project, contains a Getting Started article and links to several Norwegian online resources.

The National Archives of Norway hosts a digital archive at http://digi-talarkivet.uib.no/cgi-win/WebFront.exe?slag=vis&tekst=mel dingar&spraak=e. The site includes digitized parish registers, real estate registers, and probate records, It also has a tutorial on Gothic handwriting, a photo album of farms, and information on the Archive's holdings.

If you're looking for research help, the DIS-Norge site www.disnorge.no/ cms/en/eng/english-pages) has a message board to answer questions, a Nordic dictionary to help with common terms, and a database containing genealogists who are working in a specific geographic area.

FamilySearch has some burial, census, baptism, and marriage records available at https://familysearch.org/search/collection/list#page= 1&countryId=1927171.

Sweden

The Federation of Swedish Genealogical Societies/Sveriges Släktforskarförbund hosts the site Finding Your Swedish Roots (www. genealogi.se/index.php?option=com_content&view=article&id= 167&Itemid=852) that includes helpful articles on church, legal, and tax records; information on the collection in the Swedish Archives; and a brief history of Sweden.

The Swedish DISBYT database (www.dis.se/) contains 22.2 million Swedes who lived before 1910. Genline.com (www.genline.com, now part of Ancestry.com, has more than 20 million scanned Swedish church records from 1860. Ancestry.se (www.ancestry.se) is a subscription site that contains 30 databases, including emigration lists from 1783 to 1751, passenger and immigration lists from the 1500s to 1900s, and some local histories and published genealogies.

Subscription databases on the Riksarkivet (http://sok.riksarkivet. se/) site include births, convicts, deaths, inventories, marriages, seamen's records, and a village and farm database. The site also contains scanned images of church and tax records.

The Sweden Genealogy site (www.rootsweb.ancestry.com/~wgsweden) contains queries, a list of surnames, and links to other Swedish resources.

FamilySearch includes several digital image collections of Swedish church records at https://familysearch.org/search/collection/list# page=1&countryId=1927041.

Iceland

A few resources are available for Icelandic research. The IcelandGenWeb site (www.rootsweb.ancestry.com/~islwgw) contains a few links to resources for your research.

The Íslenski Ættfræðivefurinn site (www.halfdan.is/aett) contains links to personal web pages of people interested in Icelandic genealogy.

FamilySearch has a couple of record sets of baptisms and marriages at https://familysearch.org/search/collection/list#page=1& countryId=1927031.

Italian Cooking

A place to begin your Italian research is the Italian Genealogy home page at www.daddezio.com. The site contains useful articles on family history research as well as links to other Italian genealogical resources. The ItalianGenealogy.com home page (?www.italiangenealogy.com/) features message boards that cover topics such as genealogy, immigration, geography, and the Italian language.

The Italian Genealogical Group (www.italiangen.org) is based in New York City. Resources on its website include naturalization and vital records databases. Ancestry.it (www.ancestry.it) contains more than 100 databases related to Italian genealogy. The bulk of these databases contain birth, marriage, and death records — although some maps and newspapers are available.

FamilySearch (https://familysearch.org/search/collection/list#page=1&countryId=1927178) has more than 100 databases mainly focused on civil registrations and Catholic Church records.

Other European Sites

Several other sites cover European countries and ethnic groups. These include the following:

- ✔ **Armenian:** FamilySearch (https://familysearch.org/search/collection/list#page=1&countryId=1927048)

- ✔ **Belarusian:** Belarusian Genealogy (www.belarusguide.com/genealogy1/index.html)

- ✔ **Belgium:** Belgium-Roots Project (http://belgium.rootsweb.ancestry.com/) and FamilySearch (https://familysearch.org/search/collection/list#page=1&countryId=1927071)

- ✔ **Bosnia-Herzegovina:** Bosnia-Herzegovina Web Genealogy Project (www.rootsweb.ancestry.com/~bihwgw)

- ✔ **Bulgarian:** BulgariaGenWeb (www.rootsweb.ancestry.com/~bgrwgw)

- ✔ **Croatian:** Croatia GenWeb (www.rootsweb.ancestry.com/~hrvwgw) and FamilySearch (https://familysearch.org/search/collection/list#page=1&countryId=1927181)

- ✔ **Czech:** Czech Republic Genealogy (`www.rootsweb.ancestry.com/~czewgw`) and FamilySearch (`https://familysearch.org/search/collection/list#page=1&countryId=1927165`)

- ✔ **Estonian:** FamilySearch (`https://familysearch.org/search/collection/list#page=1&countryId=1927007`)

- ✔ **Federation of East European Family History Societies (FEEFHS):** If you're looking for research guides for Eastern Europe, start here. The federation's pages (`http://feefhs.org`) have information on the Albanian, Armenian, Austrian, Belarusian, Bohemian, Bulgarian, Carpatho-Rusyn, Croatian, Czech, Danish, Finnish, Galician, German, Hutterite, Hungarian, Latvian, Lithuanian, Polish, Moravian, Pomeranian, Romanian, Russian, Silesian, Slavic, Slavonian, Slovak, Slovenian, Transylvanian, Ukrainian, and Volhynian ethnic groups

- ✔ **Greek:** GreeceGenWeb (`www.rootsweb.ancestry.com/~grcwgw`)

- ✔ **Hungarian:** HungaryGenWeb (`www.rootsweb.ancestry.com/~wghungar`) and FamilySearch (`https://familysearch.org/search/collection/list#page=1&countryId=1927145`)

- ✔ **Latvian:** LatvianGenWeb (`www.rootsweb.ancestry.com/~lvawgw`)

- ✔ **Maltese:** MaltaGenWeb (`www.rootsweb.ancestry.com/~mltwgw`)

- ✔ **Moldovian:** MoldovaGenWeb (`www.rootsweb.ancestry.com/~mdawgw`) and FamilySearch (`https://familysearch.org/search/collection/list#page=1&countryId=1927051`)

- ✔ **Polish:** PolandGenWeb (`www.rootsweb.ancestry.com/~polwgw`) and FamilySearch (`https://familysearch.org/search/collection/list#page=1&countryId=1927187`)

- ✔ **Romanian:** RomaniaGenWeb (`www.rootsweb.ancestry.com/~romwgw`)

- ✔ **Russian:** RussiaGenWeb (`www.rootsweb.ancestry.com/~ruswgw`) and FamilySearch (`https://familysearch.org/search/collection/list#page=1&countryId=1927021`)

- ✔ **Serbian:** Serbia GenWeb (`www.rootsweb.ancestry.com/~serwgw`)

- ✔ **Slovak:** Slovak Republic Genealogy (`www.rootsweb.ancestry.com/~svkwgw`) and FamilySearch (`https://familysearch.org/search/collection/list#page=1&countryId=1927146`)

- ✔ **Slovenian:** SloveniaGenWeb (`www.rootsweb.ancestry.com/~svnwgw`) and FamilySearch (`https://familysearch.org/search/collection/list#page=1&countryId=1927180`)

- ✔ **Ukrainian:** Ukraine GenWeb (`www.rootsweb.ancestry.com/~ukrwgw`) and FamilySearch (`https://familysearch.org/search/collection/list#page=1&countryId=1927132`)

Asian Resources

If your ancestors came from Asia or the Pacific Rim, your success at finding records greatly depends on the history of the ancestor's ethnic group and its record-keeping procedures. Currently, you don't find much online genealogical information that pertains to these areas and peoples. Here's a sampling of Asian and Pacific Rim resources:

- **Bangladesh:** BangladeshGenweb (`www.rootsweb.ancestry.com/~bgdwgw`)

- **Bhutan:** BhutanGenWeb (`www.rootsweb.ancestry.com/~btnwgw`)

- **China:** ChinaGenWeb (`www.rootsweb.ancestry.com/~chnwgw`) and FamilySearch (`https://familysearch.org/search/collection/list#page=1&countryId=1927073`)

- **India:** FamilySearch (`https://familysearch.org/search/collection/list#page=1&countryId=1927063`)

- **Indonesia:** FamilySearch (`https://familysearch.org/search/collection/list#page=1&countryId=1927029`)

- **Japan:** JapanGenWeb (`www.rootsweb.ancestry.com/~jpnwgw`) and FamilySearch (`https://familysearch.org/search/collection/list#page=1&countryId=1927172`)

- **Korea:** FamilySearch (`https://familysearch.org/search/collection/list#page=1&countryId=6118214`)

- **Lebanon:** Lebanon GenWeb (`www.rootsweb.ancestry.com/~lbnwgw`)

- **Melanesia:** MelanesiaGenWeb (`www.rootsweb.ancestry.com/~melwgw`)

- **Philippines:** FamilySearch (`https://familysearch.org/search/collection/list#page=1&countryId=1927042`)

- **Polynesia:** PolynesiaGenWeb (`www.rootsweb.ancestry.com/~pyfwgw`)

- **Saudi Arabia:** Saudi Arabia GenWeb (`www.angelfire.com/tn/BattlePride/Saudi.html`)

- **South Korea:** SouthKoreaGenWeb (`www.rootsweb.ancestry.com/~korwgw-s`)

- **Syria:** Syria GenWeb (`www.rootsweb.ancestry.com/~syrwgw`)

- **Sri Lanka:** Sri Lanka Genealogy (`www.rootsweb.ancestry.com/~lkawgw`) and FamilySearch (`https://familysearch.org/search/collection/list#page=1&countryId=1927054`)

- **Taiwan:** TaiwanGenWeb (`www.rootsweb.ancestry.com/~twnwgw`)

✔ **Tibet:** TibetGenWeb (`www.rootsweb.ancestry.com/~tibetwgw`)

✔ **Turkey:** Turkey Genealogy Web (`www.rootsweb.ancestry.com/~turwgw`)

✔ **Vietnam:** VietnamGenWeb (`www.rootsweb.ancestry.com/~vnmwgw`)

✔ **Various:** Genealogical Gleanings (genealogies of the rulers of India, Burma, Cambodia, Thailand, Fiji, Tonga, Hawaii, and Malaysia, `http://freepages.genealogy.rootsweb.ancestry.com/~royalty/`)

Researching African Ancestry

It's a common misconception that tracing African ancestry is impossible. In the past decade or so, much has been done to dispel that perception. If your ancestors lived in the U.S., you can use many of the same research techniques and records (census schedules, vital records, and other primary resources) that genealogists of other ethnic groups consult, back to 1870. Prior to 1870, your research resources become more limited, depending on whether your ancestor was a freedman or a slave. To make that determination, you may want to interview some of your relatives. They often possess oral traditions that can point you in the right direction.

If your ancestor was a slave, try consulting the slave owners' probate records (which you can usually find in local courthouses), deed books (slave transactions were often recorded in deed books — which you can also find in local courthouses), tax records, plantation records, Freedman's Bureau records, and runaway-slave records. These types of records can be helpful because they identify persons by name.

Although your first inclination may be to turn to a slave schedule in the U.S. Census (slave schedules show the owner's name and the age, sex, and color of slaves), such schedules are not as useful as other sources in your research because the *enumerators* who collected the census information didn't record the names of all slaves, nor did the government require them to do so. This fact doesn't mean that looking at slave schedules is a total waste of time; the schedules simply don't identify your ancestor by name. You need to find other resources that name your ancestor specifically.

If your ancestors served in the American Civil War, they may have service and pension records. You can begin a search for service records in an index to Civil War records of the United States Colored Troops or, if your ancestor joined a state regiment, in an Adjutant General's report. (An *Adjutant General's report* is a published account of the actions of military units from a particular state during a war; these reports are usually available at libraries or archives.) A good place to begin your search for Civil War records is the Civil War Soldiers and Sailors System at `www.itd.nps.gov/cwss`.

Two other sources of records to keep in mind are the Freedmen's Bureau and the Freedman's Savings and Trust. Following are a few sites that contain information from these two organizations:

- **The Freedmen's Bureau** (its full name was the Bureau of Refugees, Freedmen, and Abandoned Lands) was established in 1865 to assist ex-slaves after the American Civil War. For more on the Bureau, see the article by Elaine C. Everly at www.archives.gov/publications/prologue/1997/summer/freedmens-bureau-records.html.

- **The Freedmen's Bureau Online** offers examples of Freedmen's Bureau records at www.freedmensbureau.com.

- **The Freedman's Savings and Trust Company** was also established in 1865 as a bank for ex-slaves. For more information, see the article by Reginald Washington at www.archives.gov/publications/prologue/1997/summer/freedmans-savings-and-trust.html. Several of the bank's contributors were members of the United States Colored Troops during the American Civil War. The company failed in 1874; its records are now kept at the National Archives and Records Administration along with the records for the Freedmen's Bureau.

- **The National Archives and Records Administration** provides information about Freedman's Savings records (and their availability on microfilm) at www.archives.gov/research/guide-fed-records/groups/105.html.

Ancestry.com (www.ancestry.com) contains records from the Freedmen's Bureau Field Offices (1863–1878), marriages recorded by the Freedmen's Bureau (1815–1866), and Freedman's Bank records (1865–1871).

For more information on using records to research your African ancestry, try the resources that follow:

- *The Source: A Guidebook of American Genealogy,* Third Edition, edited by Loretto Dennis Szucs and Sandra Hargreaves Luebking (Ancestry, Inc.). In particular, see Chapter 14, "African American Research," written by Tony Burroughs. This is available online at www.ancestry.com/wiki/index.php?title=Overview_of_African_American_Research.

- *Black Roots: A Beginner's Guide to Tracing the African American Family Tree*, written by Tony Burroughs (Touchstone).

- *Black Family Research: Records of Post-Civil War Federal Agencies at the National Archives,* available online at www.archives.gov/publications/ref-info-papers/rip108.pdf.

- *Slave Genealogy: A Research Guide with Case Studies,* written by David H. Streets (Heritage Books).

Mailing lists focusing on African research

When you look for key records specific to African ancestral research, it's a good idea to interact with other researchers who may already be knowledgeable about such resources. One place to start is the AfriGeneas mailing list. This mailing list focuses primarily on African genealogical research methods; see Figure 8-4. On the web page for the mailing list (www.afrigeneas.com), you find the following resources:

- ✔ A beginner's guide to researching genealogy
- ✔ Links to census schedules and slave data on the Internet
- ✔ A digital library of transcribed resources
- ✔ A link to a database of African-American surnames and their corresponding researchers

Figure 8-4: The AfriGeneas site aids in finding your African ancestors.

Here's how to subscribe to the AfriGeneas mailing list:

1. **Start your favorite e-mail program.**

2. **Create a new e-mail message.**

3. **Type** majordomo@lists.msstate.edu **in the To line.**

   Make sure that you type *only* **majordomo@lists.msstate.edu** in the To line. You subscribe to AfriGeneas at this listserv e-mail account. If you type anything more, your e-mail message won't be delivered and your attempt to subscribe fails.

4. **Make sure that your e-mail address is in the From line.**

   Most e-mail programs automatically fill in your e-mail address in the From line. In that case, just make sure that it's correct. Otherwise, type the e-mail address where you want to receive messages from the AfriGeneas mailing list.

5. **In the body of the message, type** subscribe afrigeneas **or** subscribe afrigeneas-digest. **You can leave the subject line blank.**

   Use **subscribe afrigeneas-digest** if you want to receive fewer e-mail messages a day from the list. In the digest form, the listserver compiles all the messages that people post throughout the day into one e-mail. For example, if April subscribes to the mailing list in its regular format, where each posting arrives separately, she'd type **subscribe afrigeneas** in the body of her message. Again, don't type anything more than this line in the message body or you confuse the automatic program that adds you to the mailing list — and it rejects your attempt to subscribe.

6. **Send the e-mail message.**

Genealogical resource pages on the web

In addition to the AfriGeneas website, a number of online resources are available to assist you in finding your African ancestry.

You can find a high-level overview of the subject at African American Lives (www.pbs.org/wnet/aalives). The site is the companion to the PBS show that originally aired in early 2006. Items on the site include

✔ Profiles of individuals featured on the show

✔ Tips on how to effectively use documentation in researching African ancestral roots

✔ A brief primer on DNA testing

✔ An introduction to some of the issues and pitfalls surrounding research

✔ A list of stories from other researchers

For a brief list of resources that you can use, see the University of Pennsylvania African Studies Center bibliography page, at `www.africa.upenn.edu/Bibliography/menu_Biblio.html`.

Other sites with helpful content include

- ✔ Sankofa's Slave Genealogy Wiki (`http://sankofagen.pbworks.com/w/page/14230533/FrontPage`)
- ✔ Slave Archival Collection Database (`http://rootsweb.ancestry.com/~ilissdsa/text_files/database_intro2.htm`)

Transcribed records pertaining to ancestors with African roots

Many genealogists recognize the benefits of making transcribed and digitized records available for other researchers. More and more of these websites are popping up every day. A few websites have transcribed records that are unique to the study of African ancestry online. Some examples are

- ✔ **Cemetery records:** For a transcribed list of cemeteries, see African American Cemeteries Online at `http://africanamericancemeteries.com`.
- ✔ **Freedmen's Bureau records:** You can find transcribed Freedmen's Bureau records at the Freedmen's Bureau Online at `www.freedmensbureau.com/index.html`.
- ✔ **Manumission papers:** For examples of *manumission papers* — documents reflecting that a slave was granted freedom — see the Bourbon County Deeds of Manumission Abstracts site at `www.rootsweb.ancestry.com/~kyafamer/Bourbon/manumissions.htm`.
- ✔ **Registers:** At The Valley of the Shadow site, you can view transcribed Registers of Free Blacks in Augusta County, Virginia at `http://valley.lib.virginia.edu/VoS/govdoc/free.html`.
- ✔ **Slave schedules:** You can find digitized versions of slave schedules at Ancestry.com's subscription site (`www.ancestry.com`).
- ✔ **Wills and probate records:** Slaves were often mentioned in the disposition of wills. A list of slaves mentioned in probate records of Noxubee County, Mississippi, can be found at `http://earphoto.tripod.com/SlaveNames.html`.

The preceding sites are a few examples of transcribed records that you can find on the Internet. To see whether online records exist that pertain specifically to your research, visit a comprehensive genealogical site and look under the appropriate category.

Special ethnic pages about African ancestry

Many websites include information on a particular subset of individuals of African ancestry. Here are some you may want to visit:

- ✔ The African-Native Genealogy Homepage provides details on blended families in Oklahoma (www.african-nativeamerican.com).
- ✔ You can find information on French Creoles on the French Creoles Free People of Color website (www.frenchcreoles.com/CreoleCulture/freepeopleofcolor/freepeopleofcolor.htm).

Original records

You can find digitized original records online at some subscription sites. For example, Fold3.com (www.fold3.com) has the federal and Supreme Court case files for the case involving the seizure of the Amistad, a ship carrying slaves seized by the U.S. Navy in 1839.

American Indian Resources

Tracing your American Indian heritage can be challenging. Your ancestor may have moved frequently, and most likely, few written records were kept. However, your task isn't impossible. With a good research strategy, you may be able to narrow your search area and find primary resources to unlock some of the mysteries of your ancestors.

One key to your research is old family stories that have been passed down from generation to generation. Interviewing your family members is a good way to find out what tribe your ancestor belonged to and the geographic area in which that ancestor lived. After you have this information, a trip to your local library is well worth the effort to find a history of the tribe and where it migrated throughout time. From this research, you can then concentrate your search on a specific geographic area and gain a much better chance of finding records of genealogical value.

Fortunately, the U.S. government did compile some records on American Indians. For example, you can find annual census lists of American Indians, dating from 1885 to 1940, in the National Archives — as well as digitized copies of the censuses on Ancestry.com, as shown in Figure 8-5. You can also find probate and land records at the federal level, especially for transactions occurring on reservations. In federal repositories, you can also find school records for those who attended schools on reservations. Additionally, the Bureau of Indian Affairs has a vast collection of records on American Indians. For more information about American Indian resources that are available from the National Archives and Records Administration, visit `www.archives.gov/research/alic/reference/native-americans.html`.

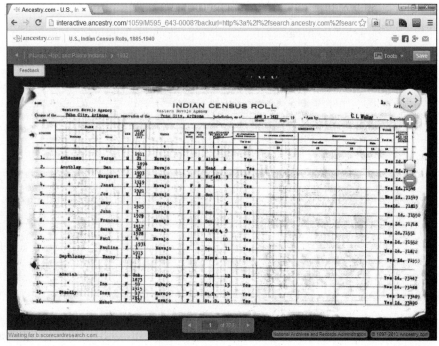

Figure 8-5:
Image of an Indian census record at Ancestry.com.

You may also be able to find records on your ancestor in one of the many tribal associations in existence. To find out how to contact tribes recognized in the U.S., go to the American Indian Tribal Directory, at `http://tribaldirectory.com/`.

For more information about researching American Indian records, see the following resources:

✔ *The Source: A Guidebook of American Genealogy,* Third Edition, edited by Loretto Dennis Szucs and Sandra Hargreaves Luebking (Ancestry, Inc.). In particular, see Chapter 19, "Native American Research," written by Curt B. Witcher and George J. Nixon. You can find this online at `www.ancestry.com/wiki/index.php?title=Overview_of_Native_American_Research`.

✔ *Native American Genealogical Sourcebook,* edited by Paula K. Byers and published by Thomas Gale.

✔ *Guide to Records in the National Archives of the United States Relating to American Indians,* published by the National Archives and Records Services Administration.

Where to begin looking for information about American Indians

For a general look at what Internet resources are available on American Indians, see NativeWeb (www.nativeweb.org). NativeWeb includes a resource center with hundreds of links to other Internet sites on native peoples around the world.

When you're ready to dive into research, you may want to join the INDIAN-ROOTS-L mailing list, which is devoted to discussing American Indian research methods. To subscribe to the list, type **SUB INDIAN-ROOTS-L** *your first name your last name* in the body of an e-mail message and send it to listserv@listserv.indiana.edu.

Another resource worth exploring is the National Archives and Records Administration's Online Public Access (OPA), at http://research.archives.gov/search. OPA contains indexes to a small portion of the archive's holdings. Among the Native American collections in OPA are

✔ Images of the Index to the Final Rolls of the Citizens and Freedmen of the Five Civilized Tribes in Indian Territory

✔ Images of the Index to Applications Submitted for the Eastern Cherokee Roll of 1909 (Guion Miller Roll)

✔ Records of the Bureau of Indian Affairs Truxton Canon Agency

✔ Record of Applications under the Act of 1896 (1896 Citizenship Applications) received by the Dawes Commission

✔ Descriptions for records of the Cherokee Indian Agency and the Seminole Indian Agency

✔ Descriptions for records of the Navajo Area Office, the Navajo Agency, and the Window Rock Area Office of the Bureau of Indian Affairs

✔ Some images of Cherokee, Chickasaw, Creek, and Seminole Applications for Enrollment to the Five Civilized Tribes (Dawes Commission)

✔ Images of the Kern-Clifton Roll of Cherokee Freedmen

- Images of the Wallace Roll of Cherokee Freedmen in Indian Territory

- Surveys of Indian Industry, 1922

- Classified Files of the Extension and Credit Office, 1931–1946

- Selected Documents from the Records of the Bureau of Indian Affairs, 1793–1989

- American Indians, 1881–1885

To search OPA, try this:

1. **Go to** `http://research.archives.gov/search`.

2. **Place a search term into the Search Online Public Access field and click Search.**

   We type Annie Abbott in the box.

3. **Click a link to content that interests you.**

   We click the link for the Enrollment for Cherokee Census Card M1394 that shows more information about the record.

At this point, OPA contains descriptions of only a portion of the Archives' total holdings. So, if you don't find something, it doesn't mean it doesn't exist.

You can find a brief outline of how to trace American Indian ancestry at the U.S. Department of the Interior site (`www.doi.gov/tribes/trace-ancestry.cfm`).

American Indian resource pages on the web

Researching American Indian roots would be much easier if some sites were dedicated to the genealogical research of specific tribes. If your ancestor's tribe passed through the state of Oklahoma, you may be in luck. Volunteers with the Oklahoma USGenWeb project developed the Twin Territories site, at `www.okgenweb.org/~itgenweb`.

Some links to various tribes available on the web are

- Cherokee Nation, Indian Territory (`www.rootsweb.ancestry.com/~itcherok`)

- Cherokee Archival Project (`www.rootsweb.ancestry.com/~cherokee`)

- NC Cherokee Reservation Genealogy (`www.ncgenweb.us/cherokeereservation`)

- Cheyenne-Arapaho Lands of Oklahoma Genealogy (www.rootsweb.
  ancestry.com/~itcheyen)

- Chickasaw Nation, Indian Territory, 1837–1907 (www.rootsweb.
  ancestry.com/~itchicka)

- Choctaw Nation, Indian Territory (www.felihkatubbe.com/
  ChoctawNation/index.html)

- Kiowa-Comanche-Apache Indian Lands (www.genealogynation.com/kiowa)

- Muscogee (Creek) Nation of Oklahoma (www.genealogynation.com/
  creek)

- Native Genealogy People of the Three Fires (Chippewa, Ottawa, and
  Potawatomi; www.rootsweb.ancestry.com/~minatam)

- Osage Nation Genealogical website (www.felihkatubbe.com/
  OsageNation)

- Quapaw Agency Lands of Indian Territory (www.rootsweb.ancestry.
  com/~itquapaw)

- Seminole Nation in Indian Territory (www.seminolenation-
  indianterritory.org)

- The Kansas/Kanza/Kaw Nation (www.okgenweb.org/~itkaw/
  KanzaNation.html)

Transcribed American Indian records

Some websites have transcribed records that are unique to researching
American Indian roots. Two examples are

- **The Chickasaw Historical Research Page:** This page contains transcriptions of a few records, such as guardianship records and land sales, at
  www.chickasawhistory.com.

- **1851 Census of Cherokees East of the Mississippi:** This site provides
  a transcription of the census, including names, family numbers, ages,
  and relationships to head of household, all at http://freepages.
  genealogy.rootsweb.ancestry.com/~gilmercountyrecords/
  1851silerrollforgilmercounty.htm.

Many families have legends that they are descended from famous American
Indians. These claims should always be researched carefully and backed up with
appropriate proof. One of the most prolific legends is descent from Pocahontas.
If that legend runs through your family, you may want to visit the Pocahontas
Descendants page for resources that can help you prove your heritage. You can
find it at http://pocahontas.morenus.org/poca_gen.html.

Part III

Making Sure Your Family History Checks Out

Review the article "Sources for Learning about DNA" online at www.dummies.com/extras/genealogyonline.

In this part...

- ✔ Learn how to use DNA tests to assist researching your direct male and female lines.

- ✔ Discover the probability of your ethnicity with DNA tests.

- ✔ Discover off-the-beaten-path records that add color to your research.

Chapter 9

Specializing in Your Family History

Many people who are familiar with genealogy know to use vital records, census returns, tax lists, and wills to find information about their ancestors. These records offer historical snapshots of an individual's life at particular points in time. But as a family historian, you want to know more than just when your ancestors paid their taxes — you want to know something about them as people.

For example, April once came across a photograph of her great-great-grandfather while she was looking through an old box full of pictures and letters. He was dressed in a uniform with a sash and sword, and he was holding a plumed hat. As far as April knew, her great-great-grandfather hadn't been in the military, so she decided to dig for some information about the uniform. Although part of the picture was blurry, she could make out three crosses on the uniform. One was on his sleeve, the second was on the buckle of his belt, and the third was a different kind of cross that was attached to his sash. April suspected that the symbols were Masonic. She visited a few Masonic sites on the web and found that the crosses indicated that her great-great-grandfather had been a member of the Order of the Temple in the Masonic organization. She may not have discovered that he was a member of that organization had she depended solely upon the usual group of records used by genealogists.

This chapter looks at some examples of unique or hard-to-find records that can be useful in family history research, including records kept by religious groups and fraternal orders, photographs, and adoption records.

Researching Religious Group Records

In the past, several countries required attendance at church services or the payment of taxes to an ecclesiastical authority. Although your ancestors may not have appreciated those laws at the time, the records that were kept to ensure their compliance can benefit you as a genealogist. In fact, before governments started recording births, marriages, and deaths, churches kept the official records of these and other events (such as baptisms and lists of vestrymen). You can use a variety of records kept by church authorities or congregations to develop a sketch of the everyday life of your ancestor.

Some common records that you may encounter include baptismal records, parish registers, lists of people holding positions in the church (vestrymen, deacons, elders, lay ministers), marriage records, death or burial records, tithes, welfare rolls, meeting minutes, and congregation photographs. Each type of record may include several different bits of information. For example, a baptismal record may include the date of birth, date of baptism, parents' names, and where the parents lived. Parish registers may have names of household members and addresses, and possibly an accounting of their tithes to the church. The amount of data present on the records depends on the church.

Several sites provide general information and links to all sorts of resources that pertain to specific religions and sects. Here are a few examples:

- **Anabaptist:** The Global Anabaptist Mennonite Encyclopedia Online (GAMEO) site (www.gameo.org) has an extensive collection of articles related to Amish, Mennonite, Hutterite, and Brethren in Christ congregations, as well as confessions and faith statements from some church members. It also has links to other resources for Anabaptist-Mennonite research. Additionally, you can find genealogical databases of Anabaptists at the Swiss Anabaptist Genealogical Association site (www.saga-omii.org/index.html).

- **Baptist:** The Baptist History & Heritage Society site (www.baptisthistory.org/bhhs) contains an overview of the Society and information about Baptists in the American Civil War.

- **Catholic:** The Local Catholic Church History & Genealogy Research Guide (http://localcatholic.webs.com) includes links to information on diocese and genealogy, categorized by location.

- **Church of the Brethren:** The Fellowship of Brethren Genealogists website (www.cob-net.org/fobg) contains information on the organization and the current projects sponsored by the Fellowship.

- **Church of Scotland:** The General Register Office for Scotland site (www.scotlandspeople.gov.uk) features searchable indexes of births, baptisms, banns, marriages, deaths, and burials from the Old Parish Registers dating from 1553 to 1854.

- ✔ **Huguenot:** The Huguenots of France and Elsewhere site (`http://huguenots-france.org/english.htm`) contains genealogies of several Huguenot families. Also, you find a surname index at the Australian Family Tree Connections site (`www.aftc.com.au/Huguenot/Hug.html`).

- ✔ **Hutterite:** The Hutterite Genealogy Home Page (`www.feefhs.org/links/hutterites.html`) gives an introduction and links to resources for this denomination found in Austria, Bohemia, Moravia, Slovakia, Hungary, Romania, Canada, the United States, and the Ukraine. For links to a variety of Hutterite resources, see Hutterite Reference Links at `http://home.westman.wave.ca/~hillmans/BU/hutterite.html`.

- ✔ **Jewish:** The JewishGen site (`www.jewishgen.org`) has information about the JewishGen organization and FAQs about Jewish genealogy, as well as indexes of other Internet resources, including searchable databases, special interest groups, and JewishGen family home pages.

- ✔ **Lutheran:** Lutherans Online — Genealogy (`www.lutheransonline.com/lutheransonline/genealogy`) has a registry of researchers looking for information about Lutheran ancestors and a message board to which you can post questions about your research.

- ✔ **Mennonite:** The Mennonite Research Corner (`www.ristenbatt.com/genealogy/mennonit.htm`) features general information about Mennonites and a collection of online resources for researchers. For a Canadian perspective, visit the Mennonite Genealogy Data Index at `http://mgdi.mennonitehistory.org`.

- ✔ **Methodist:** The Researching Your United Methodist Ancestors site (`www.gcah.org/site/pp.aspx?c=ghKJI0PHIoE&b=2901109`) contains general advice on getting started with your research and links to online resources.

- ✔ **Moravian Church:** The Moravian Church Genealogy Links page (`https://sites.google.com/site/moravianchurchgenealogylinks`) features links to articles on the history of the church, as well as links to genealogical resources.

- ✔ **Quaker:** The Quaker Corner (`www.rootsweb.com/~quakers`) contains a query board, a list of research resources, and links to other Quaker pages on the web.

- ✔ **Seventh-day Adventist:** The Center for Adventist Research at Andrews University site (`www.andrews.edu/library/car`) contains information on the university's archives and research center and databases including a periodical index, obituary index, bibliographies, and photographs.

A few church organizations have online descriptions of their archives' holdings:

- ✔ **Archives of Brethren in Christ Church:** `www.messiah.edu/archives`

- ✔ **Catholic Archives of Texas:** `http://catholicarchivesoftx.org`

- ✔ **Fresno Pacific University's Mennonite Library and Archives:** `www.fresno.edu/library/cmbs`

✔ **Concordia Historical Institute Department of Archives and History (Lutheran Church — Missouri Synod):** `www.lutheranhistory.org`

✔ **General Commission on Archives and History for the United Methodist Church:** `www.gcah.org/index.htm`

✔ **Greek Orthodox Archdiocese of America Department of Archives:** `www.goarch.org/archdiocese/departments/archives`

✔ **Moravian Archives:** `www.moravianchurcharchives.org`

✔ **United Church of Canada Archives:** `www.united-church.ca/local/archives/on`

The following sites can give you a better idea of the types of information available on the Internet for religious groups:

✔ **Baptism records:** You can find a list of those baptized in the Wesleyan Methodist Baptismal Register at `http://freepages.genealogy.rootsweb.ancestry.com/~wjmartin/wm-index.htm`.

✔ **Cemetery records:** The Quaker Burying Ground Cemetery, Galesville, Anne Arundel County, Maryland, site is `www.interment.net/data/us/md/anne_arundel/quaker.htm`. This web page is part of the Interment.net: Cemetery Records Online site, which provides transcribed burial information, including the person's name and dates of birth and death, as well as some other information, as shown in Figure 9-1.

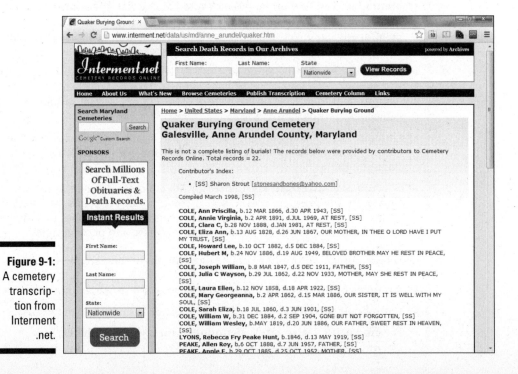

Figure 9-1: A cemetery transcription from Interment.net.

✔ **Marriage records:** The Moravian Church, Lititz Marriages 1742–1800 page (`http://files.usgwarchives.net/pa/lancaster/church/moravianlititz.txt`) contains a list of marriage dates along with the names of the bride and groom married in the church located in Lancaster County, Pennsylvania.

✔ **Parish directories:** The Holy Trinity Church, Boston, Massachusetts site (`http://homepages.rootsweb.com/~mvreid/bgrc/htc.html`) has a searchable 1895 parish directory, an ongoing project to identify and post information about church members who served in the Civil War, and a list of church members who served in World War I.

In addition to sites that focus specifically on one type of record, you may run across sites that collect digitized copies of all sorts of records pertaining to a particular church. For example, the goal of Genline (`www.genline.com`) is to place all digital copies of Swedish church records online.

Ancestry.com (`www.ancestry.com`) has a few collections of church records on its subscription site.

FamilySearch (`www.familysearch.org`) also has a growing number of church records, especially Catholic Church records in countries outside the U.S.

Finding Fraternal Orders and Service Clubs

Were any of your ancestors members of fraternal orders or service clubs? These groups are organized around a feature or attribute (such as a religion, military service, occupation, and so forth) and generally work toward a common good. Many such organizations exist and, chances are, you have at least one ancestor who was a member of an order or club. Although most of the better-known organizations are for men, affiliated organizations for women exist, too. A few general-information sites on fraternal orders and service clubs are

✔ **The American Legion:** www.legion.org

✔ **Ancient and Mystical Order Rosae Crucis:** www.amorc.org

✔ **Ancient Order of Hibernians in America:** www.aoh.com

✔ **DeMolayInternational:** www.demolay.org

✔ **Eagles (Fraternal Order of Eagles):** www.foe.com

✔ **Elks (Benevolent and Protective Order of the Elks):** www.elks.org

✔ **Freemasonry:** The Philalethes Society (`www.freemasonry.org`) and A Page About Freemasonry (`http://web.mit.edu/dryfoo/www/Masons/index.html`)

- ✔ **Improved Order of Red Men:** www.redmen.org
- ✔ **Job's Daughters International:** www.jobsdaughtersinternational.org
- ✔ **Kiwanis International:** www.kiwanis.org
- ✔ **Knights of Columbus:** www.kofc.org/un/en/index.html
- ✔ **Lions Clubs'LionNet:** www.lionnet.com
- ✔ **Military Order of the Loyal Legion of the United States:** www.suvcw.org/mollus/mollus.htm
- ✔ **Modern Woodmen of America:** www.modern-woodmen.org/Pages/HomePage.aspx
- ✔ **MooseInternational:** www.mooseintl.org/public/default.asp
- ✔ **Odd Fellows (Independent Order of Odd Fellows):** www.ioof.org
- ✔ **Optimist International:** www.optimist.org
- ✔ **Order of the Eastern Star (Grand Chapter Order of the Eastern Star):** www.easternstar.org
- ✔ **Orioles (Fraternal Order of Orioles):** http://fraternalorderorioles.homestead.com/
- ✔ **Rainbow for Girls (International Order of the Rainbow for Girls):** www.iorg.org
- ✔ **Rebekahs:** http://www.ioof.org/IOOF/About_Us/Whats_an_Odd_Fellow/Rebekah/IOOF/Rebekah.aspx?hkey=b56bd9ab-9e56-4eec-a8bc-8faeee1420e3
- ✔ **Rotary International:** https://www.rotary.org
- ✔ **Shriners International:** www.shrinersinternational.org
- ✔ **Veterans of Foreign Wars of the United States:** www.vfw.org

Most sites related to fraternal orders provide historical information about the clubs and current membership rules. Although the sites may not provide you with actual records (membership lists and meeting minutes), they do give you an overview of what the club is about and an idea of what your ancestor did as a member. The sites also provide you with the names and addresses of local chapters — you can contact them to see whether they have original resources available for public use or whether they can send you copies of anything pertaining to your ancestor.

Having information about a fraternal order doesn't necessarily make a particular site the organization's *official* site. This is particularly true for international organizations. You may find web pages for different chapters of a particular club in several different countries, and although each site may have some general club information in common, they are likely to have varying types of information specific to that chapter of the organization.

If you're looking for sites that contain information on fraternal organizations, you may want to try some of the comprehensive genealogy sites. If you can't find sufficient information there, try one of the general Internet search engines.

Finding clues on gravestones

You might notice a unique marker on your ancestor's gravestone when visiting the cemetery or looking at photos. The marker may indicate your ancestor's membership in one of these fraternal orders or service clubs. The Pennsylvania USGenWeb Archives has a resource that may be helpful in just such a situation. The Guide to Identifying Grave Markers in Pennsylvania Social and Fraternal Organizations (http://www.usgwarchives.net/pa/1pa/tscarvers/veteran-markers/social-fraternal/social-fraternal-organizations.htm) contains information and illustrations that pertain to more than just Pennsylvania.

A Photo Is Worth a Thousand Words

In Chapter 2, we discuss the value of photographs in your genealogical research. But a lot of us don't have photographs of our family beyond two or three generations, though it sure would be great to find at least an electronic copy of a picture of your great-great-grandfathers. Such pictures may exist. Another researcher may have posted them on a personal site, or the photographs may be part of a collection belonging to a certain organization. You may also be interested in pictures of places where your ancestors lived. Being able to describe how a certain town, estate, or farm looked at the time your ancestor lived there adds color to your family history.

You can find various types of photographic sites on the Internet that can assist you with your research. Some of these sites explain the photographic process and the many types of photographs that have been used throughout history. Some sites contain collections of photographs from a certain geographic area or time period in history, and some sites contain photographs of the ancestors of a particular family. Here are some examples:

✔ **General information:** City Gallery's Learning page (www.city-gallery.com/learning) has a brief explanation of the types of photography used during the nineteenth century (see Figure 9-2), a photography query page, and a gallery of photographs from one studio of the period.

Figure 9-2:
Find out
about pho-
tographic
methods of
the past at
City Gallery.

✔ **Photograph collections:** You can find general collections of images online at sites such as American Memory Collections: Orginal Format: Photos and Prints at `http://memory.loc.gov/cgi-bin/query/S?ammem/collections:@field(FLD003+@band(origf+Photograph)):heading=Original+Format%3a+Photos+&+Prints`. You can find pictures also at sites that have a specific focus, such as the Civil War (`www.flickr.com/photos/usnationalarchives/collections/72157622495226723/`), or images of people and places in Florida (`www.floridamemory.com/PhotographicCollection`).

✔ **Photograph identification:** The DeadFred Genealogy Photo Archive contains more than 99,000 photographs at `www.deadfred.com`. Each photograph includes descriptive information, including where the photograph was taken, the names of the subjects, and an approximate time frame; see Figure 9-3.

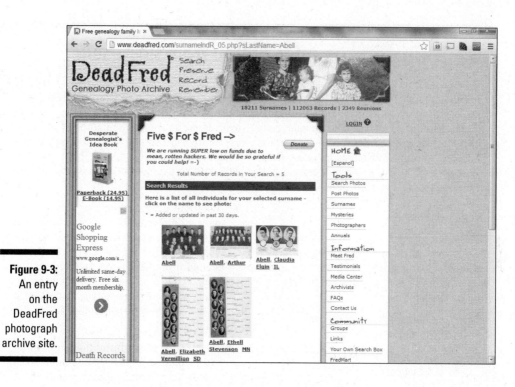

Figure 9-3:
An entry
on the
DeadFred
photograph
archive site.

> ✔ **Personal photographs:** The Harrison Genealogy Repository site is
> an example of a personal website with a photo gallery: `http://`
> `freepages.genealogy.rootsweb.com/~harrisonrep/Photos/`
> `harrphot.htm`. The gallery includes the likenesses of several famous
> Harrisons, including Benjamin Harrison V, President William Henry
> Harrison, and President Benjamin Harrison.

To find photographic sites, you may want to visit one of the comprehensive
genealogy sites or general Internet search engines.

For more information on using photography in genealogy, see the
FamilySearch Tech Tips page at `https://familysearch.org/techtips/`
`series/digital-photography-for-the-genealogist`. Also, take a
look at Maureen Taylor's blog at `www.maureentaylor.com/blog` for tips
on using photographs in your research.

Digging up information from the grave

Most genealogists recognize what a valuable resource a cemetery can be when researching family history. Your ancestors' gravestones (or tombstones) may contain an abundance of clues for you to use in further research. But traveling to visit all of the cemeteries where your ancestors' are buried may not be possible because of financial, health, or physical constraints. Luckily, there is an online resource designed to help!

Billion Graves (`http://billiongraves.com`) is an effort to collect photos of gravestones, transcribe and index the information on them, and post the photo and transcription online for all to use.

The basic search interface is easy to use. Follow these steps:

1. Go to Billion Graves at `http://billiongraves.com`.

2. In the Headstone Search box, enter some basic information about your ancestor, including first name (in the Given Names field), last name (in the Family Names field), Birth Year, and Death Year.

   If you don't know the years of birth and/or death, you can leave those fields blank.

3. Click the Search button.

4. Sort through any results and click on any that look promising.

   If you want to specify a location, you can refine your search using the Advanced Search functionality.

It's important to note that this site is relatively young and still growing. Not all gravestones in all cemeteries are included at the site. And even those that are photographed may not yet be transcribed and indexed. Much of the content relies on volunteers. There are several ways to get involved with Billion Graves. Volunteers can:

✔ Take and upload photos of gravestones near where they live or travel using an iPhone or Android smart-phone camera application. The application can be downloaded from the iPhone AppStore or the Google Play site. The application maps the photo to the cemetery (provides the global positioning information embedded in the photo's code).

✔ Transcribe the information contained in the photos of the gravestones. This makes the information easily indexed for searching, which helps others who are looking for family history information on the site.

✔ Offer to photograph particular cemeteries or specific gravestones that other users are looking for. The website has a Request Board where people can post "look-up" needs.

While you can search for headstones without registering at the site, you will need to register if you want to volunteer in any way. Registration is fast and free. Just fill out the Register box on the home page for Billion Graves, then click Register.

Accessing Adoption Records

Adoption records are of interest to a lot of genealogists, including those who were adopted themselves, those who gave up children for adoption, and those who have ancestors who were adopted. With the advent of DNA testing as a genealogy tool, even those who are not adopted may become interested in researching a person who is a match with them who was adopted and may not have much information on how they fit into the family. For example, Matthew is an administrator of a surname DNA project. During the course of testing, he found two individuals who were adopted that are a close match in DNA. So, for them, participation in the surname DNA project became a project to find how the two individuals fit into the family lines.

If you fall into the first two groups (you were adopted or gave up a child for adoption), some online resources may help you find members of your birth family. The online resources include registries, reference materials, advice and discussion groups, and information on legislation pertaining to adoption. Registries enable you to post information about yourself and your adoption, with the hope that a member of your birth family may see the posting and contact you. (Likewise, if you're the birth parent of an adoptee, you can post a message with the hope that the adoptee sees it and responds.)

It is also worthwhile to look for information on how to use DNA testing to jump-start your research. For example, the International Society of Genetic Genealogy has published the brief article Utilizing DNA Testing to Break Through Adoption Roadblocks at `www.isogg.org/adoption.htm`. The article points to a few other sites that can help in your research and contains some success stories.

Unfortunately, you won't find online sites that contain actual adoption records — for legal reasons, generally. Instead, you need to rely on registries and other resources that point you toward more substantial information about adoption. If you have a successful reunion with your birth parent(s) by registering with an online site, you can, with any luck, obtain information about their parents, grandparents, and so on — so that you know where to begin your genealogical pursuit of that family line.

Here are some online sites that have adoption registries, reference materials, advice and discussions, or legislative information:

- **Child Welfare Information Gateway: Access to Adoption Records:** `https://www.childwelfare.gov/systemwide/laws_policies/statutes/infoaccessap.cfm`
- **Adoption.org:** `www.adoption.org`

✔ **Adoption Registry Connect: Worldwide Adoptee and Birth Parent Search Database:** `www.adopteeconnect.com/index.htm`

✔ **About.com Genealogy: Adoption Resources for Your Family Tree:** `http://genealogy.about.com/od/adoption/Adoption_Resources_for_Your_Family_Tree.htm`

If you're interested in adoption records because you have ancestors who were adopted, finding information may be more difficult. Although some article- and blog-type sites exist that give general research information relating to adoption, we have yet to discover any sites specifically designed to aid in research for adopted ancestors. Most likely, you'll have to rely on the regular genealogical resources — particularly query pages and discussion groups — and the kindness and knowledge of other researchers to find information about your adopted ancestors.

If you're searching for general types of adoption resources, using a general Internet directory such as Yahoo! may be the best course of action. To find resources using Yahoo!, try this:

1. **Open your web browser and go to Yahoo! at** `http://dir.yahoo.com`.

2. **Click the Society and Culture link.**

3. **Click the Families link.**

   Here's a second way to find items in Yahoo! (that may be a lot faster): Type a search term in the box near the top of the screen and have Yahoo! search for the topic. For example, you can type **Adoption** in the box and click Search, which produces a results page that has links to take you directly to the appropriate page in Yahoo! that contains adoption links.

4. **Under the Families category, click the Adoption link.**

   This takes you directly to the adoption page — even though it's a few levels down in the directory's hierarchy.

5. **Click a link to another subdirectory in Yahoo! or a link to an Internet site that contains information that interests you.**

   Descriptions follow most of the links in Yahoo! to give you an idea of what kind of information is on the sites. Figure 9-4 shows an example of a Yahoo! page.

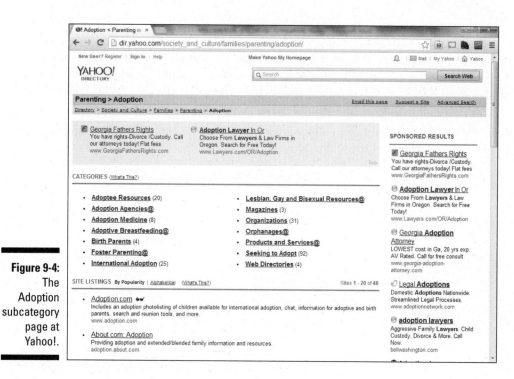

Figure 9-4:
The
Adoption
subcategory
page at
Yahoo!.

Preparing to Be Schooled

Relatively few readily available records chronicle the early years of an individual. Educational records can help fill in the gaps. These records can take a number of forms, including enrollment records, transcripts, yearbooks, directories, and fraternity and sorority records.

The first step is to find out what educational institution your ancestor attended. If you're looking for an elementary or secondary school, you might visit the USGenWeb page (www.usgenweb.org) for the county where your ancestor lived to see whether information is available on the location of schools. If the USGenWeb page doesn't have the information, try to find the website of the local historical or genealogical society.

You might also discover this information by finding a reference to your ancestor and a school in a newspaper article available on a subscription newspaper site. For example, on a routine search on a subscription site, Matthew found a brief article in a local newspaper that listed the participants in a play in a school. From that, he was able to gather the school name, teacher's name, and the names of classmates.

After you discover the name of the institution, find out who has the records for that school. Some schools — such as colleges and universities — have their own archives. For primary and secondary schools, you may need to contact the school district or the overarching parish. Or, if the school no longer exists, you need to find out where the records for that school were transferred.

To see whether a college or university has an archive, look at the list of archives at the Repositories of Primary Sources site (`www.uidaho.edu/special-collections/Other.Repositories.html`). If you're not sure where the records are located, you can use WorldCat, at `www.worldcat.org`, by following these steps:

1. **Use your web browser to pull up `www.worldcat.org`.**

2. **In the search field, enter your criteria and then click Search Everything.**

   We search for Harvard enrollment records.

3. **Select a result that looks promising.**

   Figure 9-5 shows the results of our WorldCat search.

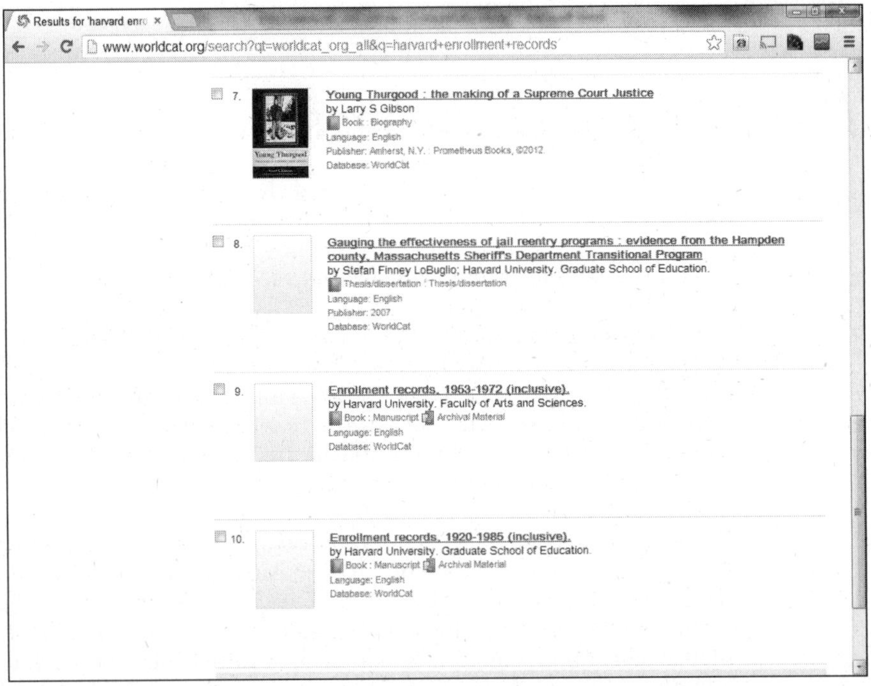

Figure 9-5: Results from the WorldCat search for Harvard enrollment records.

Turning to Bible Records

Bible records are a great source of birth, death, and marriage information for time periods before vital records were required. Because most Bible records are held by private individuals, it's sometimes difficult to locate them. Recognizing the importance of these records, groups have created websites to share the information contained in the Bibles. A few sites worth visiting are

- **Ancestor Hunt Family Bible Records:** www.ancestorhunt.com/family_bible_records.htm

- **Bible Records Online:** www.biblerecords.com

- **Family Bible Records in Onondaga County:** www.rootsweb.ancestry.com/~nyononda/BIBLE.HTM

- **Maine Family Bible Archives:** www.rootsweb.com/~meandrhs/taylor/bible/maine.html

Similar to looking for educational records, you can also find Bible records in some archives. You can use WorldCat (www.worldcat.org) to see what is available in different institutions. For details on how to use WorldCat, see the preceding section. Some subscription sites might also have Bible records. For example, Ancestry.com (www.ancestry.com) has Bible records from New York, Tennessee, Missouri, and Virginia, as well as a collection called Old Southern Bible Records.

Snooping through Great-Grandma's Diary

Another excellent source of information that can add color to your family history is a diary, journal, or memoir kept by your ancestor. Diaries and journals are books in which a person writes his or her thoughts and experiences, typically within a short time of events occurring. Memoirs are written reflections on one's life. Like Bibles and photos online, finding these personal memory keepers on the Internet is somewhat hit-and-miss. Individuals and organizations tend to place online digital images or transcriptions from these resources for their own family members or people from whom an organization has inherited the document. You can search for such records in the same way that you look for Bibles and photos: Look by location or surname using a site such as USGenWeb (www.usgenweb.org) or a search engine such as Google (www.google.com). Some example sites to check out, which may give you an idea of what you can expect from these types of records, are

- **Diaries, Memoirs, Letters, and Reports Along the Trails West:** www.over-land.com/diaries.html

- **Historical Journals and Diaries Online:** www.aisling.net/journaling/old-diaries-online.htm

- **The Civil War Women: Women and the Homefront:** http://library.duke.edu/specialcollections/bingham/guides/cwdocs.html

Nosing through Newspaper Records

A lot of the day-to-day details of your ancestor's life can be filled in by reading local newspapers. You can find obituaries, marriage announcements, social activities, and tax assessments information. Also, you can find background information on the locality that he or she lived in so that you gain a better perspective of your ancestor's life.

A lot of effort has been expended to digitize newspapers over the last few years. Ancestry.com (www.ancestry.com) has partnered with NewspaperArchive.com (www.newspaperarchive.com) to offer a collection of more than 1,000 newspaper databases online. The newspapers featured in the collection are digitized images that have been indexed by *optical character recognition (OCR)* — a software method in which letters in an image are translated into characters (typically letters of the alphabet) that a computer can read. Each page of the newspaper is searchable. When a search result is found, the text is highlighted on the page. The optical character recognition system doesn't always know the context of the words on the page — so the system sometimes generates false-positive search results. Figure 9-6 shows the interface for the newspaper collection at Ancestry.com.

Figure 9-6:
The Decatur Daily Review newspaper image at Ancestry.com.

Several large newspapers have also begun to place their back issues online —
often with a subscription service. For example, you can find the *Los Angeles
Times* back to 1881 online at `http://pqasb.pqarchiver.com/latimes/
advancedsearch.html`, the *Washington Post* from 1877 at `http://pqasb.
pqarchiver.com/washingtonpost/search.html`, and the *Chicago
Tribune* from 1852 at `http://pqasb.pqarchiver.com/chicagotribune/
advancedsearch.html`.

You can find more about using newspapers in your research in Chapter 7.

Chapter 10

Fitting into Your Genes: Molecular Genealogy

In This Chapter

▶ Signing up for a DNA primer

▶ Determining the right test to use

▶ Searching for DNA sites

*I*t sounds like something right out of a crime scene investigation: You swab your cheek or spit in a tube, send the sample to a lab, the results are analyzed, and presto! You find the identity of someone super-important. However, instead of identifying some master-minded criminal, you find the identity of that long-lost ancestor for whom you've been searching. Although the science behind molecular genealogy traces its roots to identifying individuals from crime scenes, it hasn't advanced to the point where you can simply take the test and watch your entire genealogy unfold. But it can provide you with valuable evidence that can help you confirm that you're related to a particular family line.

Although *deoxyribonucleic acid* (DNA) testing is just one of many tools to use in documenting your research, it holds great potential for the future of genealogy. You may be familiar with the use of DNA testing in identifying the remains of Nicholas, the last Czar of Russia, and his family; in debating the last resting place of Christopher Columbus; or in determining the true fate of Jesse James. The methods used in these investigations are the same methods that you can use to complement your documentary research.

In this chapter, we provide an overview of how DNA testing works, where you can order tests, and what to do with the information that you discover during the testing process.

Delving into DNA

Some people might think that we're attempting the impossible — explaining how DNA testing works in one mere chapter. However, we feel it is our duty to at least give you a basic introduction to genetic research so that you can use all the technological means available to you when digging for information on your ancestors.

You need an understanding of the terminology and how the testing process works to interpret your test results. If you find that our elementary explanations just whet your appetite, you can get a healthy dose on the subject with *Genetics For Dummies*, 2nd Edition, by Tara Rodden Robinson.

A friendly word of caution

Before you embark into the world of molecular genealogy, we want you to consider two things. First, by taking a DNA test, you might find out something that you would rather not know. For example, some people have discovered that they're not biologically related to the family from which they've always claimed descent. Sometimes this occurs due to a "nonpaternal event," where the biological father was not the person listed on the birth record. (This may have occurred in the immediate family or in a past generation.) Others have discovered that they may not have the racial or ethnic composition that they've always identified themselves with. Also, some testing services provide probabilities that a particular disease or medical condition might occur. If you prefer not to know that, you can skip that portion of the results.

The second thing to remember is that molecular genealogy is a science, but not an absolute one. DNA test results show the probability that something is true. (*Probability* is the likelihood that a specific fact or outcome will occur.) Nothing is ever 100 percent certain. In addition, sometimes (but rarely) mistakes are made by the testing facility, or new research is discovered that changes the way a test result is viewed. DNA testing for genealogy is still undergoing development and being refined. As long as you can adapt to change and accept new technology, you'll be just fine in the world of DNA genealogy.

What can molecular genealogy do for you?

Have you ever thought about the applications of genetic testing in genealogical research? It's a brave new world in which some of your family riddles may be answered and the brick walls in your research could be torn down. Molecular genealogy offers hope in many research realms, not the least of which are

- Determining whether two people are related when one or both were adopted
- Identifying whether two people are descended from the same ancestor

✔ Discovering whether you are related to others with the same surname

✔ Proving or disproving your family tree research

✔ Providing clues about your ethnic origin

✔ Finding out about inherited traits from your family

Getting down to bases

There's no doubt about it: DNA is hard to explain. We do our best to keep it simple but informative here. Being a family historian, most likely you've taken a research trip to a particular town to find the burial location for an ancestor. When you reached that town, your first stop was probably the local library. Entering the library, you quickly made your way to the reference room. You leafed through the reference room collection, looking for a cemetery index for that area. Finding an index, you located the chapter that contained a list of gravestones for the cemetery where your ancestor is buried. Thumbing through the chapter, you found your ancestor's name, which is typed with some combination of 26 letters (assuming that it contains no special characters and that the book is in English).

You can think about the components of DNA like the preceding library. (Figure 10-1 shows a model of the components of DNA.) The basic building blocks of humans are *cells* that function like little towns. Within each cell is a *nucleus,* which is the structure that contains all the DNA. This nucleus acts as the library for the cell. Within the nucleus is the *genome* (the complete set of instructions for how the cell will operate). You can think of the genome as the reference book collection of the library.

The human genome contains 23 pairs of chromosomes. A *chromosome* is the container that holds the strands of DNA. Each type of chromosome has a different set of instructions and serves a different purpose. Sticking with our analogy, like a library's reference collection has several types of reference books, the genome has several types of chromosomes. Particular sections of a chromosome are called genes. *Genes* contain specific sequences of information that determine a particular inheritable characteristic of a human. Where a chromosome is the reference book, genes are the chapters in the book.

A particular gene can come in different forms called *alleles.* For example, the gene for eye color might come in a blue eye allele or a brown eye allele. To use our book analogy, a particular chapter of a book can be laid out in different ways. Alleles would be different layouts that a particular chapter could have.

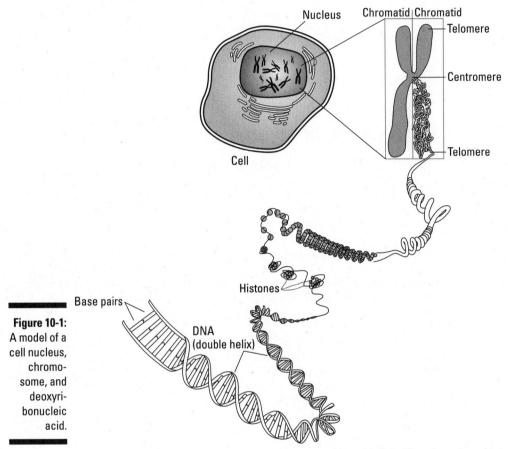

Courtesy of the National Human Genome Research Institute

Figure 10-1:
A model of a cell nucleus, chromosome, and deoxyribonucleic acid.

Genes are composed of *bases,* also called *nucleotides,* which form the rungs of the DNA ladder that hold the DNA molecule together. You find four types of bases: adenine (A), guanine (G), cytosine (C), and thymine (T). When forming the rungs of the DNA molecule, bases attach in only one way. Adenine always pairs with thymine on the opposite strand, and guanine always pairs with cytosine. The attachment of bases is called *base pairing.* The bases are the language of DNA. You read the sequence of the base pairs to determine the coding of the allele — just like reading the sequence of letters in a book forms a recognizable sentence.

Please understand that our DNA-library analogy is a very simplistic explanation of the molecular parts that are considered in genetic testing. DNA plays a much more complicated role in genetics than what we just covered. However, for the purpose of this chapter, our basic presentation on genetic structure should be sufficient for understanding the broader implications in DNA testing for molecular genealogy.

Selecting the Right Test for You

After you gain a basic understanding of molecular structure, you may find your curiosity piqued — are you ready to jump right in and gather DNA samples willy-nilly? Slow down! You have more to discover so that you don't lose time and momentum by submitting your swabs for the wrong types of tests.

Four types of tests are commonly available from DNA testing companies:

- **Y chromosome DNA testing:** Humans have 23 pairs of chromosomes. Of these 23, males and females have 22 pairs in common and one pair not in common. In that one pair, males have one X and one Y chromosome, whereas females have two X chromosomes. The Y chromosome DNA test explores the Y chromosome in this uncommon pair of chromosomes. As you might suspect at this point, this particular test is available only for men because females do not carry the Y chromosome. However, just because you — the reader — might be female, don't fail to read the following section on Y chromosome DNA testing. You can always have a male relative (such as your father, brother, uncle, or cousin) take this test for you to discover the hidden secrets in your familial Y DNA.

- **Mitochondrial DNA testing:** The mitochondrion is considered by some to be the "power plant" of the cell. (Remember, the cell is the basic building block of the human body.) It sits outside the nucleus of the cell, and it contains its own distinct genome — that means its genome is separate from the genome found in the nucleus of the cell. This distinct genome is known as mtDNA in genetic testing. The mtDNA is inherited only from the female parent, is passed to all offspring (male and female), and mutates (or changes) at a slow rate over generations. All of these aspects of the mtDNA make it good for identifying genetic relationships over hundreds of generations.

- **Autosomal DNA testing:** Autosomal DNA consists of 22 pairs of non–sex-specific chromosomes that are found in the cell nucleus — this means that they don't contain the X or Y chromosome. Autosomal DNA is found in males and females and is the part of the DNA responsible for characteristics such as height and eye color. This DNA is inherited from both parents. Autosomal testing, also called admixture or biogeographical testing, is used to determine paternity, indicate ethnicity, and diagnose potential health problems.

- **X chromosome DNA testing:** As we mention earlier, males have one X and one Y chromosome, whereas females have two X chromosomes. This test looks at the mixture of the X chromosomes inherited over several generations.

Given the complexity of molecular research, we expect the tests to be complicated as well. Hence, each test warrants its own attention. In the next sections, we explore them in a little more depth.

Y chromosome DNA testing

In the preceding section, we introduce the concept that the Y chromosome DNA test examines the Y chromosome that men receive from their male ancestors. The Y chromosome is part of the one chromosomal pair that is not common between males and females; in males, the pair has an X and a Y chromosome, whereas in females, the pair has two X chromosomes. We also mention that this test is available only for men — although women can participate in Y chromosome projects by using a father, brother, or male cousin as a proxy. (Figure 10-2 shows how the Y chromosome is passed from one male to another.) Now it's time to get into the details of the test.

Figure 10-2:
A
Y chromo-
some is
passed from
father to son
relatively
unchanged.

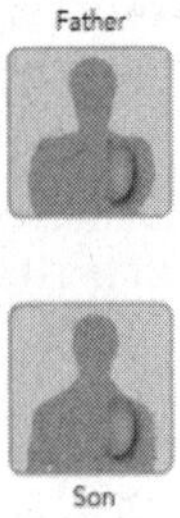

Father

Son

Courtesy of the Sorenson Molecular Genealogy Foundation, the scientific backbone of GeneTree.com

"Junk" DNA is worth something

When scientists began studying chromosomes, they discovered that not all the base pairs were used as instructions for the cell. These *noncoding regions,* sometimes referred to as "junk" DNA because they seem to just be hanging around without helping guide the cell to fulfill its larger purpose, contain alleles that differ from person to person. This means that the junk DNA has characteristics that distinguish individuals from each other. Scientists soon began to use these alleles to identify individuals, especially in criminal investigations.

As more research was performed on the Y chromosome, scientists found that the noncoding regions could be used to define not only individual characteristics but also characteristics of larger populations into which individuals with these characteristics fit. In essence, they discovered how to determine what population a particular human was a member of by using the noncoding regions of the DNA. They also discovered that the Y chromosome changes (or mutates) very little or not at all between fathers and sons. Because the Y chromosome is passed only from father to son, it is useful for tracing the direct paternal line of an individual's ancestry (as illustrated in Figure 10-3).

Figure 10-3: The path of the Y chromosome through a family.

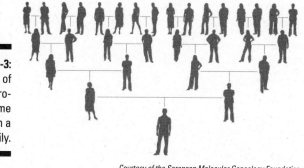

Courtesy of the Sorenson Molecular Genealogy Foundation, the scientific backbone of GeneTree.com

The testing process

The process of testing the Y chromosome starts with a man swabbing the inside of his cheek with a sample collection device that usually looks something like a Q-Tip cotton swab. The swab collects cheek cells, which serve as the source for the DNA. After the laboratory receives the swab, the DNA is extracted using a process called polymerase chain reaction (PCR). This process makes thousands of copies of the DNA so that it can be analyzed.

After the copies are made, sequences of DNA at specific locations on the chromosome are analyzed. These sequences are called *markers,* and the location of the markers on the chromosome is called the *locus* (or plural *loci*). The markers are read by the sequence of the bases. (Remember, as we mention in the section "Getting down to bases," earlier in this chapter, the bases are abbreviated A, G, C, and T.) The sequence for the bases shown in Figure 10-4 is

```
ATGCTAATCGGC
```

Each marker is given a name that usually begins with *DYS* — short for DNA Y Chromosome Segment. When analyzing the markers, laboratory technicians look for the number of times that a segment of bases (usually three to five bases long) repeats. These segments of repeating bases are called *short tandem repeat polymorphisms* (STRPs).

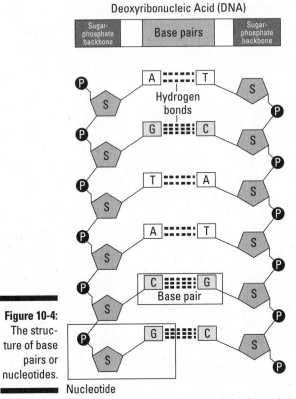

Deoxyribonucleic Acid (DNA)

Figure 10-4:
The structure of base pairs or nucleotides.

Courtesy of the National Human Genome Research Institute

Is your head spinning yet from all the definitions? Try using the book analogy again: Think of this book as the Y chromosome and this chapter as a gene on the chromosome. This page would be the locus where the segment is located — that is easily found by using the page number. The DNA Y Chromosome Segment is the following sentence:

I like this book VERY VERY VERY much.

The Short Tandem Repeat is the phrase *VERY VERY VERY* in the sentence — a set of letters that repeat.

Now see whether you can make sense of a real sequence of bases for the marker DYS393, keeping in mind that you can refer to the book example if needed:

gtggtcttctacttgtgtcaatac AGAT AGAT AGAT AGAT AGAT AGAT AGAT AGAT AGAT AGAT AGAT AGAT AGAT AGAT AGAT atgtatgtcttttctatgagacatac ctcatttttggacttgagttc

To make it easier for you to see, we capitalized the letters and inserted spaces between the base segments composing the STR (which are AGAT). If you count the number of times the bases AGAT repeat, you find that the number of repeats for DYS393 for this individual is 15.

Comparing the results

After the number of repeats within a marker is calculated, we can compare the results of that marker plus a few other markers to see whether two or more individuals are related. Most labs try to compare at least 12 markers. Table 10-1 shows a comparison between the markers of four individuals.

Table 10-1	A Comparison of 12 Markers for Four Individuals										
ID	DYS393	DYS390	DYS19/394	DYS391	DYS385a	DYS385b	DYS426	DYS388	DYS439	DYS389-1	DYS392	DYS389-2
A	13	25	14	11	11	11	12	12	13	13	13	29
B	13	25	14	11	11	11	12	12	12	13	13	29
C	13	25	14	11	11	11	12	12	12	13	13	29
D	13	25	14	11	11	11	12	12	12	13	13	29
Modal	13	25	14	11	11	11	12	12	12	13	13	29

If you compare the results between Individuals A and B in Table 10-1, you can see that they have the same number of repeats in 11 of the 12 markers. Only at DYS439 is there a difference in the number of repeats, commonly called a *mutation*. Based on this information, we would say that a genetic distance of 1 exists between these two individuals. At 12 markers, a genetic distance of 1 would indicate that these two individuals are probably related; however, testing more markers would certainly give a better indication of how closely they may be related. A higher probability exists that Individuals B, C, and D are related because they match on all 12 markers.

The result of a set of markers for an individual is called a *haplotype*. So, in the preceding chart, the haplotype for Individual A is DYS393 – 13, DYS390 – 25, DYS19/394 – 14, DYS391 – 11, DYS385a – 11, DYS395b – 11, DYS426 – 12, DYS388 – 12, DYS439 – 13, DYS389-1 – 13, DYS392 – 13, DYS 389-2 – 29.

After you have haplotype results for an individual, it's important to get results from relatives of that individual. More specifically, it's important to get the haplotype results for relatives whose relationships can be documented by primary sources, including those in the extended family. These results help confirm the results of Individual A and establish an overall specific haplotype for the family. For example, say that all the individuals in Table 10-1 are related, and the fact is well documented with primary sources. After analyzing the results, a *modal haplotype* can be calculated by looking at the number of repeats that have the highest occurrence for each marker. Because all the results are the same for 11 out of 12 markers, the modal values for these are the same as the number of repeats for that marker. That leaves only one marker to calculate — DYS439. The results for DYS439 include one 13 and four 12s. That makes the modal value for that marker 12 — because it appears the most. So, the row marked *Modal* in Table 10-1 shows the haplotype for Individual A's family.

The modal haplotype for a family can be used to compare that family to other families with the same surname to determine the probability that the two families are related. A good way to see these relationships is to join a surname DNA project — we talk about how to find these projects in the section "Helpful DNA Sites," later in this chapter.

Assessing the probability of a relationship

After the test is taken and the results compared, it's time to figure out the probability that two individuals are related. This probability is calculated by determining how often a change might occur to a marker over time. Fortunately, the testing companies calculate this for you and typically give you a tool (in the form of an online chart or written instructions) to compare two results.

Reviewing the data in Table 10-1, say that you want to determine how closely related Individual A may be to Individual B. To do this, you need to identify the *Time to Most Recent Common Ancestor* (TMRCA) for the two individuals. The TMRCA is pretty much what it sounds like — a calculation to determine when two individuals may have shared the same ancestor. As you'll see from this example, the calculation is not extremely precise, but it is close enough to point you in the right direction as you begin looking for supporting documentation. By the way, if you want a more in-depth explanation of how TMRCA works, see the article by Bruce Walsh at `http://nitro.biosci.arizona.edu/ftdna/TMRCA.html`.

The easiest way to determine the TMRCA between two individuals is to use an online utility. If your testing company doesn't have one — or you're comparing results from more than one testing company — you can use the Y-Utility: Y-DNA Comparison Utility at `www.mymcgee.com/tools/yutility.html`. You have a lot of options with this utility, so we take it a step at a time.

1. **Point your web browser to the Y-Utility website at `www.mymcgee.com/tools/yutility.html`.**

   The page has a number of options and ways of displaying the data. We adjust some of these to make it easier to see the results.

2. **Ensure that the Marker table includes those markers necessary for the calculation.**

   In the table at the top of the screen, you can see 100 markers. In this example, you work with the first 13 markers from the left. Make sure that the following markers are selected for Exists and Enable: DYS393, DYS390, DYS19/394, DYS391, DYS385a, DYS385b, DYS426, DYS388, DYS439, DYS389-1, DYS392, and DYS 389-2. Be sure that DYS19b is not selected. You can leave the rest of the markers selected.

3. **Select the options that provide the appropriate calculation.**

   You are looking only for the TMRCA, so deselect the check boxes next to Ysearch, SMGF, Ybase, Yhrd, and Genetic Distance. Under the General Setup column, deselect the Create Modal Haplotype check box.

4. **Enter the marker values into the Paste Haplotype Rows Here field.**

   Make sure that you separate the values with a space, as shown here:

   ```
   A 13 25 14 11 11 11 12 12 13 13 13 29
   B 13 25 14 11 11 11 12 12 12 13 13 29
   ```

5. **Click Execute.**

   A new browser window appears with the calculation. In this example, the time to most recent common ancestor between Individuals A and B is estimated at 1,110 years. (The box with the TMRCA contains a blue background.)

Figure 10-5 shows the estimated TMRCA for Individuals A and B. Essentially, the results show a 50 percent probability that Individuals A and B shared a common ancestor within the past 1,110 years. So, as you can see, just testing on 12 markers doesn't give you conclusive evidence of how closely two people are related. However, it can certainly indicate that two individuals are not related — especially if more than 2 markers out of 12 don't match.

Haplogroups

We mention earlier in this chapter that haplotypes are a set of results of markers for a particular individual. When several similar haplotypes are categorized together, they compose a *haplogroup*. Haplogroups are useful for deep ancestry research (that is, research that is further back than the advent of surnames) and for placing a geographical context around the possible origin of the individuals in the haplogroup.

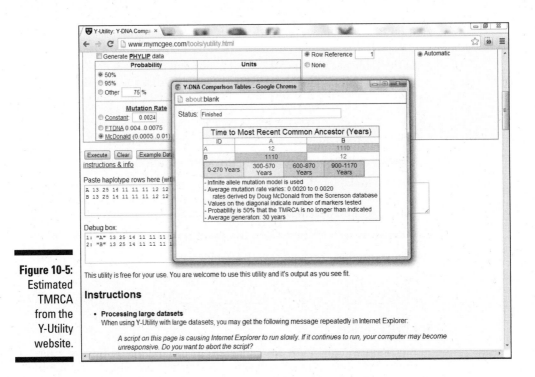

Figure 10-5:
Estimated
TMRCA
from the
Y-Utility
website.

Y chromosome haplogroups are categorized by the letters A through T. You can find the current Haplogroup Tree at `www.isogg.org/tree/`. These letter designations are based on mutations of certain locations of the Y chromosome. For instance, if an individual has a mutation at the M89 locus, that individual falls into a haplogroup between F and J. If the individual has a mutation at both the M89 and M170 loci, the individual is classified in the I haplogroup.

When you submit a sample to a DNA testing company, the results you receive usually include your haplogroup. You can then take that haplogroup and go to the National Geographic Genographic Project page to find out more about the origins of the haplogroup. Follow these steps:

1. **Point your web browser to the National Geographic project site at** `https://genographic.nationalgeographic.com`.

   In the top portion of the page are links to the different sections of the site, including About, News, Results, Buy the Kit, and Resources.

2. **Point your cursor at the Resources tab.**

   A menu drops down.

3. **Click Map of Human Migration.**

   A map appears showing the probable migration routes.

4. **Hover your mouse pointer over the segments of the migration route.**

   A pop-up box appears over the migration route lines.

5. **Click the route line to see additional information about the haplogroups.**

Figure 10-6 shows a map of the migration path of haplogroups from Southeastern Europe to Northern Europe.

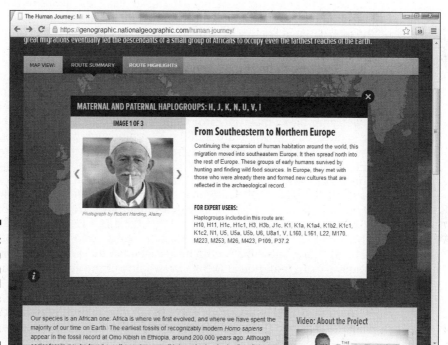

Figure 10-6:
Migration
Paths from
the National
Geographic
Genographic
Project site.

Haplogroups can also be used to show the genetic distribution of individuals in a particular geographic area. For example, Doug McDonald maintains a map of the distribution of haplogroups at www.scs.uiuc.edu/~mcdonald/ WorldHaplogroupsMaps.pdf. So, if you're interested in finding out the distribution of Haplogroup I in Europe, you can match the color (pink) on the pie charts to determine how prevalent the haplogroup is in a particular area. From this chart, you can see that Haplogroup I has a strong concentration in Scandinavia and Northwest Europe.

Because haplogroups are large collections of haplotypes, it is useful to break down haplogroups into subgroups that have common traits. These subgroups are referred to as *subclades.* Subclades can help genealogists get a clearer picture of the geographical setting of that portion of the haplogroup.

Although the typical Y chromosome test can suggest a haplogroup and perhaps a high-level subclade, it normally takes additional testing to refine the subclade. In these additional tests, particular positions of the Y chromosome are examined for differences called *single nucleotide polymorphisms* (SNPs, or *snips*). Some SNPs are common and apply to a large population of people within a haplogroup. Other SNPs can be unique to an individual or a family — referred to as private SNPs. New SNPs are constantly being discovered, and that sometimes results in changes to the labels of subclades or the discovery of new subclades. To find the most up-to-date list of subclades, take a look at the International Society of Genetic Genealogy (ISOGG) Y-DNA Haplogroup Tree at `www.isogg.org/tree/`.

To illustrate how subclades work, look at the Haplogroup I example. Haplogroup I has a concentration in Northern Europe and a concentration in the Balkans. If you're in that haplogroup, you might be curious about which region your direct male ancestor came from. To find this out, SNP tests would be conducted on several areas of the Y chromosome and compared with the Y-DNA Haplogroup I and Its Subclades – 2013 chart at `www.isogg.org/tree/ISOGG_HapgrpI.html`. (See Figure 10-7.) If the individual had mutations at the positions L41/PF3787, M170/PF3715, M258, P19_1, P19_2, P19_3, P19_4, P19_5, P38, P212, U179, that individual would be in the Haplogroup I (also referred to as I-M170). If further mutations were found at locations L64, L75, L80, L81, L118, L121/S62, L123, L124/S64, L125/S65, L157.1, L186, L187, L840, M253, M307.2/P203.2, M450/S109, P30, P40, S63, S66, S107, S108, S110, S111, the individual would be classified in the subclade I1 (or I-M253). Discovery of a mutation at DF29/S438 would put the individual in the subclade I1a (or I-DF29), and so on.

With the subclade in hand, you can consult a haplogroup distribution map to see where the subclade has the highest distribution. Figure 10-8 shows the distribution of Haplogroup I from a map on Wikipedia (`http://en.wikipedia.org/wiki/File:Haplogroup_I.png`). Note that subclade I1 is listed as I-M253 on the map and that its greatest concentration is found in Norway, Sweden, and Denmark, with lesser concentrations in eastern England and Normandy. This information can give you a hint as to where your ancestors may have originated.

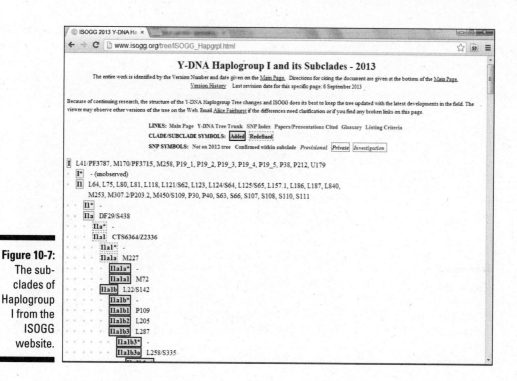

Figure 10-7:
The sub-
clades of
Haplogroup
I from the
ISOGG
website.

After you discover the haplogroup of your results, you can join a Y chromosome project for a particular haplogroup. Through a haplogroup project, you might be able to find out more about the origins of the haplogroup or the subclade within the haplogroup and communicate with others who are studying the same genetic group. To find a project for your haplogroup, see whether your DNA testing company already has a project for it or do a search using a general Internet search engine, such as Google, for something like *"Y-DNA Haplogroup I project"* or look for a haplogroup project hosted by the company that conducted your testing.

Getting tested

Have you decided it's time to take the plunge and get a Y chromosome test? If you're female (or if you're a male but not a direct-line descendant from the family for which you want to test), you need to find a male relative that is a direct-line descendant of the family you're researching. Then it's just a matter of selecting a testing company and following its instructions.

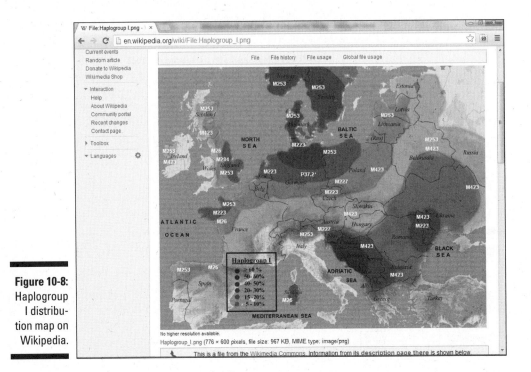

Figure 10-8: Haplogroup I distribution map on Wikipedia.

A number of testing companies offer Y chromosome testing. Some of these are

- ✔ **23andMe:** www.23andme.com (includes Y chromosome testing in its product)
- ✔ **African Ancestry:** http://africanancestry.com
- ✔ **AncestryDNA:** http://dna.ancestry.com/learnMorePaternal. aspx
- ✔ **Family Tree DNA:** www.familytreedna.com
- ✔ **Genebase:** www.genebase.com
- ✔ **Oxford Ancestors:** www.oxfordancestors.com

Locating others with the same results

Spending the money to perform a Y chromosome test doesn't do you much good unless you have something to compare the results with. To find others who have tested and received results, you should first look for a surname project currently under way for your direct male line. Some of the testing companies have established mechanisms for people to set up the projects that are housed on the testing companies' servers. For example, you can find a list of projects at the Family Tree DNA site at `www.familytreedna.com/projects.aspx`.

Even if you're a member of a surname project, you may want to distribute your results to a wider audience in the hopes of locating others with matching results. Ysearch (`www.ysearch.org`) allows you to enter your results, which can be then searched by other researchers.

If you don't want your results to be publicly accessible, you can use these sites to search for others with your same haplotype and contact them directly. Say that you want to see whether any matches exist for the surname Abell in Ysearch. Follow these steps:

1. **Open your web browser and go to** `www.ysearch.org`.

   At the top of the page are blue tabs with labels such as Create a New User, Edit an Existing User, Alphabetical List of Last Names, Search by Last Name, Search for Genetic Matches, Search by Haplogroup, Research Tools, and Statistics.

2. **Click the Search by Last Name tab.**

   The resulting page contains two ways to search. You can search by entering a surname or by using a user ID. Also, you can limit the search to a specific geographic area.

3. **In the Type Last Names to Search For field, type the surname you're researching, type the two words in the Captcha box, and click Search.**

   Note that you can search for multiple names at the same time using commas to separate them. It's a good idea to do this if the last name has some common derivations. For the purposes of this example, type **Abell, Abel, Able.**

4. **Click the numeral in the Name or Variants results box.**

5. **Choose a match by clicking a link in the results table.**

   In our example, the results page shows six results. When we click the Abell result, the screen shows us brief information on each name, including an Abell from Maryland in Haplogroup I1.

6. **Click the User ID link to see the DNA results for this individual.**

   Figure 10-9 shows the test results for this individual. You also find a link on the page where you can e-mail the individual who submitted the result to Ysearch.

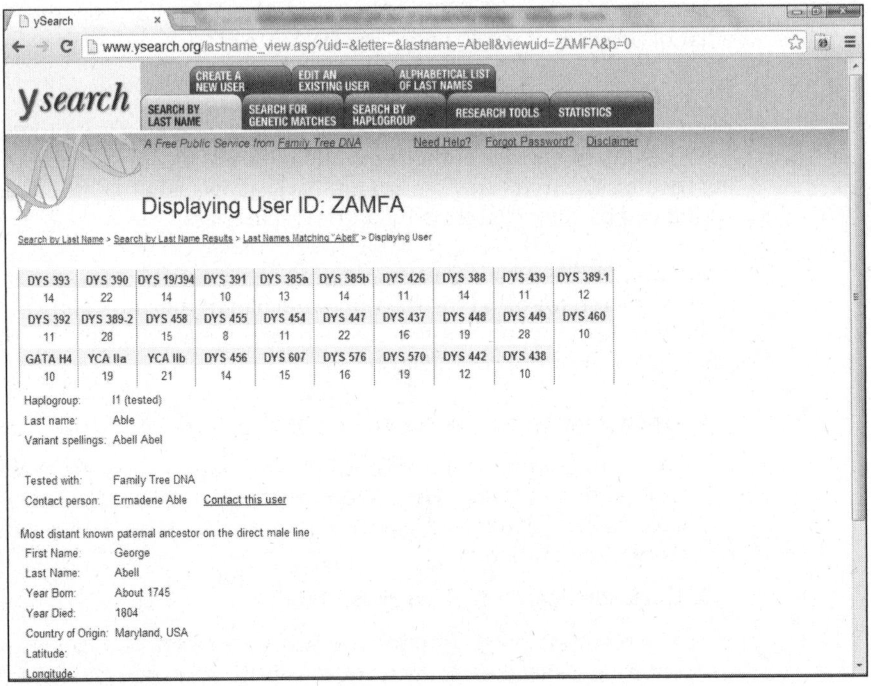

Figure 10-9:
Results from
Ysearch.org
for the sur-
name Abel.

Although you can't add your own results to the database, you can search the Sorenson Molecular Genealogy Foundation Y-Chromosome Database at www.smgf.org/pages/sorensondatabase.jspx. The database allows searches by surname or by haplotypes. The results in the database include pedigree charts submitted by the participants of the study. Unfortunately, one limitation of the database is that you don't have a direct way of contacting the participant to share research findings. A few other searchable Y chromosome databases are also available. The Y Chromosome Haplotype Reference Database, at www.yhrd.org, allows you to see the distribution of a particular haplotype. However, it is a scientific database geared toward DNA researchers, so it doesn't contain a lot of information useful to genealogists. Oxford Ancestors also allows you to search its database if you log in as a guest. The database is located at www.oxfordancestors.com/content/view/72/105.

Whole-genome testing

Although the genealogical prospects of whole-genome testing are not yet clear, some companies are now offering the sequencing of the entire Y chromosome. Full Genomes Corporation (https://www.fullgenomes.com) introduced the service in 2013; however, the price of the test is still beyond the reach of most genealogists.

Mitochondrial DNA testing

In the preceding section, you look at Y chromosome DNA testing that assists in the genetic identification of the direct male line of a family. In this section, you look at mitochondrial DNA testing, which allows the identification of the genetic information of the direct female line of a family.

The mitochondrion is the power plant of the cell. It's outside the nucleus and has its own distinct genome, called mtDNA, which is inherited from the female parent by both male and female children. (See Figure 10-10 shows the inheritance.) Because it also mutates at a very slow rate, the mtDNA is good for identifying genetic relationships over many, many years and generations, as shown in Figure 10-11.

Figure 10-10: Mitochondrial DNA is passed from the mother to her children.

Courtesy of the Sorenson Molecular Genealogy Foundation, the scientific backbone of GeneTree.com

Figure 10-11: The path of the mitochondrial DNA through a family.

Courtesy of the Sorenson Molecular Genealogy Foundation, the scientific backbone of GeneTree.com

Testing method

For testing, mitochondrial DNA is divided into three regions — a coding region, a Hyper Variable Region One (HVR1), and a Hyper Variable Region Two (HVR2). Genealogical tests are usually conducted on a sequence of Hyper Variable Region One or a sequence of both Hyper Variable Regions One and Two. Some testing facilities also fully sequence the entire mitochondrial DNA. The results from these sequences are compared with a sample known as the Cambridge Reference Sequence (CRS). The CRS is the mitochondrial sequence of the first individual to have her mitochondrial DNA sequenced. The differences between the sample and the CRS are considered mutations for the purposes of assigning a haplogroup to the sample.

How is this accomplished in practical terms? At the beginning of the chapter, we mention that DNA testing was used to identify the remains of the family of the last Czar of Russia. The results of the remains thought to be Czarina Alexandra were compared with Prince Philip, and the results matched. (Prince Philip and Czarina Alexandra were both descended from Queen Victoria.) The results were listed as the following:

```
HVR1: 16111T, 16357C HVR2: 263G, 315.1C
```

Earlier in this chapter, in the "Getting down to bases" section, we talk about how DNA is coded. In that section, we mention that a DNA sequence contains four bases: adenine (A), guanine (G), cytosine (C), and thymine (T). These same bases are used in sequencing mitochondrial DNA.

The first result for Czarina Alexandra was 16111T. This result is interpreted as the substitution of thymine in the location 16111 of the Hyper Variable One region. The second result translates as the substitution of cytosine at location 16357 of the same region. The next result, 263G, shows a substitution of guanine at location 263 in the Hyper Variable Two region. The fourth result is a bit different in that it contains a .1, indicating that an extra base was found at that location. This means that the fourth result shows that an extra cytosine is found at the 315 location in the Hyper Variable Two region. Based on the changes between Czarina Alexandra's sequence and the Cambridge Reference Sequence, her sample was classified in mitochondrial Haplogroup H.

Keep in mind that although they're named in the same manner, Y chromosome haplogroups and mitochondrial haplogroups are two different entities.

Making sense of the results

Mitochondrial DNA changes (or mutates) at a slow rate. This makes its uses for genealogical purposes very different than the uses for Y chromosomes, which change at a faster rate and can link family members together at closer intervals. However, mtDNA is useful for determining long-term relationships, as in the case of the Romanov family.

When two individuals have the same mutations within the Hyper Variable One region, it is considered a *low-resolution match*. If the individuals have a low-resolution match and are classified in the same haplogroup, there is about a 50 percent chance that they shared a common ancestor within the past 52 generations (or about 1,300 years). If they have a low-resolution match and the haplogroups are not the same, it is considered a coincidence, and the probability is that the two individuals did not share a common ancestor within a measurable time frame. Depending on your result set, you might get a lot of low-resolution matches. To see whether a connection really exists, it is useful to test both the Hyper Variable One and Hyper Variable Two regions.

A *high-resolution match* occurs when two individuals match exactly at both Hyper Variable One and Hyper Variable Two regions. Individuals having high-resolution matches are more likely to be related within a genealogically provable time frame. With a high-resolution match, there is about a 50 percent probability of sharing a common ancestor within the past 28 generations (about 700 years).

Testing companies

A lot of the same companies that provide Y chromosome tests also provide mitochondrial DNA tests. In fact, if you are male, you can have the tests performed at the same time on the same sample. Here are some sites to consider:

- ✔ **23andMe:** www.23andme.com
- ✔ **African Ancestry:** http://africanancestry.com/matriclan.html
- ✔ **AncestryDNA:** http://ldna.ancestry.com/learnMoreMaternal.aspx
- ✔ **Family Tree DNA:** www.familytreedna.com
- ✔ **Genebase:** www.genebase.com
- ✔ **Oxford Ancestors:** www.oxfordancestors.com/content/view/35/55

Finding others with the same results

Similar to Y chromosome testing, you might want to post your mitochondrial DNA results to some public databases. One place to post results is at www.mitosearch.org, shown in Figure 10-12. If you want to find results of mitochondrial tests performed by the Sorenson Molecular Genealogy Foundation, see the Mitochondrial Database at www.smgf.org/mtdna/search.jspx. To find more information on mitochondrial DNA scientific databases, check out MITOMAP at www.mitomap.org.

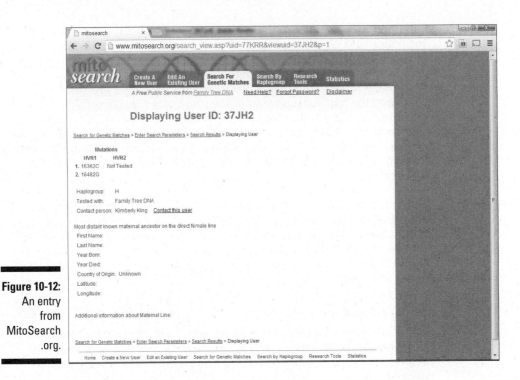

Figure 10-12:
An entry
from
MitoSearch
.org.

Autosomal DNA testing

To investigate DNA from ancestors who were not direct-line paternal or maternal, you would use autosomal testing. Earlier in the chapter, we talk about 22 pairs of nonsex chromosomes found in the cell nucleus. These nonsex chromosomes are known as *autosomes*. Autosomes are found in both males and females and are the part of the DNA that is responsible for physical characteristics of an individual, such as height and eye color.

For each pair of autosomes that an individual has, one came from the father and the other from the mother. The process where a parent contributes half of his or her child's DNA, creating a new genetic identity, is called *recombination*. Similarly, each of the individual's parents received a set of autosomes from their parents and so forth through the generations, as shown in Figure 10-13.

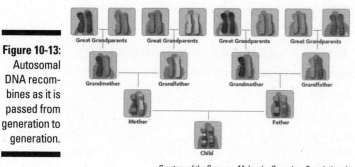

Courtesy of the Sorenson Molecular Genealogy Foundation, the
scientific backbone of GeneTree.com

Figure 10-13:
Autosomal
DNA recom-
bines as it is
passed from
generation to
generation.

Autosomal testing traditionally has been used for paternity testing, in forensic investigations, and to predict percentages of ethnicity for genealogical
purposes. But recent work has expanded the use of autosomal testing within
genealogy to test for relationships between individuals who have more recent
common ancestors.

Ethnicity testing

When forensic scientists began looking into DNA, they recognized that certain genetic markers were common to particular ethnicities. After enough
markers were identified with ethnicities, they could begin to assess what percentage of ethnicity a particular person might possess. Genealogists picked
up on this and believed that the same types of tests might be able to shed
some light on the ethnicities of their ancestors — especially in the areas of
identifying Native American, Jewish, and African ancestry.

The controversial weakness with autosomal testing is that the DNA in each
individual recombines differently. This means that two children born from
the same two parents could measure with different ethnicities because their
DNA does not recombine exactly the same way. Also, the percentages quoted
by testing companies can often have a significant error rate or change over
time as new research comes to light.

If you take an ethnicity test, you can expect to receive a copy of the
sequences examined and an interpretation of the results. The interpretation
usually comes in the form of a percentage of a certain ethnicity. For example,
Figure 10-14 shows a view of a person's ethnicity at 23andMe. In this case, it
shows the following general ethnic percentages:

European: 96.5%

Sub-Saharan African: 2.5%

East Asian & Native American: 0.6%

Middle Eastern & North African: 0%

South Asian: 0%

Oceanian: 0%

Unassigned: 0.3%

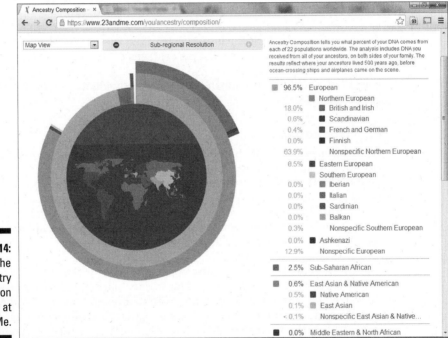

Figure 10-14:
The
Ancestry
Composition
screen at
23andMe.

The results further breakdown the ethnic groups into regional and sub-regional percentages:

British and Irish: 18.0%

Scandinavian: 0.6%

French and German: 0.4%

Nonspecific Northern European: 63.9%

Eastern European: 0.5%

Iberian: 0%

Italian: 0%

Sardinian: 0%

Balkan: 0%

Nonspecific Southern European: 0.3%

Ashkenazi: 0%

Nonspecific European: 12.9%

Native American: 0.5%

East Asian: 0.1%

North African: 0%

Middle Eastern: 0%

If you're interested in taking an autosomal test, here are some companies to look at:

- ✔ **AncestrybyDNA:** www.ancestrybydna.com
- ✔ **DNA Tribes:** www.dnatribes.com
- ✔ **23andMe:** www.23andme.com/ancestry/origins
- ✔ **AncestryDNA:** http://dna.ancestry.com
- ✔ **Family Tree DNA:** www.familytreedna.com

Relationship testing

As we mention earlier, Y chromosome testing is useful for tracing the direct male line. Mitochondrial testing is good for tracing a direct female line Autosomal testing can be used to provide evidence for relationships between people who may share a recent ancestor, as shown in Figure 10-15.

Figure 10-15:
People who are more closely related share more autosomal DNA than those more distantly related.

Closer Relatives

More Distant Relatives

Courtesy of the Sorenson Molecular Genealogy Foundation,
the scientific backbone of GeneTree.com

How does it work, you ask? Within each generation, the autosomal DNA recombines using half of the DNA from each parent. Over time, the DNA contains more and more changes. By comparing the amount of similar DNA in two autosomal DNA samples, testing companies can suggest how closely two people are related.

For example, Family Tree DNA has introduced the Family Finder test. This test can be used to provide evidence on the relationship of two individuals if they are descended from the same great-great grandparent. The results of the test are kept in a database that is constantly searched for matches. According to Family Tree DNA, the Family Finder can detect 99 percent of a person's second cousins, 90 percent of third cousins, 50 percent of fourth cousins, and about 10 percent of fifth cousins. Another company that provides autosomal testing and matching of relatives is 23andMe, with its DNA Relatives functionality (www.23andme.com/you/relfinder/). Figure 10-16 shows the results page from the DNA Relatives page. The page indicates the sex of the matching individual (and name, if the individual has shared his or her genome), whether the match is on the maternal or paternal side, the estimated relationship, number of shared segments, percent chromosome shared, haplogroup, and locations and names of ancestors.

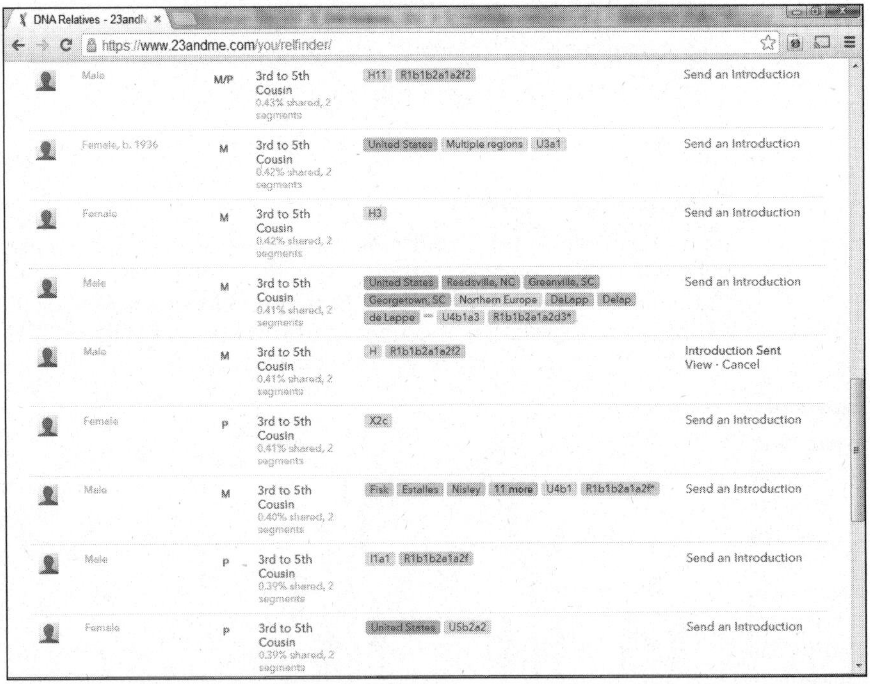

Figure 10-16: DNA Relatives matching page on 23andMe.

Because the recombination of autosomal DNA is random, an autosomal test might fail to recognize cousins. This is because a person does not necessarily inherit exactly 25 percent of his or her DNA from each grandparent. Plus, due to the random inheritance of DNA, nothing guarantees that two cousins would inherit enough of the same DNA to appear as a match.

X chromosome DNA testing

X chromosome testing can fill in some of the gaps between what Y chromosome and mitochondrial testing can show. As we mention earlier, females have two X chromosomes and males have one X and one Y chromosome. The mother's X chromosomes act like autosomes in that the two X chromosomes recombine, and one X chromosome is passed from the mother to each child, regardless of sex. The father passes a copy of his X chromosome only to his daughters. Because he has only the one X chromosome, no recombination takes place. (See Figure 10-17.)

Figure 10-17: Mothers pass a recombined X chromosome to their children. Fathers pass a non-recombined X chromosome only to their daughters.

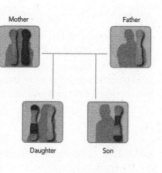

Courtesy of the Sorenson Molecular Genealogy Foundation, the scientific backbone of GeneTree.com

By looking at the X chromosome, relationships can be established for a larger population of individuals that share genetic material than can be traced through Y chromosome or mitochondrial testing. (See Figure 10-18.)

Figure 10-18:
X chromosome testing can link a larger population of individuals than Y chromosome or mitochondrial testing.

Courtesy of the Sorenson Molecular Genealogy Foundation, the scientific backbone of GeneTree.com

Finding Helpful DNA Sites

Within this chapter, we were able to cover only the tip of the iceberg in using DNA testing for genealogical purposes. Some websites can provide additional information to help you decide whether DNA testing is useful for your research or to keep abreast of the current developments in DNA research.

If you're looking for some basic information on using DNA testing in genealogy, see the International Society of Genetic Genealogy DNA-Newbies page at `www.isogg.org` or at the Sorenson Molecular Genealogy Foundation's Why Molecular Genealogy page at `www.smgf.org/pages/why_genetic_genealogy.jspx`. The Sorenson Molecular Genealogy Foundation has some videos on its site that provide a clear and concise explanation of the fundamental concepts of molecular genealogy.

Because DNA testing methods and capabilities change on a frequent basis, it's a good idea to consult some sites that provide updates on the technology and issues related to using the technology. A few sites to consult include

✔ **Genealogy-DNA mailing list archives:** `http://lists5.rootsweb.ancestry.com/index/other/DNA/GENEALOGY-DNA.html` (You can also subscribe to the mailing list from this page.)

✔ **Genetic Genealogist blog:** `www.thegeneticgenealogist.com`

✔ **Your Genetic Genealogist:** `www.yourgeneticgenealogist.com`

Part IV
Doing Things the Genealogical Way

Take a look at "Vacationing with Genealogy" online at www.dummies.com/extras/genealogyonline.

In this part...

- Explore methods of doing genealogical research.
- Learn how to share your data with the genealogical community.
- Locate online resources to network with other genealogists.
- Locate genealogical and historical societies that can help your research.
- Learn how to hire a researcher.
- Discover items to take on your family history trip.

Chapter 11

Share and Share Alike

*Y*ou've loaded your genealogical database with information about your relatives and ancestors. Now you may begin feeling that it's time to start sharing the valuable information you discovered — after all, sharing information is one foundation of a solid genealogical community. When you share information, you often get a lot of information in return from other researchers. For example, shortly after we began the Helm/Helms Family Research web page, several other Helm researchers throughout the world contacted us. We discovered that several Helm lines existed that we didn't even know about. Plus, we received valuable information on our own line from references that other researchers discovered during their research, not to mention that we connected with some really nice folks we probably wouldn't have met otherwise.

You can find many online outlets for sharing information. In the early days of Internet use for genealogy, our advice to readers was to create from scratch and post your own home page (website) where you could open the doors to guests, inviting others to come to you for information and advice. But these days, there are much easier and friendlier options than mastering HyperText Markup Language (HTML) and other coding programs. Online communities exist where all you have to do is use a template to create a snazzy-looking site. After your site is up and running, you can invite all your family and friends over. You can even make your site available to the general public so that others you don't know who might be researching the same families can find you on the Internet.

In this chapter, we focus on methods you can use to share information and explore networking sites, blogs, and even basic home-grown HTML web pages (for the die-hard do-it-yourselfers) where you can post your information. Also we review how to use genealogical utility programs to help put content in specific formats on your site.

Why Would Anyone Want Your Stuff?

Why would anyone want my stuff? seems like a logical first question when you stop and think about making the many tidbits and treasures you collected available to others. Who would want a copy of that old, ratty-looking photograph you have of Great-grandpa as a dirty-faced toddler in what appears to be a dress? Nobody else wanted it in the first place, and that's probably how you ended up with it, right? The picture has sentimental value only to you. Wrong! Some of Great-grandpa's other descendants may be looking for information about him. They, too, would love to see a picture of him when he was a little boy — even better, they'd love to have their own electronic copy of that picture!

As you develop more and more online contact with other genealogists, you may find a lot of people who are interested in exchanging information. Some may be interested in your research findings because you share common ancestors, and others may be interested because they're researching in the same geographical area where your ancestors were from. Aren't these the same reasons that you're interested in seeing other researchers' stuff? Sharing your information is likely to encourage others to share theirs with you. Exchanging information with others may enable you to fill in some gaps in your own research efforts. Even if the research findings you receive from others doesn't directly answer questions about your ancestors, they may give you clues about where to find more information to fill in the blanks.

Also, just because you haven't traced your genealogy back to the Middle Ages doesn't mean that your information isn't valuable. Although you should not share information on living persons without their explicit permission, you should feel free to share any facts that you do know about deceased ancestors. Just as you may not know your genealogy any further than your great-grandfather, someone else may be in the same boat — and with the same person! Meeting with that fellow researcher can lead to a mutual research relationship that can produce a lot more information in a shorter amount of time.

Developing Your Marketing Plan

You're at the point where you recognize the value in sharing your genealogical information online. How do you begin letting people know what you have? Well, the first thing to do is to come up with a marketing plan for your information — much like a business does when it decides to sell a product.

A *surname marketing plan* is simply a checklist of places and people to contact to effectively inform the right individuals about the information that you have to contribute to the genealogy community. As you devise your plan, ask yourself the following questions:

- ✔ **What is the best method for me to post my research? Blog? Web page?**

- ✔ **Which social networks should I join? How can I best use them for sharing information?**

- ✔ **Which existing sites are interested in my information? Surname sites (see Chapter 6)? Geographical sites (see Chapter 7)? Association sites (Chapters 6 and 7)?**

TIP

You may want to use all available Internet resources to let people know about your information, including your favorite networking site, a blog, and websites.

For example, let's say April has information on a McSwain family that lived in Madison, Estill, Jessamine, and Nicholas counties in Kentucky. She wants to shout to the world about her research successes and share some of the more interesting findings with her social networks. This allows other genealogy researchers and relatives to quickly know what she's found. And if she created a blog or a research web page on her McSwain ancestors, she would want to identify sites where she may post excerpts of her findings with a link to her blog or web page. These sites might include one-name study pages on the surname McSwain and personal pages that have connections to the McSwain family, as well as sites for each of the four counties in Kentucky that the McSwains resided in. Some of the sites she would find might include family societies or county genealogical or historical societies in Kentucky that look for information on their past inhabitants. Finally, she could look for general-query sites and GEDCOM repositories (more about GEDCOM later in this chapter) that may accept her information. Outlining all of these actions constitutes April's surname marketing plan.

Perfecting the Art of Networking via Facebook

If you're an average person who likes to use the Internet to aid in your research but who doesn't have time to learn a whole computer programming language, the past decade has probably been like a dream to you. The growing number of websites intended to help people find other people with the same interests, talents, backgrounds, and locations is amazing!

One of these social networking sites — Facebook (www.facebook.com) has become a household name. Facebook touts itself as a social utility meant to connect people with a common strand in their lives, whether that's working together, attending the same school, or living in the same or nearby communities. Facebook lends itself well to genealogists connecting with relatives and other researchers. Let's explore how to use this general social networking site for our family history purposes.

Jumping on the Facebook bandwagon

Before we can explore how to use Facebook for genealogy-related connections, you have to register for a free Facebook account. It's easy. Just follow these steps:

1. **Open your favorite web browser and go to www.facebook.com.**

2. **In the Sign Up section on the right side of the screen (see Figure 11-1), type your First Name and Last Name in the appropriate fields.**

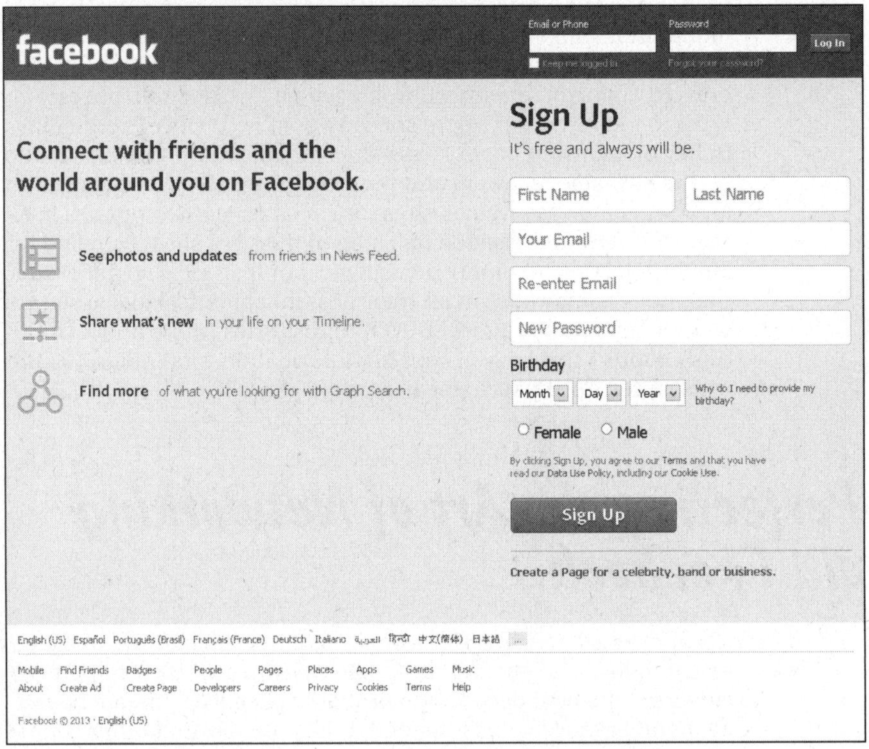

Figure 11-1: Complete the Facebook signup form to start the process of registering for an account.

3. **Provide your e-mail address in both the Your Email and Re-enter Email fields.**

4. **Select a password and type it in the New Password field.**

   As with any site, your password should consist of characters that you can remember but that someone else cannot easily figure out. A combination of upper- and lower-case letters, numbers, and special characters make a strong password.

5. **Using the drop-down lists, select the month, day, and year of your birthday.**

6. **Click the appropriate radio button next to your gender.**

7. **Click the Sign Up button.**

   This takes you to the Step 1: Find Your Friends form. You'll have the chance to look for Facebook friends later, so we'll skip this step for now.

8. **Click the Skip This Step link at the bottom right. If you get a Find Your Friends pop-up, click Skip.**

   This takes you to the Step 2: Fill Out Your Profile Info form.

9. **Complete one or more of the fields: High School, Current City, and Hometown. Next to each, use the drop-down list to choose the settings for who can see this information about you.**

   Your privacy options for each piece of information include: Public, Friends, Only Me, Custom, or you can select a pre-set list of Close Friends, Family, or Acquaintances.

10. **Click the Save & Continue button.**

    This takes you to Step 3: Get Interesting Stories In Your News Feed. This is the first opportunity to scroll through the lists of Interests and select those you wish to receive updates about in your Facebook News Feed. Because we can always add interests later, skip this step for this example.

11. **Click the Skip link at the bottom right.**

    This takes you to Step 4: Set Your Profile Picture.

12. **If you want to add a picture of yourself, here's where you can do so. Click the Upload a Photo button and select an existing image from your computer using the prompts, or click the Take a Photo button to take a picture using the camera on your computer.**

13. **Click Save & Continue.**

    You're taken to the Welcome to Facebook page (see Figure 11-2) where you have another opportunity to search for friends on Facebook, take an online tour of how to control who sees your information with your privacy settings, and complete any missing profile information. Each of these things can be completed later by choosing options from the navigation menu on the left side of the screen, if you don't want to go through them now.

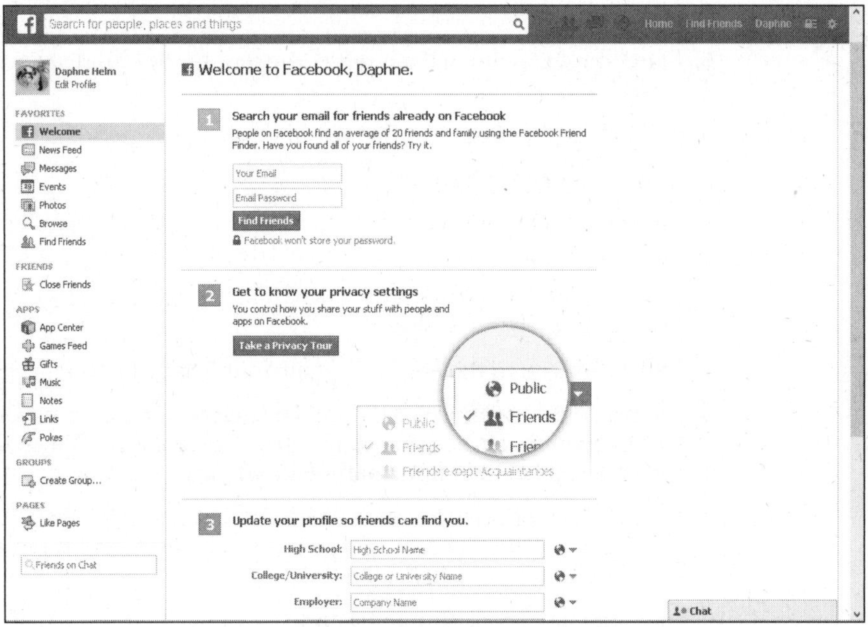

Figure 11-2:
The
Welcome to
Facebook
page.

At this point, you should receive an e-mail from Facebook informing you that your account was created successfully. From this point forward, when you return to use Facebook, you can sign in using your e-mail address and password that you created here.

Making Facebook friends

The main purpose of Facebook is to connect with people — old and new friends, relatives, and acquaintances. Finding friends is relatively easy. Follow these steps anytime you sign in to Facebook:

    1. If you're not already signed in to Facebook, fire up your computer, open a web browser, and head over to `www.facebook.com`.

2. **Click your name in the top navigation bar to get to your main profile page.**

   This takes you to the page with your timeline and profile information. This is where you can select any interests you want to share on Facebook, as well as set up other profile information, upload photos, and lots more.

3. **Click the Friends tab under your timeline photo.**

4. **Click the Find Friends button near the top of the Friends view.**

   This opens the Find Friends from Different Parts of Your Life page.

5. **Use the fields on the left to identify locations, educational institutions, or employers with which you have ties. Or if you prefer, enter the name of a friend in the Search for People, Places, and Things field at the top of the window.**

   Facebook immediately starts identifying other users who match your search criteria.

6. **Scroll through the list of matches to see if you recognize anyone.**

   You can click the person's name to see her Facebook page to learn more about her.

7. **If you find someone you know who you want to add to your friends list, click the Add Friend button by the person's name.**

An alternative way to search for friends is to use the Add Personal Contacts as Friends option on the Friends page. This allows you to enter your e-mail address (and password), which enables Facebook to access the contact list in your e-mail folder. It then looks for users with matching e-mail addresses, and presents them to you to extend Friend invites.

After you've friended a few people, Facebook continues to look for other users that have experiences, interests, and locations in common with you, and presents them in a the People You May Know list. Periodically, you should look through the list to see if there's anyone new that you'd like to extend a Friend invite to.

Sorting your Facebook friends

After you've connected with a few friends, you may find that you want to categorize them. This makes it easier to post genealogical triumphs and questions to only those friends with whom you share a research interest. It also makes it easier to restrict posts to only family members, if you so desire. To set up specific lists in Facebook, follow these steps:

1. **If you're not already signed in to Facebook, fire up your computer, open a web browser, and head over to `www.facebook.com`.**

2. **Click the Home link in the top navigation menu (upper right).**

3. **Hover the mouse cursor over the Friends section on the left side of the screen until the More link appears (see Figure 11-3), and click it.**

   This takes you to a page displaying the default and existing lists for categorizing your friends. The defaults are Close Friends, Acquaintances, Family, and Restricted.

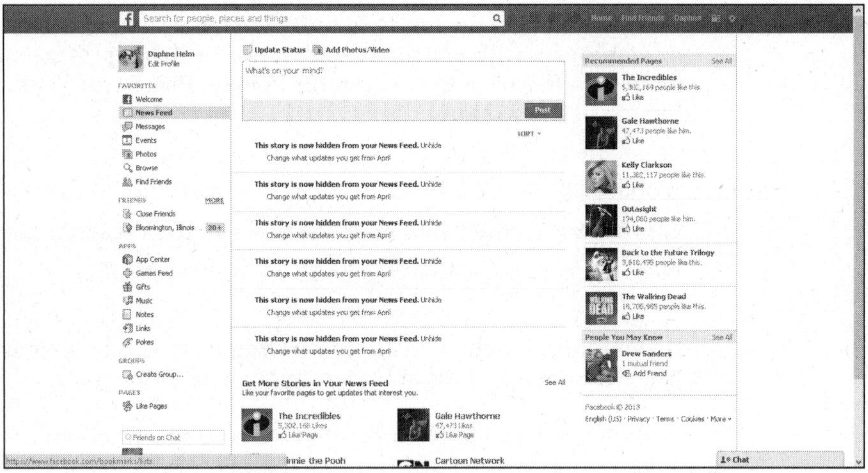

Figure 11-3:
The More link pops up if you hover the cursor over the Friends section.

4. **Click the Create List button at the top of the screen.**

   The Create New List dialog box pops up.

5. **Type the name of your list in the List Name field.**

   For our example, we type the word Genealogy in the List Name field.

6. **Start typing a friend's name in the Members section.**

   Facebook starts anticipating the name you're typing and offers suggestions. Click your friend's name if it comes up.

7. **Repeat Step 6 as many times as you want, adding all of your friends that you want to include in this list.**

8. **After you've added everyone you want, click the Create button.**

   The page for your new list opens and offers you the opportunity to post a status to the friends in this list, or add photos to share with this group. See Figure 11-4 for an example of this page.

Figure 11-4:
You can
post a sta-
tus or add
photos to
share with
the friends
on your
Genealogy
list.

You can always come back to this page for your Genealogy list if you want to post messages about your genealogical research, or to add new or additional friends to the list.

If you've already been on Facebook for a while and you have lots of genealogy-related friends, you might consider setting up more restricted lists. For example, you could create lists based on the surnames or locations you're researching.

Anytime you want to return to your Genealogy list page, click the Home link at the top of your Facebook page, then find the link to your list in the left navigation menu.

Posting statuses and messaging on Facebook

Right about now, you might be wondering what the difference is between posting a status and sending a message.

A *status* is a quick update on your Facebook page that tells the world what you're doing, thinking, or celebrating. When you post a status, Facebook sends out a notice to some or all of your friends, and it appears in their News Feeds. Likewise, when your friends post statuses, some of them may appear in your News Feed, which is typically on the first page that you access in Facebook.

You can post a status to multiple places. Just look for the What's On Your Mind? field. On the Profile page, this field is on the right under the People You May Know section. On the Home page and on special list pages, it's in the top center.

A *private message* is a personal note that you send to just one or maybe multiple people, but not to your entire list of friends. Here's how to send a private message to another person:

1. **If you're not already signed in to Facebook, fire up your computer, open a web browser, and head over to** www.facebook.com.

2. **Click the Home link in the top navigation menu (upper right).**

3. **Click the Messages link in the left navigation menu.**

   The Messages page opens, showing any past conversations that you've had with Facebook friends.

4. **Click the New Message button at the top.**

   A New Message section opens.

5. **In the To field, type the name of your friend(s) to whom you want to send this note.**

   As you begin to type a name, Facebook tries to suggest names to speed things along for you. If your friend's name pops up in the list of options that Facebook generates, you can click directly on it.

6. **In the Write a Message field, type your message.**

7. **When you're satisfied with the message, click the Send button.**

   The message section gives you the Add Files or Add Photos options if you'd like to use them. Just click the appropriate icon and follow the prompts to add an object to your message.

   You can check out the New Message screen in Figure 11-5.

After you click Send, your message appears in the box above the Write a Message field, and that field becomes titled Write a Reply and the Send button becomes a Reply button. When your friend replies to you, the response will appear in this box below your original message.

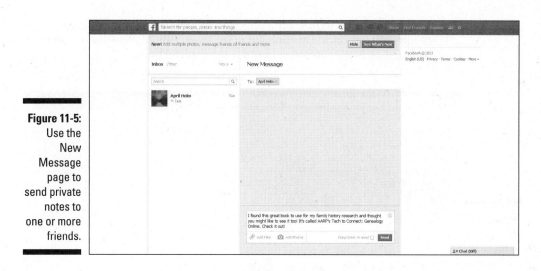

Figure 11-5:
Use the New Message page to send private notes to one or more friends.

Sharing photos via Facebook

Facebook is an easy way to share photos with your family and fellow researchers with whom you are Facebook friends. You might wish to share current photos from reunions and research trips, or you might want to share treasured family photos of ancestors that you've digitized (scanned a copy into your computer). Here's how to upload photos to Facebook:

1. **If you're not already signed in to Facebook, fire up your computer, open a web browser, and head over to** www.facebook.com.

2. **Click the Photos link.**

   If you're on your timeline, the Photos link is near the top center of the page. If you're on the Home page, the Photos link is in the left navigation frame.

   This takes you to the Photos page.

3. **Click Create Album to start a new collection of photos.**

   You might want to categorize your photos in collections by surname, or ancestor, or specific research trip.

4. **Type the filename for the location on your computer where the photos you want to upload are stored. Or you can use the navigation bar at the top to click through the directory tree to find the location.**

For our example, we click the appropriate links in the left navigation menu until we get to the directory that stores the photos that we want to share with our Facebook friends. See Figure 11-6.

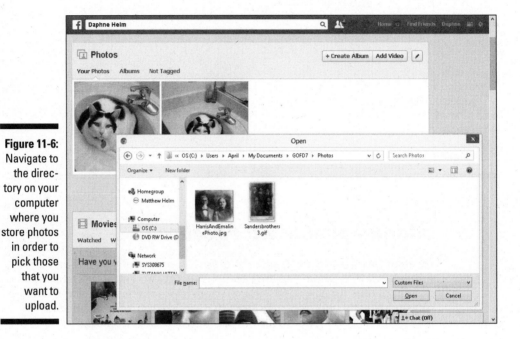

Figure 11-6:
Navigate to the directory on your computer where you store photos in order to pick those that you want to upload.

5. **Highlight the pictures you want to upload.**

   To select all of the pictures in the directory, highlight the first one, then hold the Shift key and click the last photo in the set. This should highlight all of the pictures between the first and the last. Or if you want to upload only certain photos, highlight one, and then hold the Control key while clicking the others that you wish to select.

6. **Click the Open button.**

   This begins the upload process and takes you to the album setup page; see Figure 11-7.

7. **Type the name for your album in the Untitled Album field at the top of the form.**

   Because we're uploading pictures of some of April's ancestors for our example, we'll name our album Sanders Ancestor Photos.

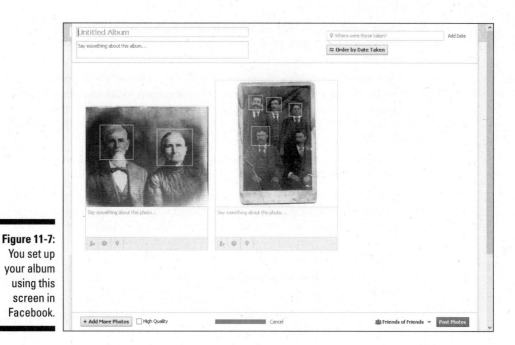

Figure 11-7:
You set up
your album
using this
screen in
Facebook.

8. **If you wish to provide a narrative or explanations about the album, type these in the Say Something about This Album field.**

9. **If you wish to say where the pictures were taken or to add a date to them, you can use the functions on the right side of the page.**

10. **If you want to sort the pictures in the order in which they were taken, you can click the Order by Date Taken button.**

11. **Under each of the photos, you can provide an explanation of who is in the picture or what the event is. You can also choose to tag locations, tag Facebook friends, or add dates using the little icons under the Say Something about This Photo field.**

    Provide as much detail as you can about the pictures so that your friends know which ancestors or relatives they're viewing, and when and where the pictures were taken. This will help add value to their genealogical research.

12. **At the bottom of the page, you find the Add More Photos option.**

    If you have additional pictures to include in this album — now or in the future — you can click this button and go through the same selection steps you followed earlier to pick the pictures to include.

13. **If you want the quality of the photos to be set higher than the typical default for a web page, then click the High Quality button at the bottom.**

    The higher the quality of the photo, the bigger the file will be on Facebook. This might make it difficult for your friends to see or download the photos, depending on their computer systems and Internet access. We recommend you leave the setting at the default and do not select the High Quality check box.

14. **Click the drop-down arrow on the Friends of Friends link at the bottom of the page and select your privacy settings.**

    You can choose to share your album with Friends of Friends (meaning your friends' friends can see it), Friends, Only Me, or Custom, or you can choose to share it with one of your lists of categorized friends, such as those who are designated as Close Friends or those in the Genealogy list that you created in an earlier part of this chapter.

15. **When you finish selecting all of the settings for your album, click the Post Photos button.**

    This takes you to a page where you can identify people who are in your photos and tag them.

16. **If you do not wish to *tag* — or identify — anyone, click the Skip Tagging Friends link at the bottom of the page. Or if you choose to tag anyone, click the Save Tags button after doing so.**

A nice feature about Facebook photo albums is that you can allow your friends to contribute to your album. This is handy for relatives who may have attended the same reunion or fellow genealogists who are researching the same family lines. You can click the Make Shared Album button at the top of the photo album in Facebook and follow the steps for adding the names of those friends who can contribute to the album. The album also becomes visible through their timelines and gives them credit anytime they add a photo to the album.

Networking Genealogy-Style

Like the number of networking sites in general, the number of genealogical-networking sites has grown at an incredible pace over the past few years. There are some significant differences between general networking or social sites, and genealogical networking sites. In particular, most genealogy-based networking sites have you start by sharing information from your Pedigree chart (also called a family tree) and research findings, rather than beginning with your profile of personal information about you. And the most interesting feature of some of these sites is that they use mathematical algorithms to link your tree(s) with trees that other people have submitted. In essence, this means they're trying to help connect you to others with the same family lines. The drawback to some of these sites is that they charge subscription fees for some of their functionality or for value-added services such as access to online records.

You might have heard of some of these:

- ✔ Geni (www.geni.com)
- ✔ Familyrelatives.com (www.familyrelatives.com)
- ✔ OneGreatFamily (www.onegreatfamily.com)
- ✔ FamilyLink.com (www.familylink.com)

If you're looking to set up a genealogy-networking site where others can discover your family lines and contribute information directly to you in a public forum, Geni is one place to start. Here's what to do to get started:

1. **Using your web browser, go to www.geni.com.**

2. **In the Start My Family Tree box, begin by selecting the option for your gender.**

3. **In the First Name field, enter your first name.**

4. **In the Last Name field, enter your last name.**

5. **In the Email Address field, type your preferred e-mail address.**

6. **Click the Start My Family Tree button.**

   The registration opens to a page where you can activate your family tree by adding relatives.

7. **Click the parent whose information you are ready to add; see Figure 11-8.**

   For this example, to enter information about your father, click the blue parental box above your box on the family tree. A dialog box appears where you can enter information.

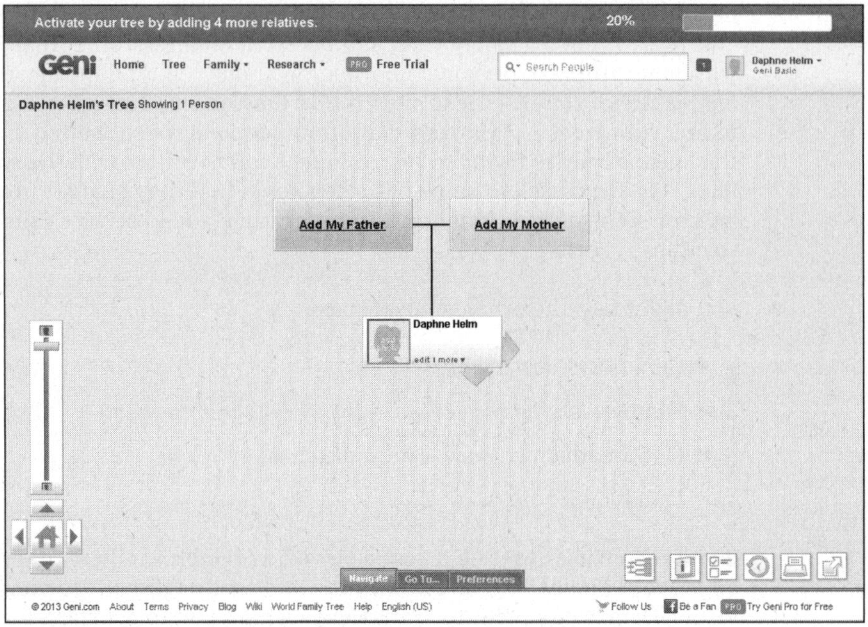

Figure 11-8:
You can navigate to other ancestors through the Geni .com family tree to add information about your family.

8. **In the First Name field, enter your father's first name.**

9. **If your father's last name is different from the one that automatically populates, fix it in the Last Name field.**

10. **Select the appropriate option to indicate whether your father is living or deceased.**

11. **If you like (and you have your dad's permission), type your father's e-mail address in the Email (Optional) field.**

   Geni.com will use this e-mail address to send this person an invitation to join Geni.com. Some relatives may consider these uninvited invitations to be spam, so be careful about entering other people's e-mail addresses at networking websites. For more information about protecting your relatives' privacy, be sure to read the section "Earning a Good Citizenship Award," later in this chapter.

12. **Click the More Fields link if you want to add more birth date information about your father.**

   If you did not enter an e-mail address, Geni.com presents you with a pop-up box offering to welcome your relative to the family tree by giving you another opportunity to add his or her e-mail address. If you don't want to see these pop-up boxes every time you enter a relative, select the Do Not Show This Message Again check box in the lower left, then click the Skip button.

13. **Click the Add button.**

After you add information about a person using one of the boxes in the family tree, the box becomes activated, and little yellow arrows surround it. You can click these arrows to navigate to that person's parents, spouse(s), and children to add more individuals to your tree.

The Geni.com site is impressive in the ways it helps you share your family tree research with others. Here's a quick overview of the various parts of the site:

- **Tree:** On this tab, you can view information about the family members included in the tree as a family tree (Pedigree chart) or a list. You can navigate in the standard Geni.com format by clicking the yellow arrows and name boxes, or you can search by name in the Go To section.

- **Family:** Several handy functions are accessible on the Family menu including Lists, Photos, Videos, Calendar, Map, Statistics, Timeline, and a Last Names Index. This is also where you can find links to share your tree and to generate the Family Tree Chart. The Lists, Photos, and Videos sections are places for you to add items to your file to enhance the content. If you enter birth dates and anniversaries for your family members, the Calendar gives you a consolidated list that helps you remember special events. The Family Map shows you where your family members currently live and were born, if you include locations in the individualized data you record on the site. The Statistics section is very interesting if you like to look for overall patterns within the family, such as average life expectancy or number of children. The Timeline gives you a quick glance of all of your Geni.com activities since registering. And the Last Name Index is just that — a list of last names in your records. Share Your Tree enables you to extend invitations to other users to view and/or contribute information. It also has a GEDCOM Export functionality so you can convert your tree for sharing. Lastly, the Family Tree Chart option builds an attractive family tree that you can then download for printing and sharing.

- **Research:** The Research menu offers services to help you connect with others to share research. It includes a Merge Center where you can see matches between people in your tree and other members' trees and online records. There are also sections for discussions with other members, projects where you can create and administer joint research with others, and documents you can upload to support your research. Additionally, there's a list of surnames in Geni.com to explore and a list of popular profiles for famous people that you can view. And if you want to order a DNA testing kit, the Research menu has information about services offered by their partner, Family Tree DNA.

- **PRO Free Trial:** The PRO Free Trial tab allows you to register to try the PRO Geni.com membership for free for 14 days. The PRO membership enables access to enhanced service features and allows you to store unlimited photos, videos, and documents. It also offers a premium level of support if you have questions or need help. Be aware that you are required to provide a credit card when you sign up for the free trial. At the end of the trial period, you will automatically be charged the one-year membership fee to continue the service if you do not notify Geni. com to end your free trial before the 14 days are over.

✔ **Profile:** The Profile section is where you can store data specifically about you — everything from your birth date and age, to educational information, to your work experience, to personal narratives about your life, aspirations, and research interests, or whatever you'd like to say about yourself in the free-form text boxes. This is also where you can track who you've invited to view and participate in your Geni tree. The data is sorted into seven tabs: Basics, Relationships, About, Personal, Contact, Work, and Schools. Depending on which setting you choose, various aspects of your profile may or may not be visible.

It's worth noting that we classify a few other sites as social networking, but don't quite fit the family-tree mold. They are interesting sites that we want to mention because they hold great potential in making your family history research a little more colorful and exciting. They are as follows:

✔ **Story of My Life (www.storyofmylife.com):** This is an online memoir site. You can record text narratives, videos, pictures, and even entire journals recounting anecdotal stories of your life. It's free to register and use the basic service, but if you want the Story of My Life Foundation to keep your stories forever, you have to pay a fee for Forever Space.

✔ **Second Life (http://secondlife.com/):** Second Life is a three-dimensional (3-D) online world of digital neighborhoods. Second Life is created by the residents and has imagery reflecting their personalities. Although its intent is not solely for genealogy, it does have interesting potential and applicability for genealogists. Imagine creating an environment to resemble your great-grandfather's world in 1850 Virginia. Or creating a presentation of an ancestor's experience on an orphan train to the western U.S. Or simply a depiction of your family tree in 3-D. You lend your creativity to present your family history in new and exciting ways. The catch — a cost is involved for services and functionality beyond the free basic membership.

Blogging for Attention

Blog is a common term around the Internet these days. But what exactly is a blog? *Blog* is an abbreviated name for a *web log,* and it's just what it sounds like: an online journal or log. Typically blogs include narratives on whatever topic the blogger (the person who maintains the blog) feels like writing about. Therefore, genealogy blogs typically contain narratives on family history research. These narratives are much like the web boards of years past, where people could go and post information about their research findings or needs, and others would post replies. The main difference is that the blogger typically updates the blog on a regular and frequent basis, anywhere from daily to weekly to monthly, and the blogger is the one who initiates the topics of discussion that are welcome on a particular blog. Some blogs even contain photos, video or audio clips, and links to other sites — all depending on the blogger's interests and abilities to include these things.

Blogs are available about all aspects of genealogy, including how-tos, news, ethnic-based research, surnames, conferences, technology, and document preservation.

Hunting blogs

Looking for genealogy blogs to aid in your family history research? A lot are available. Of course you can find them by using a general Internet search engine such as Google.com. Or you can use a couple of other simple options for finding blogs. The first is to visit the Genealogy Blog Finder search engine at `http://blogfinder.genealogue.com`. Here's how to use it:

1. **Open your web browser and go to `http://blogfinder.genealogue.com`, as shown in Figure 11-9.**

Figure 11-9:
Genealogy
Blog Finder
helps you
locate blogs
of interest.

2. **In the Search field, enter the name of the family or location you're researching.**

3. **Click Search.**

   You see a list of results with links to each. Click any that interest you.

If you're not sure of a spelling or if you just want to browse to see what's available, you can also use the menu system to navigate the Genealogy Blog Finder. All the topics under which the blogs are organized are accessible from the main web page.

A second, relatively simple way to find blogs is available. Go to one of the blog-hosting sites that we mention in the next section of this chapter and use the search functionality to see whether any blogs are available through that service that fit your needs. For example, if you're looking for anything available on the Abel family in Fayette County, Illinois, you can search using the terms *Abel* and *Illinois* or *Abel* and *Fayette*. Although this method of searching is not difficult, it can become more time-consuming than the blog-specific search engine route.

Getting a blog of your own

If you're ready to start your own blog where you can share information about your research pursuits and genealogical interests, you have some options available. One is to use the blogging functionality at one of the popular networking sites — check out the section "Perfecting the Art of Networking via Facebook," earlier in this chapter, for more information. Another option is to use a site specifically designed to host your personal blog. Three that come to mind are

- ✔ Google Blogger (www.blogger.com)
- ✔ Blog.com (www.blog.com)
- ✔ WordPress.com (www.wordpress.com)

Each of these sites offers easy-to-use instructions for creating your blog. You can choose from templates for the overall design at each site and privacy controls so that you can determine who has access to your blog and what levels of permission the user has (whether the user can just read your narratives or post replies, as well as whether he or she can contribute original narratives initiating online discussions). All three also offer the ability to post photos and files.

Here's a walk-through on how to set up your own blog at Google Blogger:

1. **Open your web browser and go to** www.blogger.com.

   This opens the Google Blogger site. In the middle of the page is a box with sign-in fields. Under the box is a Create an Account link.

2. **Click the Create an Account link.**

   This brings you to the Create Your Google Account page. Setting up an account is the first step in the process. If you already have a Google account, it offers you the opportunity to log in using your existing account instead of creating a new one — just click the Sign In button in the upper right.

3. **Enter your first and last names in the appropriate fields.**

4. **Type the user name you'd like to have for your account.**

5. **Complete the Create a Password field, typing a password that's at least eight characters long.**

   Remember that when setting up a password, you want to choose a combination of letters, numbers, or characters that won't be easy for others to decipher. Don't use your pet's name or your mother's maiden name. Instead, choose something that's not common knowledge about you — such as the name of your favorite book character with your favorite number on the end or a special text character such as $, #, or %. Click the Password Strength link, if you want Google Blogger–specific information about selecting a password. Google Blogger provides some excellent hints on making your password as safe as possible.

6. **In the Confirm Your Password field, provide the same password again.**

7. **In the Birthday fields, enter your date of birth.**

8. **Select your gender from the drop-down list.**

9. **Type your mobile phone number in the appropriate field.**

10. **In the Your Current Email Address field, type your current or preferred e-mail address.**

11. **In the Type the Text box, retype the words or numbers that you see above the field.**

    The letters and numbers are usually presented in a wavy, distorted way.

12. **Select your location.**

13. **Click the Terms of Service and read through them. If you agree to Blogger's terms, select the I Accept the Google Terms of Service and Privacy Policy check box.**

14. **Click Next Step.**

    Google shows you how your profile name will appear and then takes you to the Welcome page.

15. Click the Back to Blogger button.

This brings up the Welcome to Blogger page.

16. Scroll down and click the Continue to Blogger button.

17. Click the New Blog button.

The Create a New Blog page opens. You can see this form in Figure 11-10.

18. In the Title field, enter a name for your blog.

19. In the Address (URL) field, type part of a web address for your blog.

When choosing what to use for the section of the web address that you get to designate, think about using something that fits with the title of your blog. For example, if your blog will be called Gerty's Genealogical Adventures, you might try using GenAdventure or GGAdventure in the URL.

As you type the name of your choice, the system automatically checks to see if that selection is available.

20. Scroll through the list of templates and select the one that you like best.

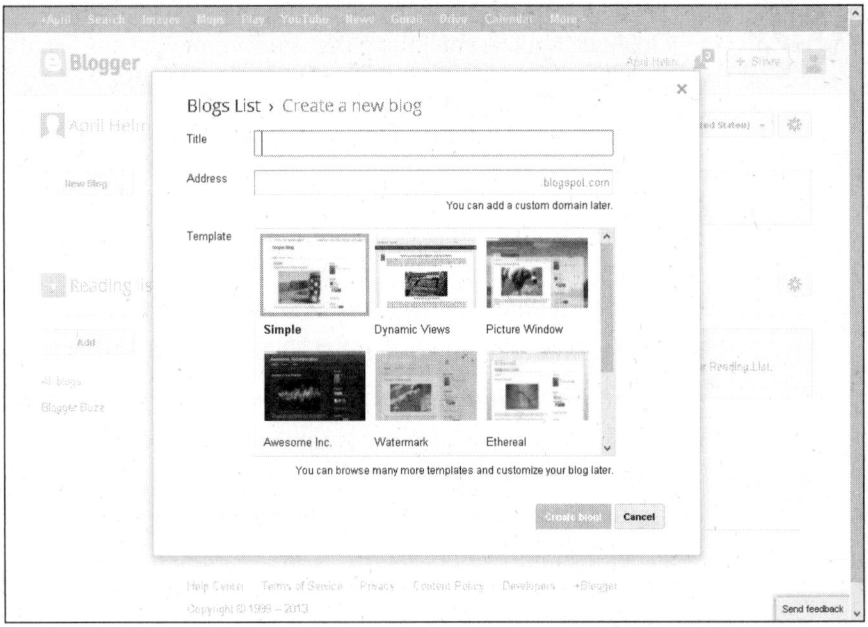

Figure 11-10:
The Create a New Blog page.

21. **Click Create Blog.**

    Congratulations! You've just created your blog. You get a message confirming that you have completed the blog-creation process, and you're now ready to begin posting to your blog.

22. **Click Start Posting Now to continue and begin adding content to your blog.**

    The Google Blogger template is easy to use for posting your blog content. You'll probably want to spend a little time exploring how it works and available options.

Building Your Own Home

When we wrote the first couple of editions of *Genealogy Online For Dummies,* the web was a very different place. Networking sites and blogs were not commonplace. Back then, we were quick to recommend designing your own home page (or website, if you will) from scratch. These days, we recommend coding your own site in HTML (HyperText Markup Language) only if you are a die-hard fan of creating things personally.

If you are that type of person, but you're not sufficiently versed in coding HTML, we recommend that you tackle one or both of the following books before venturing into the world of web-page design: *HTML, XHTML & CSS For Dummies,* 7th Edition, by Ed Tittel and Jeff Noble and *Building a Web Site For Dummies,* 4th Edition, by David A. Crowder (both published by Wiley).

Before you can build anything, you need to find a home — that is, a *host* — for it. Although you can design a basic home page on your own computer using no more than a word processor, others won't be able to see it until you put the page on a web server on the Internet. A *web server* is a computer that's connected directly to the Internet that serves web pages when you request them using your computer's web browser.

Commercial Internet service providers

If you subscribe to a commercial *Internet service provider (ISP)* such as AT&T, MSN, or Comcast, or if you subscribe to a local provider, you may already have a home for your web pages. Some commercial ISPs include a specific space allocation for user home pages in their memberships, as well as some tools to help you build your site. Check your membership agreement to see whether you have space. Then you can follow the ISP's instructions for creating your website (using the service's page builder or editor) or for getting the home page that you've designed independently from your computer to the ISP's server. If you didn't keep a copy of your membership agreement, don't fret! Most ISPs have an informational web page that you can get to from your ISP's main page; the informational page reviews membership benefits. You may as well take advantage of this service if you're already paying for it.

If your particular membership level doesn't include web space, but the ISP has other membership levels that do, hold off on bumping up your membership level. You can take advantage of some free web-hosting services that may save you money. Keep reading.

Free web-hosting services

Some websites give you free space for your home page, provided that you agree to their rules and restrictions. We can safely bet that you won't have any problems using one of these freebies because the terms (such as no pornography, nudity, or explicit language allowed) are genealogist-friendly.

If you decide to take advantage of web space, remember that the companies that provide the space must pay their bills. They often make space available free to individuals by charging advertisers for banners and other advertisements. In such cases, the web host reserves the right to require that you leave these advertisements on your home page. If you don't like the idea of an advertisement on your home page, or if you have strong objections to one of the companies being advertised on the site that gives you free space, you should find a fee-based web space for your home page.

Here are a few free web-hosting services that have been around for a while:

- ✔ Google sites (www.google.com/sites)
- ✔ Tripod (www.tripod.lycos.com)
- ✔ RootsWeb.com (http://accounts.rootsweb.com/index. cgi?op=show&page=freagree.htm)

Do you speak HTML?

HyperText Markup Language (or HTML) is the language of the web. HTML is a code in which text documents are written so that web browsers can read and interpret those documents, converting them into graphical images and text that you can see with a browser. HTML is a relatively easy language to learn, and many genealogists who post web pages are self-taught. If you prefer not to read about it and teach yourself by experimenting instead, you can surely find classes as well as other resources in your area that could teach you the basics of HTML. Check with a local community college for structured classes, local genealogical societies for any workshops focusing on designing and posting web pages, or the web itself for online courses. Or, check out *HTML, XHTML & CSS For Dummies,* 7th Edition, by Ed Tittel and Jeff Noble.

Deciding which treasures to include

Although the content of genealogical web pages with lots of textual informa-tion about ancestors or geographic areas may be very helpful, all-text pages won't attract the attention of your visitors. Even we get tired of sorting through and reading endless narratives on websites. We like to see things that personalize a website and are fun to look at. Graphics, icons, and pho-tographs are ideal for this purpose. A couple of nice-looking, strategically placed photos of ancestors make a site feel more like a home.

If you have some photographs that have been scanned and saved as `.jpg` or `.gif` images or some media clips (such as video or audio files) in a format that meets the compatibility requirements for your web-hosting service, you can post them on your website.

Just as you should be careful about posting factual information about living relatives, be careful about posting photos or recordings of them. If you want to use an image that has living relatives in it, get their permission before doing so. Some people are sensitive about having their pictures posted on the web. Also, use common sense and good taste in selecting pictures for your page. Although a photo of little Susie at age 3 wearing a lampshade and dancing around in a tutu may be cute, a photo of Uncle Ed at age 63 doing the same thing may not be so endearing!

Including Your GEDCOM

Suppose that you contact others who are interested in your research find-ings. What's the best way to share your information with them? Certainly, you can type everything, print it, and send it to them. Or, you can export a copy of your genealogy database file — which the recipients can then import into their databases and create as many reports as they want — and save a tree in the process.

Most genealogical databases subscribe to a common standard for exporting their information called *GEenealogical Data COMmunication,* or *GEDCOM.* Beware that some genealogical databases deviate from the standard a little — making things somewhat confusing.

A *GEDCOM file* is a text file that contains your genealogical information with a set of tags that tells the genealogical database importing the information where to place it within its structure. For a little history and more information about GEDCOM, see Chapter 1.

You may be asking, "Why is GEDCOM important?" It can save you time and energy in the process of sharing information. The next time someone asks you to send your data, you can export your genealogy data into a GEDCOM file and send it to him or her instead of typing it or saving a copy of your entire database.

Privatizing your database before sharing

If you plan to share the contents of your genealogical database online by generating and exporting a GEDCOM file, make sure that your file is ready to share with others. By this, we mean be sure that it's free from any information that could land you in the doghouse with any of your relatives — close or distant!

Some genealogical software programs enable you to indicate whether you want information on each relative included in reports and GEDCOM files. Other programs don't allow you to do this. This may mean that you need to manually scrub your GEDCOM file to remove information about all living persons.

After you have a GEDCOM file that is free of information about all living persons, you're ready to prepare it for the web. You can choose from several programs to help you convert your GEDCOM file to HTML. GED2HTML may be the most commonly known GEDCOM-to-HTML converter available, and you can download it at www.starkeffect.com/ged2html. Here's how to use it with your cleaned GEDCOM file:

1. **Open the GED2HTML program that you downloaded from www. starkeffect.com/ged2html.**

   A dialog box asks you to enter the location of your GEDCOM file. (You can browse if you can't remember the path for the GEDCOM file.)

2. **Type the path for your GEDCOM file, and then click Go.**

   A typical path looks like this: c:\my documents\helm.ged. GED2HTML runs a program using your GEDCOM file. You can watch it going through the file in a black window that appears.

3. **After the program is finished, press Enter to close the program window.**

   GED2HTML saves the output HTML files in a folder (appropriately called HTML) in the same directory where the GED2HTML program is saved.

4. **Use your web browser to open any of the HTML output files.**

   After seeing what your output looks like and reviewing it to make sure that it doesn't contain any information that shouldn't be posted, you're ready to add it to your website (or link to it as its own web page).

5. **Follow any instructions from your web host, and upload your GED2HTML files to your web server. Put any links to those files on your home page so that you can share your GEDCOM information online.**

   For example, suppose that GED2HTML saved an HTML-coded index of all the people in your GEDCOM file to a file called persons.html. After uploading or copying this file to your web host's server, you can use a link command such as <A HREF = "[directory path]/persons. html"> from your main home page to this index of persons to share it on the web.

Generating GEDCOM files

Making a GEDCOM file using most software programs is quite easy. This is true for RootsMagic Essentials, too. If you have not yet downloaded and installed RootsMagic Essentials, flip back to Chapter 1. After you have the program ready to go, try this:

1. **Open RootsMagic Essentials.**

   Usually, you can open your software by double-clicking the icon for that program or by choosing Start➪Programs (or Start➪All Programs) and selecting the particular program.

2. **Use the default database that appears, or choose File➪Open to open another database.**

3. **After you open the database for which you want to create a GEDCOM file, choose File➪Export.**

   The GEDCOM Export dialog box appears.

4. **Choose whether you want to include everyone in your database in your GEDCOM file or only selected people. You can also choose the output format and what types of information to include. Then click OK.**

   If you choose to include only selected people in your GEDCOM file, you need to complete another dialog box marking those people to include.

Highlight the individual's name and then select Mark People➪Person to include him or her. After you select all the people you want to include, click OK.

5. In the File Name field, type the new name for your GEDCOM file and then click Save.

Your GEDCOM file is created.

After a GEDCOM file is created on your hard drive, you can open it in a word processor (such as WordPad or Notepad) and review it to ensure that the information is formatted the way you want it. See Figure 11-11 for an example. Also, reviewing the file in a word processor is a good idea so you can be sure that you did not include information on living persons. After you're satisfied with the file, you can cut and paste it into an e-mail message or send it as an attachment using your e-mail program.

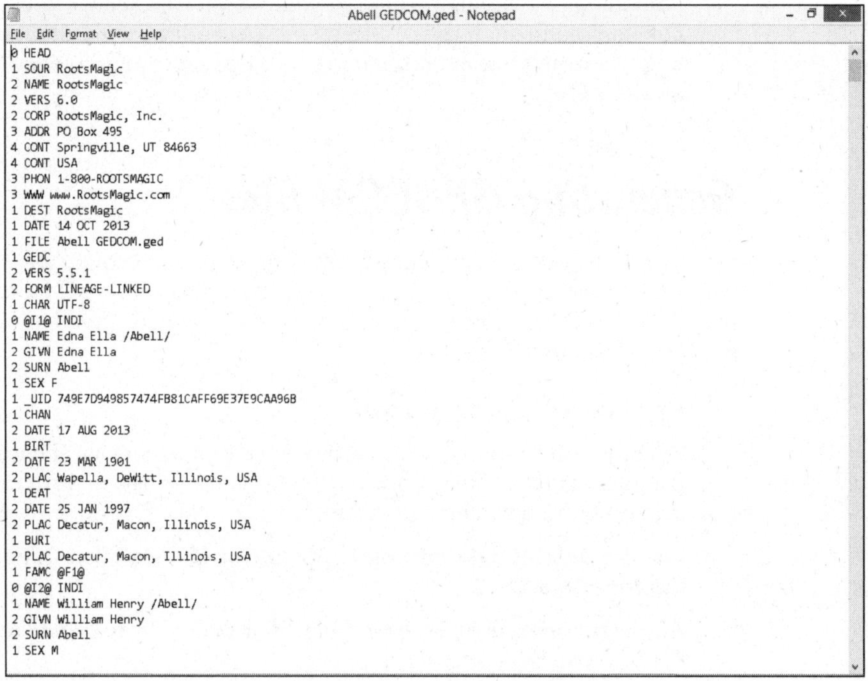

Figure 11-11: An example of a GEDCOM file opened in Notepad.

```
Abell GEDCOM.ged - Notepad
File  Edit  Format  View  Help
0 HEAD
1 SOUR RootsMagic
2 NAME RootsMagic
2 VERS 6.0
2 CORP RootsMagic, Inc.
3 ADDR PO Box 495
4 CONT Springville, UT 84663
4 CONT USA
3 PHON 1-800-ROOTSMAGIC
3 WWW www.RootsMagic.com
1 DEST RootsMagic
1 DATE 14 OCT 2013
1 FILE Abell GEDCOM.ged
1 GEDC
2 VERS 5.5.1
2 FORM LINEAGE-LINKED
1 CHAR UTF-8
0 @I1@ INDI
1 NAME Edna Ella /Abell/
2 GIVN Edna Ella
2 SURN Abell
1 SEX F
1 _UID 749E7D949857474FB81CAFF69E37E9CAA96B
1 CHAN
2 DATE 17 AUG 2013
1 BIRT
2 DATE 23 MAR 1901
2 PLAC Wapella, DeWitt, Illinois, USA
1 DEAT
2 DATE 25 JAN 1997
2 PLAC Decatur, Macon, Illinois, USA
1 BURI
2 PLAC Decatur, Macon, Illinois, USA
1 FAMC @F1@
0 @I2@ INDI
1 NAME William Henry /Abell/
2 GIVN William Henry
2 SURN Abell
1 SEX M
```

XML: GEDCOM's successor?

Although GEDCOM was designed to help researchers exchange information with each other using various genealogical software programs, it isn't necessarily the best way to present information on the web. Over the past several years, people have tried to create a better way to display and identify genealogical information on the web. Eventually, these efforts could produce the successor to GEDCOM.

One of the possible successors to GEDCOM is *eXtensible Markup Language,* more commonly recognized by the acronym *XML.* XML is similar to HyperText Markup Language (HTML) in that it uses tags to describe information. However, the purpose of XML is different than that of HTML. HTML was designed to tell a web browser, such as Firefox or Internet Explorer, how to arrange text and graphics on a page. XML is designed not only to display information, but also to describe the information. An early version of XML for the genealogical community was *GedML,* developed by Michael Kay. GedML uses XML tags to describe genealogical data on the web, much like GEDCOM does for genealogical software. Here's an example of information provided in a GEDCOM file and its GedML equivalent:

GEDCOM:

```
0 @I0904@ INDI
1 NAME Samuel Clayton /ABELL/
1 SEX M
1 BIRT
```

```
2 DATE 16 Mar 1844
2 PLAC Nelson County, KY
1 FAMS @F0397@
```

GedML:

```
<INDI ID="I0904">
<NAME> Samuel Clayton
    <S>ABELL</S></NAME>
<SEX>M</SEX>
<EVEN EV='BIRT'>
<DATE>16 Mar 1844</DATE>
<PLAC> Nelson County, KY</
    PLAC> </EVEN>
<FAMS REF="F397"/>
</INDI>
```

XML, whether it's GedML or some other XML structure, promises an enhancement of the searchability of genealogical documents on the web. Right now, it's difficult for genealogically focused search engines to identify what's genealogical in nature and what's not (for more on genealogically focused search engines, see Chapter 6). Also, tags allow search engines to determine whether a particular data element is a name or a place. XML also provides an efficient way to link genealogical data between websites, giving users more control over how particular text is displayed (such as notes), and allows genealogists to place information directly on the web without using a program to convert databases or GEDCOM files to HTML. For more information on GedML, see http://users.breathe.com/mhkay/gedml.

Reporting Your Results

The purpose of finding an online community is to share information on ancestors or on geographical areas about which you have researched. It's hard to write and rewrite every detail in an e-mail message or online post. And although GEDCOM is a great option when two individuals have genealogical software that supports the standard, what about all those people who are new to genealogy and haven't invested in software yet? How do you send them information that they can use? One option is to generate reports through your genealogical software, export them into your word processor, and then print copies to mail (or attach copies of the word processing file to e-mail messages).

The process for generating a family tree or report should be similar for most genealogical software. Because we've explained in earlier parts of this book how to download and install RootsMagic Essentials, that's the software we use to demonstrate the process of creating reports. If you've not yet installed it or entered or imported some data into it, you might want to check out Chapter 1. It gives step-by-step instructions for entering all your detailed family information into RootsMagic Essentials.

Before you can generate a report, you have to find the person who will be the focus of that report. Here's a quick refresher on how to get to the appropriate person's record:

1. **Open RootsMagic Essentials and select the family file for which you want to generate a chart or report by highlighting the filename and clicking Open.**

   Usually, you can open your software by double-clicking the icon for that program or by choosing Start⇨Programs (or Start⇨All Programs) and selecting the particular program.

2. **Highlight the name of the person who will serve as the focus for your report.**

   On the Pedigree tab, highlight the name of the focal person of the family you select. For example, if Matthew wants to generate a report for his ancestor Samuel Clayton Abell, he highlights the Samuel Abell file.

3. **On the Reports menu, select a chart or report.**

   Some report types are not available in the RootsMagic Essentials version. You have to purchase the full product to generate them.

4. **Select the content to include in the report.**

   You can choose whether to generate the report on the current family or only selected people. You can also choose what information to include (such as spouses and children, photos, and notes) in the output. And you can manipulate some formatting options, such as layout, title, fonts, and sources.

5. **Click Generate Reports.**

   RootsMagic Essentials generates the report and displays it on your screen.

Earning a Good Citizenship Award

To be a good genealogical citizen, you should keep a few things in mind, such as maintaining privacy, respecting copyrights, and including adequate citations. In this section, we discuss these key topics.

Mandatory lecture on privacy

Sometimes, we genealogists get so caught up in dealing with the records of deceased persons that we forget one basic fact: Much of the information we've collected and put in our databases pertains to living individuals and thus is considered private. In our haste to share our information with others online, we often create our GEDCOM files and reports, and then ship them off to recipients without thinking twice about whether we may offend someone or invade his or her privacy by including personal information. The same thing goes for posting information directly to websites and in our blogs — we sometimes write the data into the family tree or include anecdotal information in our blog narratives without thinking about the consequences to living individuals. We need to be more careful.

Why worry about privacy? Ah, allow us to enlighten you:

✔ **You may invade someone's right to privacy.** We've heard horror stories about Social Security numbers of living individuals ending up in GEDCOM files that are available on the Internet. We've also heard of people who didn't know that their biological parents weren't married (to each other, anyway) and found out through an online database. Your relatives may not want you to share personal information about them with others, and they may not have given you permission to do so. The same is true for photos and video clips. Just because you're gung ho to show the world the group photo from your family reunion does not mean that every one of your parents, siblings, aunts, uncles, and cousins feels the same way. So don't share the information or the image without the permission of everyone involved.

✔ **Genealogists aren't the only people who visit genealogical Internet sites.** Private detectives and other people who search for information on living persons frequently use genealogical databases to track people. They are known to lurk about, watching for information that may help their cases. Estranged spouses may visit sites looking for a way to track down their former partners. Also, people with less-than-honorable intentions may visit a genealogical website looking for potential scam or abuse victims. And some information, such as your mother's maiden name, may help the unscrupulous carry out fraud. For these reasons, it is illegal in some states and countries to share information about living persons on the Internet without first getting each person's written permission.

When sharing genealogical information, your safest bet is to clean out (exclude) any information on living individuals from your GEDCOM file or report when sharing it with others and include only the data that pertains to people who have long been deceased — unless you've obtained written consent from living persons to share information about them. By *long been deceased,* we mean deceased for more than ten years — although the time frame could be longer depending on the sensitivity of the information. You may also want to keep in mind that the U.S. Government standard dictates that no record covered under the Privacy Act is released until it's at least 72 years old.

Respecting copyrights

Copyright is the controlling right that a person or corporation owns over the duplication and distribution of a work that the person or corporation created. Although facts themselves can't be copyrighted, *works in which facts are contained* can be. Although the fact that your grandma was born on January 1, 1900, can't be copyrighted by anyone, a report that contains this information and was created by Aunt Velma may be. If you intend to include a significant portion of Aunt Velma's report in your own document, you need to secure permission from her to use the information.

With regard to copyright and the Internet, remember that just because you found some information on a website (or other Internet resource) does not mean that it's not copyrighted. If the website contains original material along with facts, it is copyrighted to the person who created it — regardless of whether the site has a copyright notice on it!

To protect yourself from infringing on someone's copyright and possibly ending up in a legal battle, you should do the following:

✔ Never copy another person's web page, e-mail, blog, or other Internet creation (such as graphics) without his or her written consent.

✔ Never print an article, a story, a report, or other material to share with your family, friends, genealogical or historical society, class, or anyone else without the creator's written consent.

✔ Always assume that a resource is copyrighted.

✔ Always cite sources of the information in your genealogy and on your web pages. (See the next section in this chapter for more information.)

✔ Always *link* to other web pages rather than copying their content on your own website.

If you don't understand what copyright is or if you have questions about it, be sure to check out the U.S. Copyright Office's home page at `www.copyright.gov`. Two U.S. Copyright Office pages of particular interest at the site are Copyright Basics and Frequently Asked Questions (FAQs).

Citing your sources

We can't stress enough the importance of citing your sources when sharing information — online or through traditional means. Be sure to include references that reflect where you obtained your information; that's just as important when you share your information as it is when you research it. Not only does referencing provide the other person with leads to possible additional information, but it also gives you a place to double-check your facts if someone challenges them. Sometimes, after exchanging information with another researcher, you both notice that you have conflicting data about a particular ancestor. Knowing where to turn to double-check the facts (and, with any luck, find out who has the correct information) can save you time and embarrassment.

Here are some examples of ways to cite online sources of information:

✔ **E-mail messages:** Matthew Helm, [<ezgenealogy@aol.com> or 111 Main Street, Anyplace, Anystate 11111]. "Looking for George Helm," Message to April Helm, 12 October 2009. [Message cites vital records in Helm's possession.]

✔ **Newsgroups:** Matthew Helm, [<ezgenealogy@aol.com> or 111 Main Street, Anyplace, Anystate 11111]. "Computing in Genealogy" in soc.genealogy.computing, 05 June 2006.

✔ **Websites:** Matthew Helm, [<ezgenealogy@aol.com> or 111 Main Street, Anyplace, Anystate 11111]. "Helm's Genealogy Toolbox." <genealogy.tbox.com> January 2004. [This site contains numerous links to other genealogical resources on the Internet. On July 12, 2010, located and checked links on Abell family; found two that were promising.]

With a note like the preceding one in brackets, you expect that your next two citations are the two websites that looked promising. For each site, you should provide notes stating exactly what you did or did not find.

Although most genealogical software programs now enable you to store source information and citations along with your data, many still don't export the source information automatically. For that reason, double-check any reports or GEDCOM files you generate to see whether your source information is included before sharing them with other researchers. If the information isn't included, create a new GEDCOM file that includes sources.

Chapter 12

Finding Your Research Path

*T*alking about the methods for working on genealogy or family history research isn't very exciting. However, we would be doing an injustice to you if we sent you out into the jungle that is online research without giving you some advice from the traditional world of research.

This chapter is designed to provide a research foundation that will help you spend your time online as efficiently as possible. In the following pages, we look at how to develop a plan to research your ancestors and cover the phases of research. In the latter parts of the chapter, we go through some gentle reminders that can help you keep your research as relevant as possible.

Introducing the Helm Online Family Tree Research Cycle

We introduced the original *Helm Online Family Tree Research Cycle* in the first edition of this book. In the 15 years that followed, we didn't make a single change to the steps of the cycle. It was a sound methodology for research in the traditional sense. But the genealogical world has changed significantly over the past few years, and it is high time that we adapt our research cycle to better fit some of those changes. So, sit back and prepare yourself for the new and improved research cycle.

Your question at this point is probably, what is the *Helm Online Family Tree Research Cycle*? All great projects start with a plan, and starting a genealogical project is no exception. A well-thought-out plan can help you make efficient use of your time and keep you focused on the goals that you've set for a particular research session. Now, we realize that not everyone enjoys coming up with a plan. Finding your ancestors is the fun part — not the planning. So, to help speed things along, we've come up with a basic process that we hope helps you make the most of your research time. We call this plan the *Helm Online Family Tree Research Cycle.* Most of our plan is common sense. Figure 12-1 shows the six phases of the cycle: planning, collecting, researching, consolidating, validating, and distilling.

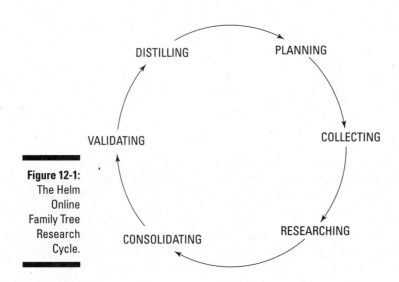

Figure 12-1:
The Helm
Online
Family Tree
Research
Cycle.

Sticking with the *family tree* motif here, we liken the cycle to the steps you take to plant and sustain a tree:

- ✔ **Planning:** The first step in planting a tree is figuring out what kind of tree you want and then finding a good place in your yard for the tree to grow. This step in the cycle is the *planning* phase. In genealogy, the planning phase consists of selecting a family that you know enough about to begin a search and thinking about the resources that can provide the information that you're looking for.

- ✔ **Collecting:** After you plan for the tree, you go to a nursery and pick a suitable sapling and other necessary materials to ensure that the tree's roots take hold. The second phase of the cycle, *collecting,* is the same — you collect information on the family that you're researching by conducting interviews in person, on the phone, or through e-mail, and by finding documents in attics, basements, and other home-front repositories.

- ✔ **Researching:** The next step is to actually plant the tree. You dig a hole, place the tree in it, and then cover the roots. Similarly, you spend the *researching* phase of the cycle digging for clues, finding information that can support your family tree, and obtaining documentation. You can use traditional and technological tools to dig — tools such as libraries, courthouses, your computer, and the web.

✔ **Consolidating:** You planted the tree and covered its roots. However, to make sure that the tree grows, you put mulch around it and provide the nourishment that the tree needs to survive. The *consolidating* phase of the cycle is similar in that you take information you find and place it into your computer-based genealogical database or your filing system. These systems protect your findings by keeping them in a centralized location and provide an environment in which you can see the fruits of your labor.

✔ **Validating:** To ensure that you're providing your tree with all the nutrition and care that it needs, you might pick up a book or watch a gardening show to confirm that your actions will nurture the tree. The *validating* phase in genealogy allows you to do the same with your research. By using additional research tools and by finding multiple sources, you can feel more confident that your discoveries are placing your research on the right track.

✔ **Distilling:** After your tree takes root and begins to grow, you need to prune the old growth, allowing new growth to appear. Similarly, the *distilling* phase is where you use your computer-based genealogical database to generate reports showing the current state of your research. You can use these reports to prune from your database those individuals you've proven don't fit into your family lines — and perhaps find room for new genealogical growth by finding clues to other lines with which you want to follow up.

We think that using our research model makes looking for genealogical information a lot easier and more fulfilling. However, this model is merely a guide. Feel free to use whatever methods work best for you — as long as those methods make it possible for someone else to verify your research (through sources you cite and so on).

Planning your research

Your computer puts the world at your fingertips. Discovering all the wonderful online resources that exist makes you feel like a kid in a candy store. You click around from site to site with wide eyes, amazed by what you see, tempted to record everything for your genealogy — whether it relates to one of your family lines or not.

Because of the immense wealth of information available to you, putting together a research plan before going online is very important — it can save you a lot of time and frustration by keeping you focused. Millions of pages with genealogical content exist on the Internet. If you don't have a good idea of exactly what you're looking for to fill in the blanks in your family history, you can get lost online. Getting lost is even easier when you see a name that looks familiar and start following its links, only to discover hours later (when you finally get around to pulling out the notes you already had) that you've been tracking the wrong person and family line.

Now that we've convinced you that you need a research plan (at least we hope we've convinced you), you're probably wondering exactly what a research plan is. Basically, a *research plan* is a commonsense approach to looking for information about your ancestors online. A research plan entails knowing what you're looking for and what your priorities are for finding information.

If you're the kind of person who likes detailed organization (such as lists and steps), you can map out your research plan in a spreadsheet or word processor on your computer, write it on paper, or use a genealogical software tool. If you're the kind of person who knows exactly what you want and need at all times, and you have an excellent memory of where you leave off when doing projects, your research plan can exist solely in your mind. In other words, your research plan can be as formal or informal as you like — as long as it helps you plot what you're looking for.

For example, say that you're interested in finding some information on your great-grandmother. Here are some steps you can take to form a research plan:

1. **Write down what you already know about the person you want to research — in this case, your great-grandmother.**

   Include details such as the dates and places of birth, marriage, and death; spouse's name; children's names; and any other details you think may help you distinguish your ancestor from other individuals. Of course, it's possible that all you know at this time is Great-grandma's name.

2. **Survey a comprehensive genealogical index to get an overview of what's available.**

   Visit a site such as Linkpendium (`www.linkpendium.com`) to browse for information by name and location. Using Great-grandma's name and the names of some of the locations where she lived will allow you to see what kinds of resources are available. (Chapter 6 goes into more detail about online tips and searching for this type of information.) Make sure that you make a list of the sites that you find in a word processor document, in a spreadsheet, or on a piece of paper; bookmark them on your web browser; or record them in your genealogical software. Also, given that websites come and go frequently, you may want to consider downloading the web page for future offline browsing. Most web browsers allow you to download a Web page by selecting Save As from the File menu at the top, and then providing the path to the file where you want to save a copy.

3. **Prioritize the resources that you want to use.**

   Browsing a comprehensive genealogical index may turn up several types of resources, such as sites featuring digitized copies of original records, transcriptions of records, online genealogy databases, or an online message board with many posts about people with the same last name. We recommend that you prioritize which resources you plan to use first. You may want to visit a website that contains specific information on your grandmother's family first — rather than spending a lot of time on a website that just contains generic information on her surname. You may also want to visit a site with digitized original records first and leave a site with transcribed records or a database for later use.

4. **Schedule time to use the various resources that you identify.**

   Family history is truly a lifelong pursuit — you can't download every bit of information and documentation that you need all at once. Because researching your genealogy requires time and effort, we recommend that you schedule time to work on specific parts of your research. If you have a particular evening open every week, you can pencil in a research night on your calendar, setting aside 15–30 minutes at the beginning to review what you have and assess your goals, then spending a couple of hours researching, and ending your evening with another 15–30 minutes of review in which you organize what you found.

Here are a few resources that can help you sharpen your planning skills:

✔ **Crafting a Genealogy Research Plan:** www.youtube.com/ watch?v=iZEJC7oruT0

✔ **Sample Family History Research Plan:** www.familytreemagazine. com/article/sample-research-plan

✔ **The 5-Step Genealogical Research Process:** www.genealogyforum. rootsweb.com/gfaol/beginners/5step.htm

Collecting useful information

After you generate a research plan (see the preceding section), you may need to fill in a few details such as dates and locations of births, marriages, and deaths. You can collect this information by interviewing family members and by looking through family documents and photographs. (See Chapter 2 for tips on interviewing and using family documents and photographs.) You may also need to look up a few places in an atlas or a *gazetteer* (a geographical dictionary) if you aren't sure of certain locations. (Chapter 7 provides more information on online gazetteers.)

It's useful to jot down peripheral information such as the names of siblings, other family members, and the names of neighbors, if they're available. This extra information might be enough to determine whether the record you're looking at pertains to your ancestor. For example, if you're looking for a pension record for your ancestor, and you run across several pension records for people with the same name, then knowing the names of others with ties to your ancestor can help you determine which of the pension records is the right one. One detail to help confirm that the record relates to your ancestor may be the name of a witness. Sometimes the applicant would use neighbors or extended family members as witnesses. Recognizing the name of the witness might help speed up your search.

For a list of things that may be useful to collect, see Chapter 2. In the meantime, here are a few online resources that can help you get started with your family history:

- ✔ **National Genealogical Society, Getting Started page:** www. ngsgenealogy.org/cs/getting_started
- ✔ **Introduction to Genealogy: First Steps:** http://genealogy.about. com/library/lessons/blintro2a.htm
- ✔ **Getting Started in Genealogy and Family History:** www.genuki.org. uk/gs
- ✔ **Ancestry.com Learning Center** www.ancestry.com/cs/ HelpAndAdviceUS

Researching: Through the brick wall and beyond

A time will undoubtedly come when you run into what genealogists affectionately call the *Brick Wall Syndrome* — when you think you've exhausted every possible way of finding an ancestor. The most important thing you can do is to keep the faith — don't give up!

Websites are known to change frequently (especially as more records are digitized, indexed, and placed online). Although you may not find exactly what you need today, you may find it next week at a site you've visited several times before or at a new site altogether. The lesson here is to check back at sites that you've visited before.

Another way to get past the brick wall is to ask for help. Don't be afraid to post a message on a mailing list or e-mail other researchers you've corresponded with in the past to see whether they have answers or suggestions for finding answers. We provide more information for using mailing lists and e-mail in Chapter 1. Also, you may be able to use the expertise of members of a genealogical or historical society who can point you to specific resources that you may not have known existed. We talk more about genealogical and historical societies in Chapter 7.

Fortunately, you can also find suggestions posted online on how to get through that brick wall when you run up against it. Check out these sites:

- ✔ **Brick Wall Strategies for Dead-End Family Trees:** `http://genealogy.about.com/od/basics/a/brick_walls.htm`
- ✔ **Brick Wall Research:** `http://genealogypro.com/articles/brick-wall-research.html`
- ✔ **Overcoming "Brick Wall" Problems:** `www.progenealogists.com/brickwall.htm`
- ✔ **Breaking Through Your Genealogy Brick Walls:** `www.youtube.com/watch?v=zQLhtzYx7Bk`

Consolidating information in a database

After you get rolling on your research, you often find so much information that it feels like you don't have enough time to put it all into your computer-based genealogical database.

A *genealogical database* is a software program that allows you to enter, organize, store, and use all sorts of genealogical information on your computer. You can find more information on using a genealogical database in Chapter 1.

When possible, try to set aside some time to update your database with information you recently gathered. This process of putting your information together in one central place, which we call *consolidating,* helps you gain a perspective on the work that you've completed and provides a place for you to store all those nuggets you'll need when you begin researching again. By storing your information in a database, you can always refer to it for a quick answer the next time you try to remember something specific, such as where you found a reference to a marriage certificate for your great-great-grandparents, or where your great-grandfather lived during a particular time frame. Placing your information in a genealogical database has a bonus — you can take your research with you when you travel. You can carry your database on your laptop's hard drive, or you can even find smartphone and tablet applications that can display the contents of genealogical databases.

Validating your findings

After discovering information on your ancestor, it's critical that you take the time to validate your findings. Just because something is printed online doesn't mean that it's correct. Even primary sources can contain incorrect data, either by a clerical error or the individual who was the source of the record intentionally mislead the recorder. For example, you've probably heard stories of underage relatives who lied about their age to enlist in the army early. So, you might find that the birthdate in a recruitment record is different than the birthdate in a pension record. To ensure that you have the best evidence possible, we recommend that you find three sources to triangulate any key piece of information on your ancestor. We understand that this isn't always possible, but it is a good practice to validate any evidence that you can find.

Beyond just finding additional records to validate ancestry, we also recommend using other available tools, such as DNA testing, to validate records. Non-paternal events did happen in the past and it's possible that the father listed on a birth record was not the biological father. DNA testing can also be used when there is not enough evidence to be certain about a particular conclusion but there is some circumstantial evidence that you would like to test. For example, Matthew's progenitor, George Helm, was located in the same county at the same time as another Helm family. A few authors asserted that George may have been a disowned son of the family. However, after DNA testing several individuals including Matthew and some descendants from that Helm family, it's clear that those assertions were not true. The two families are in different haplogroups, which allows us to conclude that they were definitely two different families with the same surname. For more on DNA testing, see Chapter 10.

For more on validating your research, check out the following sites:

- **Validation of Genealogical Lineages Using DNA:** `http://ggdna.blogspot.com/2012/11/validation-of-genealogical-lineages.html`
- **Learn to Validate Your Online Research:** `www.familytree.com/learn/learn-to-validate-your-online-research/`

Distilling the information that you gather

The final step in the cycle is distilling the information that you gather into a report, a chart, an organized database, or a detailed research log that you can use to find additional genealogical leads. Frequently, you can complete the distillation process by producing a report from your computer-based genealogical database. Most genealogical software programs allow you to generate reports in a variety of formats. For example, you can pull up a Pedigree chart (a chart showing a primary person with lines representing the relationships to his or her parents, then lines connecting them to their parents, and so on) or an outline of descendants from information that you entered in the database about each ancestor. You can use these reports to see what holes still exist in your research, and you can add these missing pieces to the planning phase for your next research effort — starting the entire cycle over.

Another advantage to genealogical reports is having the information readily available so that you can *toggle* back to look at the report while researching online, which can help you stay focused. (*Toggling* is flipping back and forth between open programs on your computer. For example, in Windows, you press Alt+Tab to toggle, or you can click the appropriate item on the task-bar at the bottom of the screen. On a Macintosh, you can use ⌘+Tab or the Application Switcher in the upper-right corner of the screen.) If you prefer, printing copies of the reports and keeping them next to the computer while you're researching online serves the same purpose.

Too Many Ancestor Irons in the Research Fire

When you begin your research, take your time and don't get in a big hurry. Keep things simple and look for one piece of information at a time. If you try to do too much too fast, you risk getting confused, having no online success, and getting frustrated with online research. This result isn't encouraging and certainly doesn't make you feel like jumping back into your research, which would be a shame because you can find a lot of valuable information and research help online.

A good strategy is to focus on one person or immediate family unit at a time. With the advances in search technology on genealogical sites, it's often tempting to conduct a search to find information on a variety of family members in a single search. However, try to resist jumping from one family member to another. Although you can accumulate records on several individuals, you might miss opportunities to systematically find records on your ancestor.

Verifying Your Information

A piece of advice for you when you're researching:

Don't believe everything you read.

Well, actually, a genealogy purist might say, "Don't believe *anything* that you read." Either way, the point is the same: Always verify any information that you find online — or, for that matter, in print — with primary records. (For more on primary records, see Chapter 2.) If you can't prove it through a vital record, census record, or some other authoritative record, the information simply may not be as valuable as you think. However, don't discount something just because you can't *immediately* prove it. You might want to hold on to the information and continue to try to prove or disprove it with a primary document. At some time in the future, you may run across a record that does indeed prove the accuracy of the information; in the meantime, it might give you some leads for where to look for more about that person.

You've probably seen the courtroom dramas on television where the lawyer must prove his case before a jury. In family history, researchers go through a similar process to prove that a particular event occurred in the lives of their ancestors. At times, you won't be able to find a record that verifies that your ancestor was born on a certain date. Perhaps the birth record was destroyed in a courthouse fire or the birth was never properly recorded. Or worse yet, you may find two records that contain conflicting information about the same event.

So, how do genealogists and family historians know when they have sufficiently proved something? Well, for the longest time, no published guidelines existed on what constituted sufficient proof. To assist professional genealogists figure out the appropriate level of proof for their clients, the Board for Certification of Genealogists (BCG) created the *Genealogical Proof Standard* as part of the BCG Genealogical Standards Manual (published in 2000 by Ancestry).

The Genealogical Proof Standard contains five steps. If these five steps are completed, sufficient proof exists for a professional genealogist to create a research report stating that a certain event happened. We paraphrase the steps a bit to make them a little easier to understand:

1. Conduct a reasonably exhaustive search for all information related to a particular event.

2. Include a complete and accurate citation of the information that you use for your research.

3. Analyze the quality of the information. (For example, is the information from a primary source or is it from a reliable source?)

4. Resolve conflicts between two sources of information (such as two resources stating two different birth dates for the same person).

5. Arrive at a sound conclusion based on the information related to an event.

Although these steps were established for professional genealogists, they are good steps for you to follow to make sure that any person reading your research can follow your conclusions. Following these steps does not ensure that your conclusions are accurate 100 percent of the time. You always have the chance that a new piece of evidence will surface that may disprove your conclusions.

Chapter 13

Help Wanted!

*Y*ou can think of genealogical research as a journey. You may begin the journey by yourself, but after a while, you discover that the trip would go a lot faster if you had someone along for the ride. In your genealogical journey, these travel partners can take various forms — a single individual researching the same family, a research group searching for several branches of a family in which you're interested, or a genealogical society that coordinates the efforts of many people researching different families.

You may be saying, "A research mate sounds great! But where can I find one of my own?" Lucky you — in the next few pages, we explore just that. We look at ways that you can find (and keep) research partners, as well as ways that research groups and genealogical societies can help you meet your research goals.

Getting Out of Your Comfort Zone

We think it's a natural instinct to want to do all your own research. After all, that way you have a sense of control over how the research is conducted, whether it's documented correctly, and what piece of information you get next. For you, it may even be comfortable to be alone in your quest. We understand that you may feel this way, but we're here to tell you that it's time to step outside your comfort zone. Although researching alone some of the time is great, don't try to do all the research yourself. As you'll discover, an awful lot of people out there are digging for answers, and it would be a shame for you not to take advantage of their work and vice versa.

We can't emphasize enough the benefits of sharing genealogical data. Sharing is the foundation on which the genealogical community is built. For example, when Matthew began researching his genealogy, he went to the National Archives, Library of Congress, and several regional libraries and archives. Along the way, he found a few books that made a passing mention of some of his ancestors, and he discovered some original records that helped him put some pieces together. It wasn't until he shared his information online that he began to realize just how many people were working on his surname. During the month following the creation of his website, he received messages from 40 other Helm researchers — one of whom lived in Slovenia! Although not all these researchers were working on Matthew's specific branch (only 2 of the 40 were directly related), he received valuable information on some of the areas on which other researchers were working. Matthew may never have known that some of these researchers existed had he not taken the first step to share his information.

By knowing the family lines and regions that other researchers are pursuing, you can coordinate your efforts with theirs — not only sharing information you've already collected but also working together toward your common goal. Maybe you live closer to a courthouse that holds records relating to your ancestor than does a distant cousin with whom you're communicating online. Maybe the cousin lives near a family gravesite that you'd like to have a photo of. Rather than duplicating efforts to collect the court records and photographs, you can make arrangements for each of you to get the desired items that are closest to you and then exchange copies of them over the Internet or through traditional mail.

The Shotgun Approach

You're probably wondering how to find individuals with whom to share your information. Well, you could start by going through telephone books and calling everyone with the surname that you're researching. However, given how some people feel about telemarketers, we don't recommend this as a strategy.

Sending mass e-mails to anyone you find with your surname through one of the online white-pages sites, networking sites, or online social circles is similar to the telemarketing strategy we've just warned you against. We refer to this mass e-mail strategy as the *shotgun approach,* and many people refer to it as spamming. You shoot out a bunch of e-mail messages aimed in various directions, with hopes of successfully hitting one or two targets. Although you may find one or two people who answer you in a positive way, a lot of people may find such unsolicited e-mail irritating. And, quite honestly, gleaning e-mail addresses from online white pages is not as easy as it was even just a few years ago. Most of the online directories that allow you to search for e-mail addresses no longer give the precise address to you. Rather, they either enable you to send an e-mail from their sites to the individuals, leaving it up to the recipient to respond to you, or they require you to purchase the specific information about the person from them or one of their sponsors. This is their way of protecting that person's online privacy, and for some it's a means to earn money.

Netiquette: Using your manners online

Part of being a fine, upstanding member of the online genealogy community is communicating effectively and politely on the Internet. Online communication is often hampered by the fact that you can't see the people with whom you're corresponding, and you can't hear the intonation of their voices to determine what emotions they're expressing. To avoid misunderstandings, follow some simple guidelines — called *netiquette* — when writing messages:

- Don't send a message that you wouldn't want posted on a bulletin board at work or the library or that you wouldn't want printed in a newsletter. You should expect that every e-mail you send is potentially public.

- Make sure that you don't violate any copyright laws by sending large portions of written works through e-mail.

- If you receive a *flame* (a heated message usually sent to provoke a response), try to ignore it. Usually, no good comes from responding to a flame.

- Be careful when you respond to messages. Instead of replying to an individual, you may be replying to an entire group of people. Checking the To line before you click the Send button is always a good idea.

- Use sentence case when you write e-mail messages. USING ALL UPPERCASE LETTERS INDICATES SHOUTING! The exception to this guideline is when you send a query and place your surnames in all-uppercase letters (for example, George HELM).

- If you participate in a mailing list and you reply with a message that is most likely of interest to only one person, consider sending that person a message individually rather than e-mailing the list as a whole.

- When you're joking, use smileys or type <grins> or <g>, but use these symbols sparingly to increase their effectiveness. A *smiley* is an emoticon that looks like :-). (Turn the book on its right side if you can't see the face.) *Emoticons* are graphics created by combinations of keys to express an emotion in an e-mail. Here are a few emoticons that you may run into:

:-) Happy, smiling

;-) Wink, ironic

:-> Sarcastic

8-) Wearing glasses

:-(Sad, unhappy

:-< Disappointed

:-o Frightened, surprised

:-{) Mustache

Instead of spending hours trying to find e-mail addresses through online directories and following a three- or four-step process to send an initial message to someone, go to a site that focuses on genealogy to find the names of and contact information for researchers who are interested in your surname. This is a much gentler, better way to go about finding others with the same interests as you.

Also, note that we aren't saying that e-mail directories are completely useless in genealogy. E-mail directories can be a good means for getting in contact with a relative whose e-mail address you've lost or one you know is interested in your e-mail.

Making Friends (And Keeping Them) Online

You may be wondering where to find fellow researchers. You can find them by searching query pages on the web, forums, mailing lists, and social networking sites. (In Chapter 11, we delve into using general networking sites such as Facebook, as well as genealogy-specific networking sites such as Geni.com.)

If you decide to use e-mail to contact other researchers, send them an e-mail message introducing yourself and briefly explaining your purpose for contacting them. Be sure to include a listing of the ancestors you're researching in your message.

Before you rush out and start contacting people, however, we must offer the following sage advice:

✔ **Before sending messages to a website maintainer, look around the site to see whether that person is the appropriate one to approach.** More often than not, the person who maintains a website is indeed the one who is researching the surnames you find on that website. However, it's not unusual for site maintainers to host information on their sites for other people. If they do, they typically have separate contact addresses for those individuals and an explanation that they're not personally researching those surnames. Some even go so far as to post notices on their sites stating that they don't entertain research questions. So when you see a list of surnames on a site, don't automatically assume that the website maintainer is the person to contact. Look around a little to ensure that you're addressing the most appropriate person.

✔ **Make your messages brief and to the point.** E-mail messages that run five or six pages long can overwhelm some people. If the person you send the message to is interested in your information and responds positively to you, you can send one or more detailed messages at a future date.

✔ **Ensure that your message is detailed enough for the recipients to decide whether your info relates to their research and whether they can help you.** Include names, dates, and places as appropriate.

✔ **Use net etiquette, or *netiquette,* when you create your messages.** Remember, e-mail can be an impersonal medium. Although you may mean one thing, someone who doesn't know you may mistakenly misinterpret your message. (For more on netiquette, see the nearby sidebar, "Netiquette: Using your manners online.")

✔ **Don't disclose personal information that could violate a person's privacy.** Information such as addresses, birth dates, and Social Security numbers for living persons is considered private and should not be freely shared with other researchers. Also, we don't recommend that you send much personal information about yourself until you know the recipient a lot better. When first introducing yourself, your name and e-mail address should suffice, along with the information about the deceased ancestors you're researching.

✔ **Get permission before forwarding messages from other researchers.** Sometimes researchers may provide information that they don't want made available to the general public. Asking permission before forwarding a message to a third party eliminates any potential problems with violating the trust of your fellow researchers.

Joining a Herd: Research Groups

If your relatives are tired of hearing about your genealogy research trips or the information that you found on Great-uncle Beauford, but you'd like to share your triumphs with someone, you may be ready to join a research group.

Research groups consist of any number of people who coordinate their research and share resources to achieve success. These groups may start conducting research because they share a surname, family branch, or geographic location. Individuals who live geographically close to each other may make up a research group, or the group may consist of people who have never personally met each other but are interested in descendants of one particular person. Research groups may have a variety of goals and may have a formal or an informal structure.

A good example of a research group is one that Matthew discovered shortly after he posted his first web page many years back. An individual who was researching one of his surnames on the East Coast of the United States contacted him. After exchanging a few e-mails, Matthew discovered that this individual was part of a small research group studying the origins of several branches of the Helm surname. Each member of the group contributes the results of his or her personal research and provides any information that he or she finds, which may be of use to other members of the group. Over the years, the group has continued to work together and expanded their efforts. The group as a whole has sponsored research by professional genealogists in other countries to discover more about their ancestors there, and they've spun off a more formal research group that focuses solely on molecular research (DNA-based) of the Helm bloodlines. The vast majority of the communication for these two research groups is through e-mail.

You can find an example of an online-based research group at the Search for the Parents of the North Carolina Helms Brothers (1690–1750) site at `http://freepages.genealogy.rootsweb.ancestry.com/~helmsnc/`. The site includes information on the various branches of the Helms family, details on other branches of Helm/Helms families, and references to allied families.

To find research groups, your best bet is to visit a comprehensive genealogical website, a search engine, or a site that specializes in surnames, such as SurnameWeb at `www.surnameweb.org`.

The following steps show you how to find groups pertaining to a surname on the site:

1. **Launch your web browser and go to the SurnameWeb site at `www.surnameweb.org`.**

   After the page loads, you see a search field and the letters of the alphabet near the top center of the page.

2. **Click the letter of the alphabet that's the first letter of the surname that you're researching.**

   For example, say that the surname you're researching begins with the letter *P*. Find the link to the letter *P* and click it. This action brings up a web page with the *P* index.

3. **Click the next level link corresponding to the first and second letter of the surname you're researching.**

   We selected the link labeled Po. You see a list of surname links that begin with the letters *Po*.

4. **Scroll through the list and click a surname link.**

   We wanted to find sites relating to the surname *Pollard,* so we clicked the link for the Pollard surname, which displayed a Results page entitled Pollard Surname Resource Center.

5. **Choose a site to visit.**

   Scroll down past all the links to search other commercial websites until you reach the links you're most interested in. We wanted to see the links that would take us directly to personal and group web pages containing information about people named Pollard, so we selected the link titled Pollard Genealogy Web Pages under Pollard Surname Search.

In addition to using comprehensive genealogy sites and specialized surname sites, you can use other strategies to identify possible research groups. One way to find research groups pertaining to surnames is to visit a one-name studies index. You can find a list of one-name studies sites at the Guild of One-Name Studies page (`www.one-name.org`).

If you can't find an established online group that fits your interests, why not start one yourself? If you're interested in researching a particular topic, chances are good that others out there are interested as well. Maybe the time has come for you to coordinate efforts and begin working with others toward your common research goals. Starting an online research group can be relatively easy — just post a message stating your interest in starting a group at some key locations, such as message boards, newsgroups, or mailing lists.

Becoming a Solid Member of (Genealogical) Society

Genealogical societies can be great places to discover research methods and to coordinate your research. Several types of societies exist. They range from the more traditional geographical or surname-based societies to *cybersocieties* (societies that exist only on the Internet) that are redefining the way people think about genealogical societies.

Geographical societies

Chapter 6 introduces geography-based genealogical societies as groups that can help you discover resources in a particular area in which your ancestors lived, or as groups in your hometown that can help you discover how to research effectively. However, local genealogical societies can provide another service to their members. These societies often coordinate local research efforts of the members in the form of projects. To locate geographical societies, follow our advice in Chapter 6 or check out the site of a genealogical-society federation such as one of these:

- ✔ **Federation of Genealogical Societies, Society Hall page:** `www.fgs.org/cstm_societyHall.php`
- ✔ **Federation of Family History Societies:** `www.ffhs.org.uk`

These projects can take many forms. For example, the Illinois State Genealogical Society (`www.ilgensoc.org`) is working on several projects, including creating a database of county marriage records, updating a list of Illinois pioneers, forming a list of all cemeteries in the state (see Figure 13-1), and compiling indexes of Civil War, World War I, and World War II certificates issued.

Smaller groups of members sometimes work on projects in addition to the society's official projects. For example, you may belong to a county genealogical society and decide to join with a few members to write a history of the pioneers who settled a particular township in the county.

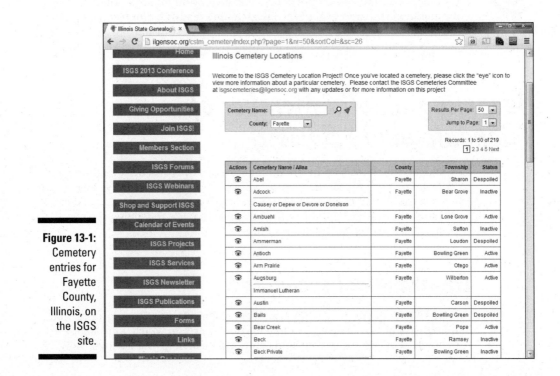

Figure 13-1: Cemetery entries for Fayette County, Illinois, on the ISGS site.

Family and surname associations

In addition to geographically based associations, you can find groups tied to particular names or family groups. Typically, they're referred to as — you've probably already guessed — surname or family associations or research groups.

Family associations also frequently sponsor projects that coordinate the efforts of several researchers. These projects may focus on the family or surname in a specific geographic area or point in time, or they may attempt to collect information about every individual possessing the surname throughout time and then place the information in a shared database.

You can find family and surname associations by using the methods and websites recommended earlier in this chapter for finding research groups. In essence, the two types of organizations are similar — the main difference is whether formal meetings are held.

If a family or surname association isn't currently working on a project that interests you, by all means suggest a project that does interest you (as long as the project is relevant to the association as a whole).

Gathering Kinfolk: Using the Family Reunion for Research

You may have noticed that throughout this book, we strongly recommend that you interview relatives to gather information about your ancestors both to use as leads in finding records and to enhance your genealogy. Well, what better way to gather information from relatives than by attending a family reunion?

Family reunions can add a lot to your research because you find many relatives all in one place, and typically most are eager to visit. A reunion is an efficient way to collect stories, photographs, databases (if others in the family research and keep their records in their computers), and even copies of records. You might even find some people interested in researching the family along with you. A family reunion can be great fun, too.

When you attend your next family reunion, be sure to take along your notebook, list of interview questions (see Chapter 2 if you haven't developed your list yet), and camera. You can take some printed charts from your genealogical database, too — we bet that lots of your relatives will be interested in seeing them.

Rent-a-Researcher

A time may come when you've exhausted all the research avenues directly available to you and need help that family, friends, and society members can't provide. Maybe all the records you need to get past a research brick wall are in a distant place, or maybe you have too many other obligations and not enough time to research personally. You needn't fret. Professional researchers are happy to help you.

Professional researchers are people to whom you pay a fee to dig around and find information for you. They can retrieve specific records that you identify, or they can prepare an entire report on a family line by using all the resources available. And, as you might expect, the amount that you pay depends on the level of service that you require. Professional researchers are especially helpful when you need records from locations to which you cannot travel conveniently.

When looking for a professional researcher, you want to find someone who is reputable and experienced in the area in which you need help. Here's a list of questions you may want to ask when shopping around for a professional researcher:

✔ **Is the researcher certified or accredited and, if so, by what organization?** In the genealogy field, certifications function a bit differently than in other fields. Rather than receiving a certification based on coursework, genealogical certifications are based on demonstrated research skills. You find two main certifying bodies in the field: the Board for Certification of Genealogists (www.bcgcertification.org) and the International Commission for the Accreditation of Professional Genealogists (www.icapgen.org). The Board for Certification of Genealogists (BCG) awards two credentials: Certified Genealogist and Certified Genealogical Lecturer.

You might also run into some old certifications such as Certified Lineage Specialist (CLS), Certified American Indian Lineage Specialist (CAILS), Certified Genealogical Records Specialist (CGRS), and Certified Genealogical Instructor (CGI), which are no longer used by the organization.

The credentials are awarded based on a peer-review process — meaning that a group of individuals possessing the credentials evaluate a research project of an applicant. The International Commission for the Accreditation of Professional Genealogists (ICAPGen) awards the Accredited Genealogist (AG) credential. The accreditation program originally was established by the Family History Department of the Church of Jesus Christ of Latter-day Saints. In 2000, the program was launched as an independent organization called ICAPGen. To become accredited, an applicant must submit a research project and take an examination. Accredited Genealogists are certified in a particular geographical or subject-matter area. So, you want to make sure that the accreditation that the researcher possesses matches your research question. Some professional researchers do not hold either of these credentials but might hold a professional degree such as a Masters in Library and Information Science or advanced history degree from an accredited college or university. Depending on the research area, they could be just as proficient as a credentialed genealogist.

✔ **How many years of experience does the researcher have researching?** In general, we tend to think of a person as improving in knowledge and efficiency as he or she has more years of experience researching. But the answer to this question needs to be considered in context of some other questions. The researcher might have only a little time actually researching genealogies for others but might have an educational degree that required historical research experience.

✔ **What is the researcher's educational background?** The methods for researching and the type of reports that you can get from an individual can be directly influenced by his or her educational background. If the researcher has a degree in history, you may get more anecdotal material relating to the times and places in which your ancestor lived. If the researcher attended the school of hard knocks (and doesn't have a formal education per se but has lots of experience researching), you may get specific, bare-bones facts about your ancestor.

✔ **Does the researcher have any professional affiliations?** In other words, does he or she belong to any professional genealogical organizations and, if so, which ones? Much like the question dealing with certification or accreditation, a researcher's willingness to belong to a professional organization shows a serious commitment. One particular organization to look for is membership in the Association of Professional Genealogists (www.apgen.org). The APG is an umbrella organization of all types of researchers and those providing professional services. It includes researchers credentialed under both BCG and ICAPGen, as well as other noncredentialed researchers. All members of the APG agree to be bound by a code of ethics and meet particular research standards.

✔ **What foreign languages does the researcher speak fluently?** This is an important question if you need research conducted in another country. Some research firms send employees to other countries to gather information, but you need the reassurance that the employee has the qualifications necessary to obtain accurate information.

✔ **What records and resources does the researcher have access to?**
Again, you want the reassurance that the researcher can obtain accurate
information and from reliable sources. You probably don't want to pay a
researcher to simply read the same documents that you have access to
at your local library and put together a summary.

✔ **What is the professional researcher's experience in the area where
you need help?** For example, if you need help interviewing distant relatives in a foreign country, has he or she conducted interviews in the past?
Or, if you need records pertaining to a particular ethnic or religious group,
does the researcher have experience researching those types of records?

✔ **How does the researcher charge?** You need to know how you're going
to be charged — by the record, by the hour, or by the project. And
it's helpful to know up front what methods of payment the researcher
accepts so that you're prepared when payment time comes. And you
should ask what you can do if you're dissatisfied with the researcher's
services (although we hope you never need to know this).

✔ **Is the researcher currently working on other projects and, if so, how
many and what kinds?** It's perfectly reasonable to ask how much time
the researcher can devote to your research project and when you can
get results. If the researcher tells you that it's going to take a year to get
a copy of a single birth certificate from an agency in the town where he
or she lives, you might want to rethink hiring that person.

✔ **Does the researcher have references you can contact?** We think that a
researcher's willingness to provide references speaks to his or her ethics.
And we recommend that you contact one or two of the references to find
out what exactly they like about this researcher and whether they see the
researcher as having any pitfalls of which you should be aware.

One way to find professional researchers is to look for them on comprehensive genealogy sites. Another is to consult an online directory of researchers, such as the Association of Professional Genealogists (`www.apgen.
org/directory/index.html`) directory or genealogyPro (`http://
genealogypro.com`).

Follow these steps to check the APG directory:

1. **Using your web browser, go to the APG site at `www.apgen.org`.**

2. **Click the link from the list in the left column of the page under the
   Find a Specialist heading.**

   For example, we looked for a researcher who specializes in adoption.

3. **Click the link for a researcher who, based on the description posted,
   looks promising.**

   Figure 13-2 shows the researchers specializing in adoption.

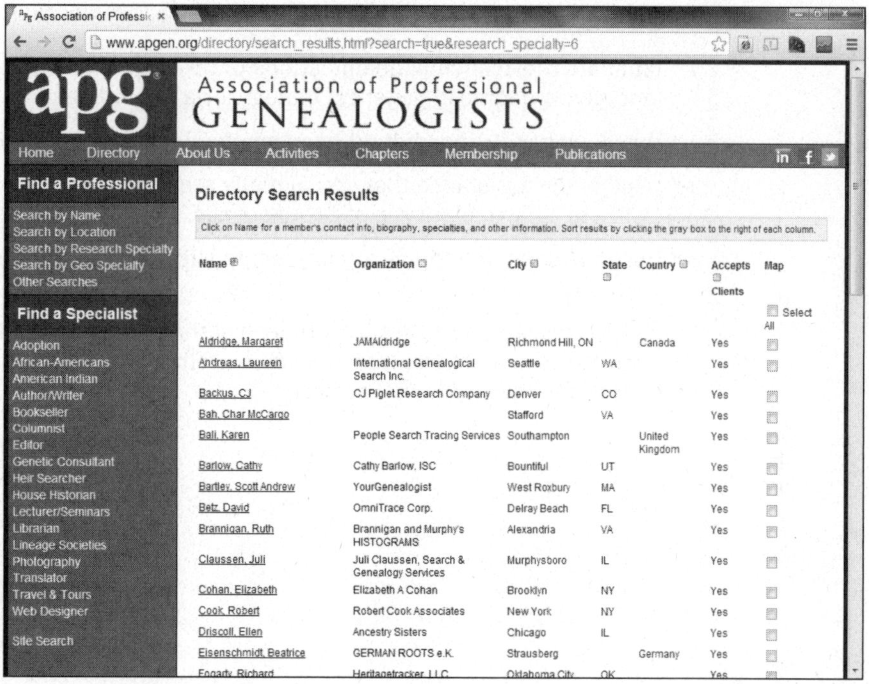

Figure 13-2:
Researchers
specializing in
adoption at the
Association of
Professional
Genealogists
site.

When you find a professional researcher, make your initial contact. Be as specific as possible about your needs. That helps the researcher pinpoint exactly what he or she needs to do and makes it easier to calculate how much it will cost you.

DNA Consulting

In addition to generalized genealogical researchers, some paid researchers specialize in helping you understand your DNA tests. If you've taken one or more DNA tests and you just don't understand what it all means, you might consider hiring one of these professional researchers in the area of DNA consulting services. Some have built companies that will create a report that interprets your DNA results after they've been processed by a lab. The International Society of Genetic Genealogy maintains a list of DNA consultants at www.isogg.org/consult.htm.

Be sure to get answers to the following questions before engaging a consultant:

- ✔ What are the academic qualifications of the consultant? Does the consultant have a degree in genetics, biology, or a related field?
- ✔ How long has the consultant been involved in genetic genealogy?
- ✔ What is the assistance that you actually require? Some consultants specialize in a particular type of DNA analysis.
- ✔ Does the consultant have a relationship with a particular testing company?
- ✔ As DNA research changes over time, will the consultant update the research as new information becomes available, and how much will the consultant charge for that service?

Chapter 14

Taking It on the Road

Researching your family history online may jump-start your genealogical pursuits, but at some point, you'll want to make a pilgrimage to your ancestor's birthplace, travel to another location to get original records or pictures, or attend a family reunion to meet some primary sources in person. In this chapter, we discuss ways you can make your trip easier by planning your travels and taking along a few aids.

Planning Your Trip Using the Web

A wealth of information is available to help you plan your travels — and it's all at your fingertips! You can surf the web to check out hotels and motels, car-rental agencies, airlines, restaurants, grocery stores, local attractions, and a host of other services related to research trips and vacations.

You can use a mapping site such as MapQuest (www.mapquest.com) to plan your basic trip. It has sections for transportation, lodging, dining, and a variety of other things you need while traveling. You can even use MapQuest to plan your route if you're driving in North America.

Follow these steps to get driving directions from MapQuest:

1. **Using your web browser, go to the MapQuest site (www.mapquest.com).**

2. **Click Get Directions in the left column.**

   Two fields appear where you can enter a starting and ending address.

3. **In the first field (marked as A), type your start location or where this part of your journey will begin.**

   In the field, you can type an address, business, or landmark.

4. **In the second field (marked as B), enter your destination or end location.**

   The items that you can enter are the same as the first field.

5. **Click Get Directions.**

   MapQuest determines the directions from your starting point to your destination. If MapQuest can't determine a route for you, it provides an explanation and recommends revising your direction information.

If you're going to drive a long distance, you might consider a site such as Roadtrippers (`https://roadtrippers.com`). Not only does it map out a path for you to take on your trip, but it also allows you to plan stops for accommodations, attractions, entertainment, history, shopping, and more.

Narrowing Your Target

Before you jump in the car and head out, you should do a little research on the places you plan to visit and what your objectives are after you get there. Fire up your computer at home and check the days and hours that repositories you plan to visit are open to the public. Review their holdings to determine exactly what types of records you're looking for at particular locations. And review their rules and policies — you do not want to haul in all your gadgets if they allow you to bring only paper and a writing utensil.

If you're traveling during cold months, you might want to see whether your destination offers lockers or a coat closet to store your jacket, umbrella, or backpack. If you plan to spend an entire day in one location, you might want to see whether it has a cafeteria or food court where you can purchase lunch, or whether it has a designated place where you can eat a lunch you bring with you. You can iron out all sorts of details before you embark on your journey.

If you're traveling within the United States, the USGenWeb Project (`www.usgenweb.com`) provides links for every state and details on many of the resources that are available.

Your time at a research site is limited, so you want to make the best of it. Before making the trip, it's a good idea to generate reports in your genealogical database that focus on your research objectives. Include items such as key dates and family relationships. For more on reporting, see Chapter 11.

For advice on planning a research trip, see the article "Planning a Genealogy Research Trip" at `www.archives.com/experts/brandt-kathleen/` `planning-a-genealogy-research-trip.html` and "Preparing for a Genealogy Research Trip" at `http://elysesgenealogyblog.com/` `preparing-for-a-genealogy-research-trip`.

Remembering Your Laptop or Notebook

It would be frustrating if you reached your destination and found that you didn't have any of your past findings and leads for research on this trip with you, and you couldn't remember much about the ancestors you set out to research. It's easy to get caught up in packing and meeting departure times and to forget some of the most important things you need to have with you. We don't expect you to have all your research memorized, so be sure to set your laptop computer or your notebook containing your genealogical database and all your family charts, pictures, and notes in an obvious place so that you don't forget to take them along. You could even keep a printed copy of the directions you just received from MapQuest (see the "Planning Your Trip Using the Web" section, earlier in this chapter) with your laptop or notebook so that you don't forget them either.

Opting for a Tablet

Although having your notebook or laptop computer with you is handy, these days you have smaller, lighter options: tablets. There are many variations on tablets these days, including devices that support iOS (such as Apple iPhone and iPad), Android (such as Google Nexus and Samsung Galaxy), Windows and Windows RT (such as Dell Latitude 10 and Microsoft Surface), and proprietary devices such as the Amazon Kindle and Barnes & Noble Nook. There are various ways to use a tablet in your research — here are a few of them:

- ✓ **Genealogy databases:** Some tablets, such as those that run the full Windows operating system, can run a full genealogy database the same way that a notebook computer can. Also, some genealogy databases or light versions of genealogy databases have been created specifically for particular tablet operating systems. For more on genealogical databases, take a peek at Chapter 1.

- ✓ **GEDCOM viewers:** In an effort to save space on the tablet, some developers have created apps that display a GEDCOM file exported from a genealogical database. Review Chapter 11 for a quick refresher on GEDCOM.

✔ **Photo storage:** Take digital copies of your family-related pictures or scanned images of records with you. This feature is especially nice at a family reunion, where you can set photos to play in a slide show. Photo storage is also handy when you're sitting in a repository and need to take a quick look at a census record. Also, some tablets allow you to take pictures of key places and documents. And some tablets even allow you to include *geocoding* — the embedding of geographic coordinates into the image — so you don't forget where you took the picture.

✔ **Map applications:** No need to carry printed copies of the maps you downloaded plotting your trip. And if you get lost, you can find your way back to the main road. You can also use map applications to identify geographic areas that might be relevant in your research. Also, you can use GPS applications to accurately note the locations of grave sites, homesteads, land parcels, and other geographical entities important to your research.

✔ **Text editors and note-taking applications:** Take notes of the things you find in your on-site research and save them to your tablet or sync them up to a cloud application such as Evernote (`http://evernote.com`).

✔ **Web browsers and e-mail access:** Stay connected to everything you use in cyberspace from home while on the road. A lot of tablets support connecting to the Internet directly through cellular phone networks or through Wi-Fi networks. If your device connects only through Wi-Fi networks, you can purchase a MiFi device from your favorite cellular provider that can act as a Wi-Fi device for your tablet.

✔ **Cloud storage:** If you don't want to put all of your documents, photos, and scanned images on your tablet, you can always use cloud storage options such as Box (`www.box.com`) and Dropbox (`www.dropbox.com`).

Flashing Your Treasures

Our title for this section caught your attention, didn't it? Well, it's really not risqué — we're talking about flash drives (also sometimes called thumb drives or jump drives). Flash drives are inexpensive devices that store from 2GB (gigabytes) to 128GB of files, scanned images, and photos. You can plug one into the USB port on any computer, as well as some tablets, and transfer files from one location to another quickly. Most flash drives fit on your keychain, so you can carry them almost anywhere. Some computers and tablets also support SD cards that are smaller and thinner than flash drives and support similar storage amounts.

A flash drive or SD card are wonderful gadgets to have if you're going to share your genealogical treasures with others at a family reunion or society meeting, need access to data at a repository that has public computers, or if you plan to give a presentation at a genealogical meeting or conference.

Capturing a Picture-Perfect Moment

If your mother is like April's mother, she drilled into your head when you were young that you should always carry a camera with you. Of course, these days, cameras are sitting at the ready on cell phones, so it's hard not to have one with you. As far as genealogical pursuits are concerned, cameras are handy to have around for many reasons — photos at family reunions, pictures of headstones in cemeteries, or snapshots of the family homestead or some landmark near it. (We won't mention how we know that they are also great to have on hand if you get into a car accident while on your genealogical excursion.) If you're visiting a library or archive that allows you to bring your camera inside with you, it might even be used to photograph documents or books (to save on photocopying costs).

Using Your Cell Phone as a Cell Phone

In the preceding section, we talk about using your cell phone as a camera. But you should take your cell phone with you on your research jaunts and ensure that it's always charged so that you can use it as a phone, too. We probably don't have to explain that you will want it if you have an emergency while traveling. A cell phone is also useful when you need to call a relative or research buddy if you have questions about a particular ancestor that you're researching in a location away from home.

For example, a few years back, we were visiting a cemetery that we had never been to before and were having trouble locating Matthew's ancestor because of conflicting information in the family file. It was a wonderful convenience to be able to call his aunt and ask her for clarification rather than having to travel home to phone her or waiting to see her and then making a return trip to the cemetery at a later date.

Positioning Yourself for Success

If you've had the opportunity to work much with land records, you know the difficulty in translating the land descriptions into an actual place on the ground. One way to help you find a specific location is to use latitudes and longitudes.

Latitude is the distance of a point either north or south of the equator, and *longitude* is the distance of a point either east or west of the prime meridian. If you want a primer on latitude and longitude, we recommend visiting the WorldAtlas.com site at www.worldatlas.com/aatlas/imageg.htm.

In genealogy, you might encounter latitude and longitude associated with descriptions of historical landmarks, land measurements, and burial locations, among other things.

Global positioning systems (GPS) pick up satellite signals that determine your precise location in terms of latitude and longitude. They're also designed to guide you to specific locations based on latitude and longitude. This feature is useful if you're looking for a plat of land where your great-great-grandfather lived but all the natural markings have changed over time.

You find many varieties of GPS devices — from handheld systems, to navigation systems built into cars, to cellular phones that can give you position readings. Although handheld GPS devices and automobile navigation systems have become less expensive over the years, cellular phones with built-in GPS are common and a good alternative. So check your cell phone to see whether it has positioning capabilities before rushing out to buy a GPS device.

After you find that your cellular phone does contain a GPS, then selecting the right GPS application is the next step. We recommend finding a GPS application that works for both driving and walking, and has the capability for storing the path that you took to get to a particular location. That might come in handy later if you forget to take a GPS reading at a location that you want to record in your genealogical database.

Have Scanner, Will Travel

At first, it may sound a bit strange to say that you should take your scanner with you on your travels — especially when you can snap a picture with your cell phone. However, many document repositories now allow you to bring in a small scanner with your laptop, and scanners can sometimes provide better resolution than your cell phone or tablet.

Scanning the documents that you discover on location saves you the cost of having them reproduced on a copier and saves you time that you'd typically lose waiting for a staff member to copy the document (if it is a large document that requires staff copying). Be sure to check the policies of the repository online to make sure that it allows a scanner on-site before trying to bring it into the repository.

When it comes to scanners, the catch is whether you have one that is small and lightweight enough to carry with you. Some flatbed scanners are thin and light but are still cumbersome to carry because of the size of the bed. This type of scanner might be a viable option if you're carrying a large computer bag or backpack. But it's likely that you'll want a handheld scanner. We recently discovered a wand-style, handheld scanner called the Magic Wand that seems made for on-site researching. It's about 10 inches long and less than 2 inches wide and deep, so it fits nicely in a bag. The battery-powered scanner stores the images to a microSD card, making it easy to swap out the card when scanning lots of documents. Another model even supports Wi-Fi. You can find out more about the Magic Wand at www.vupointsolutions.com.

Part V
The Part of Tens

Get ideas for planning your next family reunion at www.dummies.com/extras/genealogyonline.

In this part...

- ✔ Discover genealogical sites that you'll want to visit time and again.

- ✔ Seek answers from helpful genealogical sites.

Chapter 15

Ten Sites Worth Bookmarking

In This Chapter

▶ Keeping up-to-date with blogs

▶ Finding valuable information in online magazines

▶ Subscribing to mailing lists

Things can change quickly in the world of online genealogy. So how do you keep in the loop on all of the new sites and resources? Well, that's what this chapter is all about. Here we'll tell you about ten sites that you might want to bookmark to stay informed on what's going on in genealogy.

Eastman's Online Genealogy Newsletter

`http://blog.eogn.com/`

Perhaps one of the oldest sources of news on the genealogy community is Eastman's Online Genealogy Newsletter. You can read the newsletter online or you can choose to receive free daily updates through e-mail. The newsletter comes in two forms — the free Standard Edition and the subscription Plus Edition. The free edition includes press releases, book reviews, and articles about what's happening in the genealogy industry — not necessarily only online resources. The Plus Edition contains more in-depth articles on how-to topics. To get an idea of what's included in either edition, go to the blog at the address above. Any article with a (+) symbol in front of it requires a subscription. Anything else is freely available.

Family Tree Magazine

www.familytreemagazine.com

The Family Tree Magazine website is the companion to the print magazine published by F+W Media. The site contains blogs, some getting-started articles, a list of websites, and a research toolkit that includes forms and worksheets that you can use in your research. If you want more interactive communication, the site includes podcasts, webinars, and training videos.

About.com Genealogy

www.genealogy.about.com

About.com's Genealogy page has a regular blog that focuses on how-to articles. The articles fall into topics such as starting a family tree, genealogy by country or ethnicity, databases and records, DNA and genetics, education and tutorials, famous family trees, help and networking, heraldry and arms, historical research, photos and scrapbooking, relatives and reunions, software and tools, and writing and publishing.

The Ancestry Insider

www.ancestryinsider.blogspot.com

The Ancestry Insider is a blog that reports on news surrounding the Ancestry.com and FamilySearch websites. Keep in mind that the blog is reflective of the authors' feelings on both sites, but it is a way to keep up to date on what's going on with both sites.

DearMYRTLE

http://blog.dearmyrtle.comblog.dearmyrtle.com

DearMYRTLE has been providing genealogy advice since 1995. Her current blog features how-to articles and news about the genealogical world. DearMYRTLE also has webinars and a YouTube channel that's linked from the site.

Genealogy Gems

http://lisalouisecooke.com

The Genealogy Gems website contains a blog about various genealogy happenings, free podcasts, and links to its YouTube channel. There's also a premium subscription that allows members access to special podcasts, the podcast archives, and video recordings of the author's classes.

The Genealogy Guys Podcast

www.genealogyguys.com

The Genealogy Guys site takes pride in being the longest-running, regularly produced genealogy podcast. The podcasts come out about once a month and contain news about the genealogy world and answers listener's e-mails.

The Genetic Genealogist

www.thegeneticgenealogist.com

As you might suspect, The Genetic Genealogist's blog focuses on news related to the use of DNA analysis in genealogy. The blog looks at how to use DNA techniques with traditional genealogy and also includes articles on the developing area of personal genomics. Also included on the site are product reviews of the various DNA testing services that cater to genealogists.

NARAtions

http://blogs.archives.gov/online-public-access

NARAtions is the blog of the United States National Archives. You can get an insider look at what's going on with records at the Archives and see blogs on the contents of particular record groups. Also available are tips on using the National Archives website for research.

GeneaBloggers

`http://geneabloggers.com`

GeneaBloggers is a site that attempts to keep track of the many genealogical blogs. From the front page, you can see the latest topics in various blogs. If you're interested in starting your own blog, the site has some helpful hints and daily blogging prompts that can provide ideas for what to cover in your blog. For a list of almost 3,000 blogs, see the Genealogy Blog Roll section of the site.

Chapter 16

Ten Helpful Sites

In This Chapter

▶ Finding sites with general research info

▶ Getting help in the form of videos and tutorials

▶ Subscribing to mailing lists

Do censuses make you feel senseless? Panicked at the idea of using Soundex? Just plain confused about where to start? These ten sites may relieve some of the anxiety you feel about researching your genealogy.

Ancestry.com Learning Center

`www.ancestry.com/cs/HelpAndAdviceUS`

Although the purpose of Ancestry.com is to offer subscriptions to online data, the site also offers some good articles and video tutorials for free. The video tutorials cover topics such as Why Start a Family Tree and Exploring Census Records. The Learning Center provides free forms and charts, descriptions of historical record types (including census, military, and vital records), as well as advice on how to use the various resources on Ancestry.com.

You might want to investigate the Family History Wiki area, where you can find articles on many research topics. These entries come from a variety of sources, including The Source: A Guidebook to American Genealogy; Red Book: American State, County, and Town Sources; content from Ancestry. com; and user-submitted articles. By the way, a *wiki* is a collaborative website where users provide definitions and information about a topic. You'll find a link to the Family History Wiki under the Learning Center drop-down menu at the top of the Ancestry.com Learning Center page.

FamilySearch Help Center

`https://familysearch.org/ask/`

The FamilySearch Help Center contains several resources to help with your research. The Center covers support for FamilySearch products, live research assistance from individuals with expertise in particular areas, getting started tutorials, a learning center with online courses, and the FamilySearch Research Wiki. With more than 75,000 articles related to genealogical research, the FamilySearch Research Wiki is an invaluable guide to assist you with your research. Whether you're looking for guidance on a specific locality, a type of record, or an ethnic group, or you need general help with research, you should be able to find an applicable article. The site is set up like a typical wiki and is maintained by the genealogical community at large.

WeRelate

`www.werelate.org/wiki/Main_Page`

WeRelate started as a wiki developed jointly by the Foundation for On-Line Genealogy and the Allen County Public Library. It has recently added contributions from the user community, mostly in the form of pages on specific ancestors. It claims to be the largest genealogy wiki with ancestor pages numbering more than 2,500,000.

Genealogy Today: Guide to Genealogy

`www.genealogytoday.com`

Genealogy Today's Guide to Genealogy (located on the left side of the home page, near the bottom) contains tips for experienced and newbie researchers alike. The guide is divided into four categories: Getting Started, Family History, Research Tools, and Advanced Topics. Mixed with the articles are suggestions on how to use the site's other resources to contribute to your research success. Under Advanced Topics, try the News Center link, which reports on new genealogical resources. The link to the GenWeekly newsletter offers insight on research geared toward researchers with all levels of experience.

Guide to Family History Research

```
www.arkansasresearch.com/guideindex.htm
```

If you're looking for a concise overview of genealogical research methods, then the Guide to Family History Research may be for you. The site is divided into 13 topics:

- ✔ Is Family History For You?
- ✔ Home and Family Sources
- ✔ Organizing Your Family Records
- ✔ Beginning Your Research
- ✔ Federal Census Records
- ✔ Courthouse Research
- ✔ Military Records
- ✔ Ethnic Genealogy
- ✔ A Broad View
- ✔ Correspondence
- ✔ Sharing Your Heritage
- ✔ A Genealogist's Toy Box
- ✔ Glossary

GEN-NEWBIE-L

```
http://lists.rootsweb.ancestry.com/index/other/
Miscellaneous/GEN-NEWBIE.html
```

The GEN-NEWBIE-L mailing list is a forum for individuals who are new to computers and genealogy and are looking for a place to discuss a variety of topics in a comfortable environment. To subscribe to the mailing list, follow these steps:

1. **Open your favorite e-mail program and start a new e-mail message.**

2. **Type** Gen-Newbie-L-request@rootsweb.com **in the Address line.**

3. **Type only the word** subscribe **in the Subject line and in the body of your message.**

   Make sure that you turn off any signature lines in your e-mail.

4. **Send your e-mail message.**

Soon you will receive a confirmation message with additional details on unsubscribing from the mailing list (if you want to do so down the road) and other administrative items. If you have questions about the mailing list, consult the GEN-NEWBIE-L home page for help. If you've asked questions, you can search the archives of the mailing list from the mailing list's home page to see whether your questions have been answered.

National Genealogical Society

www.ngsgenealogy.org

The National Genealogical Society (NGS) is an organization for individuals whose research interests include the United States. At its website, you can find information on the society's home-study genealogy course, online and PDF courses, how to start your genealogy research, research services, the society's library catalog, and conferences. The site also has information about membership — no surprise there — and does a good job of keeping visitors abreast of genealogical news and events. You even find a bookstore that carries a lot more than just books on its virtual shelves. On the site is a free online Family History Skills course available to its members.

ProGenealogists: Genealogy Sources and Resources

www.progenealogists.com/resources.htm

ProGenealogists is a professional genealogical research firm. It provides a number of research services, for a fee, and it can access records and researchers from around the world. In addition to providing research services, ProGenealogists has posted several resources, including a list of links to online databases, how-to articles, a citation guide, resources related to specific countries, blank forms, lists of journals and magazines, genealogy news, and research tools.

Getting Started in Genealogy and Family History

```
www.genuki.org.uk/gs
```

The GENUKI (U.K. and Ireland Genealogy) website provides a list of helpful hints for starting out in genealogical research. The extensive list covers the following elements and more: deciding the aim of your research, using Family History Centers, joining a genealogical society, tracing immigrants, and organizing your information. You also find a list of reference materials — should you want to read more about the topics GENUKI discusses.

About.com Genealogy: Genealogy Learning and Guidance

```
http://genealogy.about.com/od/make_family_tree/u/learn.htm
```

If you're looking for information on a range of genealogical topics, hop over to the About.com Genealogy site. The Genealogy Learning and Guidance section has a large collection of articles categorized by subject:

- Get Started
- Organize and Record Your Research
- Analyze and Evaluate What You've Found
- Skills, Strategies, and Techniques
- Surnames and Heraldry
- How to Trace Your Family In . . .

You find many subcategories under each of these topics as well. Some of the resources in these categories include information on surname origins, mistakes you can avoid, a genealogy chat room, and publishing your family history.

Index

• *H* •